I'll work hard
in the next
volume, too!

MANGA — Atsuro Yomino

ORIGINAL STORY — Ichirou Ohkouchi / Goro Taniguchi

SCRIPT COOPERATION — Saika Hasumi

ENGLISH PRODUCTION CREDITS

TRANSLATION	Satsuki Yamashita
LETTERING	Keiran O'Leary
COORDINATOR	Yumi Dorsey
COPY EDITOR	Brian Cutts
EDITOR	Robert Place Napton
PUBLISHER	Ken Iyadomi

CODE GEASS Suzaku of the Counterattack
©Atsuro YOMINO 2007
©2006-2008 SUNRISE/PROJECT GEASS, MBS
Character Design ©2006 CLAMP

Originally published in Japan in 2007 by KADOKAWA SHOTEN PUBLISHING CO., LTD., Tokyo.
English translation published by Bandai Entertainment Inc. under the license by Sunrise, Inc.

ISBN-13: 978-1-59409-977-9

Printed in Canada
First Bandai Printing: November 2008

10 9 8 7 6 5 4 3 2 1

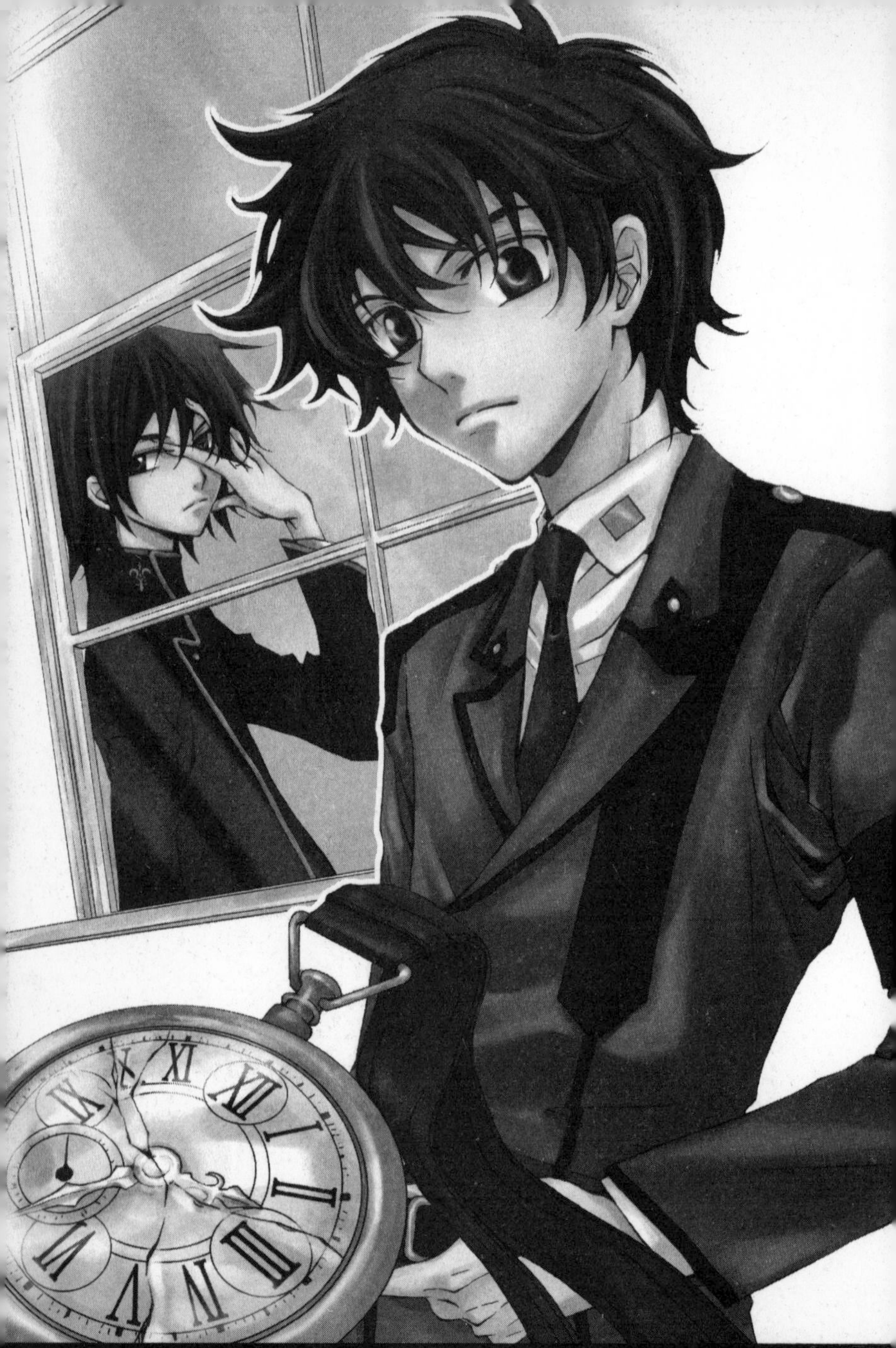

Phase 1

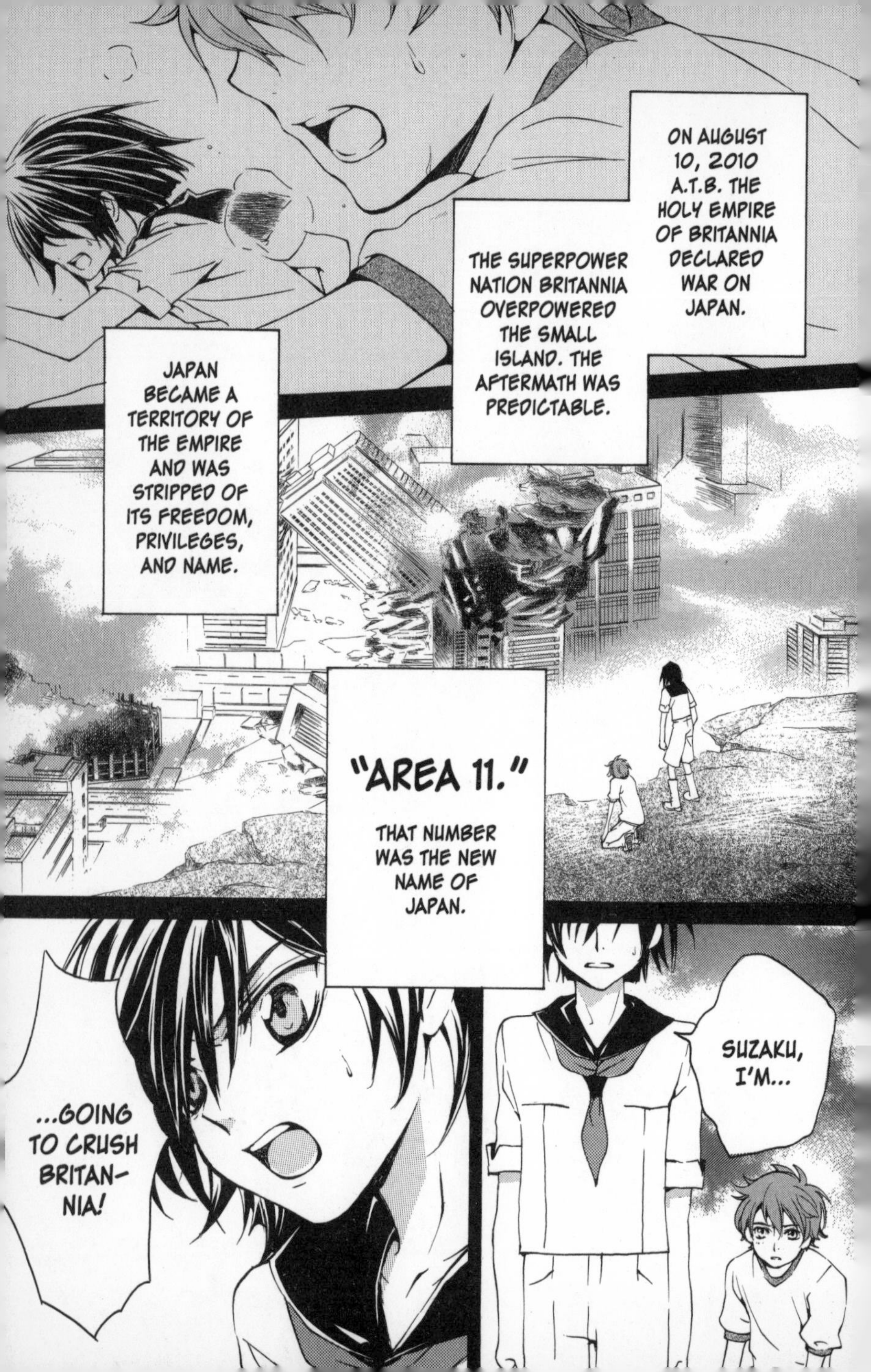
ON AUGUST 10, 2010 A.T.B. THE HOLY EMPIRE OF BRITANNIA DECLARED WAR ON JAPAN.
THE SUPERPOWER NATION BRITANNIA OVERPOWERED THE SMALL ISLAND. THE AFTERMATH WAS PREDICTABLE.
JAPAN BECAME A TERRITORY OF THE EMPIRE AND WAS STRIPPED OF ITS FREEDOM, PRIVILEGES, AND NAME.
"AREA 11."
THAT NUMBER WAS THE NEW NAME OF JAPAN.
SUZAKU, I'M...
...GOING TO CRUSH BRITAN-NIA!

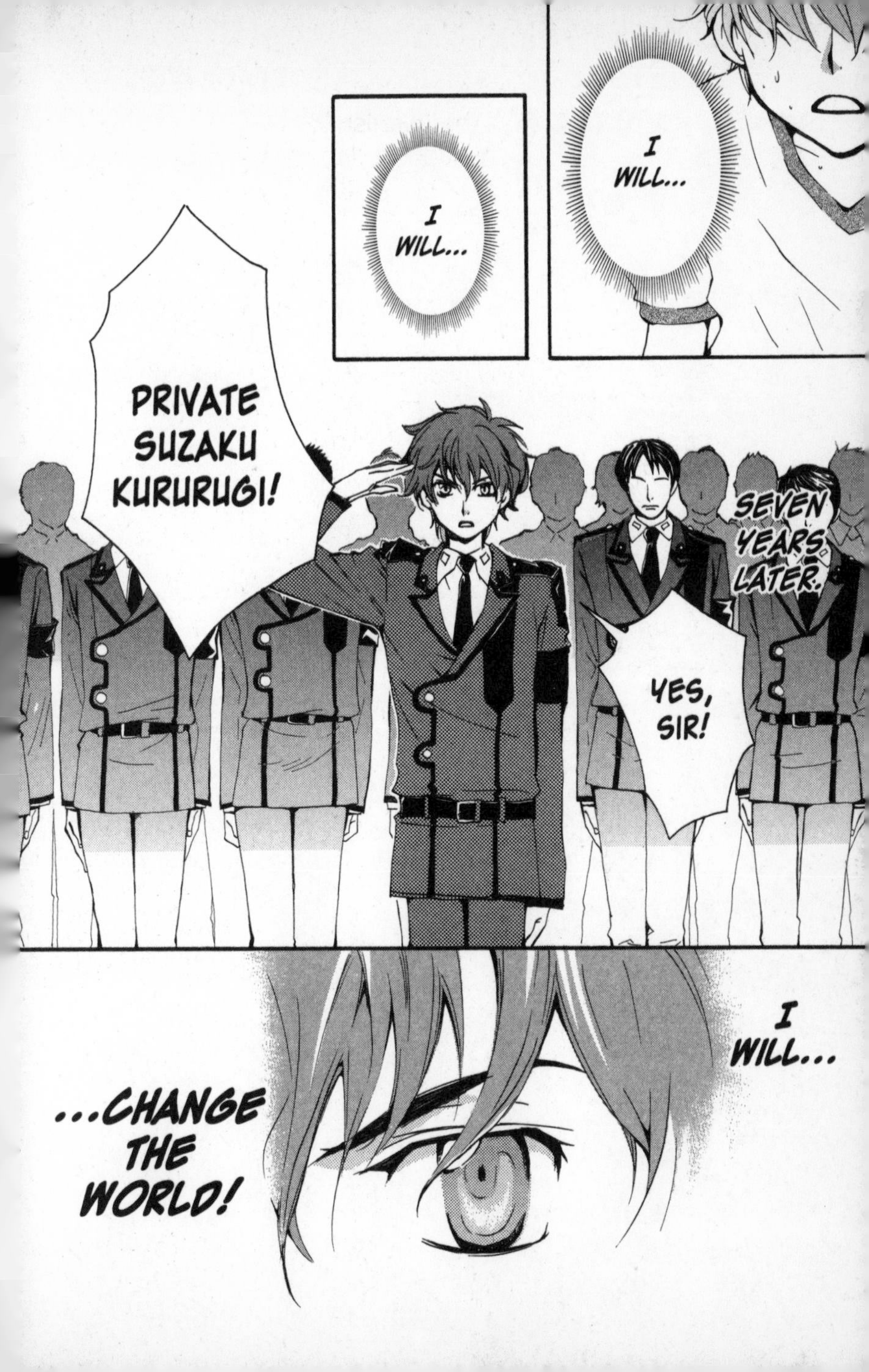
I WILL...
I WILL...
SEVEN YEARS LATER.
PRIVATE SUZAKU KURURUGI!
YES, SIR!
I WILL...
...CHANGE THE WORLD!

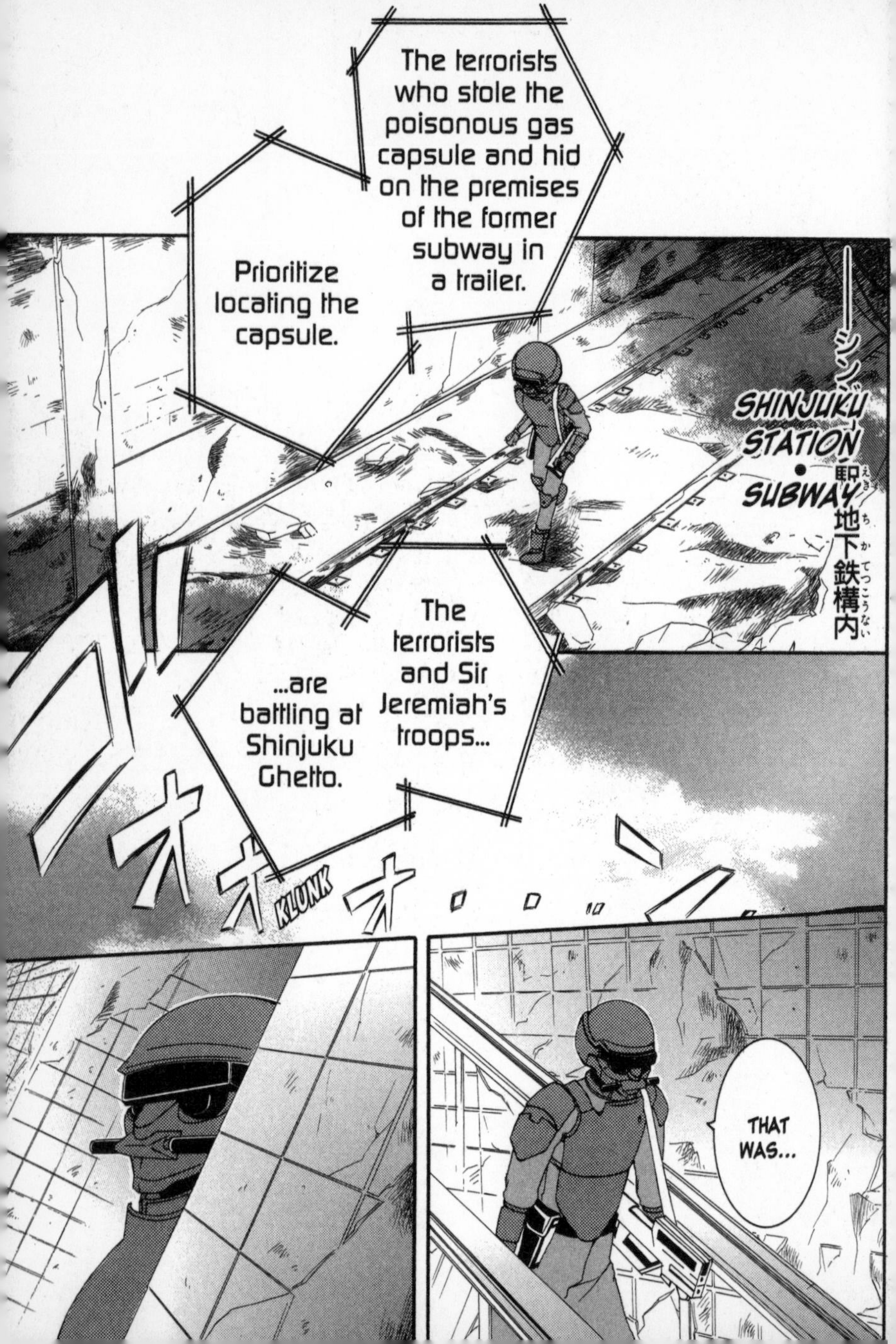
──シンジュク駅地下鉄構内
SHINJUKU STATION • SUBWAY
The terrorists who stole the poisonous gas capsule and hid on the premises of the former subway in a trailer.
Prioritize locating the capsule.
The terrorists and Sir Jeremiah's troops...
...are battling at Shinjuku Ghetto.
KLUNK
THAT WAS...

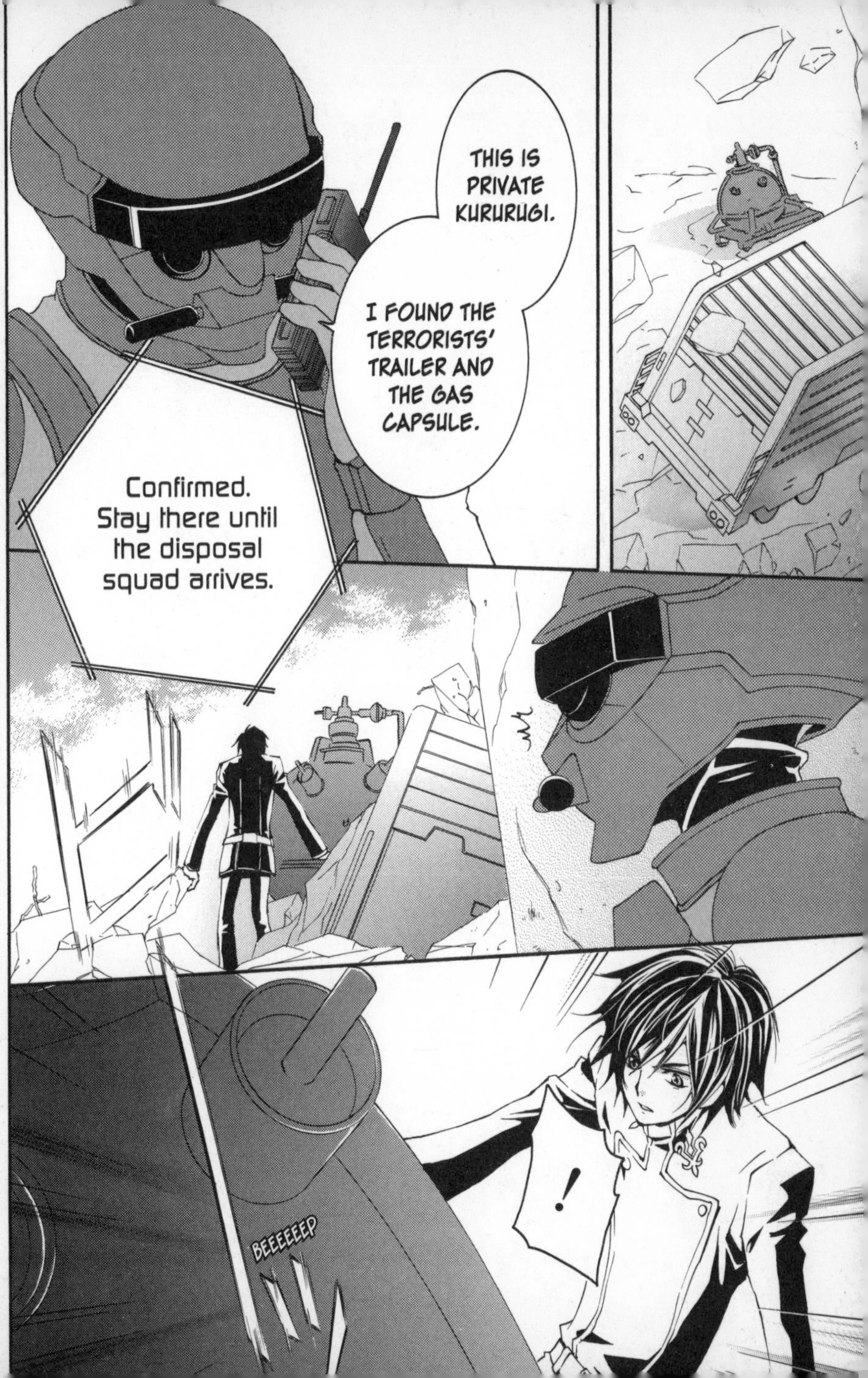
THIS IS PRIVATE KURURUGI.
I FOUND THE TERRORISTS' TRAILER AND THE GAS CAPSULE.
Confirmed. Stay there until the disposal squad arrives.
!
BEEEEEEP

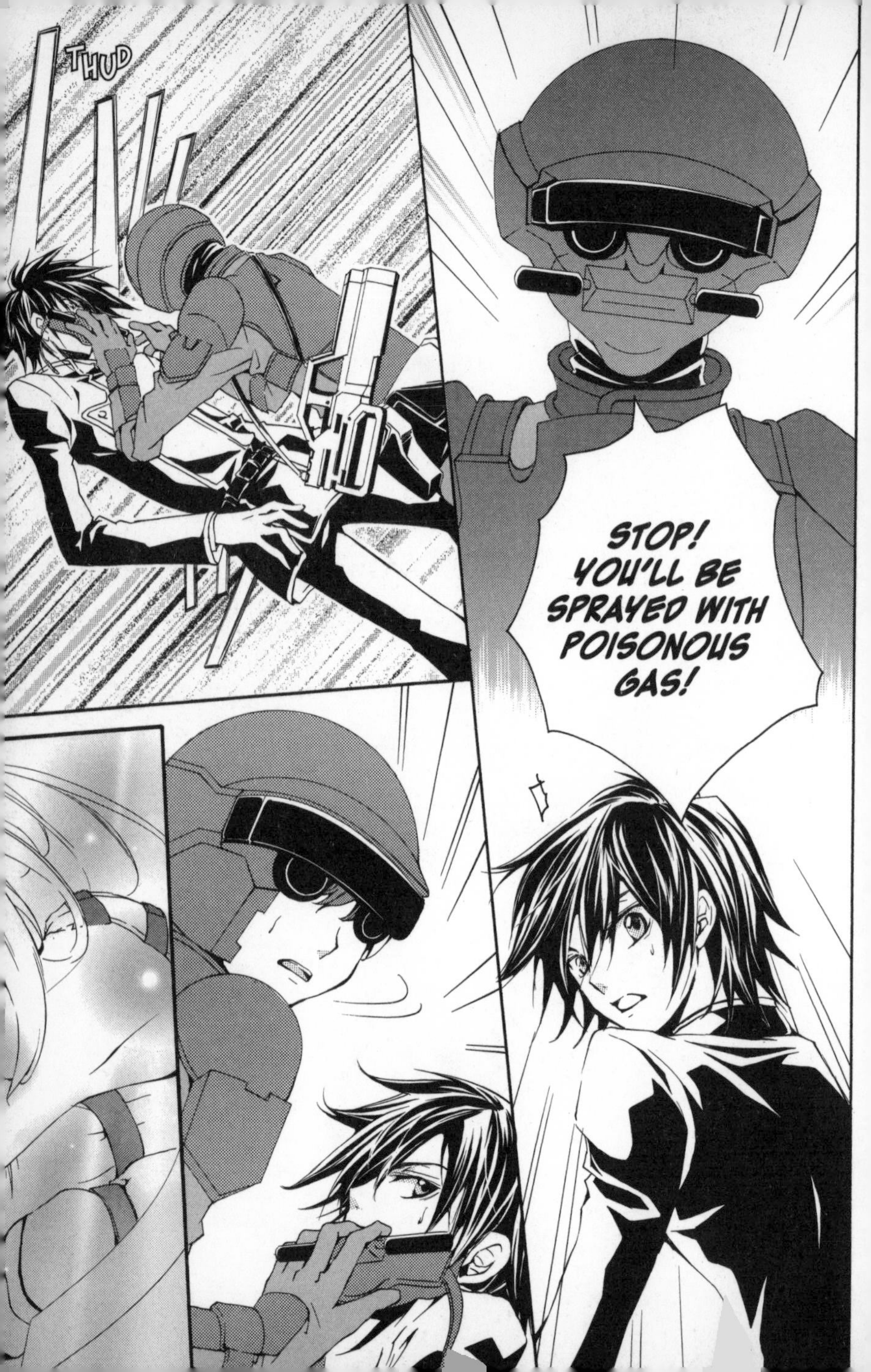
STOP! YOU'LL BE SPRAYED WITH POISONOUS GAS!
THUD

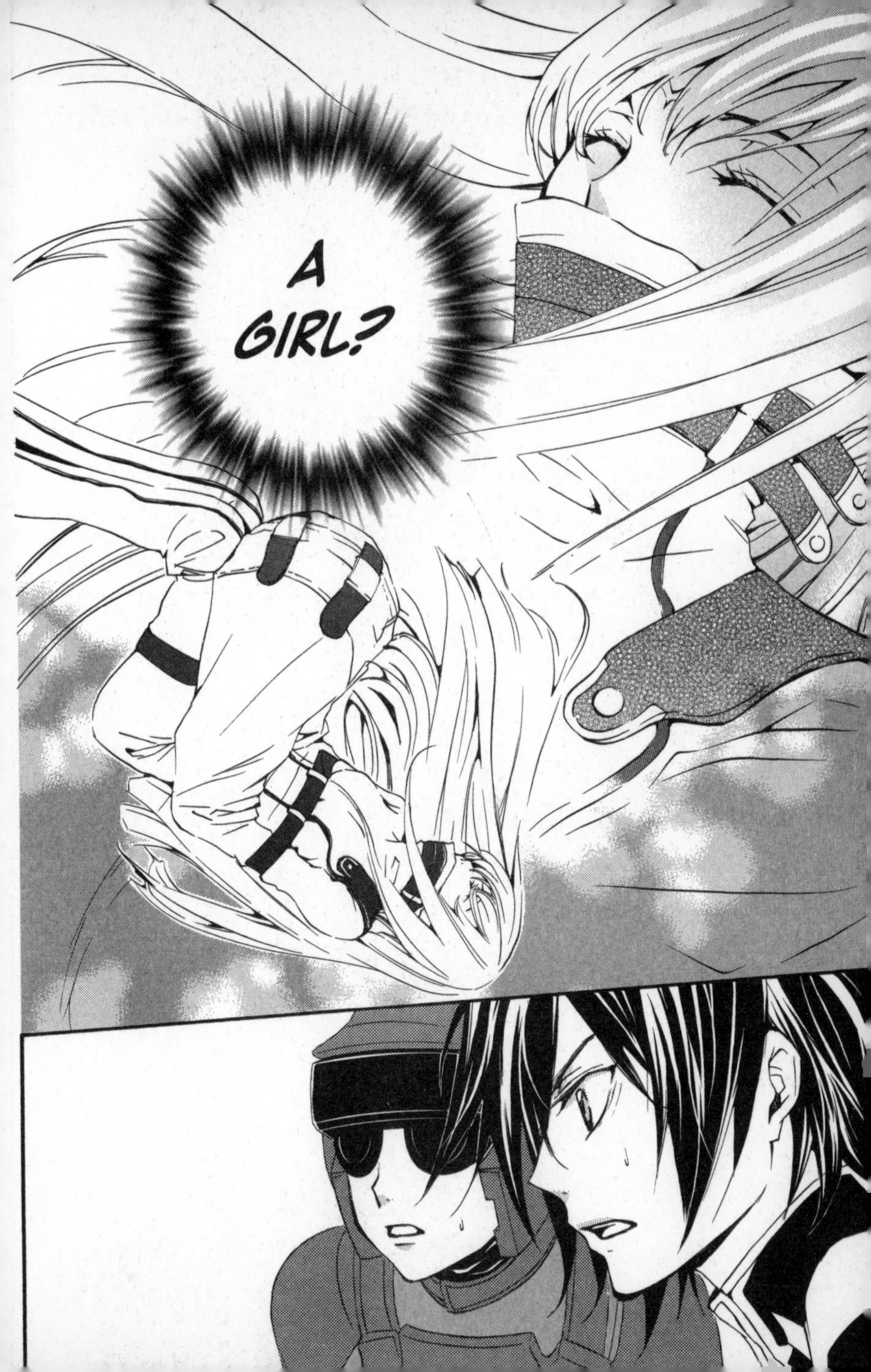
A GIRL?

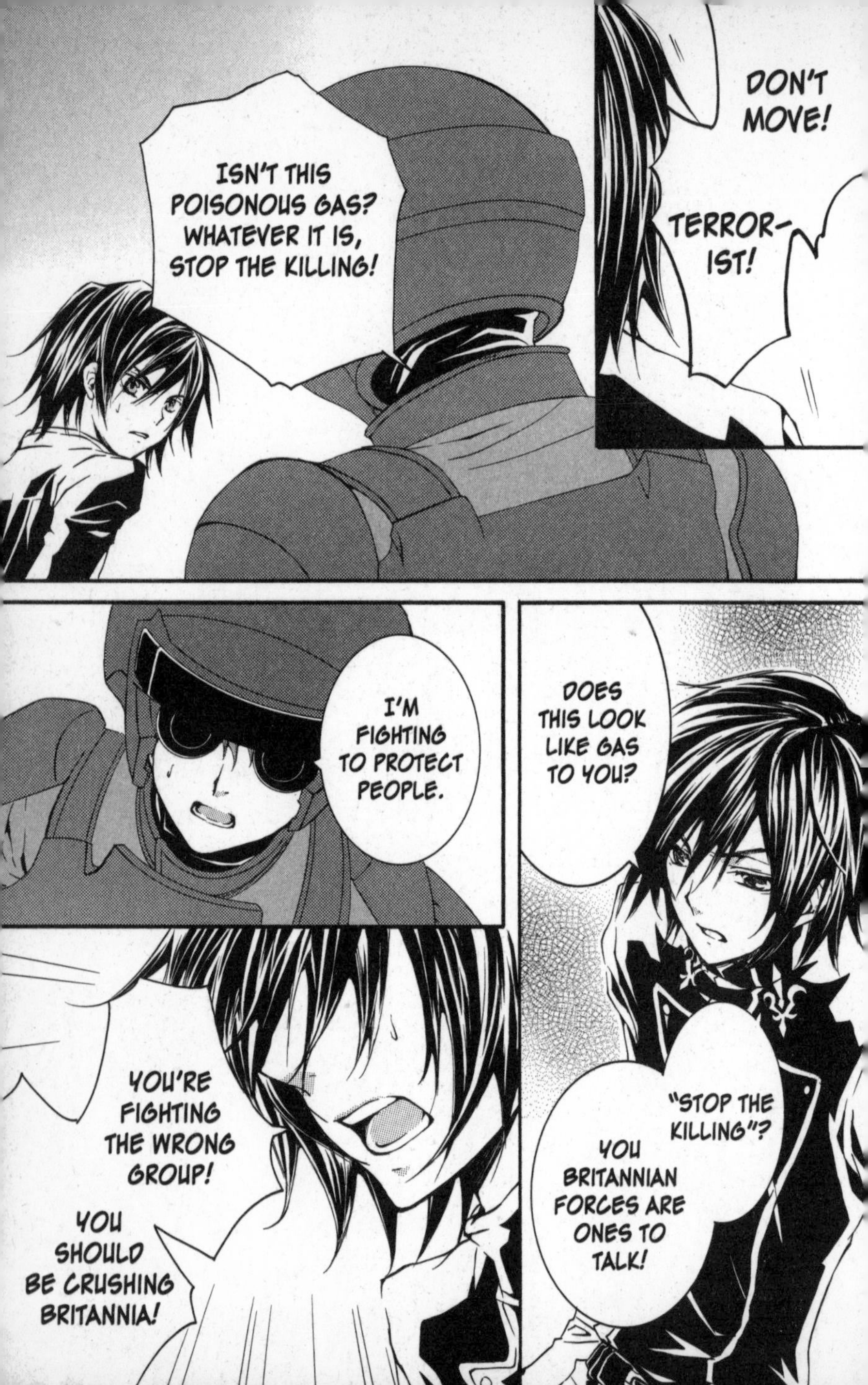
DON'T MOVE!
TERROR-IST!
ISN'T THIS POISONOUS GAS? WHATEVER IT IS, STOP THE KILLING!
DOES THIS LOOK LIKE GAS TO YOU?
"STOP THE KILLING"?
YOU BRITANNIAN FORCES ARE ONES TO TALK!
I'M FIGHTING TO PROTECT PEOPLE.
YOU'RE FIGHTING THE WRONG GROUP!
YOU SHOULD BE CRUSHING BRITANNIA!

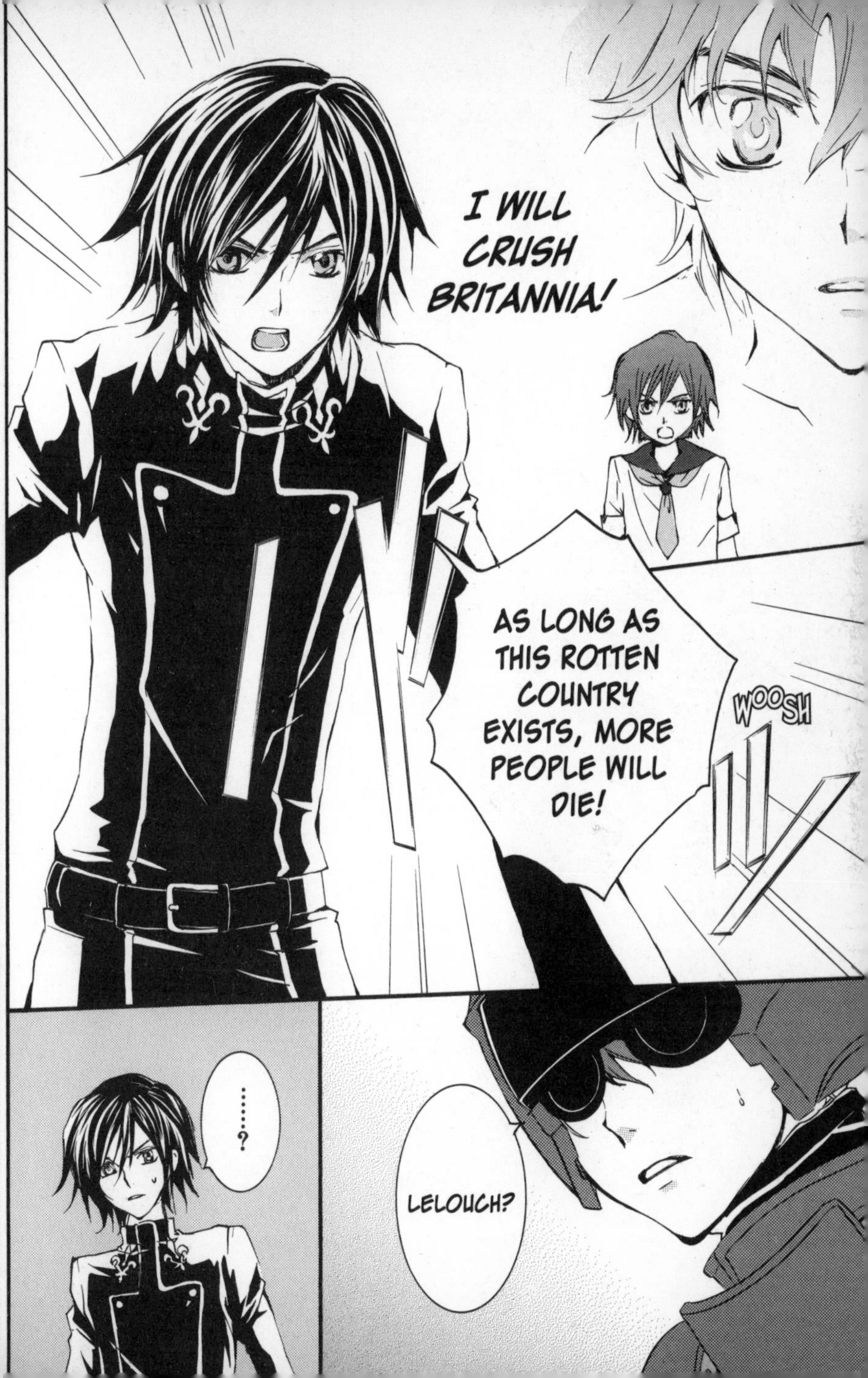
I WILL CRUSH BRITANNIA!
AS LONG AS THIS ROTTEN COUNTRY EXISTS, MORE PEOPLE WILL DIE!
WOOSH
LELOUCH?
......?

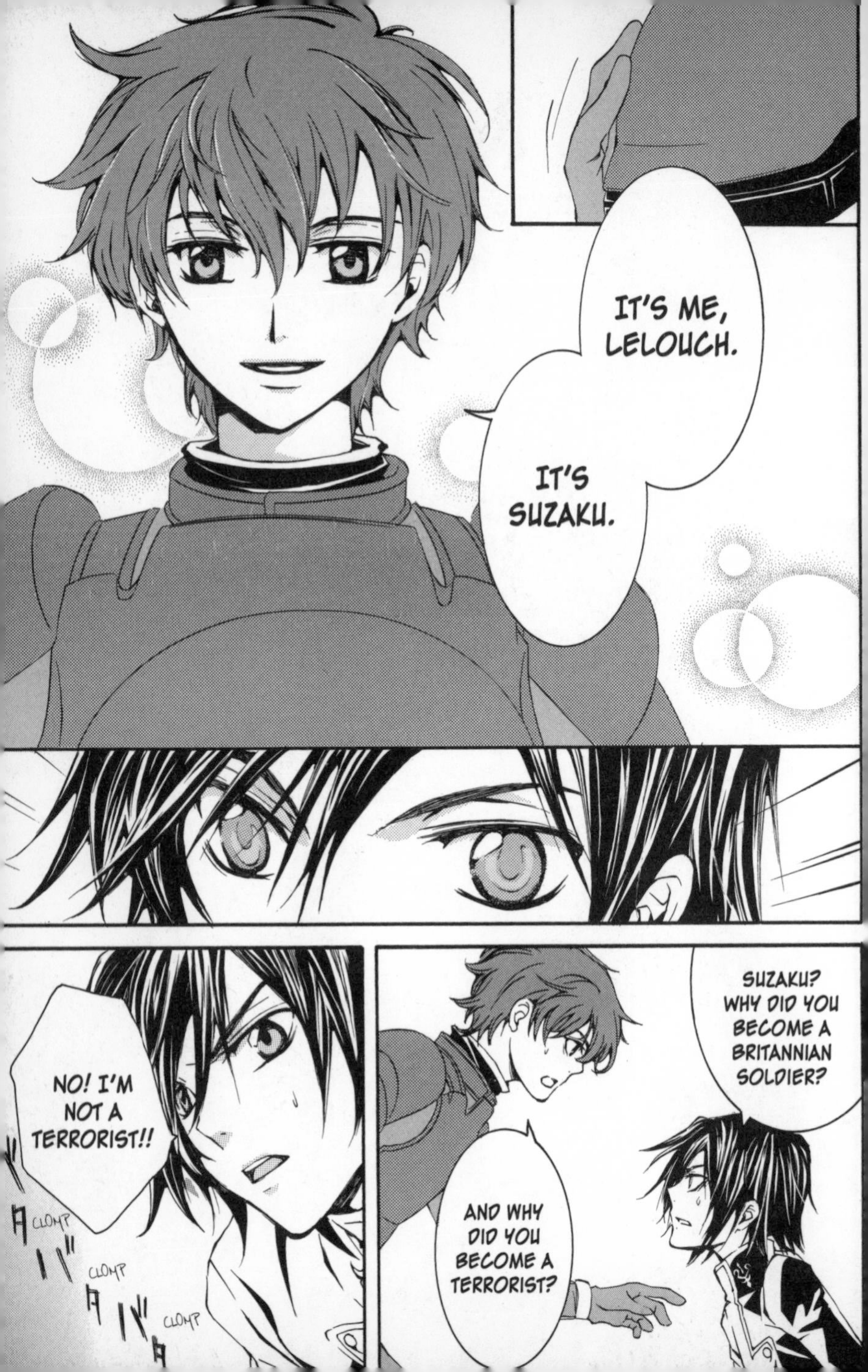
IT'S ME, LELOUCH.
IT'S SUZAKU.
SUZAKU? WHY DID YOU BECOME A BRITANNIAN SOLDIER?
AND WHY DID YOU BECOME A TERRORIST?
NO! I'M NOT A TERRORIST!!
CLOMP
CLOMP
CLOMP

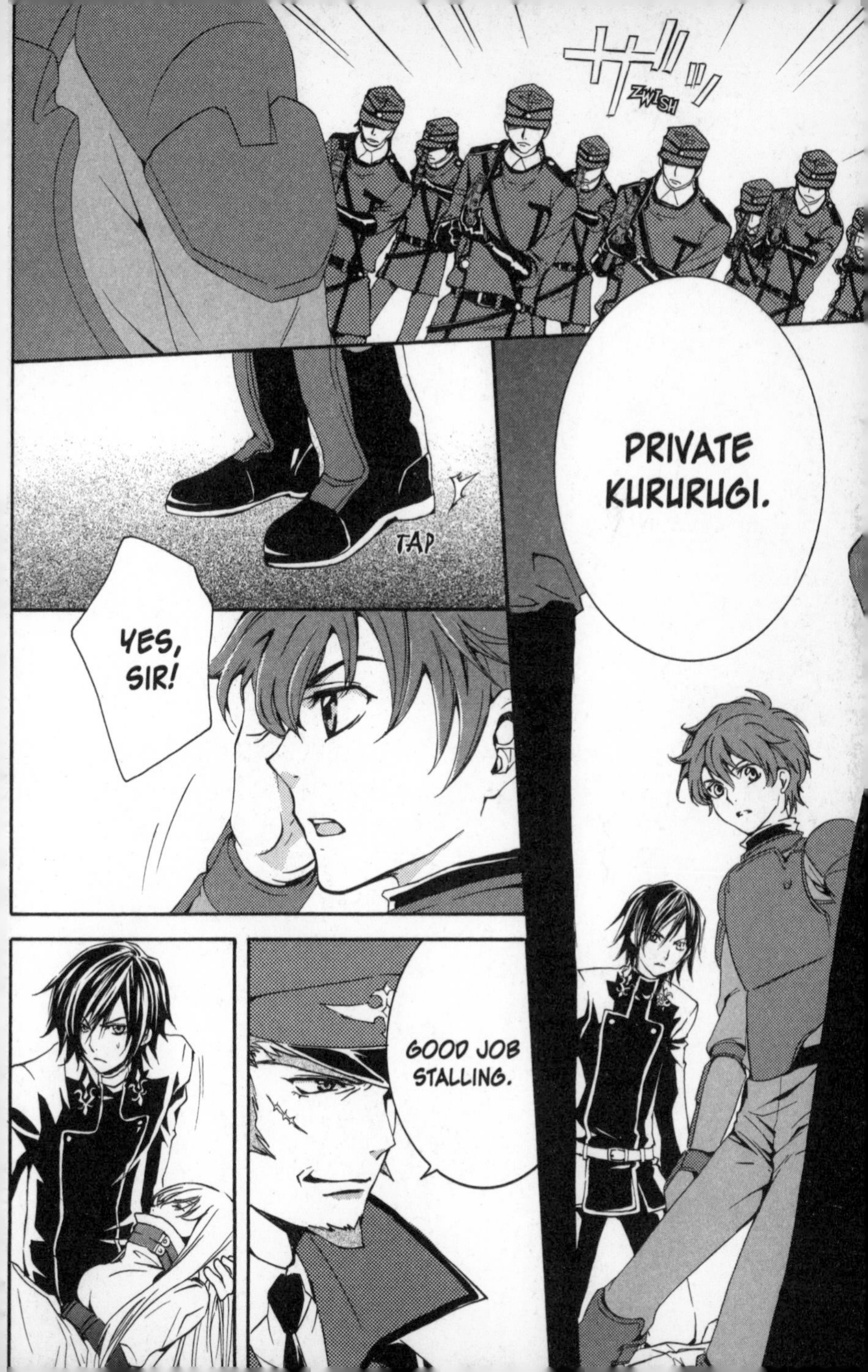
ZWISH
PRIVATE KURURUGI.
TAP
YES, SIR!
GOOD JOB STALLING.

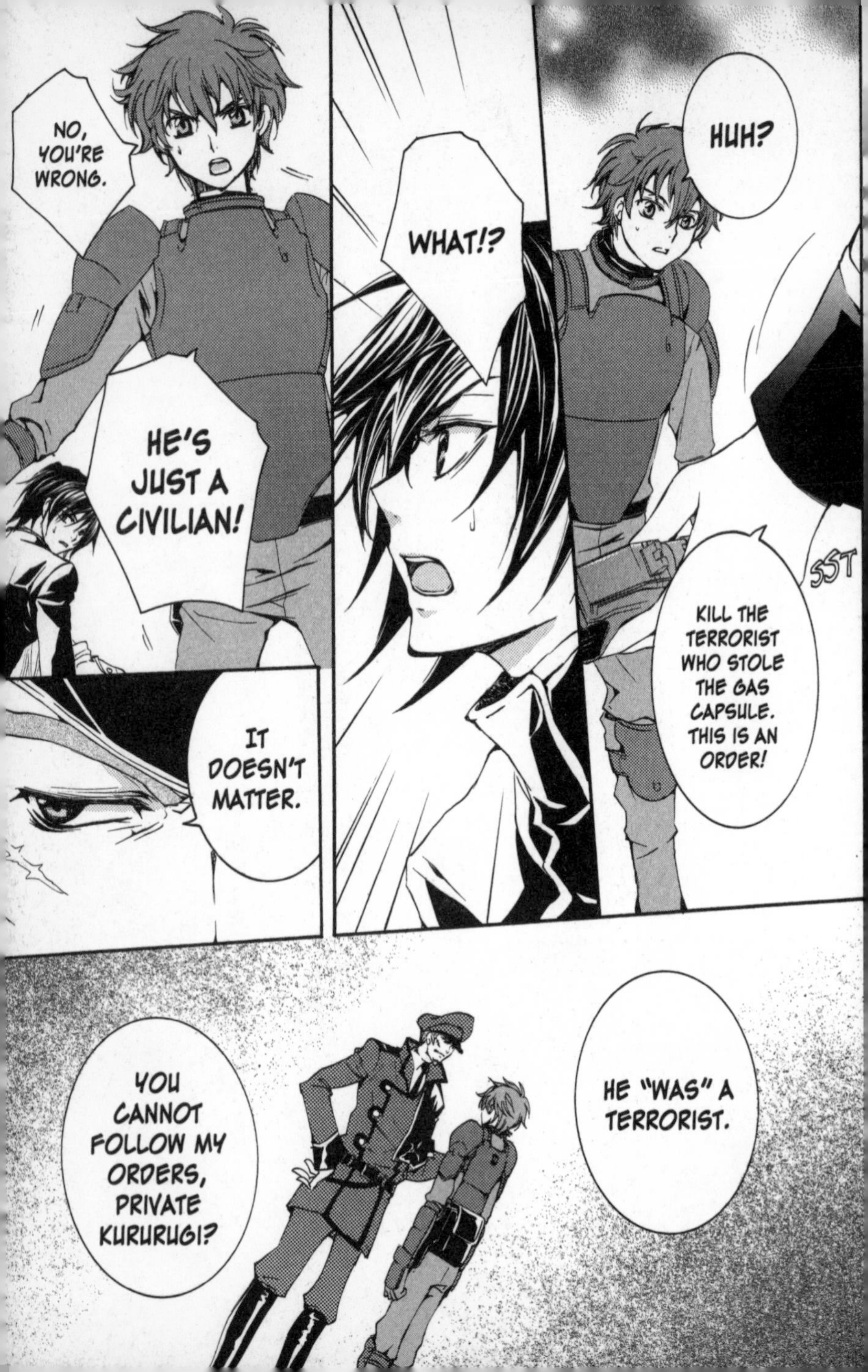
HUH?
KILL THE TERRORIST WHO STOLE THE GAS CAPSULE. THIS IS AN ORDER!
SST
WHAT!?
NO, YOU'RE WRONG.
HE'S JUST A CIVILIAN!
IT DOESN'T MATTER.
HE "WAS" A TERRORIST.
YOU CANNOT FOLLOW MY ORDERS, PRIVATE KURURUGI?

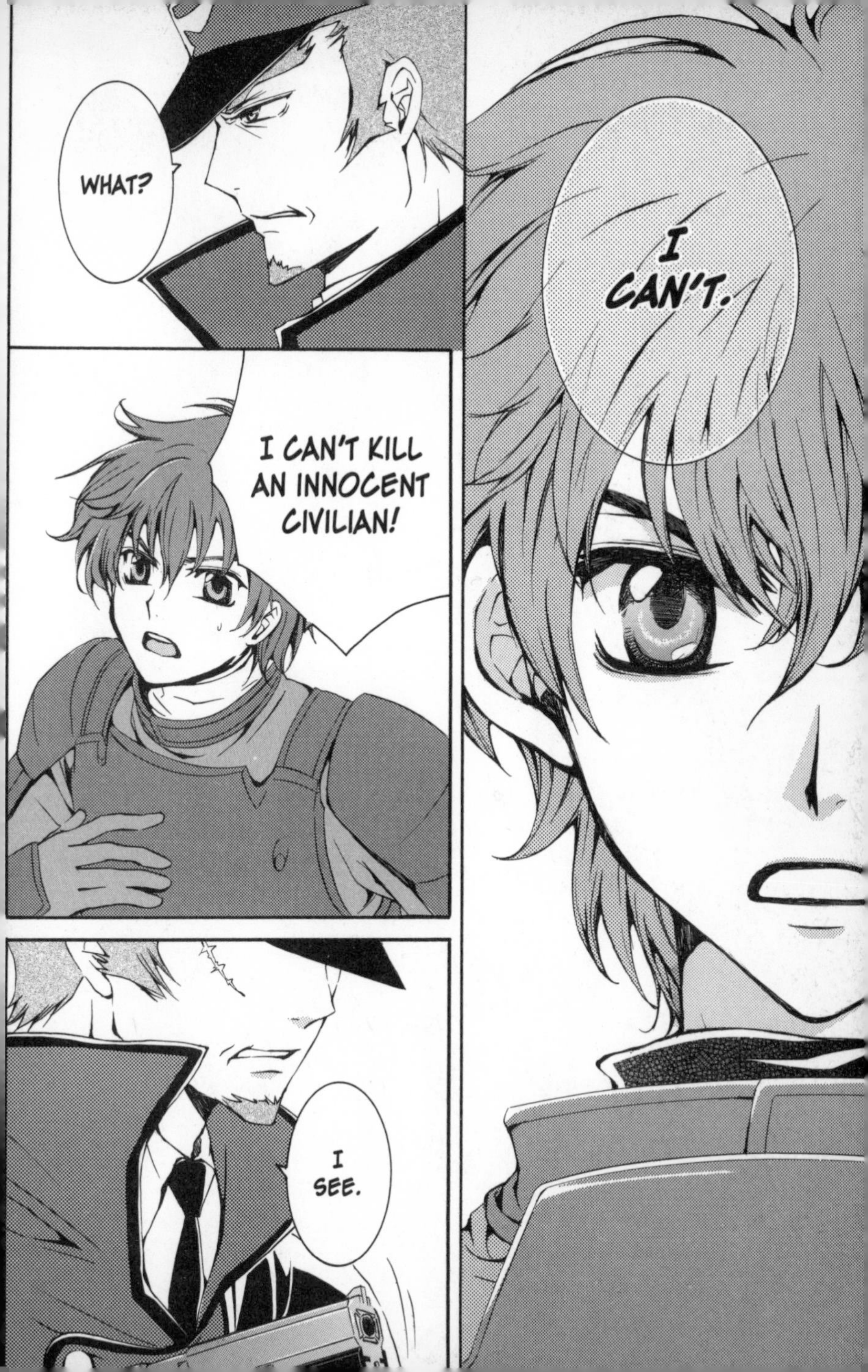
I CAN'T.
WHAT?
I CAN'T KILL AN INNOCENT CIVILIAN!
I SEE.

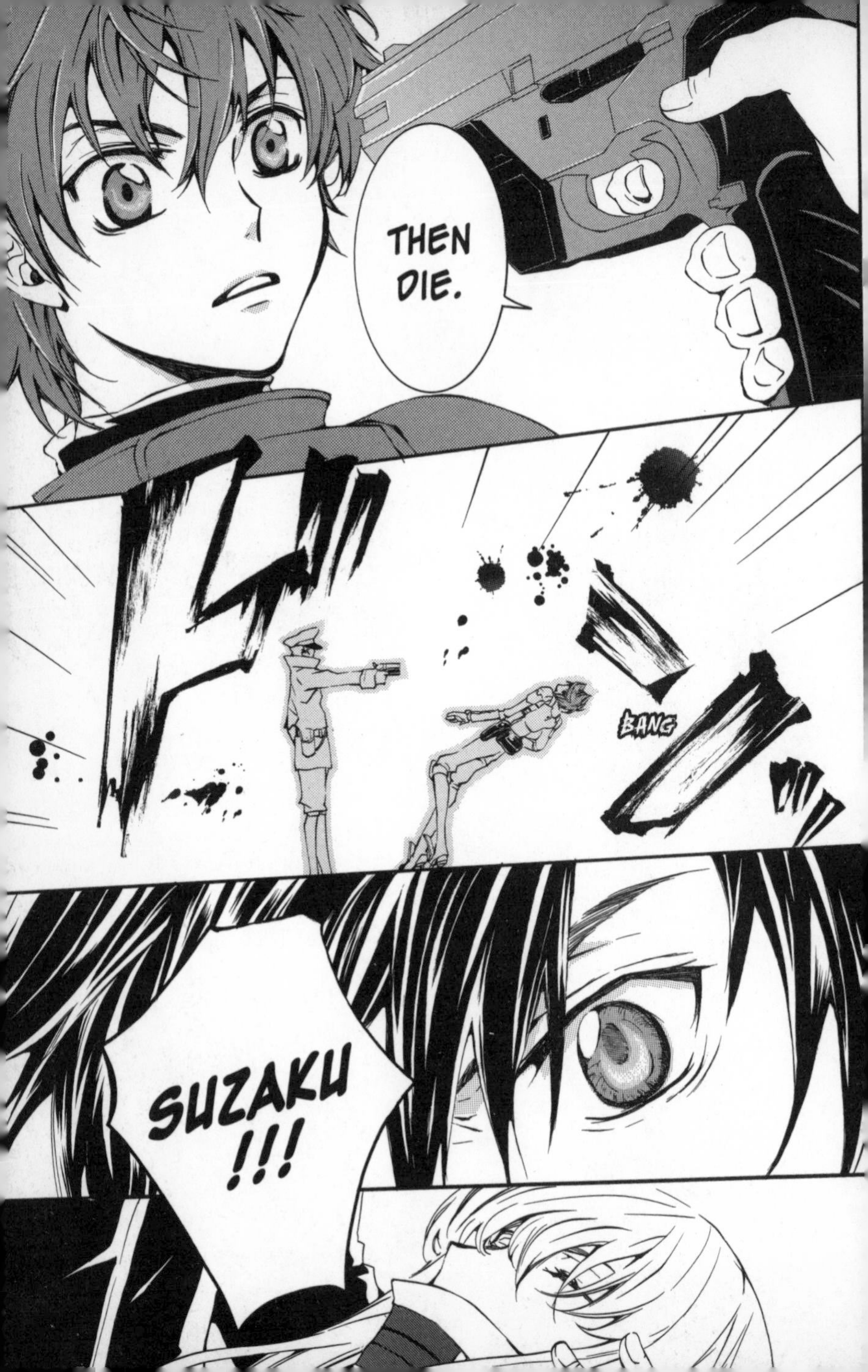
THEN DIE.
BANG
SUZAKU !!!

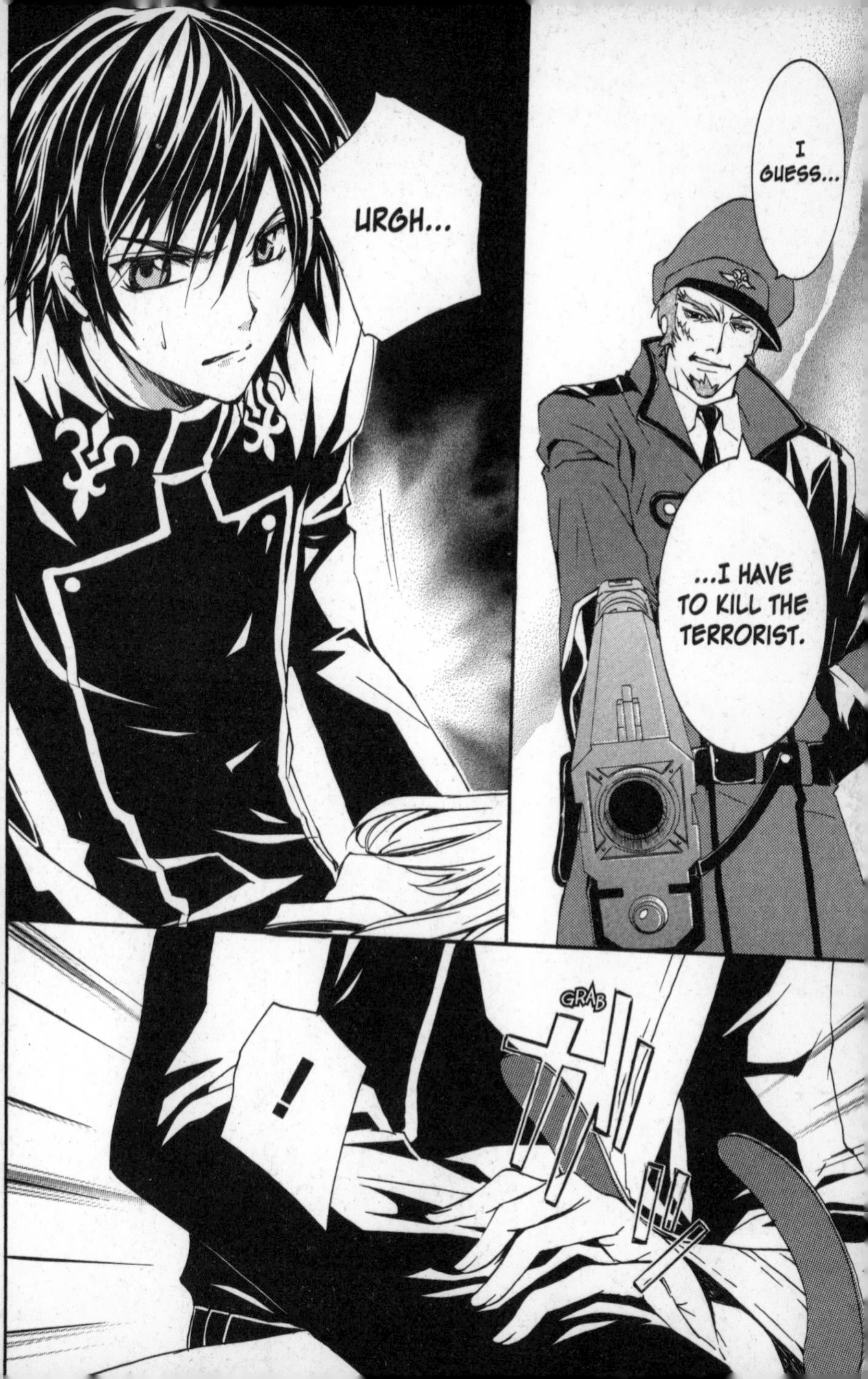
I GUESS...
...I HAVE TO KILL THE TERRORIST.
URGH...
GRAB
!

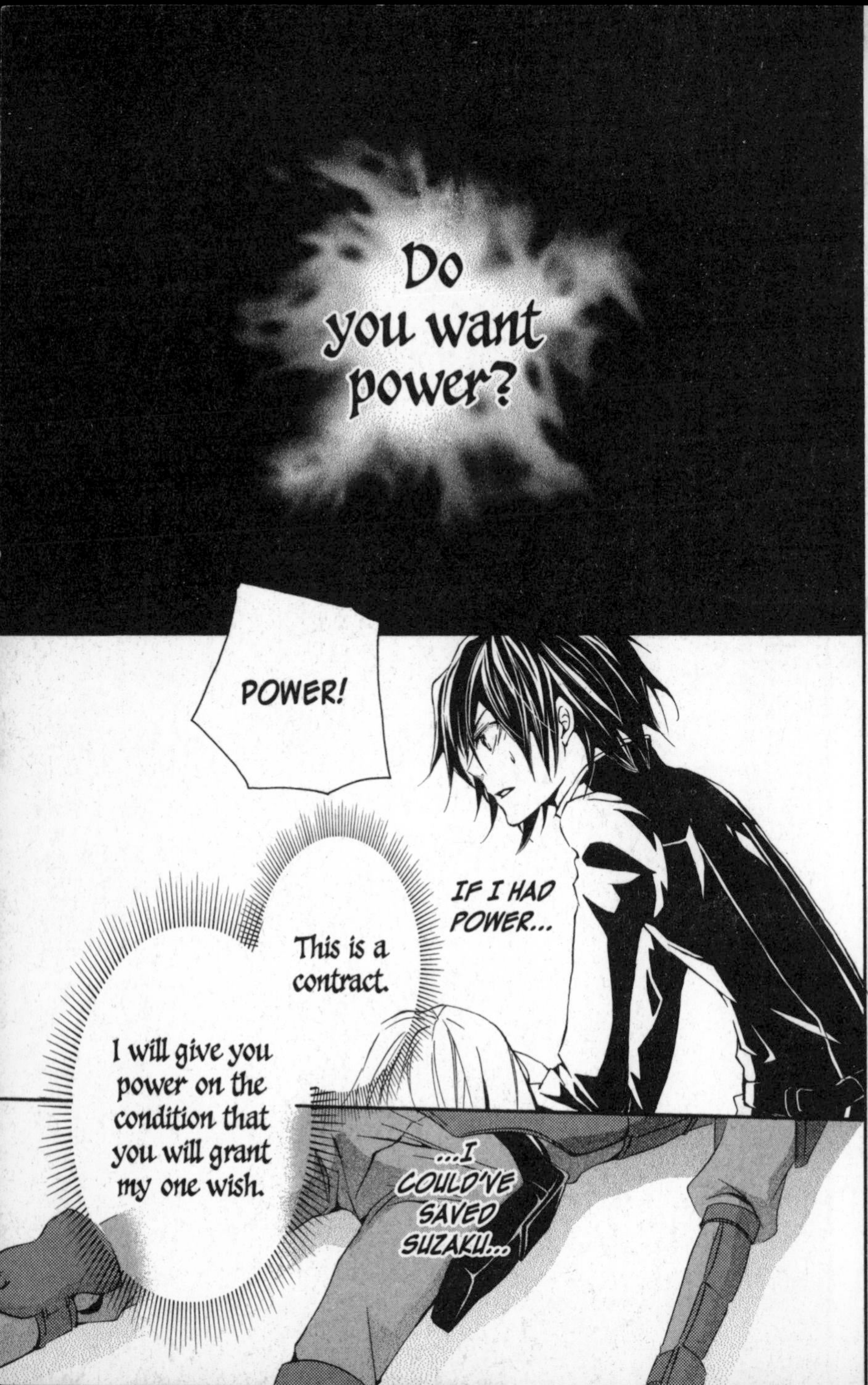
Do you want power?
POWER!
IF I HAD POWER...
This is a contract.
I will give you power on the condition that you will grant my one wish.
...I COULD'VE SAVED SUZAKU...

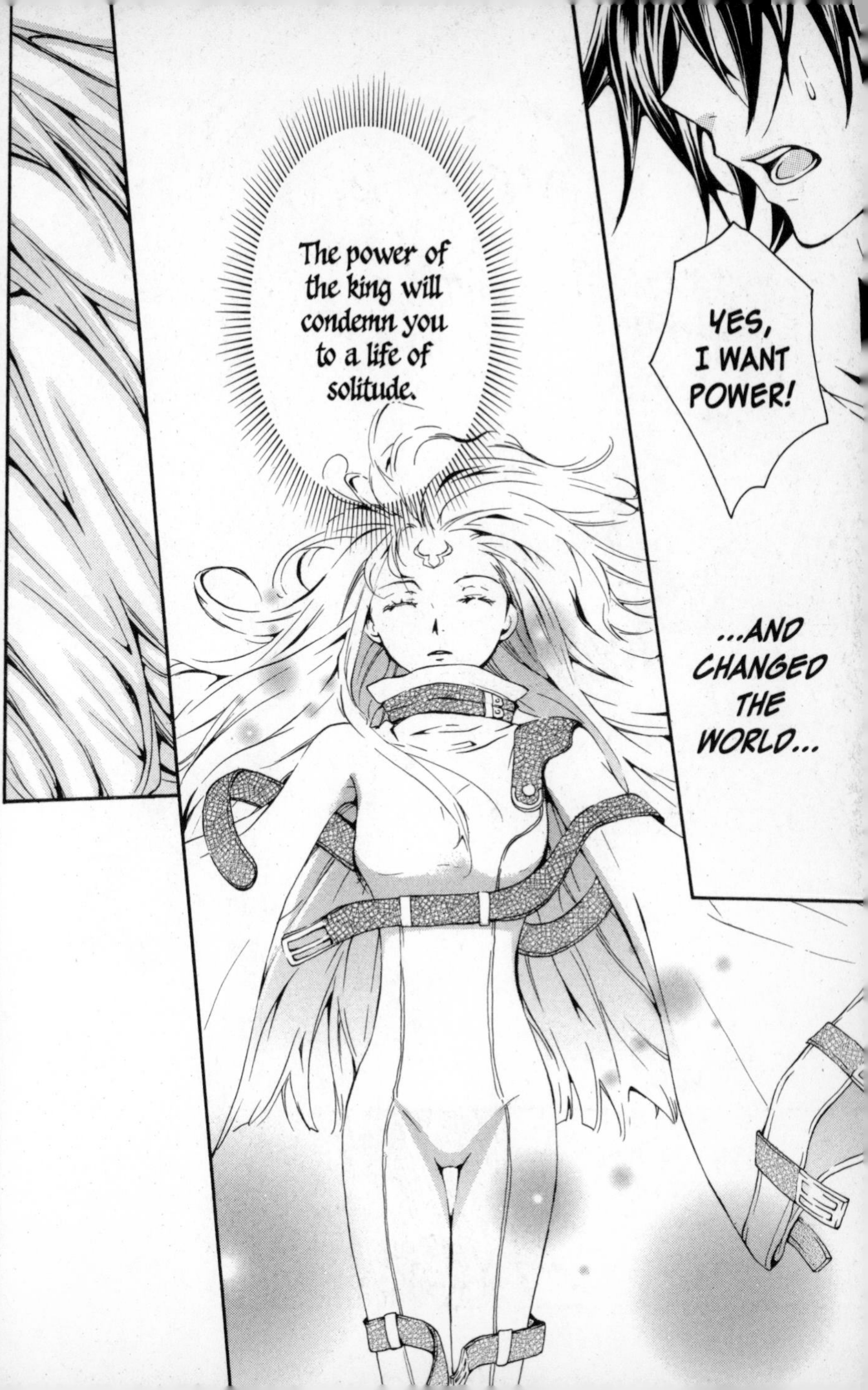
YES, I WANT POWER!
...AND CHANGED THE WORLD...
The power of the king will condemn you to a life of solitude.

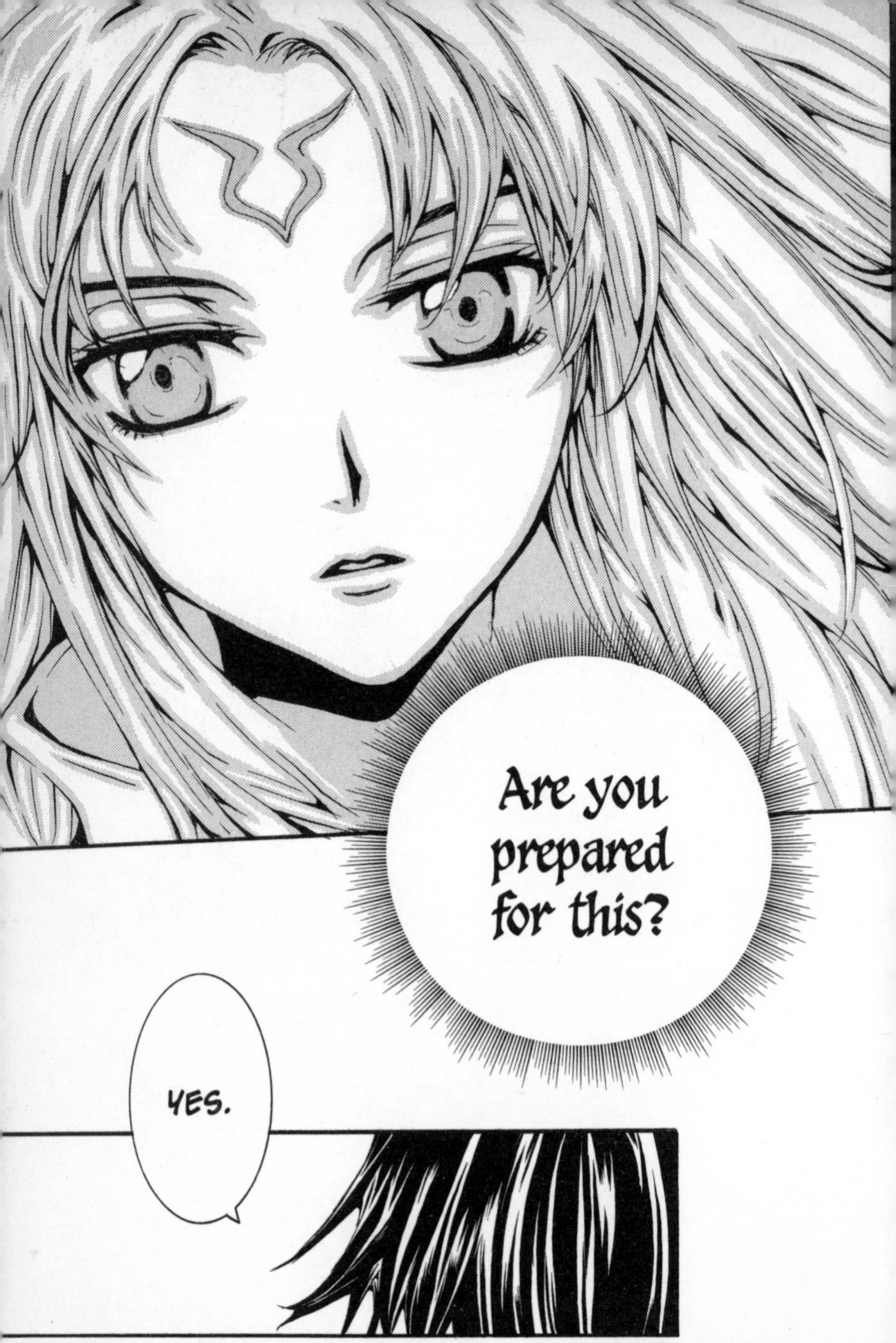
Are you prepared for this?
YES.

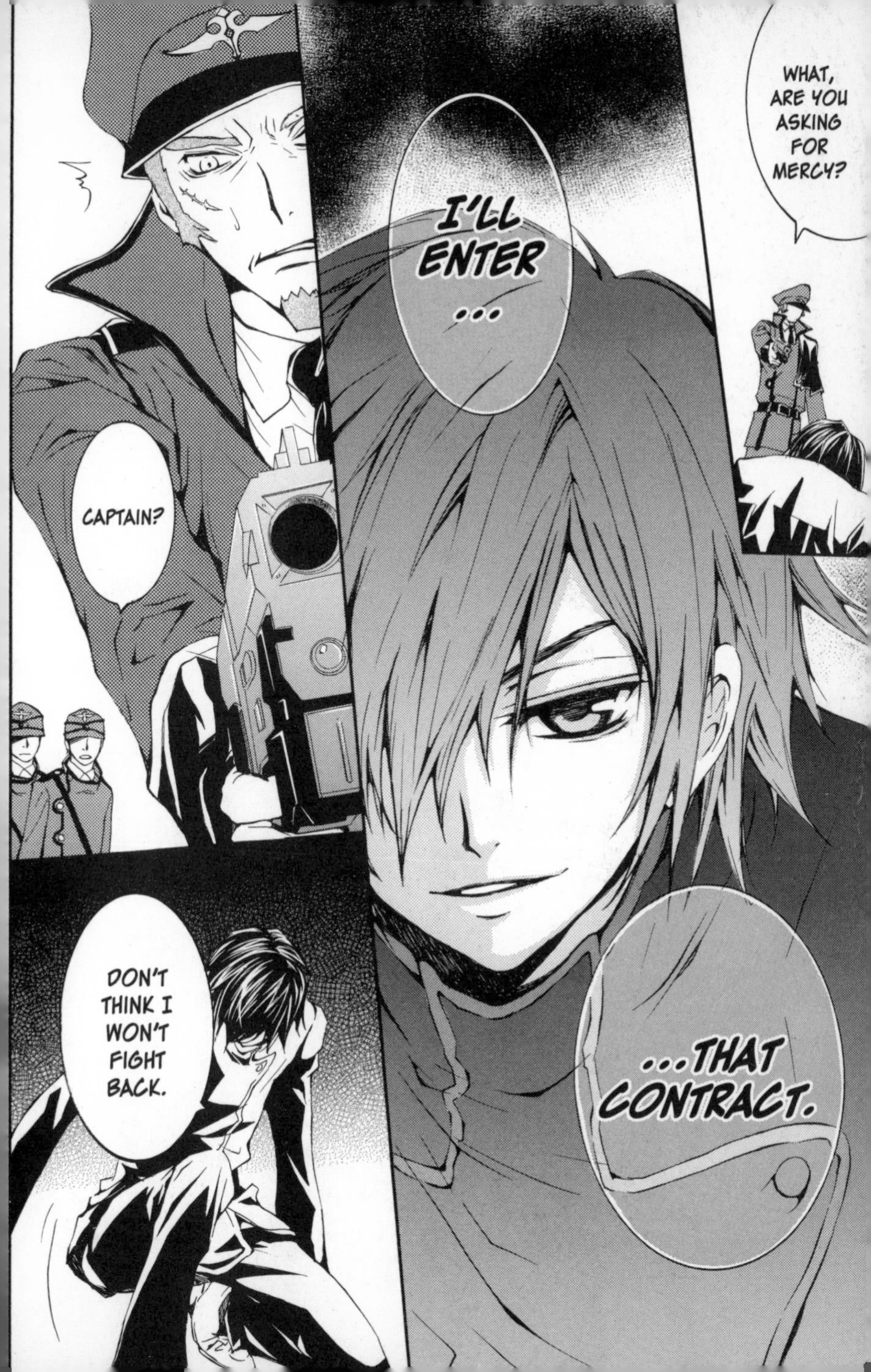
WHAT, ARE YOU ASKING FOR MERCY?
I'LL ENTER ...
...THAT CONTRACT.
CAPTAIN?
DON'T THINK I WON'T FIGHT BACK.

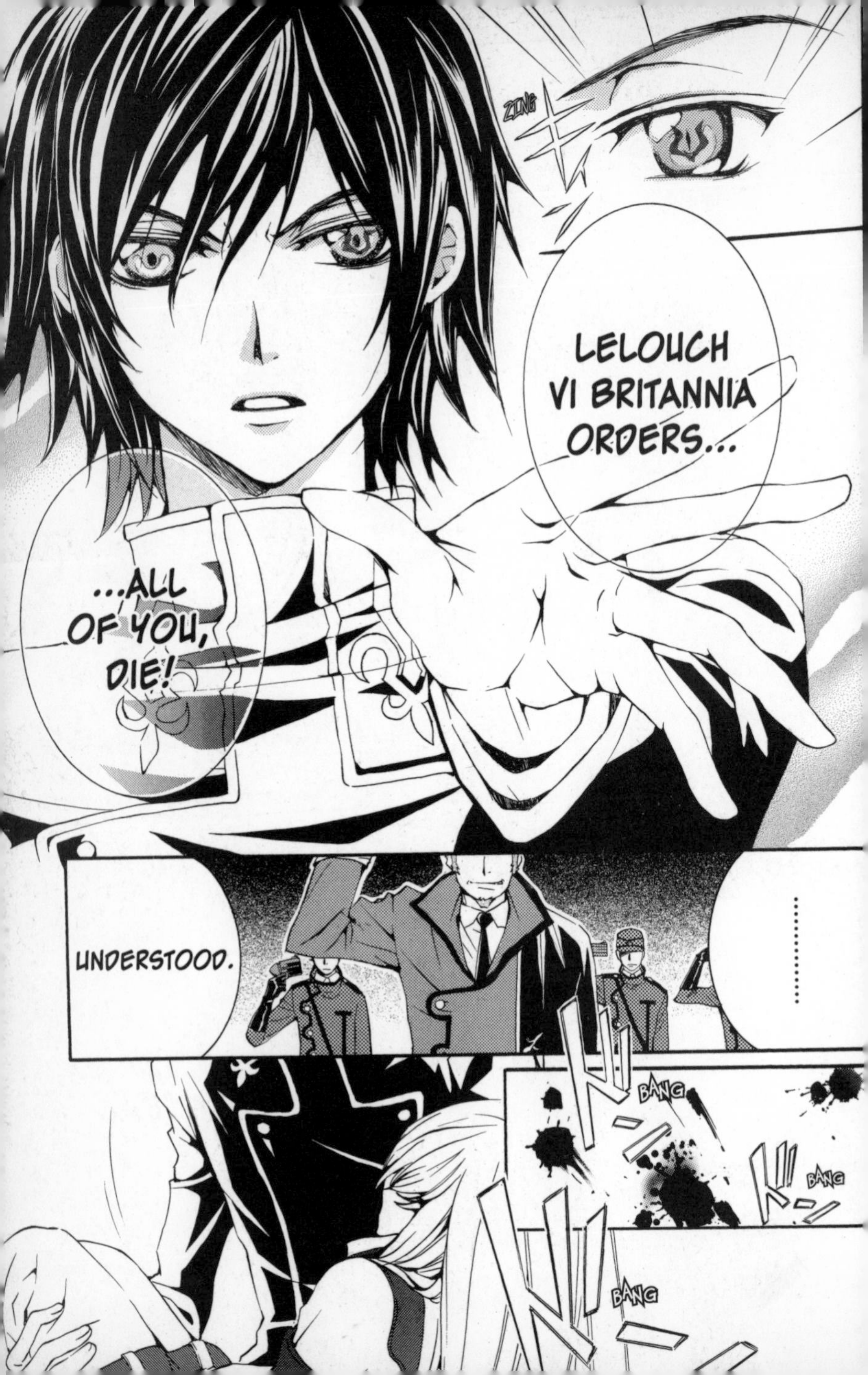
ZING
LELOUCH VI BRITANNIA ORDERS...
...ALL OF YOU, DIE!
......
UNDERSTOOD.
BANG
BANG
BANG

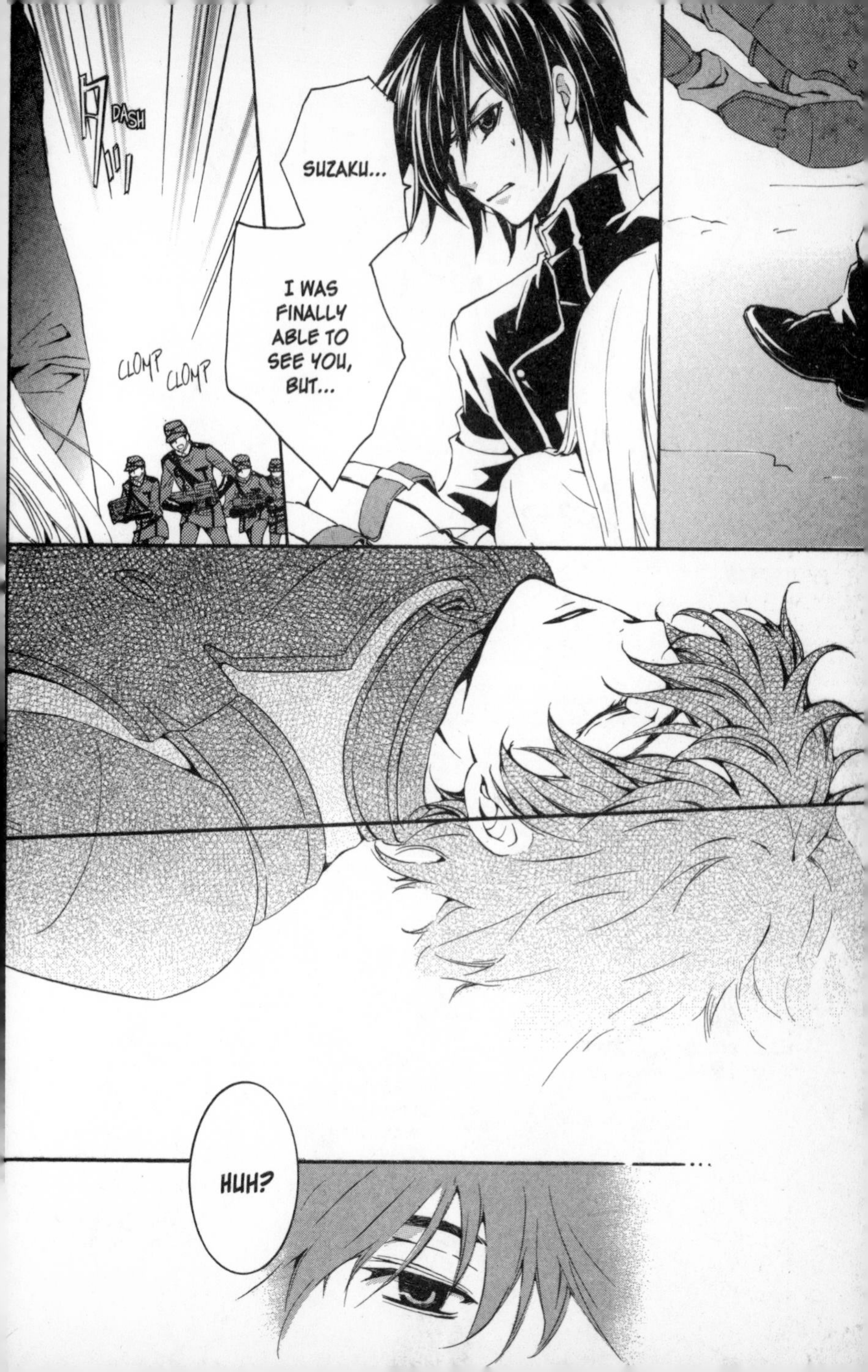
DASH
SUZAKU...
I WAS FINALLY ABLE TO SEE YOU, BUT...
CLOMP CLOMP
HUH?

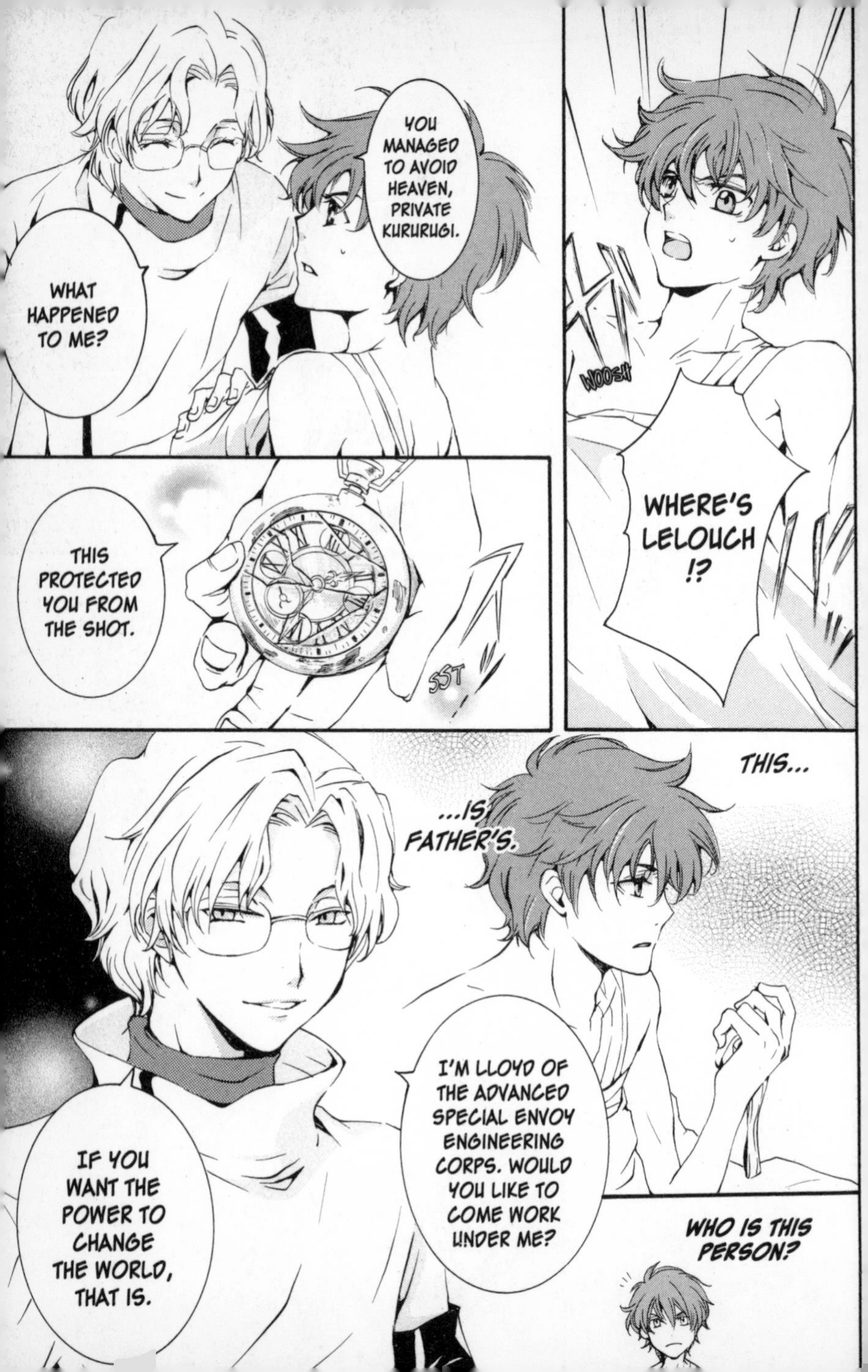
WOOSH
WHERE'S LELOUCH !?
YOU MANAGED TO AVOID HEAVEN, PRIVATE KURURUGI.
WHAT HAPPENED TO ME?
SST
THIS PROTECTED YOU FROM THE SHOT.
THIS...
...IS FATHER'S.
I'M LLOYD OF THE ADVANCED SPECIAL ENVOY ENGINEERING CORPS. WOULD YOU LIKE TO COME WORK UNDER ME?
IF YOU WANT THE POWER TO CHANGE THE WORLD, THAT IS.
WHO IS THIS PERSON?

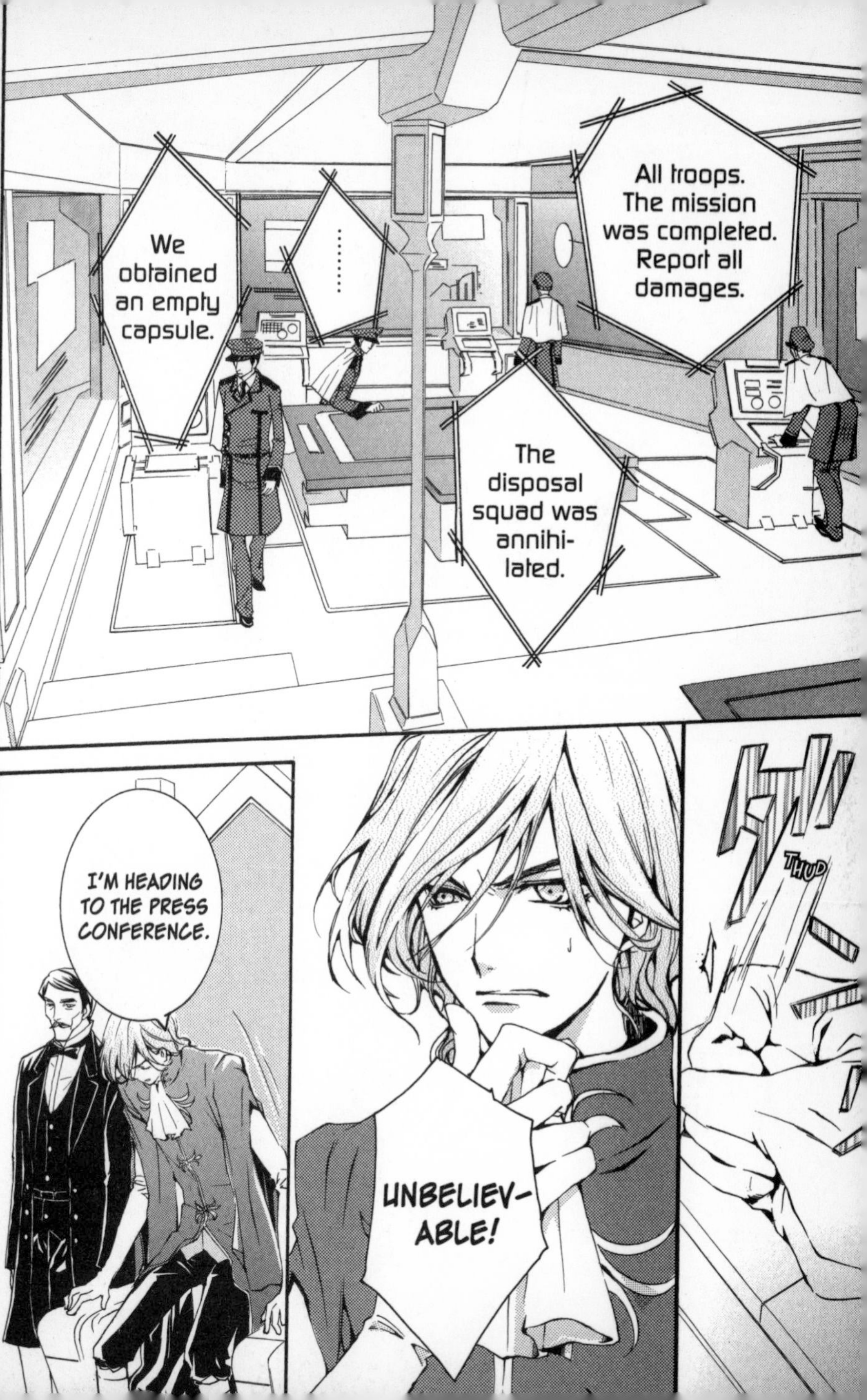

All troops. The mission was completed. Report all damages.
The disposal squad was annihi-lated.
......
We obtained an empty capsule.
THUD
UNBELIEV-ABLE!
I'M HEADING TO THE PRESS CONFERENCE.

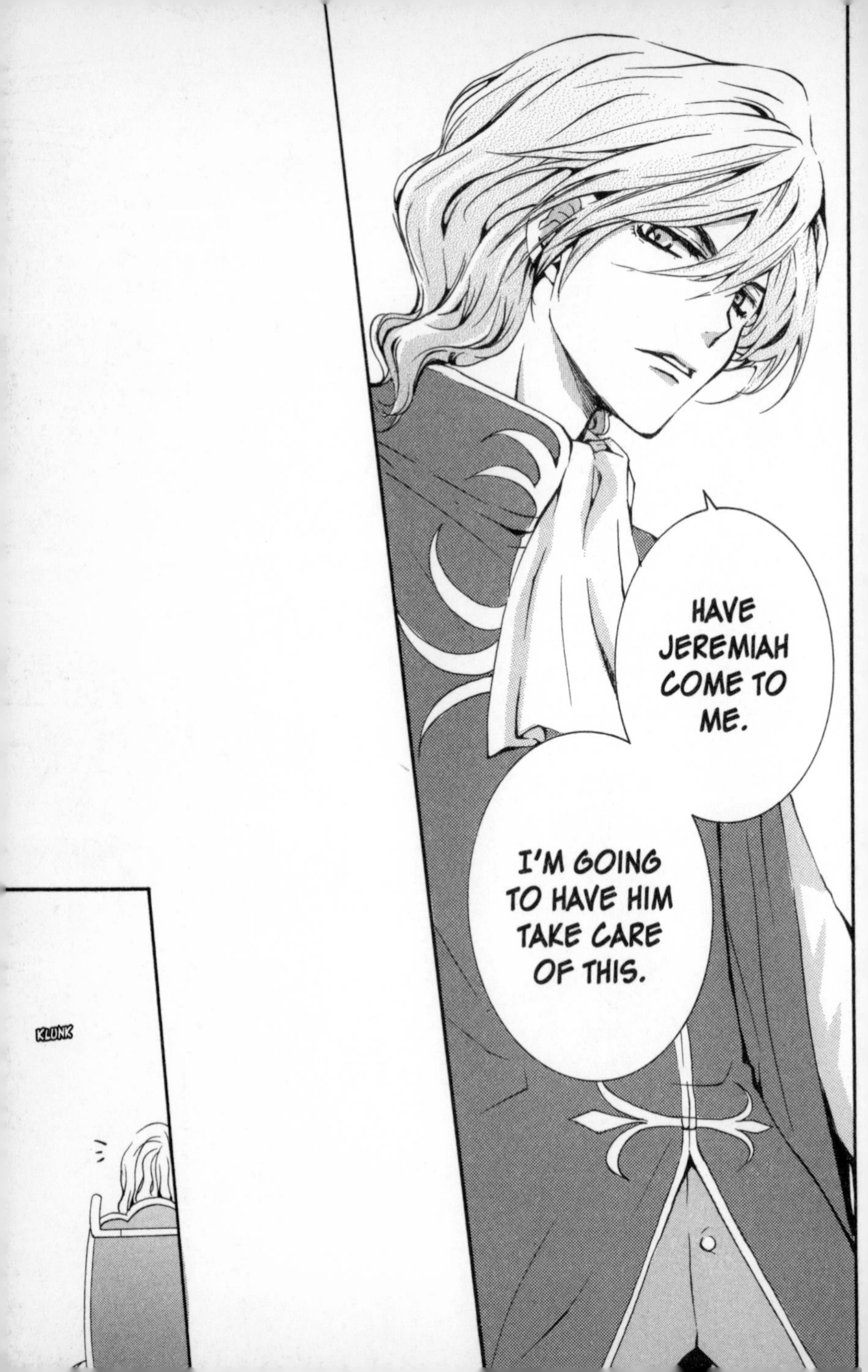
HAVE JEREMIAH COME TO ME.
I'M GOING TO HAVE HIM TAKE CARE OF THIS.
KLUNK

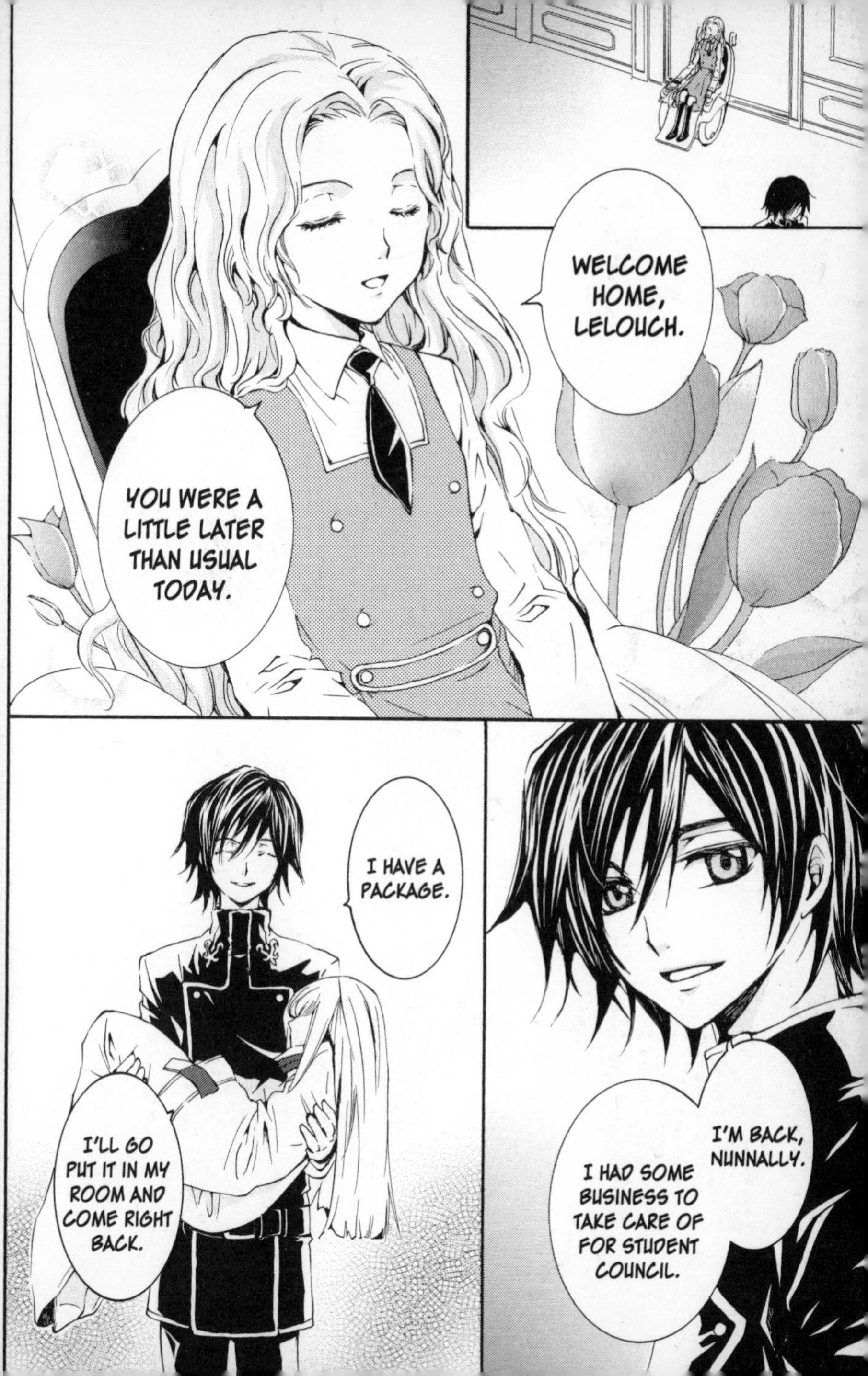
WELCOME HOME, LELOUCH.
YOU WERE A LITTLE LATER THAN USUAL TODAY.
I'M BACK, NUNNALLY.
I HAD SOME BUSINESS TO TAKE CARE OF FOR STUDENT COUNCIL.
I HAVE A PACKAGE.
I'LL GO PUT IT IN MY ROOM AND COME RIGHT BACK.

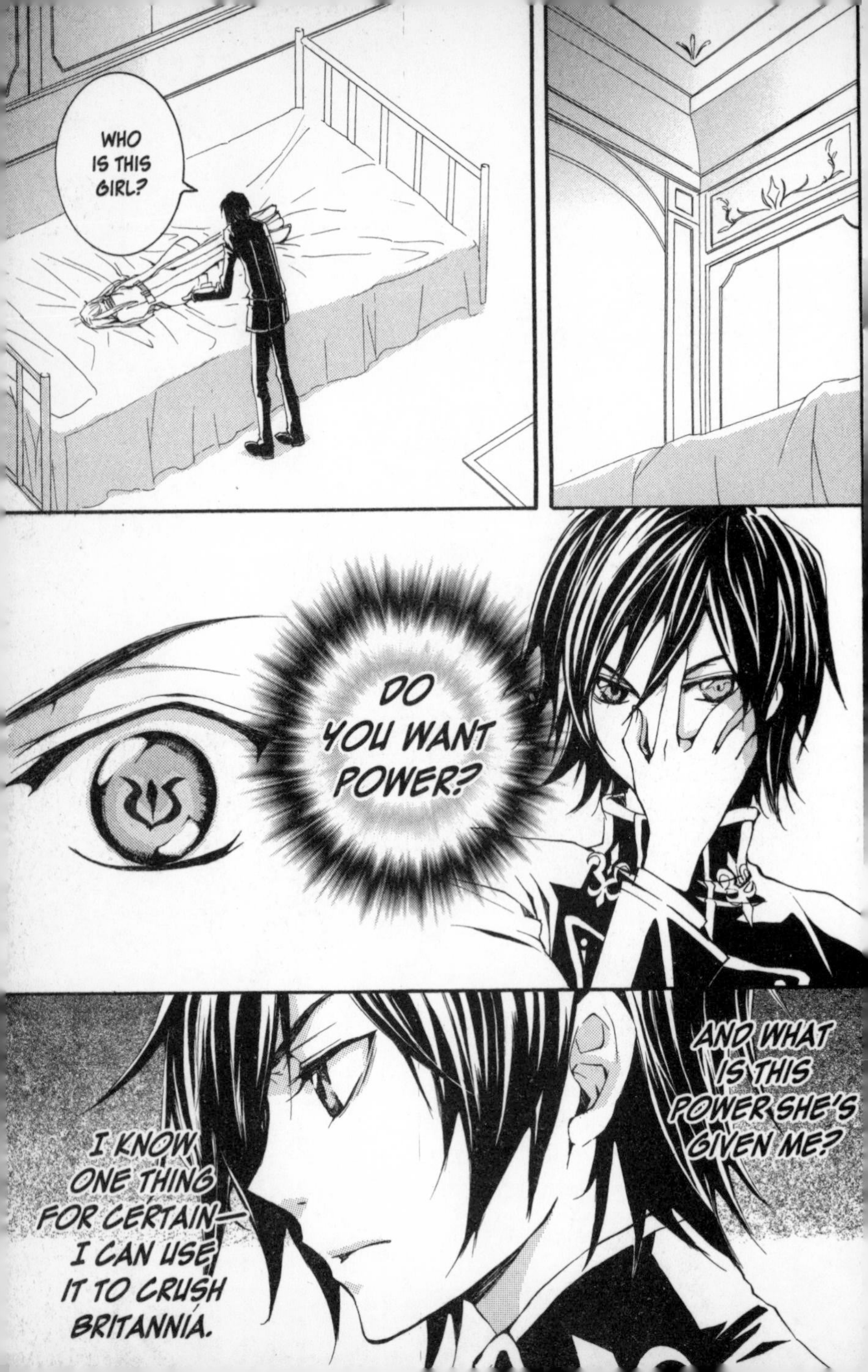
WHO IS THIS GIRL?
DO YOU WANT POWER?
AND WHAT IS THIS POWER SHE'S GIVEN ME?
I KNOW ONE THING FOR CERTAIN— I CAN USE IT TO CRUSH BRITANNIA.

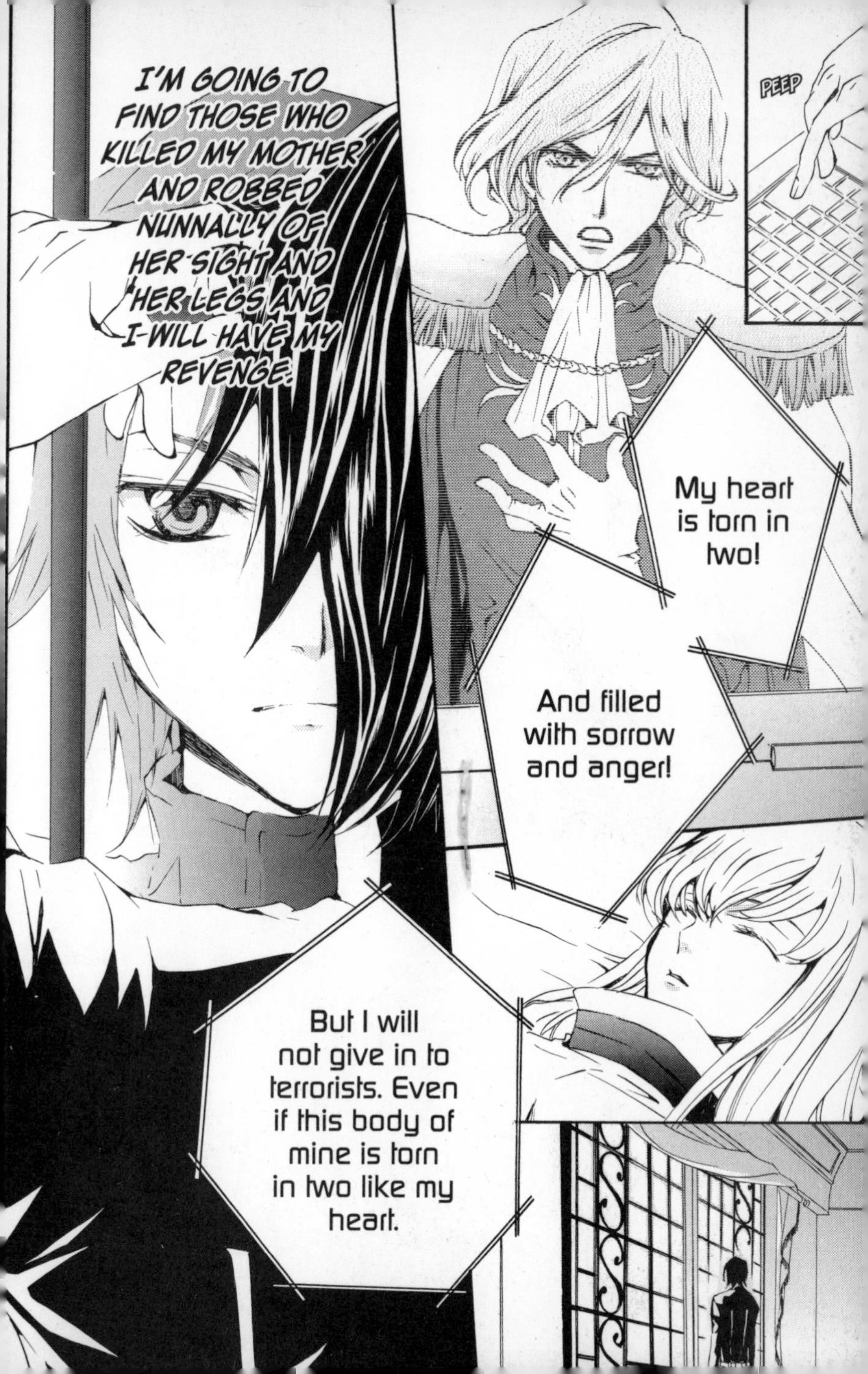
PEEP
My heart is torn in two!
And filled with sorrow and anger!
I'M GOING TO FIND THOSE WHO KILLED MY MOTHER AND ROBBED NUNNALLY OF HER SIGHT AND HER LEGS AND I WILL HAVE MY REVENGE.
But I will not give in to terrorists. Even if this body of mine is torn in two like my heart.

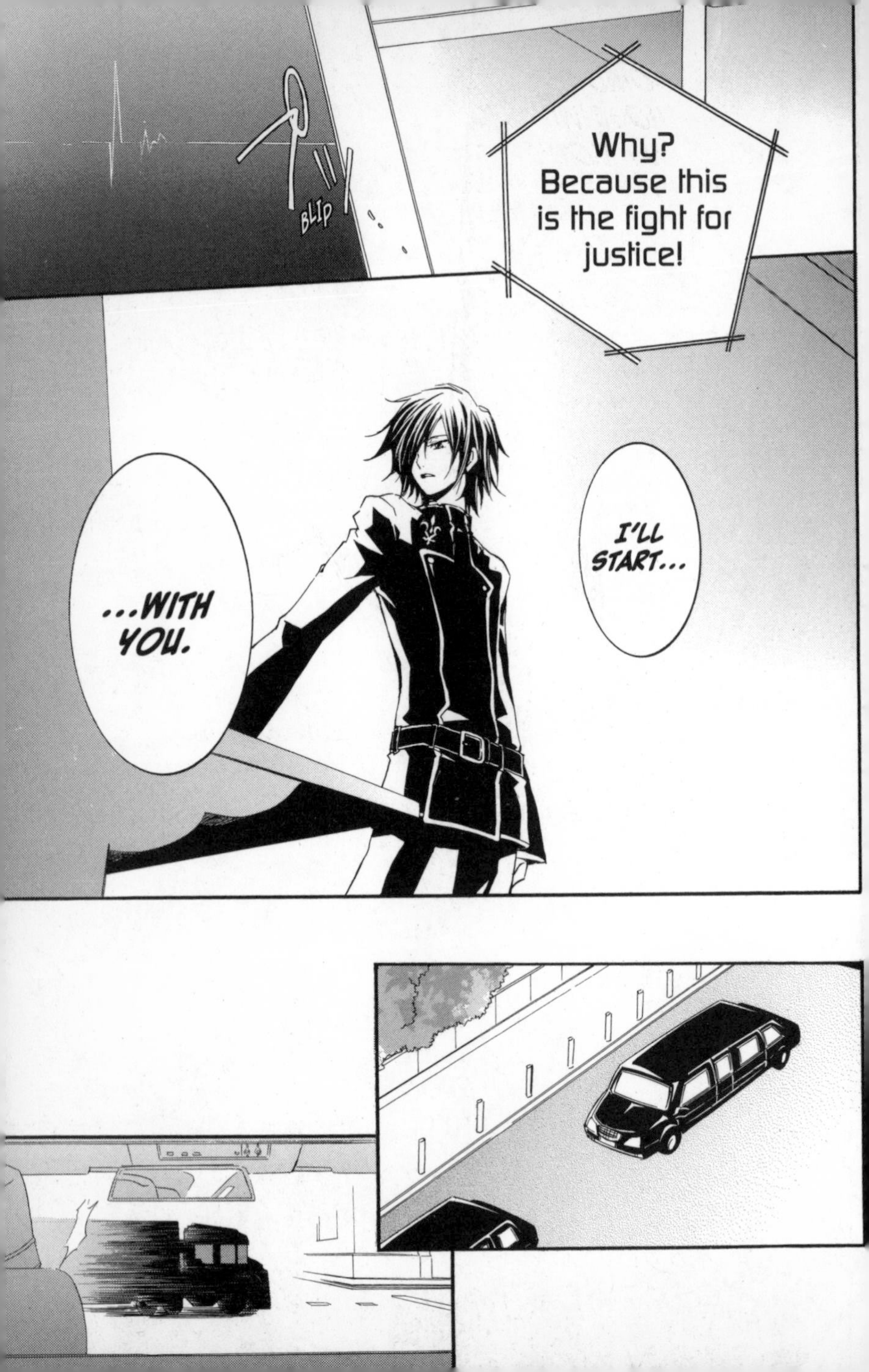
Why? Because this is the fight for justice!
BLIP
I'LL START...
...WITH YOU.

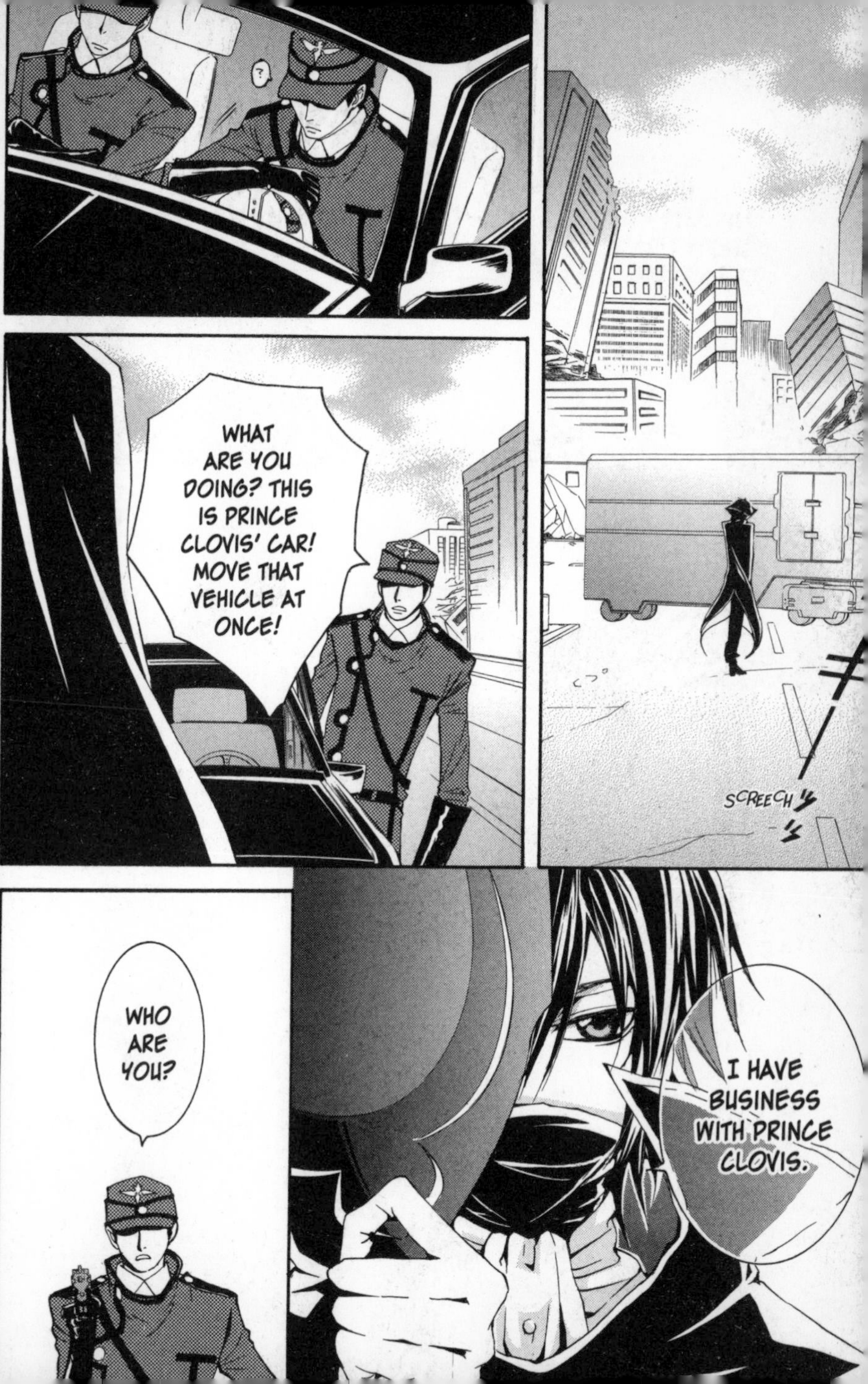
SCREECH
?
WHAT ARE YOU DOING? THIS IS PRINCE CLOVIS' CAR! MOVE THAT VEHICLE AT ONCE!
I HAVE BUSINESS WITH PRINCE CLOVIS.
WHO ARE YOU?

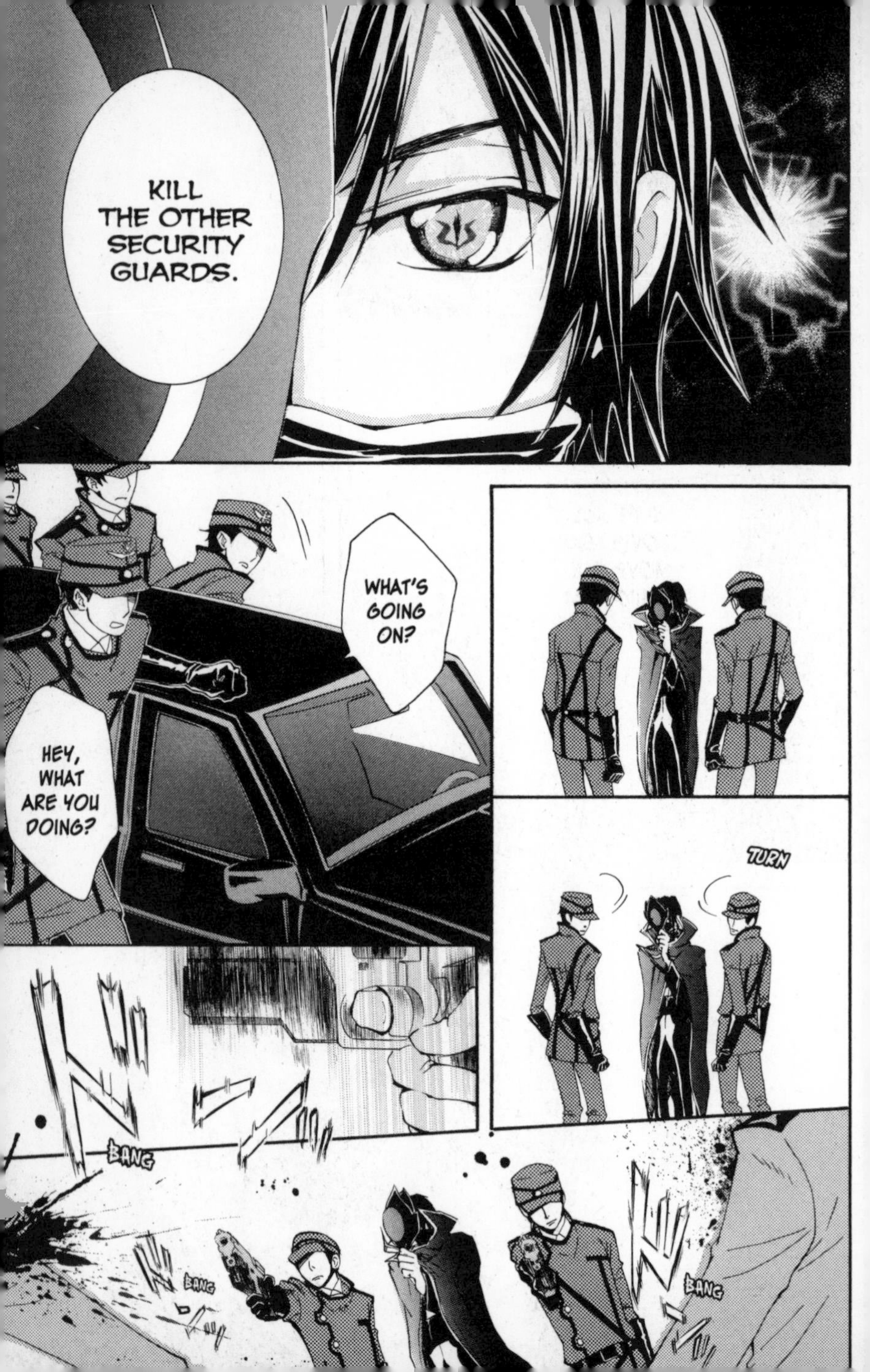
KILL THE OTHER SECURITY GUARDS.
TURN
WHAT'S GOING ON?
HEY, WHAT ARE YOU DOING?
BANG
BANG
BANG

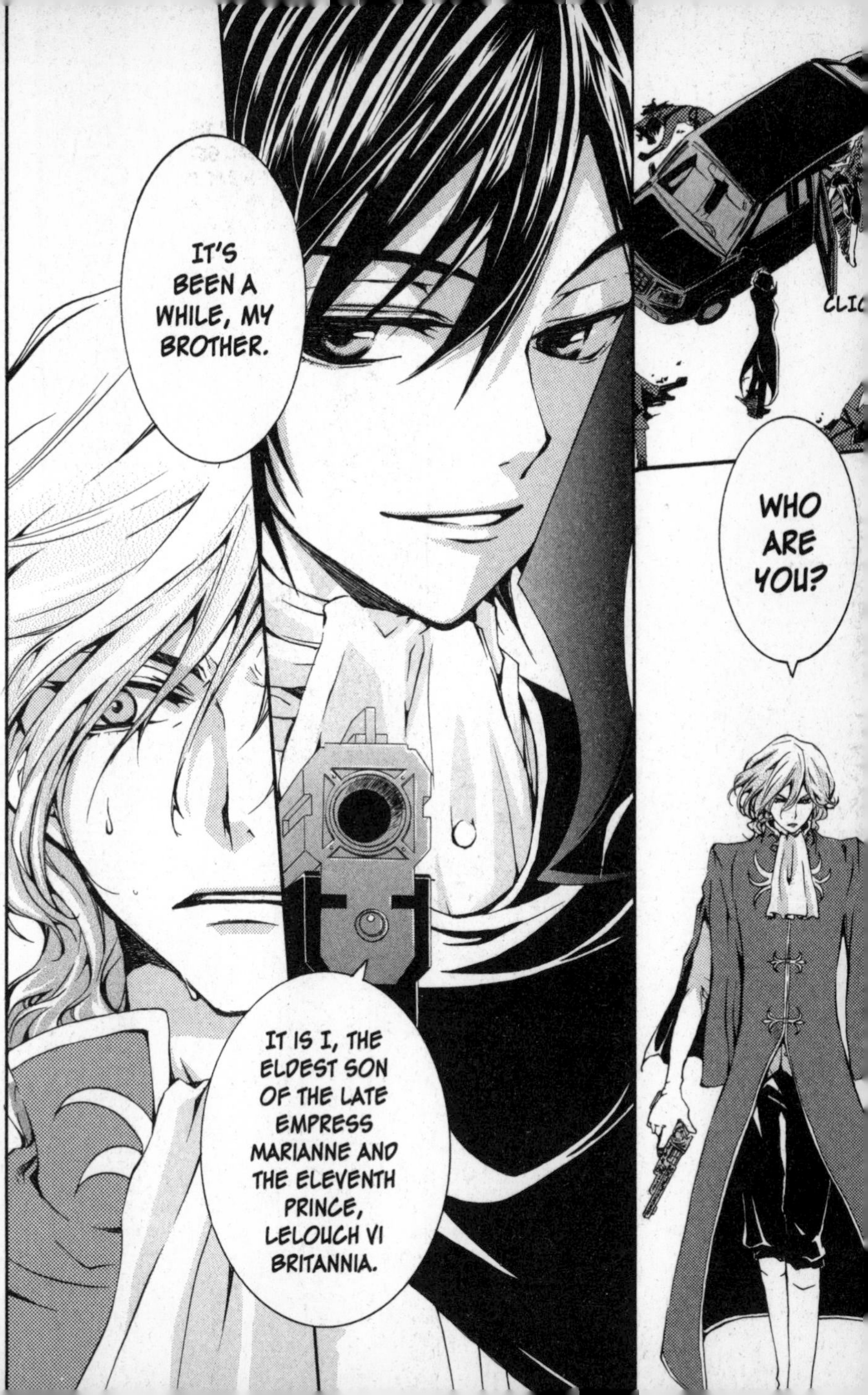
CLIC
WHO ARE YOU?
IT'S BEEN A WHILE, MY BROTHER.
IT IS I, THE ELDEST SON OF THE LATE EMPRESS MARIANNE AND THE ELEVENTH PRINCE, LELOUCH VI BRITANNIA.

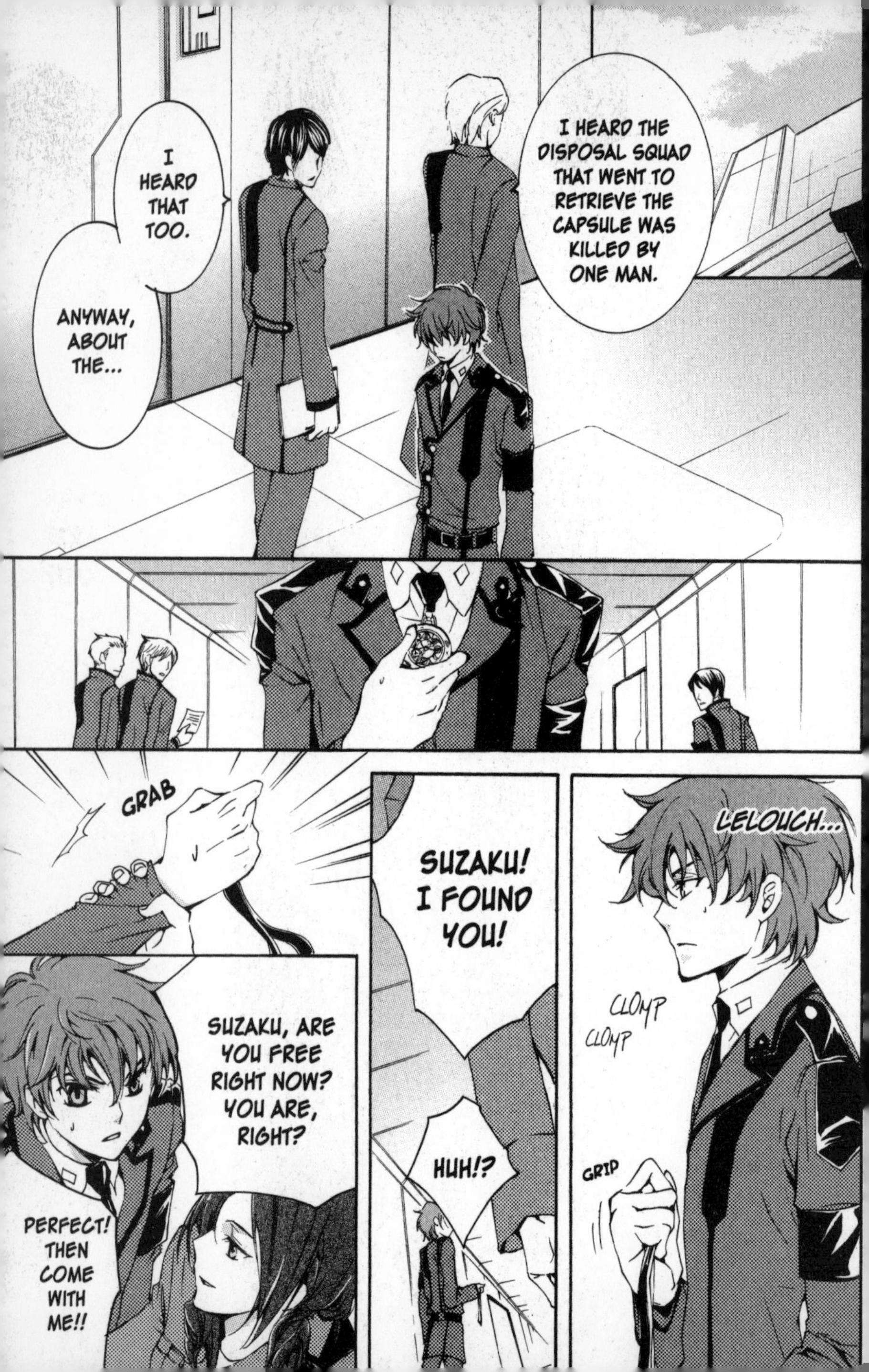
I HEARD THE DISPOSAL SQUAD THAT WENT TO RETRIEVE THE CAPSULE WAS KILLED BY ONE MAN.
I HEARD THAT TOO.
ANYWAY, ABOUT THE...
LELOUCH...
CLOMP
CLOMP
GRIP
SUZAKU! I FOUND YOU!
HUH!?
GRAB
SUZAKU, ARE YOU FREE RIGHT NOW? YOU ARE, RIGHT?
PERFECT! THEN COME WITH ME!!

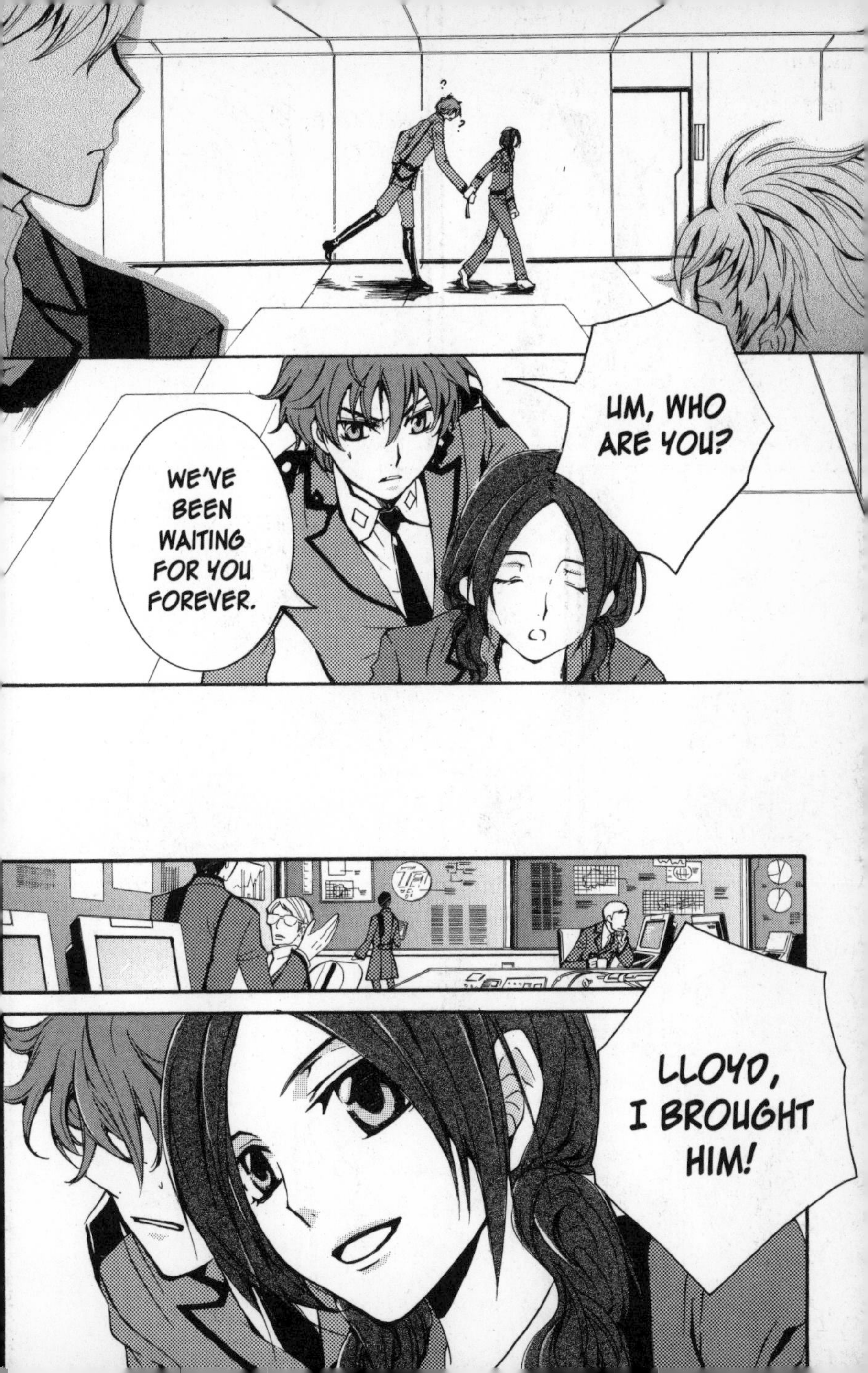
UM, WHO ARE YOU?
WE'VE BEEN WAITING FOR YOU FOREVER.
LLOYD, I BROUGHT HIM!

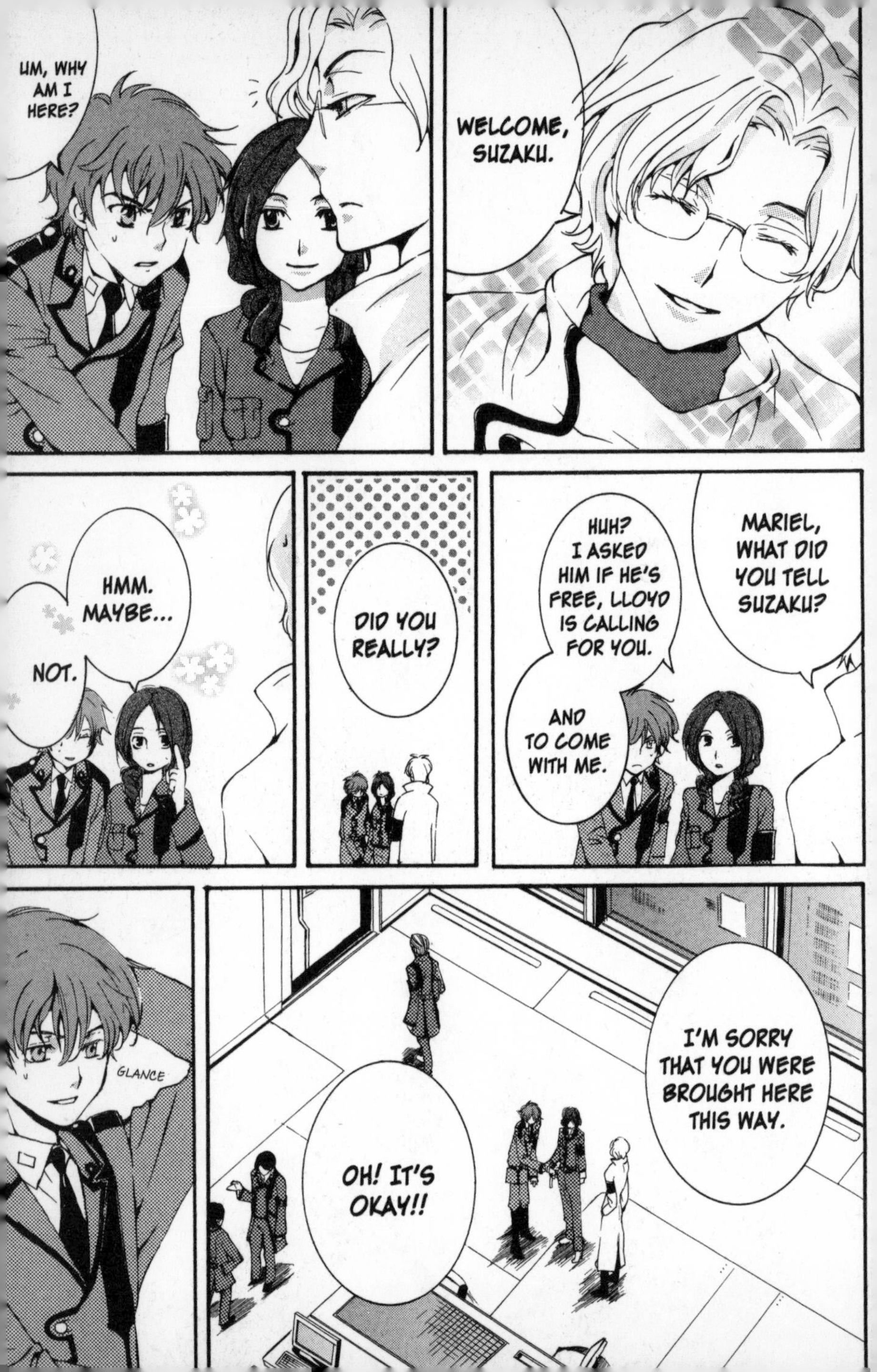
WELCOME, SUZAKU.
UM, WHY AM I HERE?
MARIEL, WHAT DID YOU TELL SUZAKU?
HUH? I ASKED HIM IF HE'S FREE, LLOYD IS CALLING FOR YOU.
AND TO COME WITH ME.
DID YOU REALLY?
HMM. MAYBE...
NOT.
I'M SORRY THAT YOU WERE BROUGHT HERE THIS WAY.
OH! IT'S OKAY!!
GLANCE

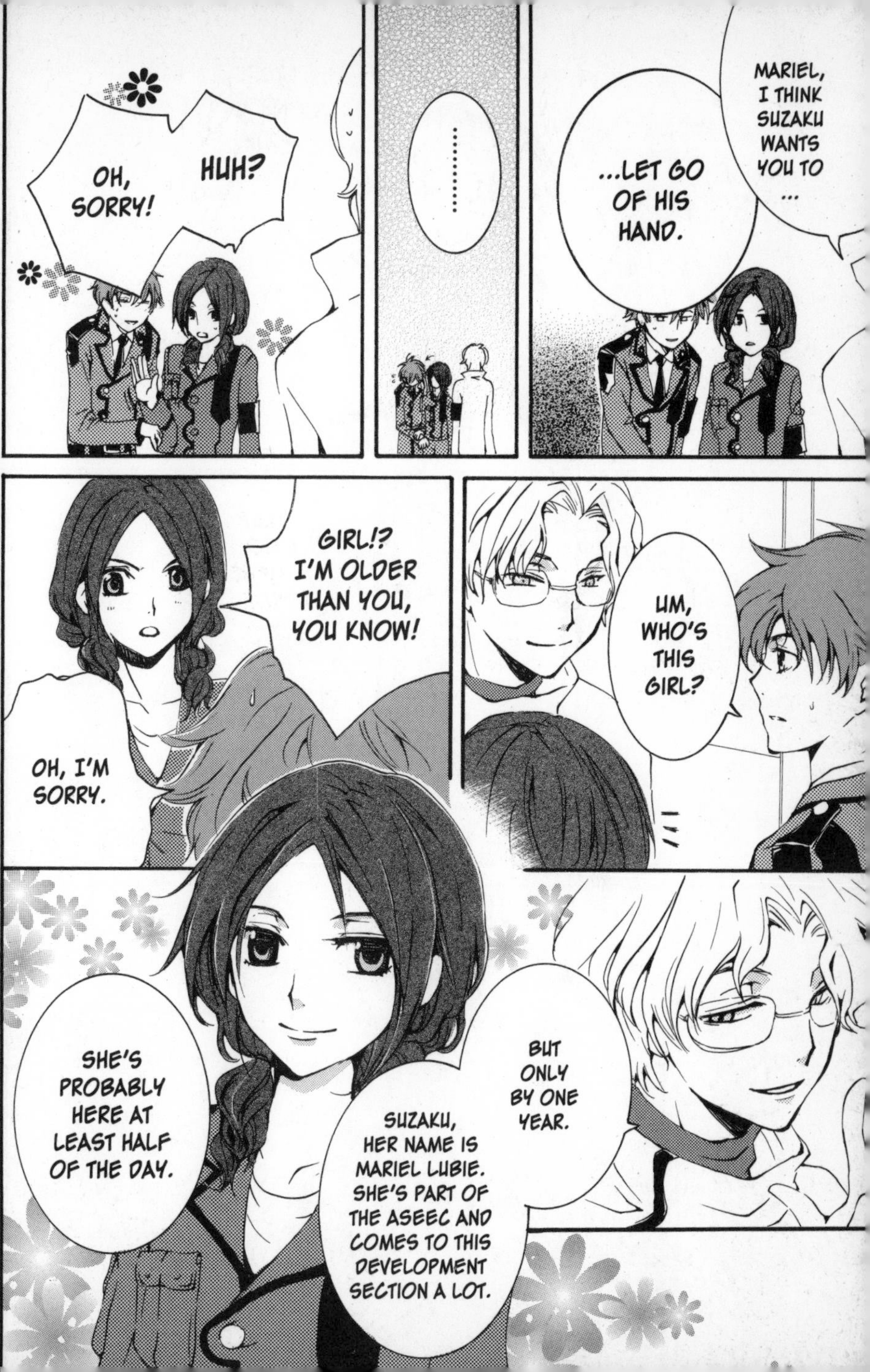
MARIEL, I THINK SUZAKU WANTS YOU TO ...
...LET GO OF HIS HAND.
....
HUH?
OH, SORRY!
UM, WHO'S THIS GIRL?
GIRL!? I'M OLDER THAN YOU, YOU KNOW!
OH, I'M SORRY.
BUT ONLY BY ONE YEAR.
SUZAKU, HER NAME IS MARIEL LUBIE. SHE'S PART OF THE ASEEC AND COMES TO THIS DEVELOPMENT SECTION A LOT.
SHE'S PROBABLY HERE AT LEAST HALF OF THE DAY.

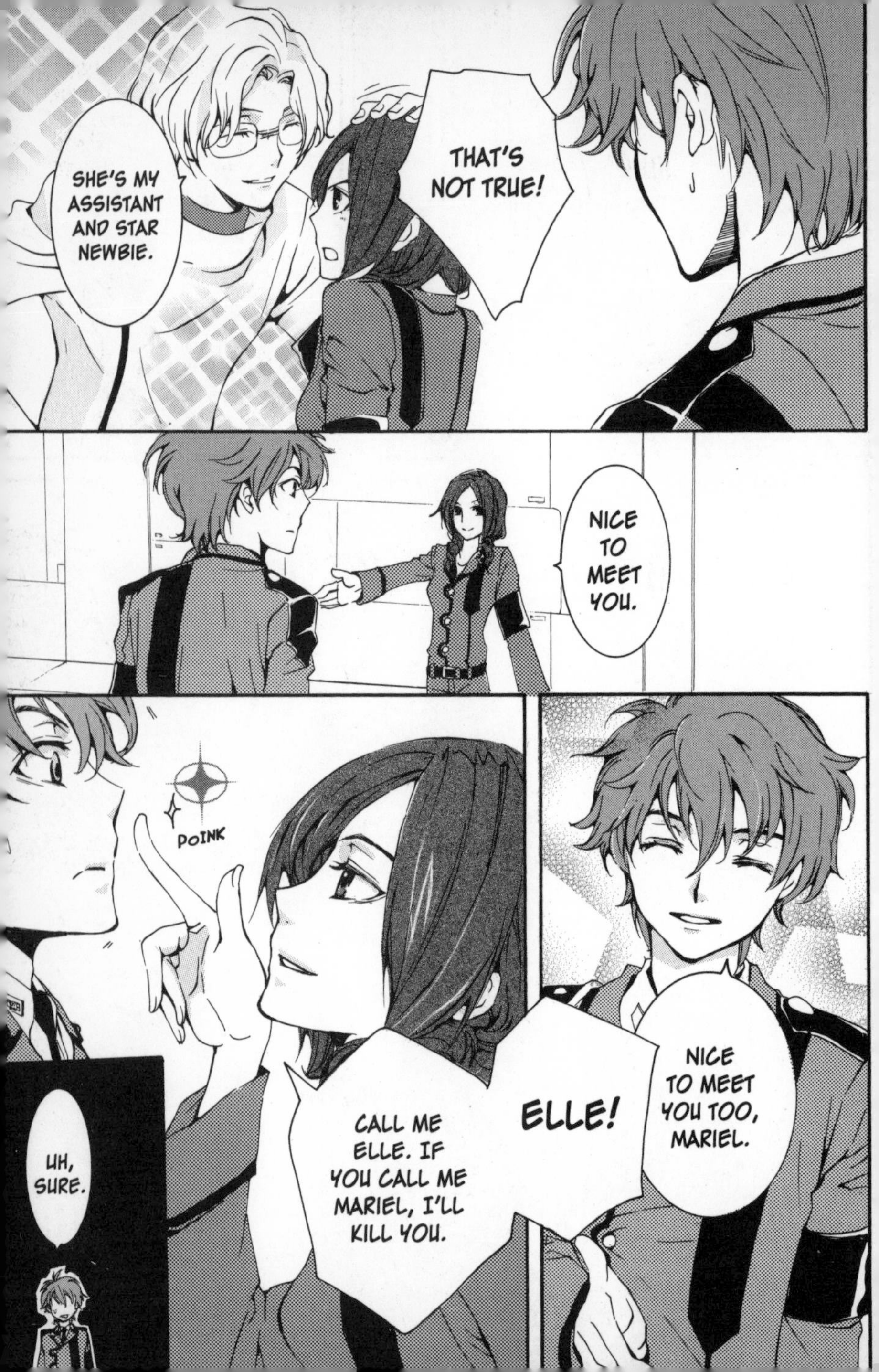
SHE'S MY ASSISTANT AND STAR NEWBIE.
THAT'S NOT TRUE!
NICE TO MEET YOU.
NICE TO MEET YOU TOO, MARIEL.
ELLE!
POINK
CALL ME ELLE. IF YOU CALL ME MARIEL, I'LL KILL YOU.
UH, SURE.

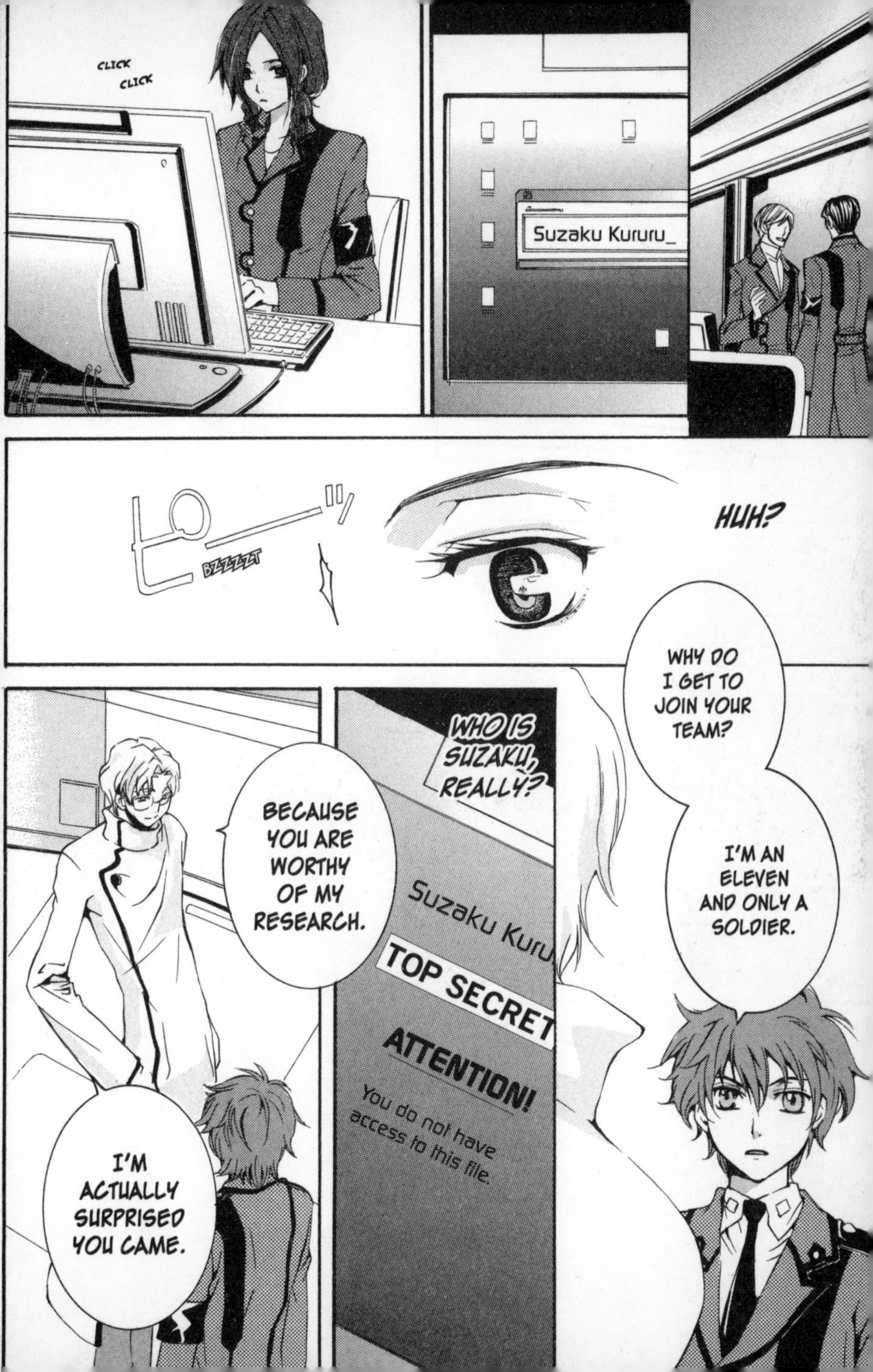
Suzaku Kururu_
CLICK
CLICK
HUH?
BZZZZT
WHY DO I GET TO JOIN YOUR TEAM?
I'M AN ELEVEN AND ONLY A SOLDIER.
WHO IS SUZAKU, REALLY?
Suzaku Kuru
TOP SECRET
ATTENTION!
You do not have access to this file.
BECAUSE YOU ARE WORTHY OF MY RESEARCH.
I'M ACTUALLY SURPRISED YOU CAME.

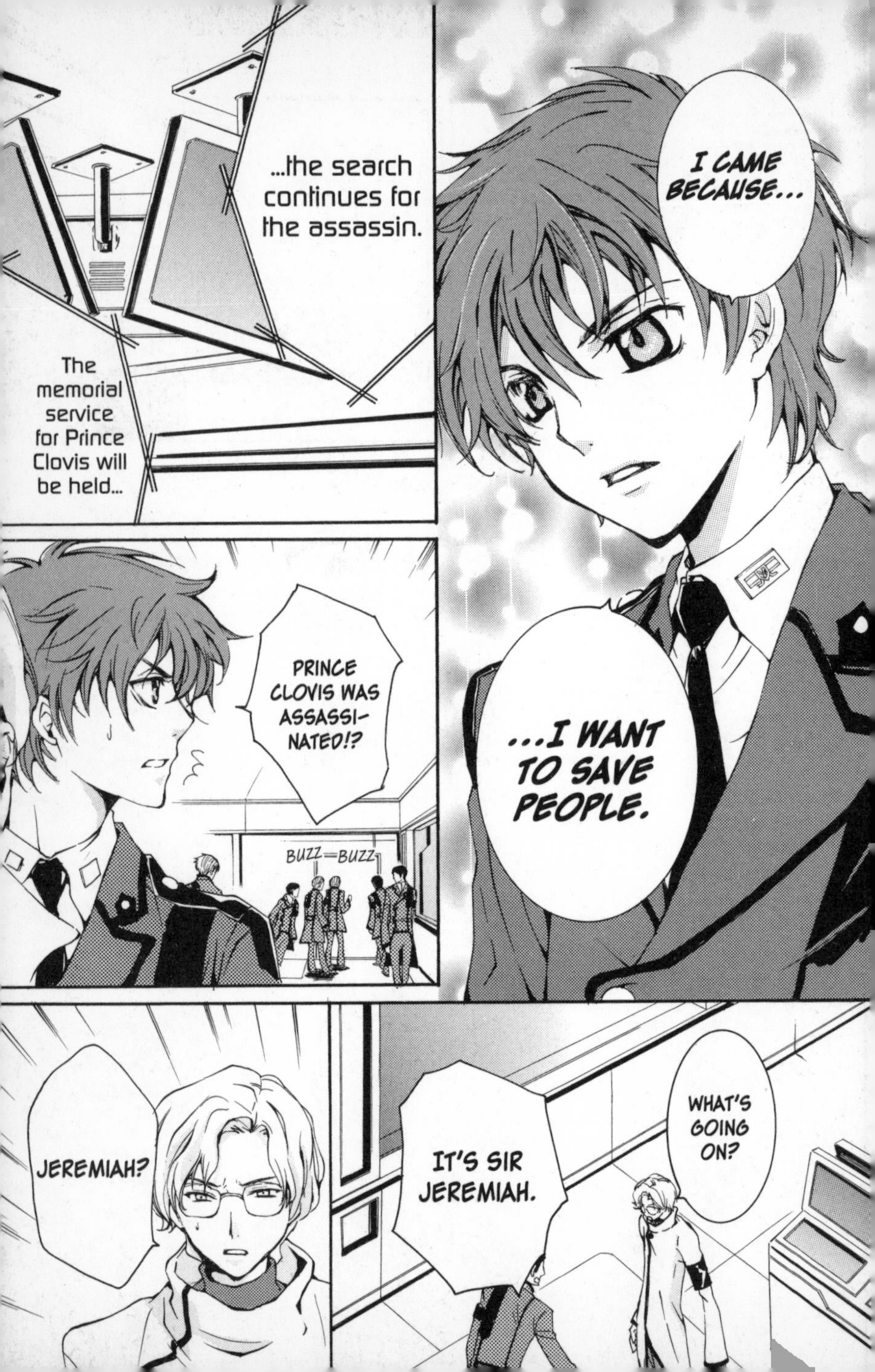
I CAME BECAUSE...
...I WANT TO SAVE PEOPLE.
...the search continues for the assassin.
The memorial service for Prince Clovis will be held...
PRINCE CLOVIS WAS ASSASSI-NATED!?
BUZZ BUZZ
WHAT'S GOING ON?
IT'S SIR JEREMIAH.
JEREMIAH?

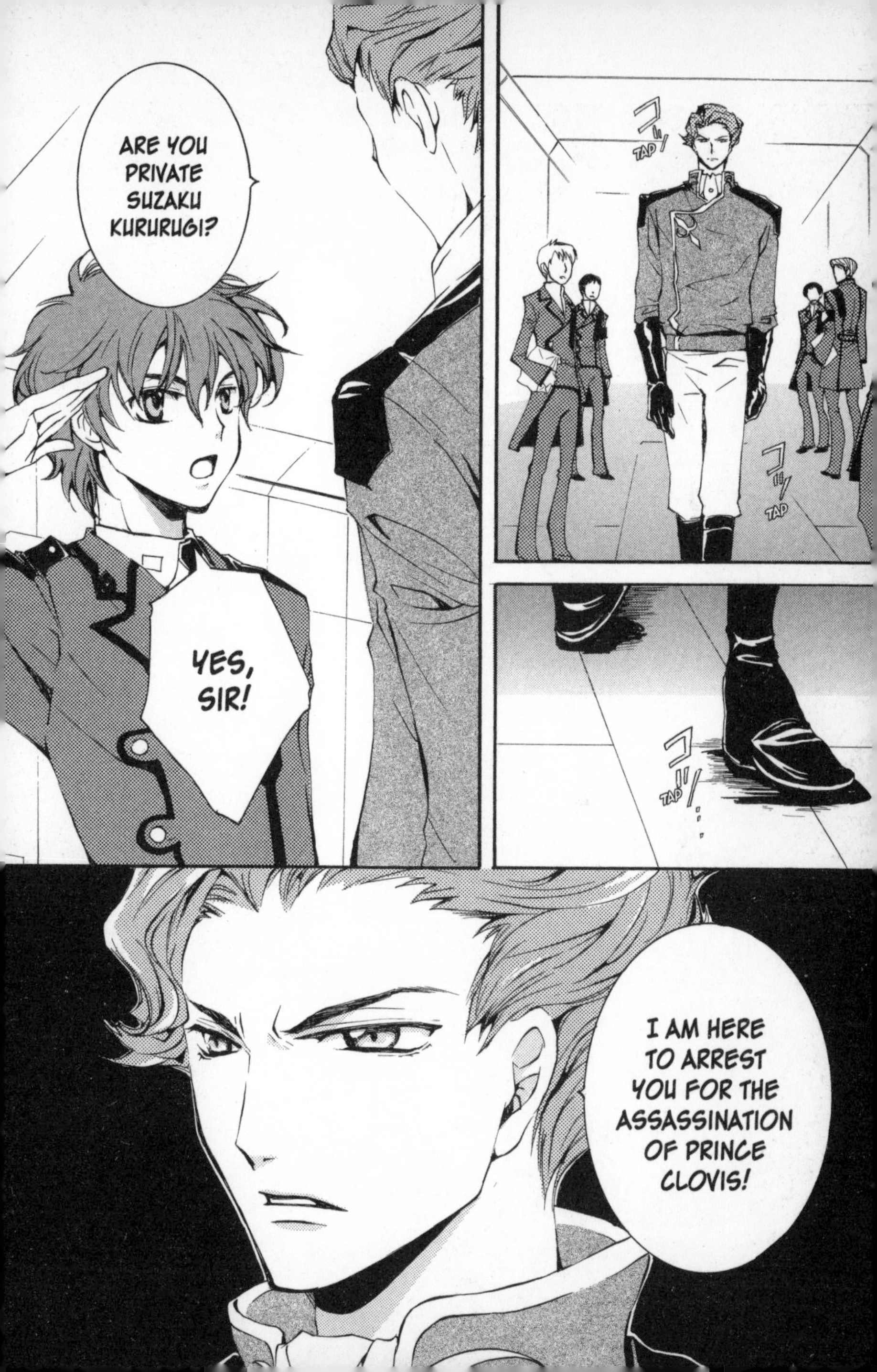
TAP
TAP
TAP
ARE YOU PRIVATE SUZAKU KURURUGI?
YES, SIR!
I AM HERE TO ARREST YOU FOR THE ASSASSINATION OF PRINCE CLOVIS!

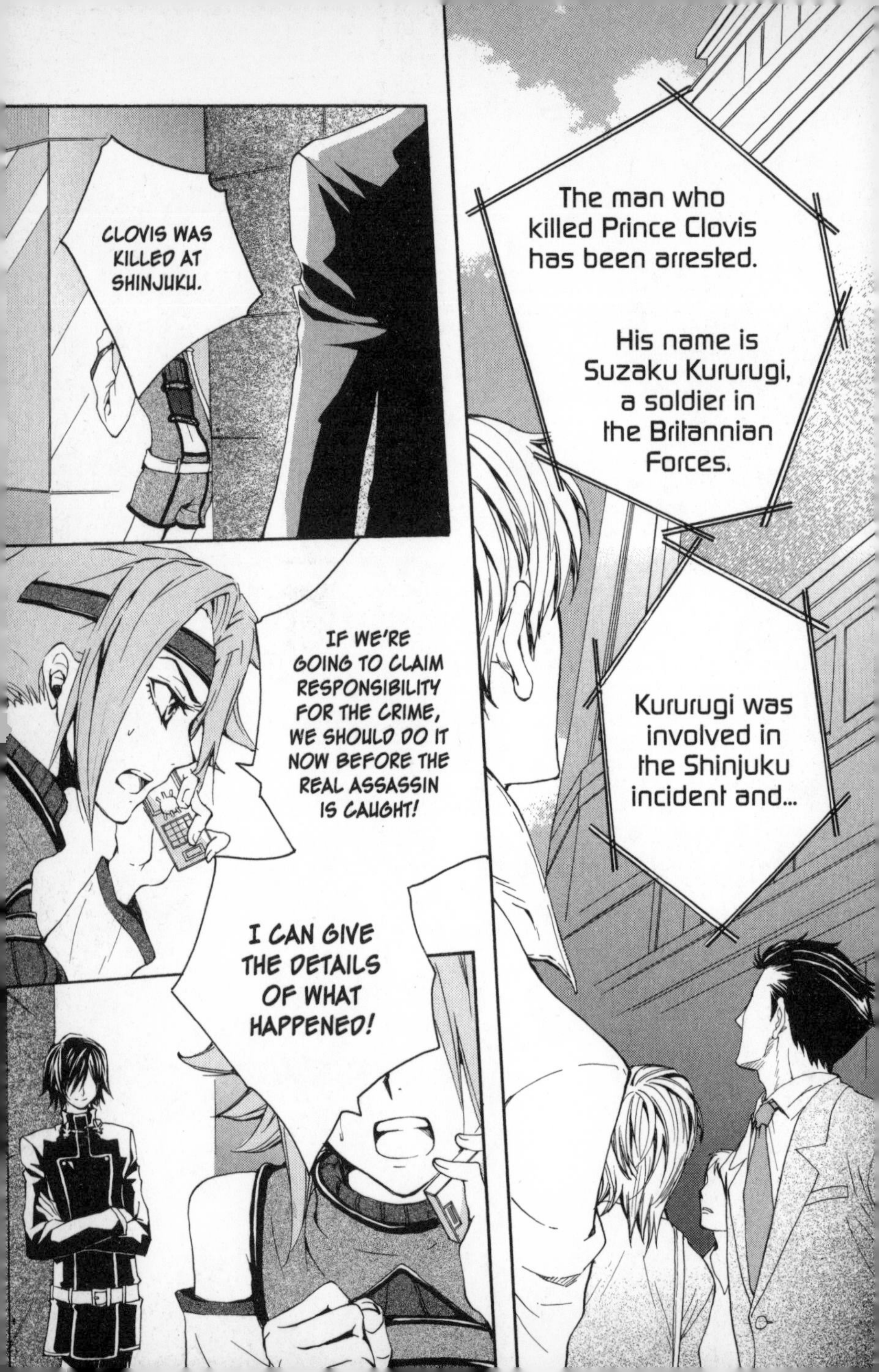
The man who killed Prince Clovis has been arrested.
His name is Suzaku Kururugi, a soldier in the Britannian Forces.
Kururugi was involved in the Shinjuku incident and...
CLOVIS WAS KILLED AT SHINJUKU.
IF WE'RE GOING TO CLAIM RESPONSIBILITY FOR THE CRIME, WE SHOULD DO IT NOW BEFORE THE REAL ASSASSIN IS CAUGHT!
I CAN GIVE THE DETAILS OF WHAT HAPPENED!

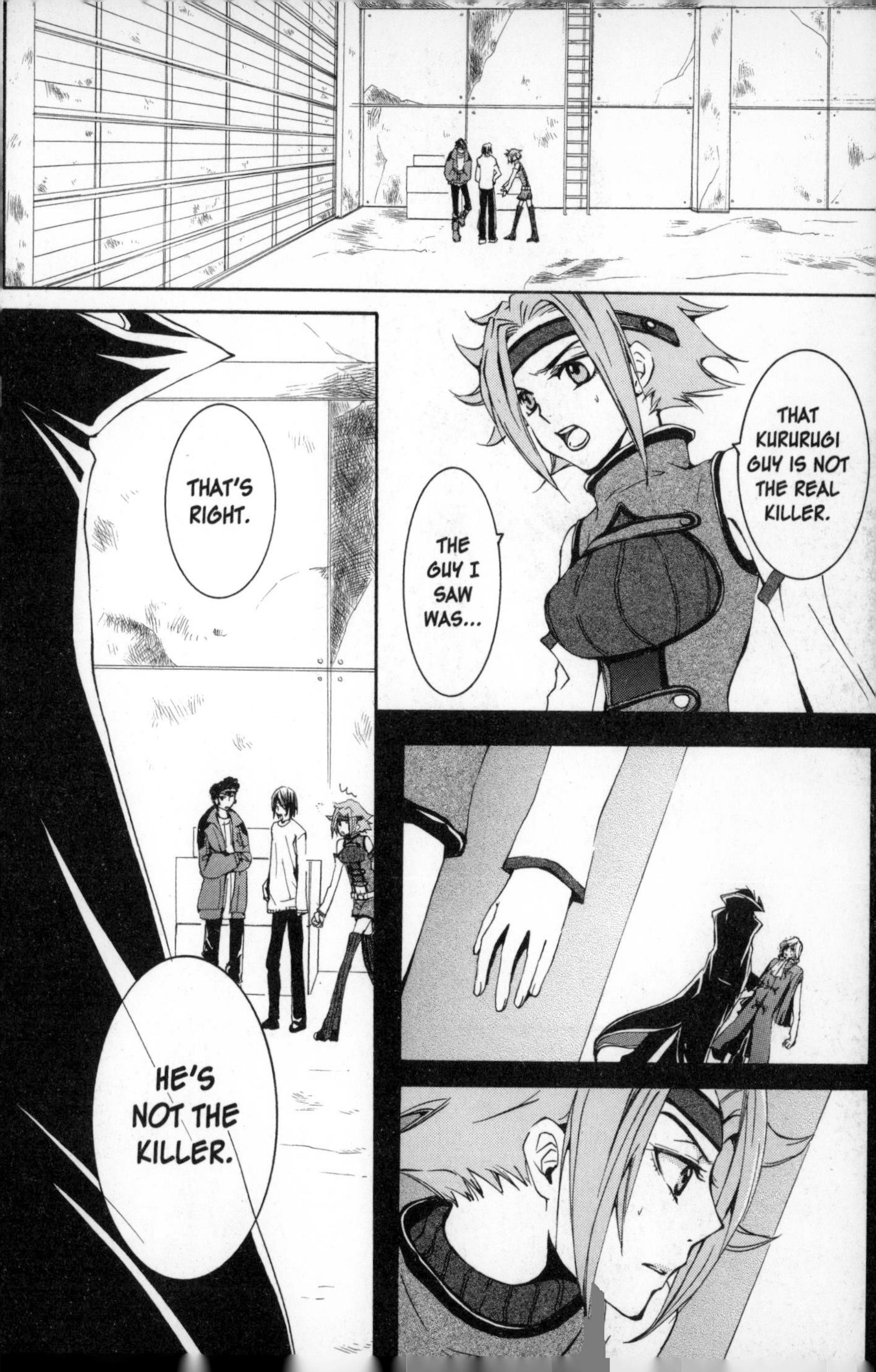
THAT KURURUGI GUY IS NOT THE REAL KILLER.
THE GUY I SAW WAS...
THAT'S RIGHT.
HE'S NOT THE KILLER.

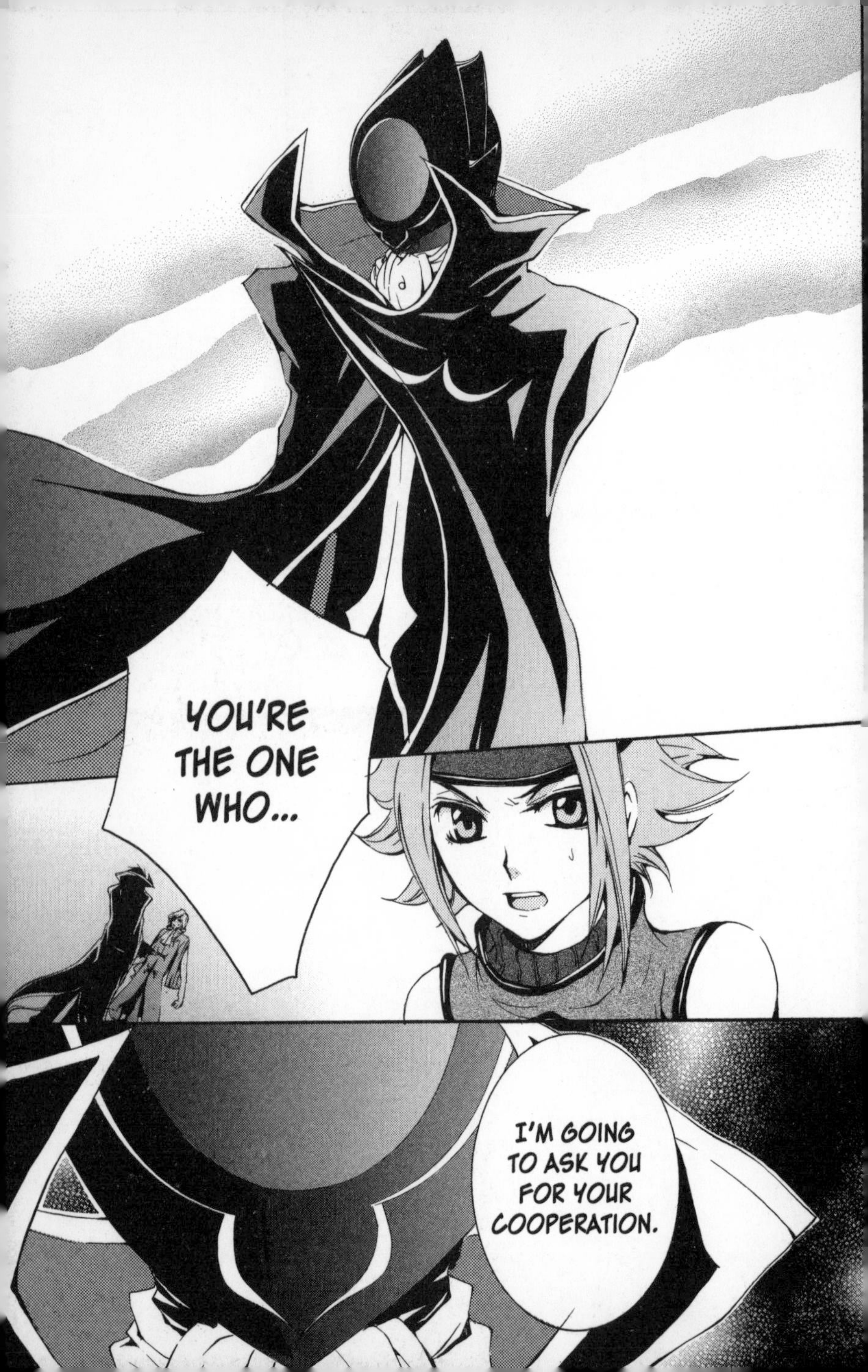
YOU'RE THE ONE WHO...
I'M GOING TO ASK YOU FOR YOUR COOPERATION.

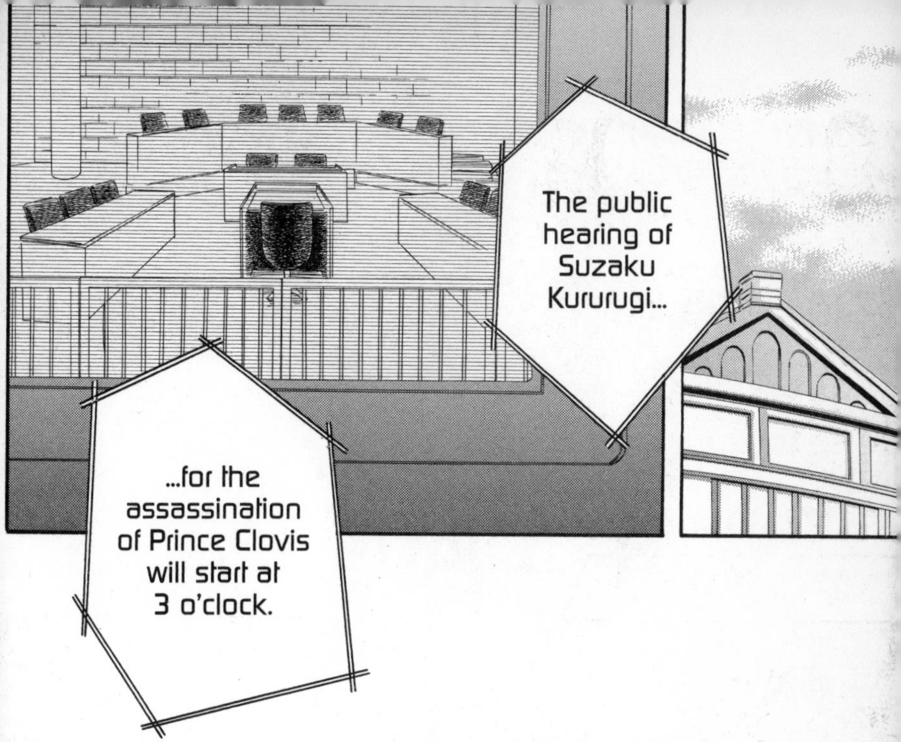
The public hearing of Suzaku Kururugi...
...for the assassination of Prince Clovis will start at 3 o'clock.

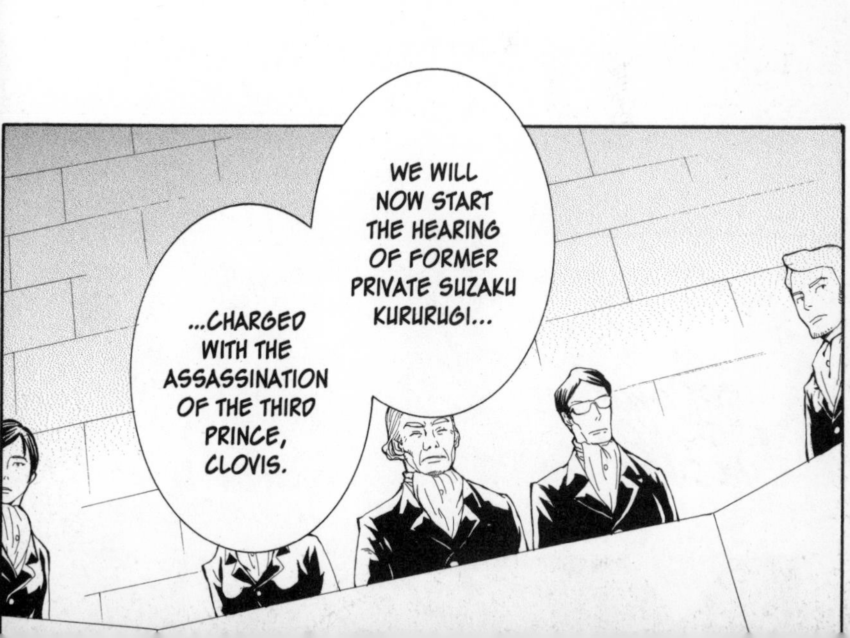
WE WILL NOW START THE HEARING OF FORMER PRIVATE SUZAKU KURURUGI...
...CHARGED WITH THE ASSASSINATION OF THE THIRD PRINCE, CLOVIS.

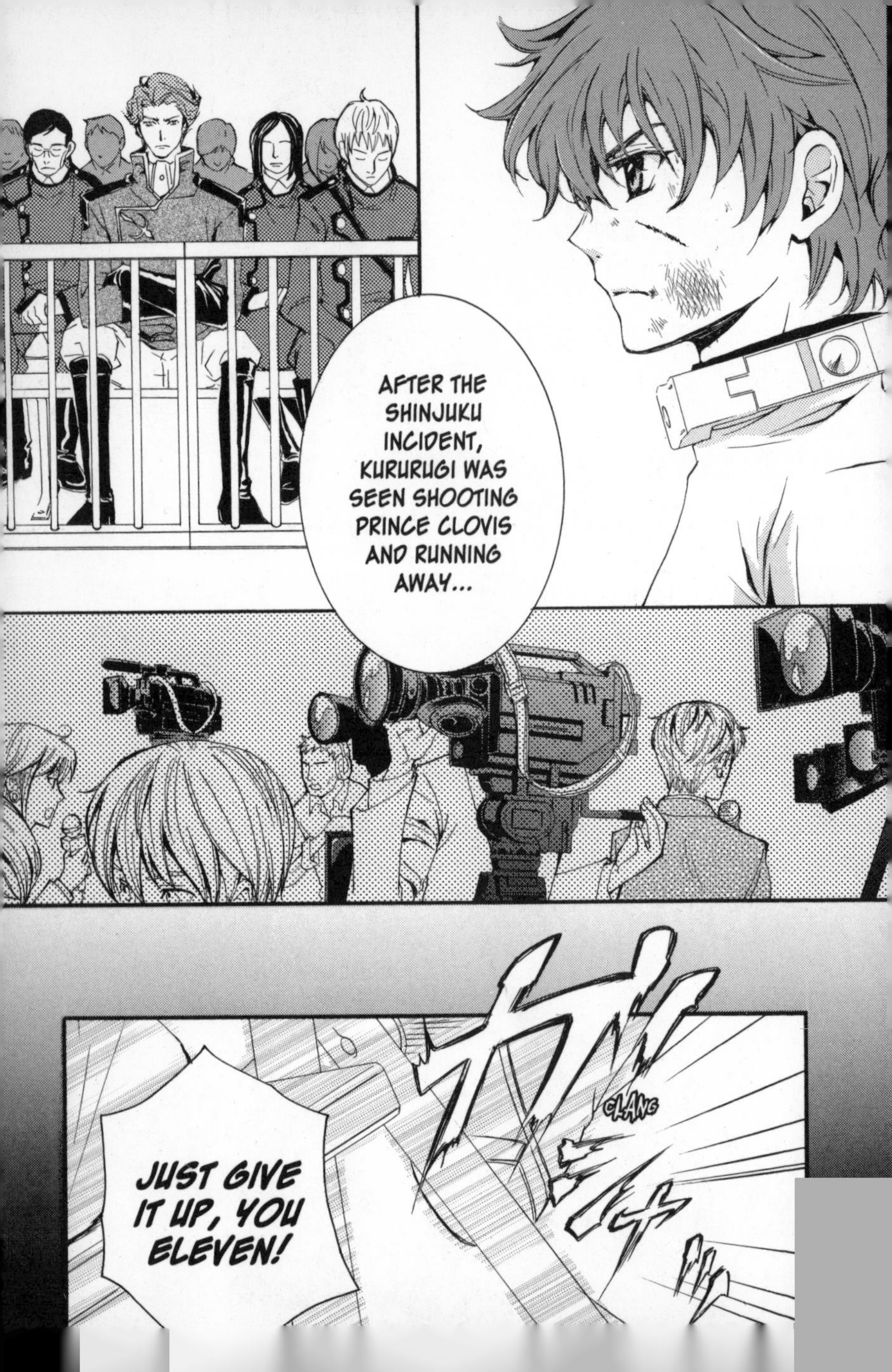
AFTER THE SHINJUKU INCIDENT, KURURUGI WAS SEEN SHOOTING PRINCE CLOVIS AND RUNNING AWAY...
CLANG
JUST GIVE IT UP, YOU ELEVEN!

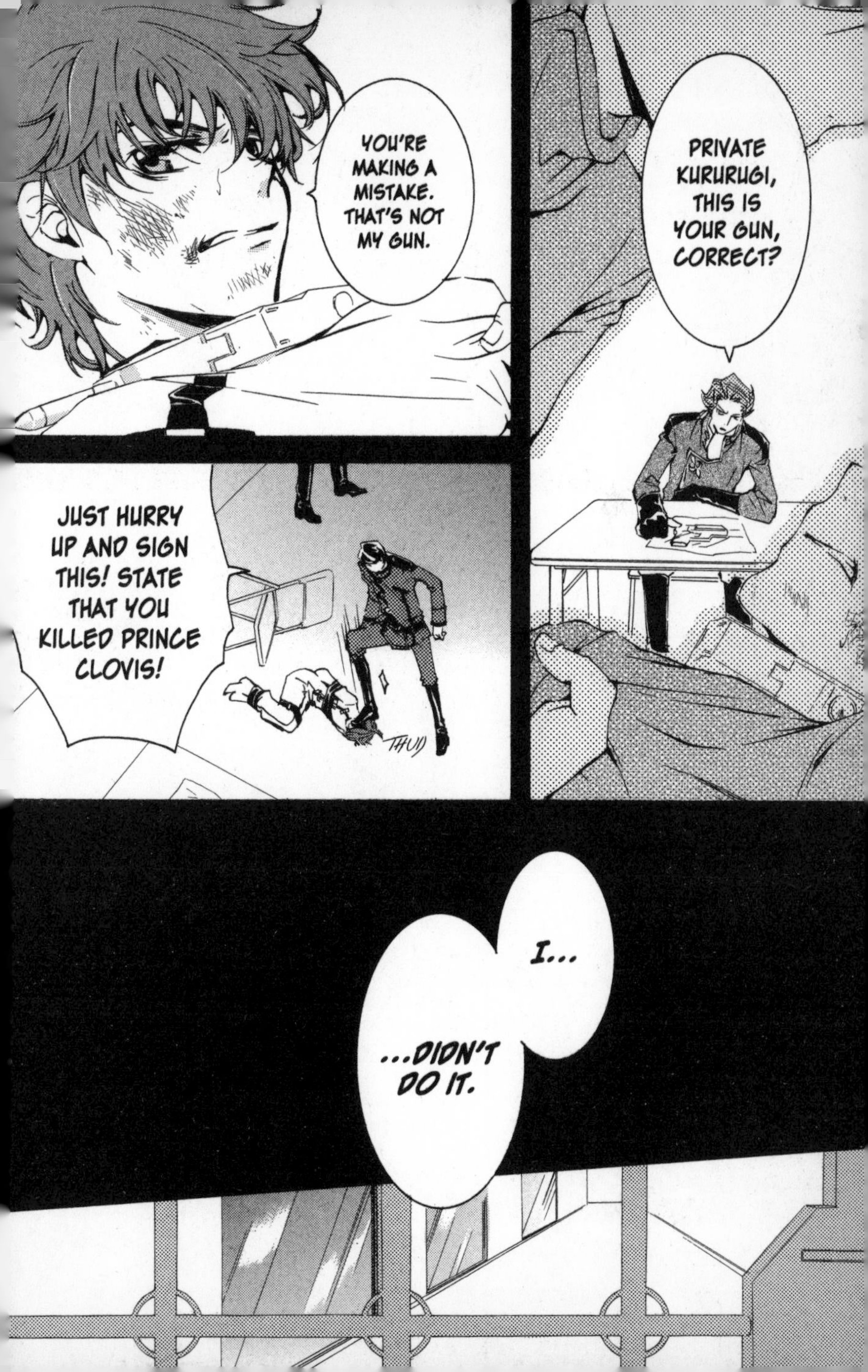
PRIVATE KURURUGI, THIS IS YOUR GUN, CORRECT?
YOU'RE MAKING A MISTAKE. THAT'S NOT MY GUN.
JUST HURRY UP AND SIGN THIS! STATE THAT YOU KILLED PRINCE CLOVIS!
THUD
I...
...DIDN'T DO IT.

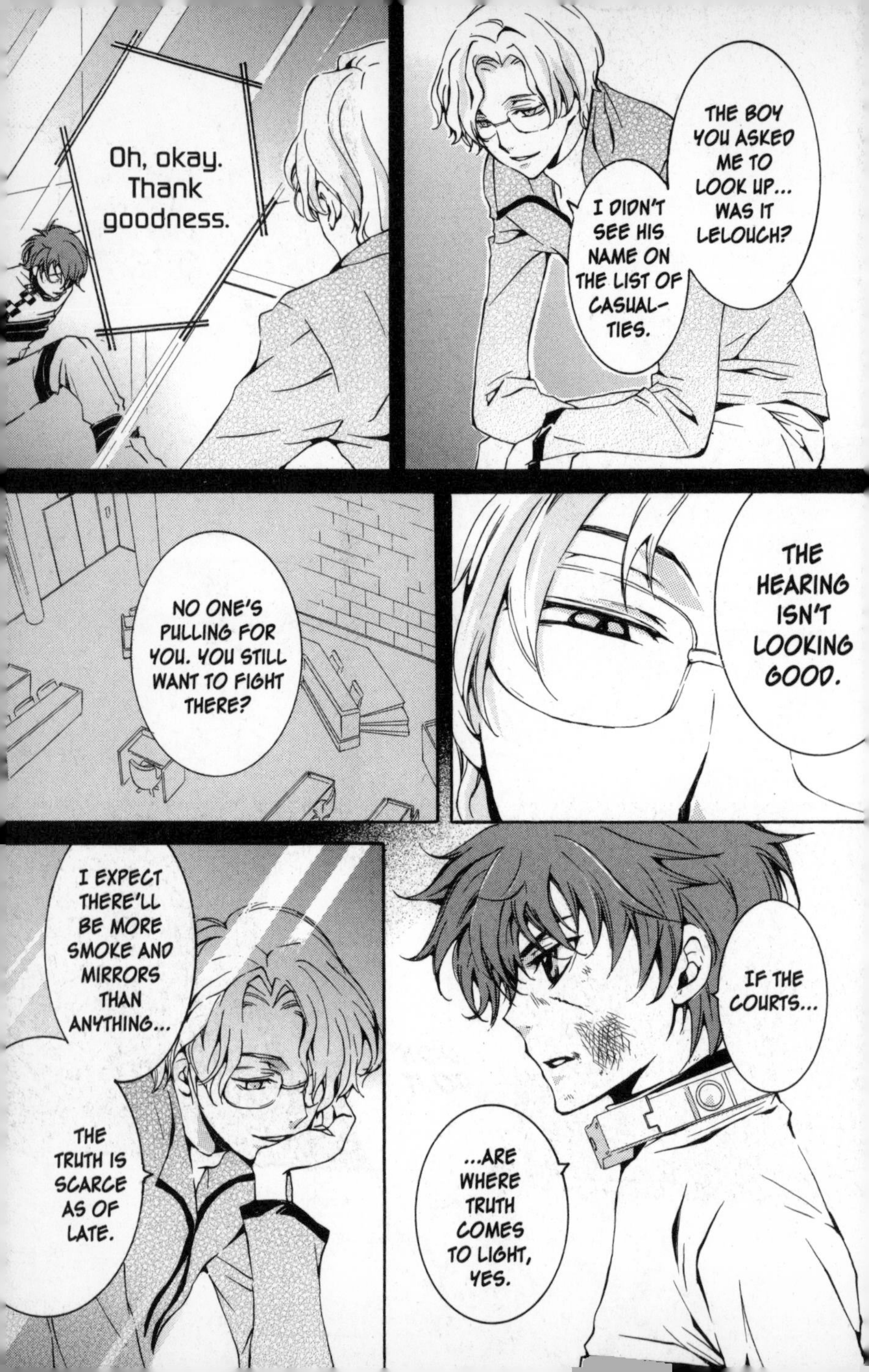
THE BOY YOU ASKED ME TO LOOK UP... WAS IT LELOUCH?
I DIDN'T SEE HIS NAME ON THE LIST OF CASUAL-TIES.
Oh, okay. Thank goodness.
THE HEARING ISN'T LOOKING GOOD.
NO ONE'S PULLING FOR YOU. YOU STILL WANT TO FIGHT THERE?
IF THE COURTS...
...ARE WHERE TRUTH COMES TO LIGHT, YES.
I EXPECT THERE'LL BE MORE SMOKE AND MIRRORS THAN ANYTHING...
THE TRUTH IS SCARCE AS OF LATE.

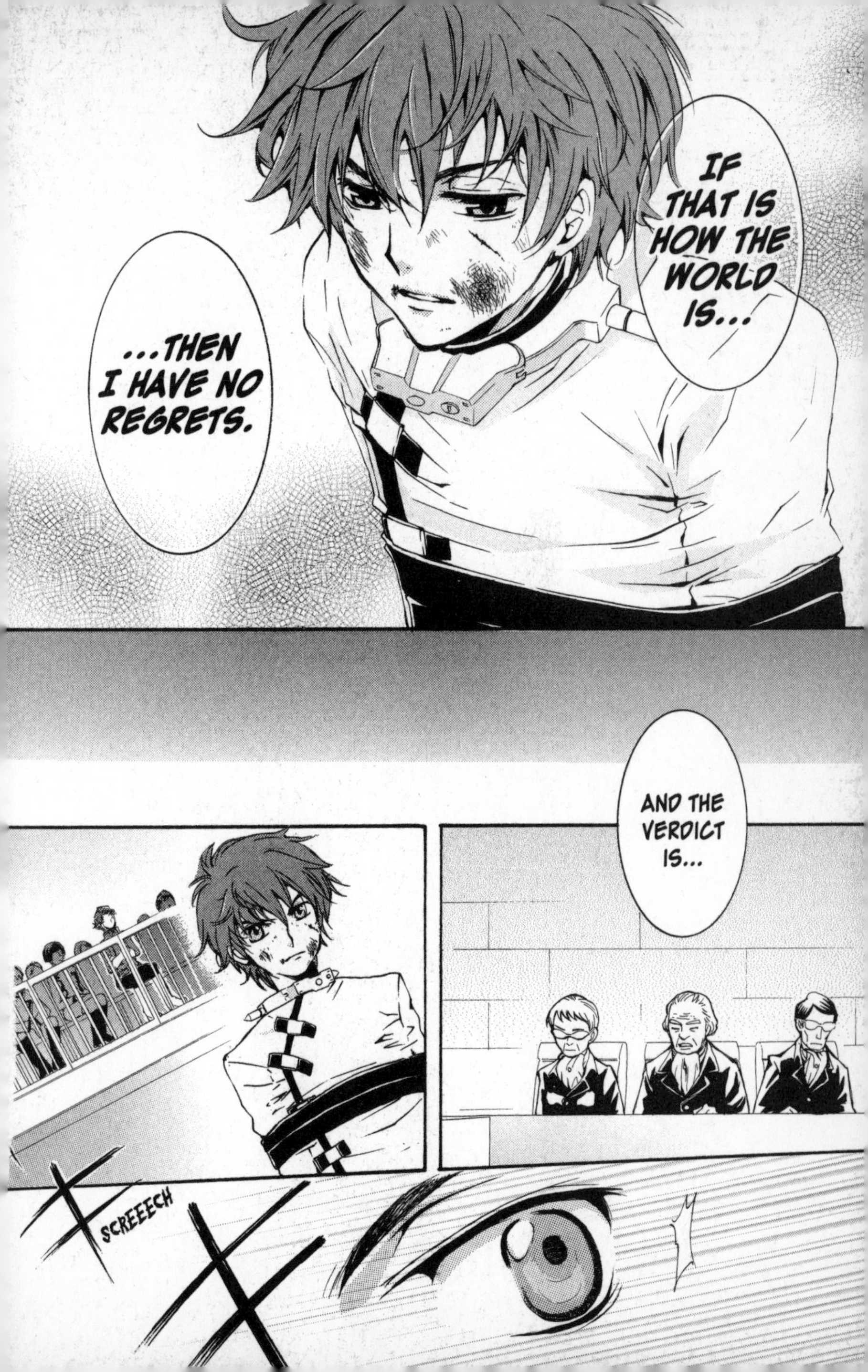
IF THAT IS HOW THE WORLD IS...
...THEN I HAVE NO REGRETS.
AND THE VERDICT IS...
SCREEECH

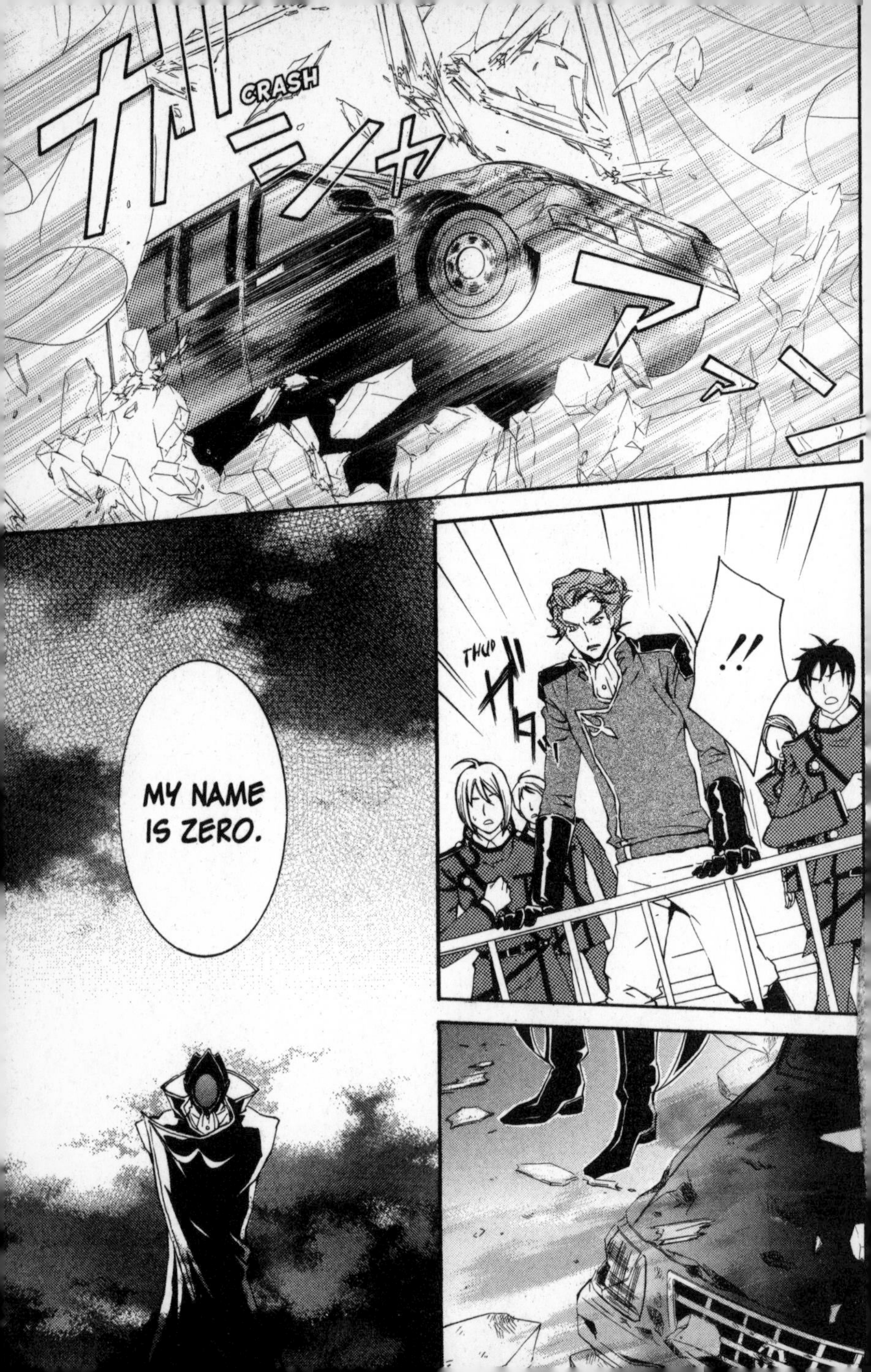
CRASH
THUD
!!
MY NAME IS ZERO.

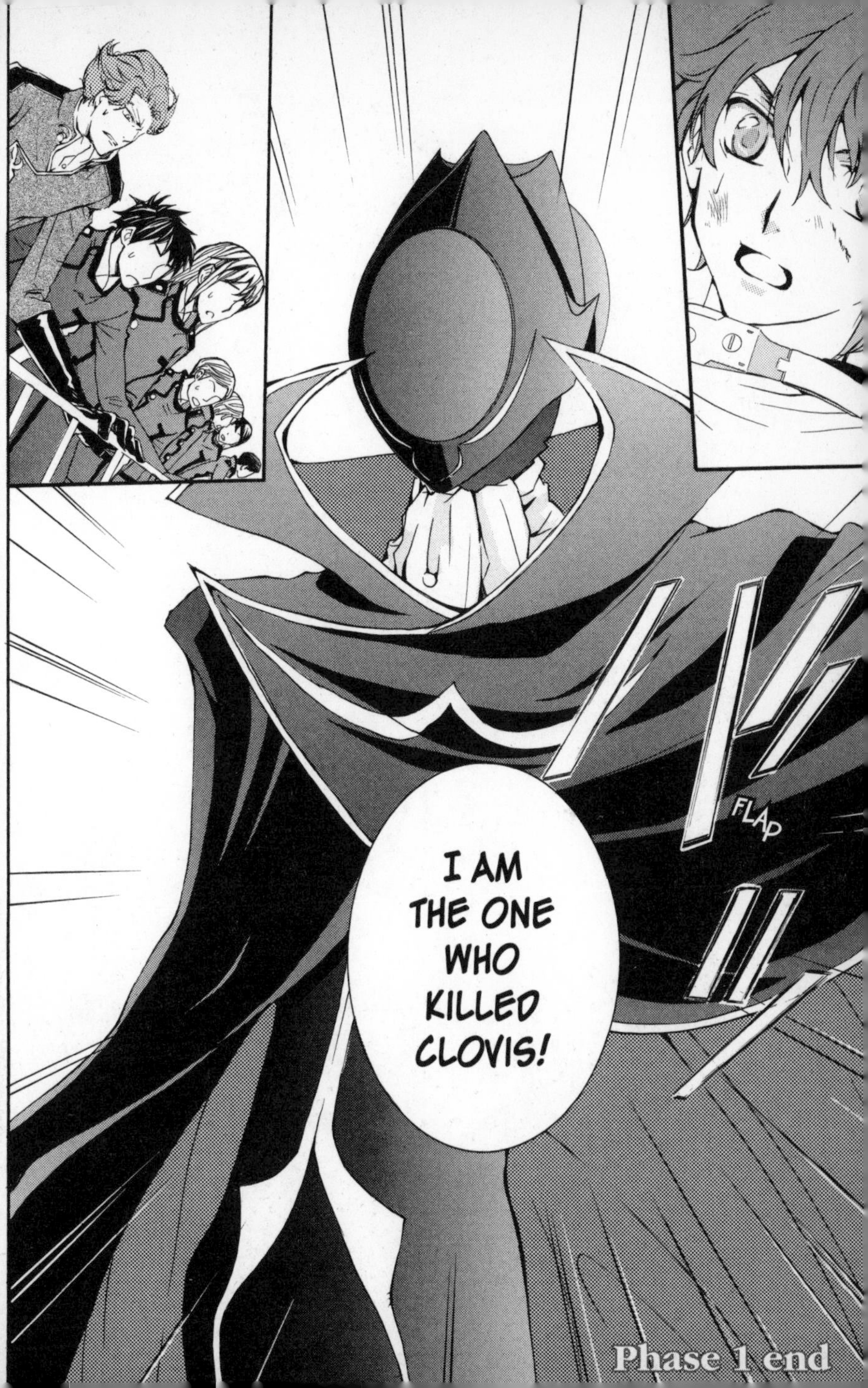
FLAP
I AM THE ONE WHO KILLED CLOVIS!
Phase 1 end

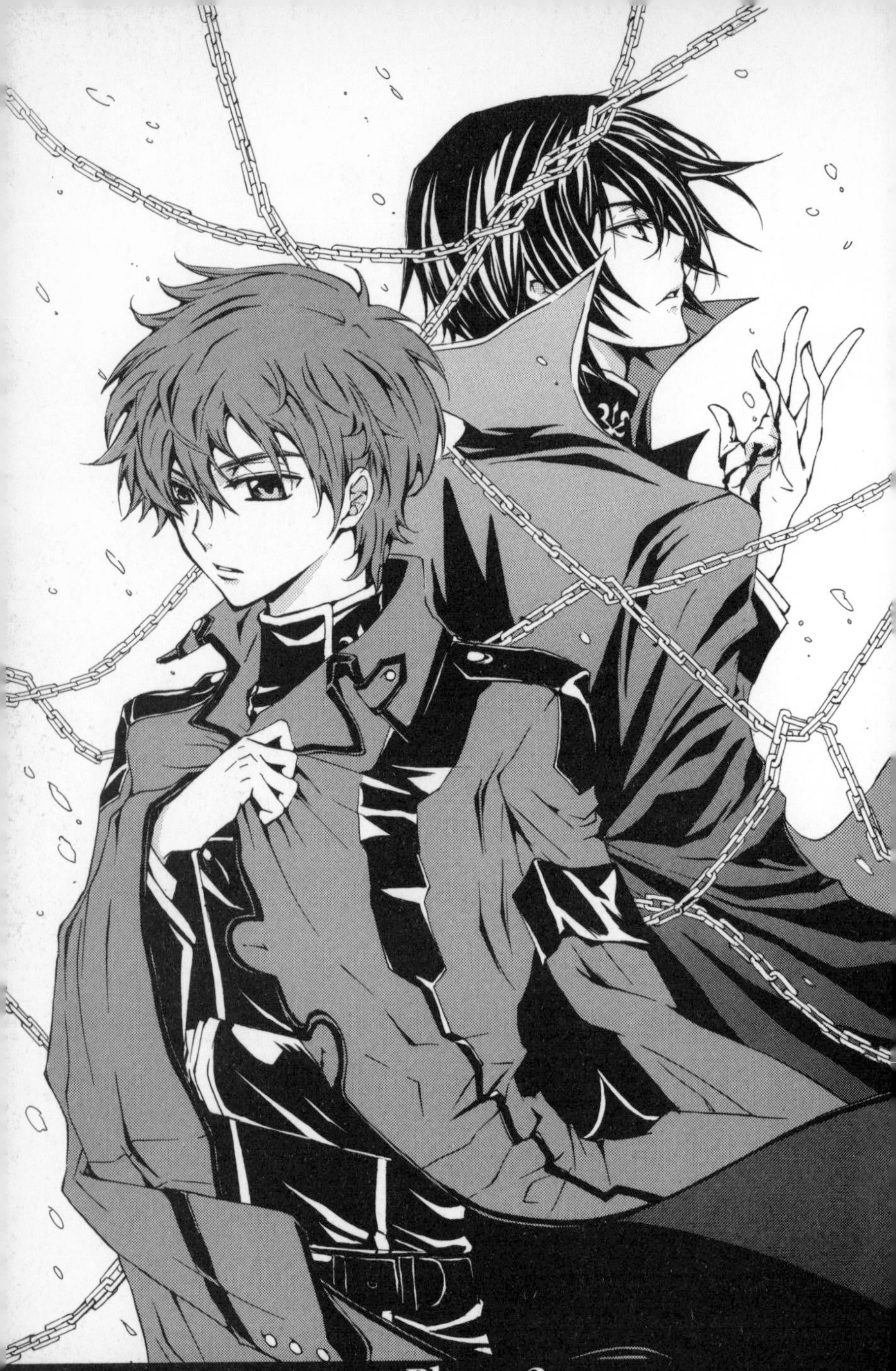

Phase 2

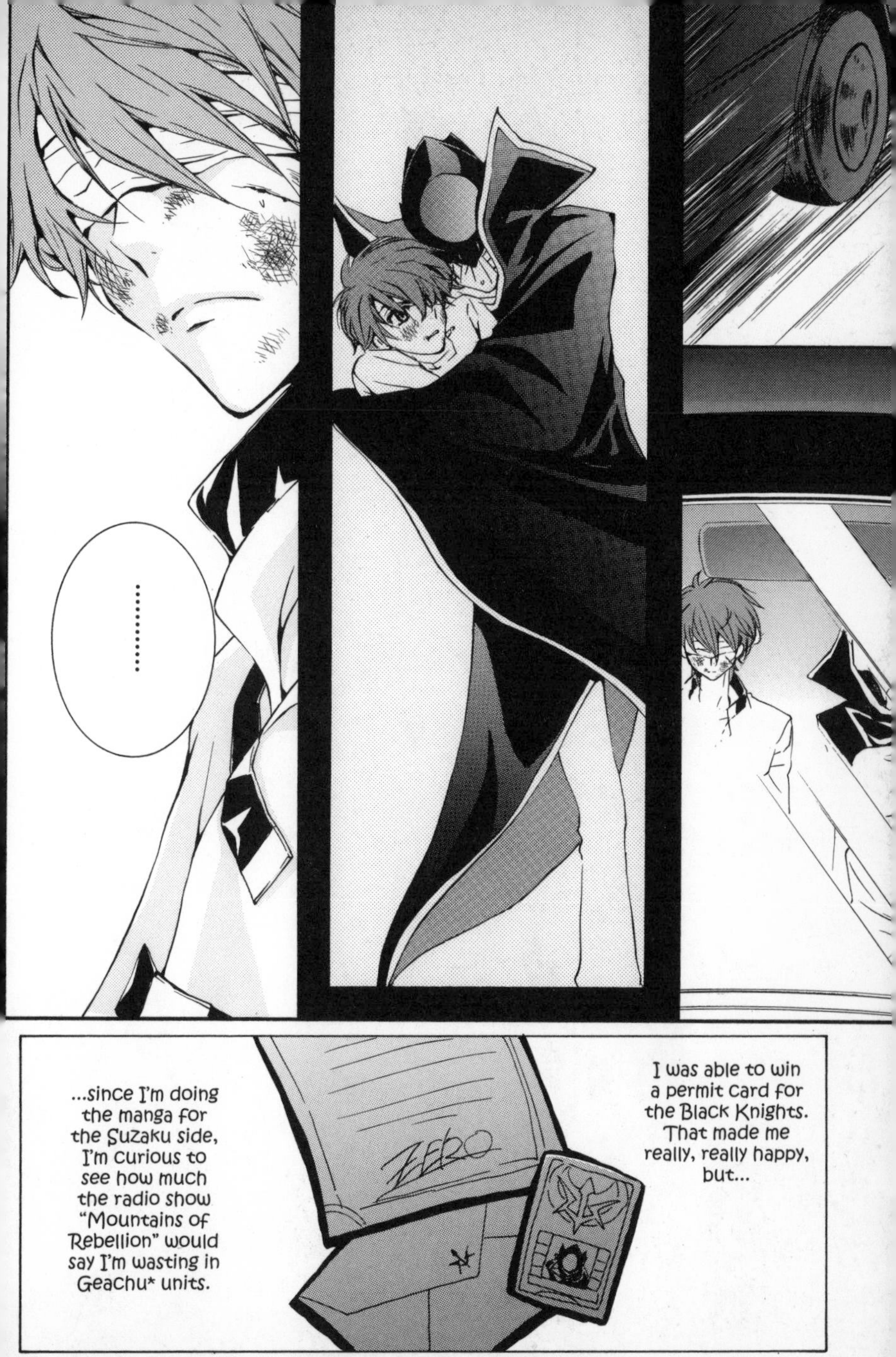
......
I was able to win a permit card for the Black Knights. That made me really, really happy, but...
...since I'm doing the manga for the Suzaku side, I'm curious to see how much the radio show "Mountains of Rebellion" would say I'm wasting in Geachu* units.
ZERO

* Geachu is a unit used in the Code Geass radio show, "Mountains of Rebellion." It determines how much energy is wasted if a specific instance was caused by Lelouch's Geass.

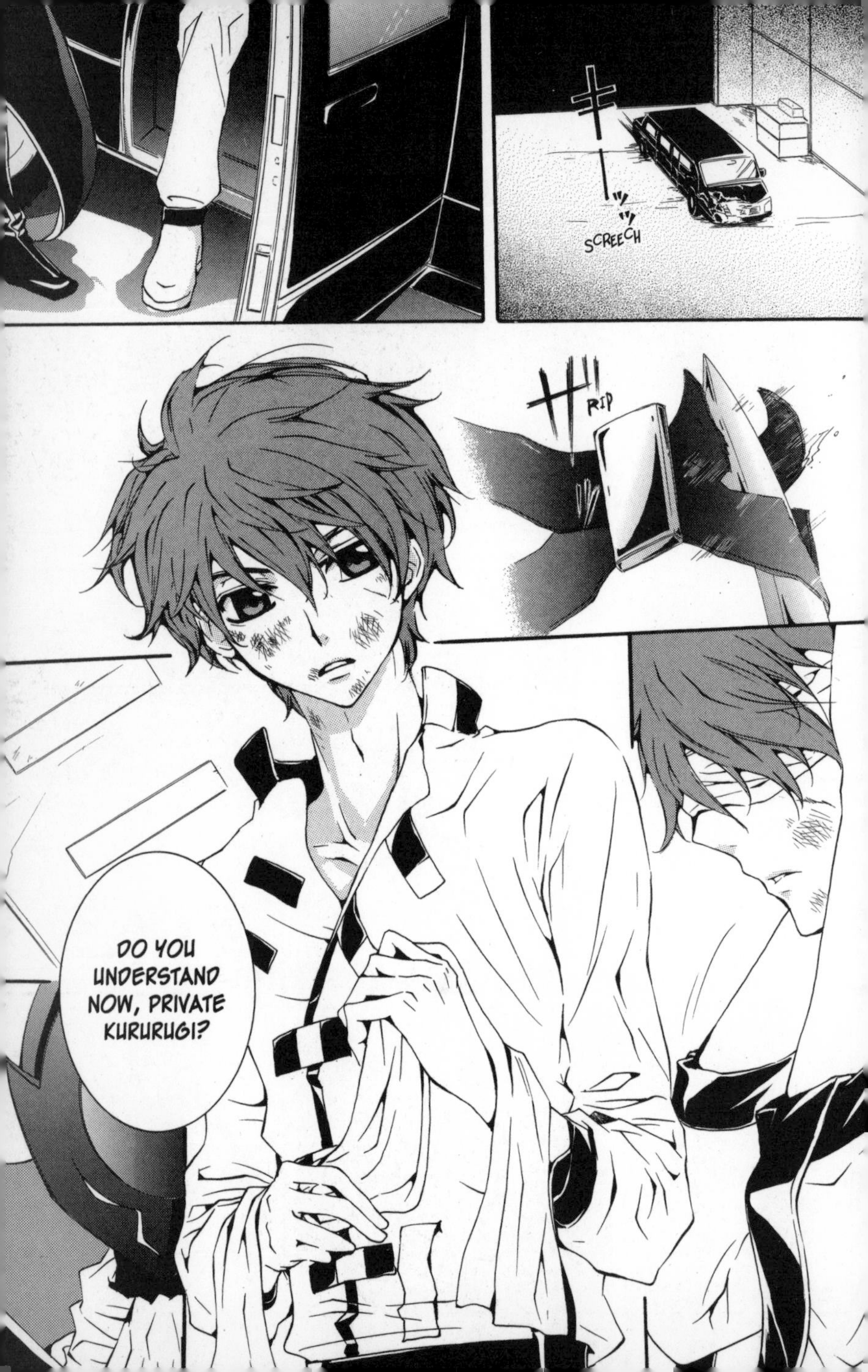
SCREECH
RIP
DO YOU UNDERSTAND NOW, PRIVATE KURURUGI?

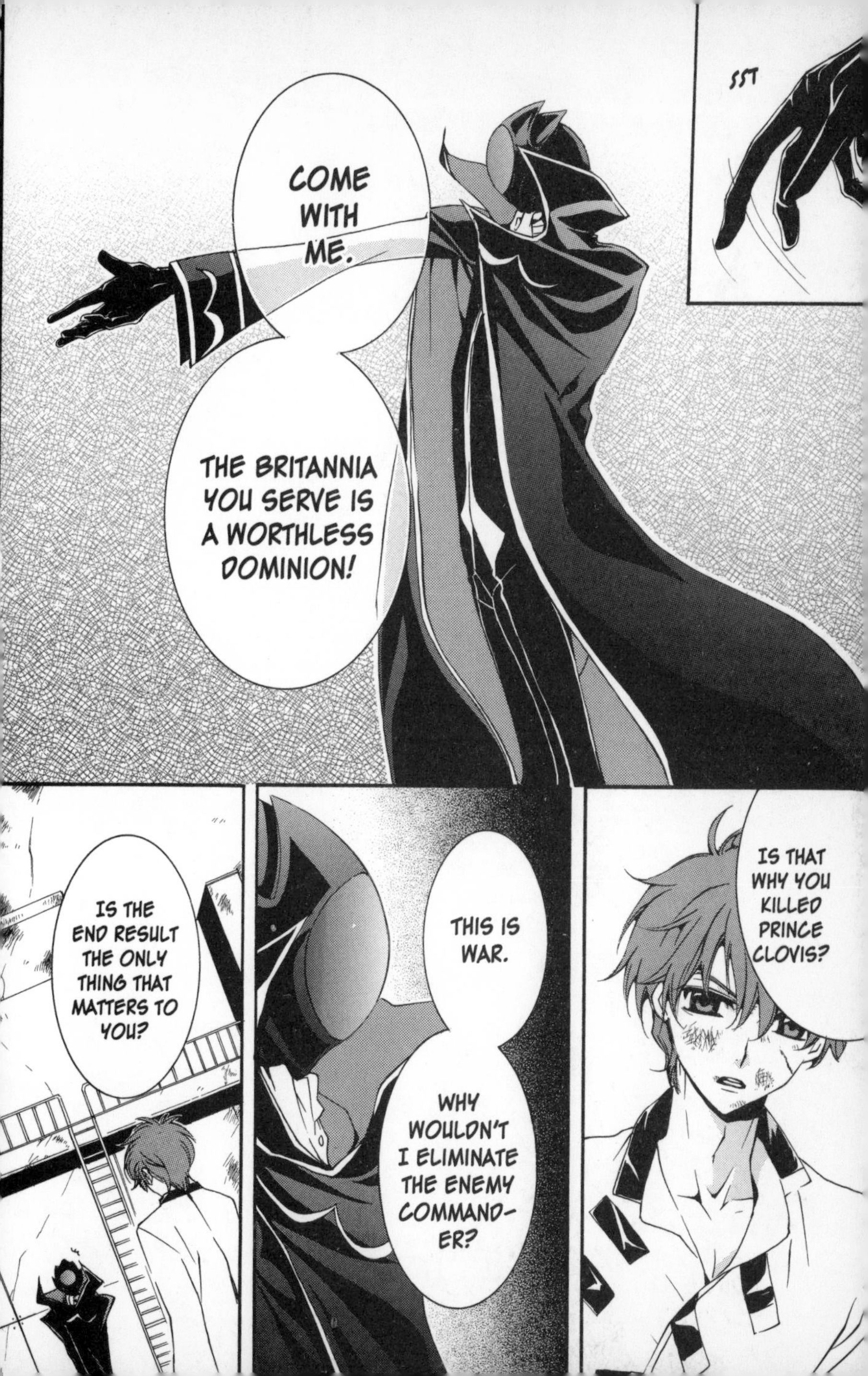
SST
COME WITH ME.
THE BRITANNIA YOU SERVE IS A WORTHLESS DOMINION!
IS THAT WHY YOU KILLED PRINCE CLOVIS?
THIS IS WAR.
WHY WOULDN'T I ELIMINATE THE ENEMY COMMAND-ER?
IS THE END RESULT THE ONLY THING THAT MATTERS TO YOU?

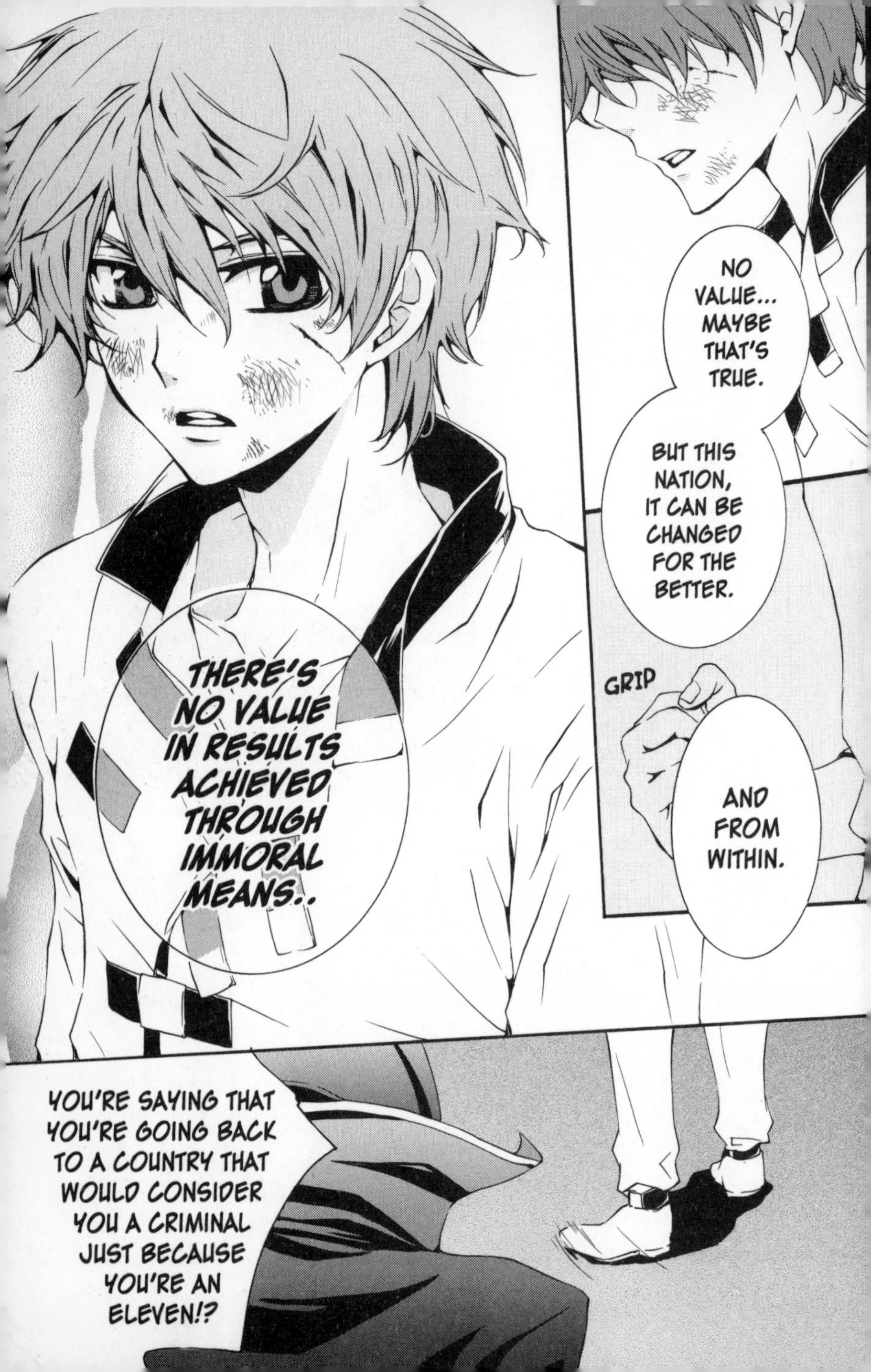
NO VALUE... MAYBE THAT'S TRUE.
BUT THIS NATION, IT CAN BE CHANGED FOR THE BETTER.
GRIP
AND FROM WITHIN.
THERE'S NO VALUE IN RESULTS ACHIEVED THROUGH IMMORAL MEANS..
YOU'RE SAYING THAT YOU'RE GOING BACK TO A COUNTRY THAT WOULD CONSIDER YOU A CRIMINAL JUST BECAUSE YOU'RE AN ELEVEN!?

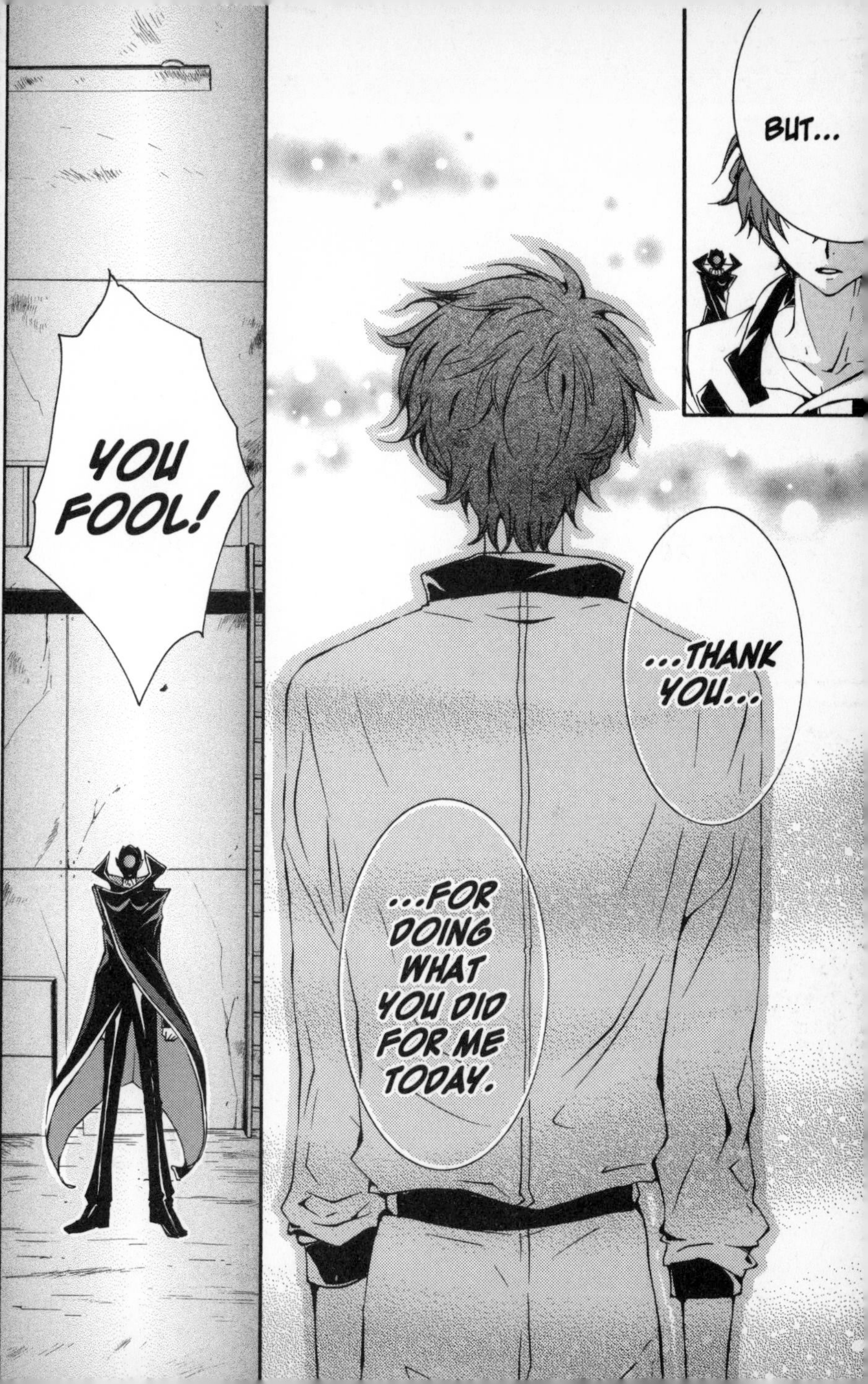
BUT...
...THANK YOU...
...FOR DOING WHAT YOU DID FOR ME TODAY.
YOU FOOL!

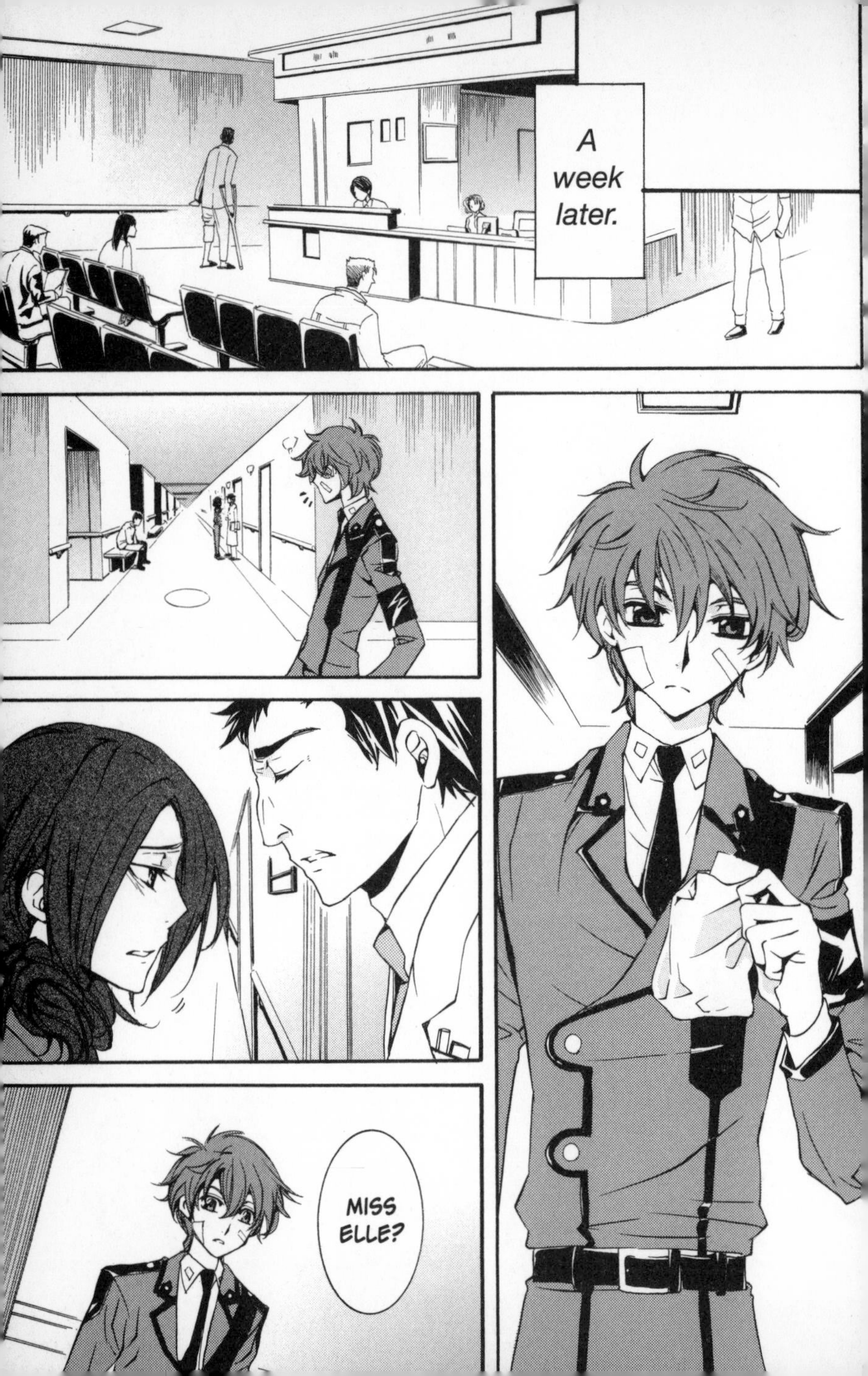
A week later.
MISS ELLE?

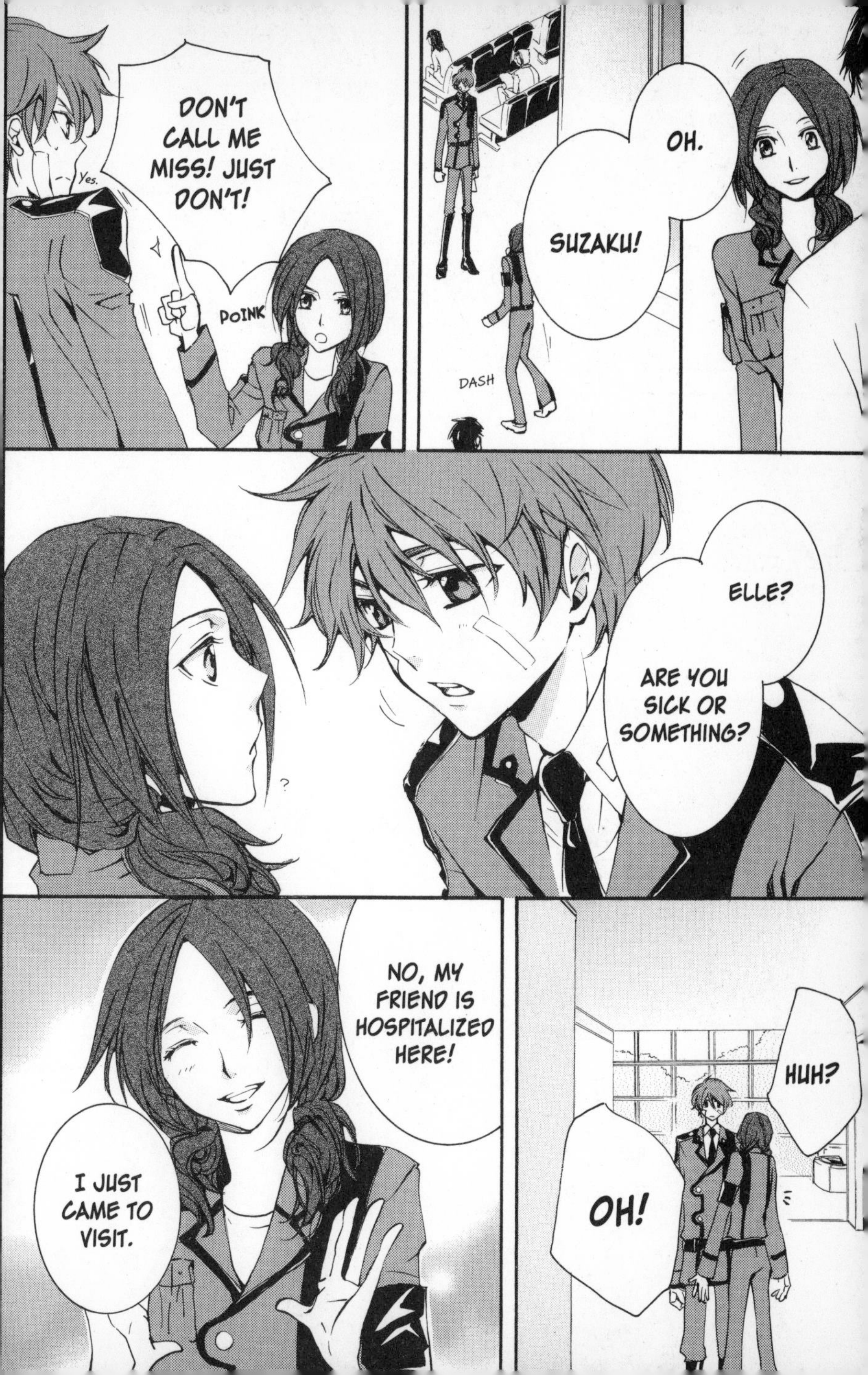
OH.
SUZAKU!
DASH
DON'T CALL ME MISS! JUST DON'T!
Yes.
POINK
ELLE?
ARE YOU SICK OR SOMETHING?
?
HUH?
OH!
NO, MY FRIEND IS HOSPITALIZED HERE!
I JUST CAME TO VISIT.

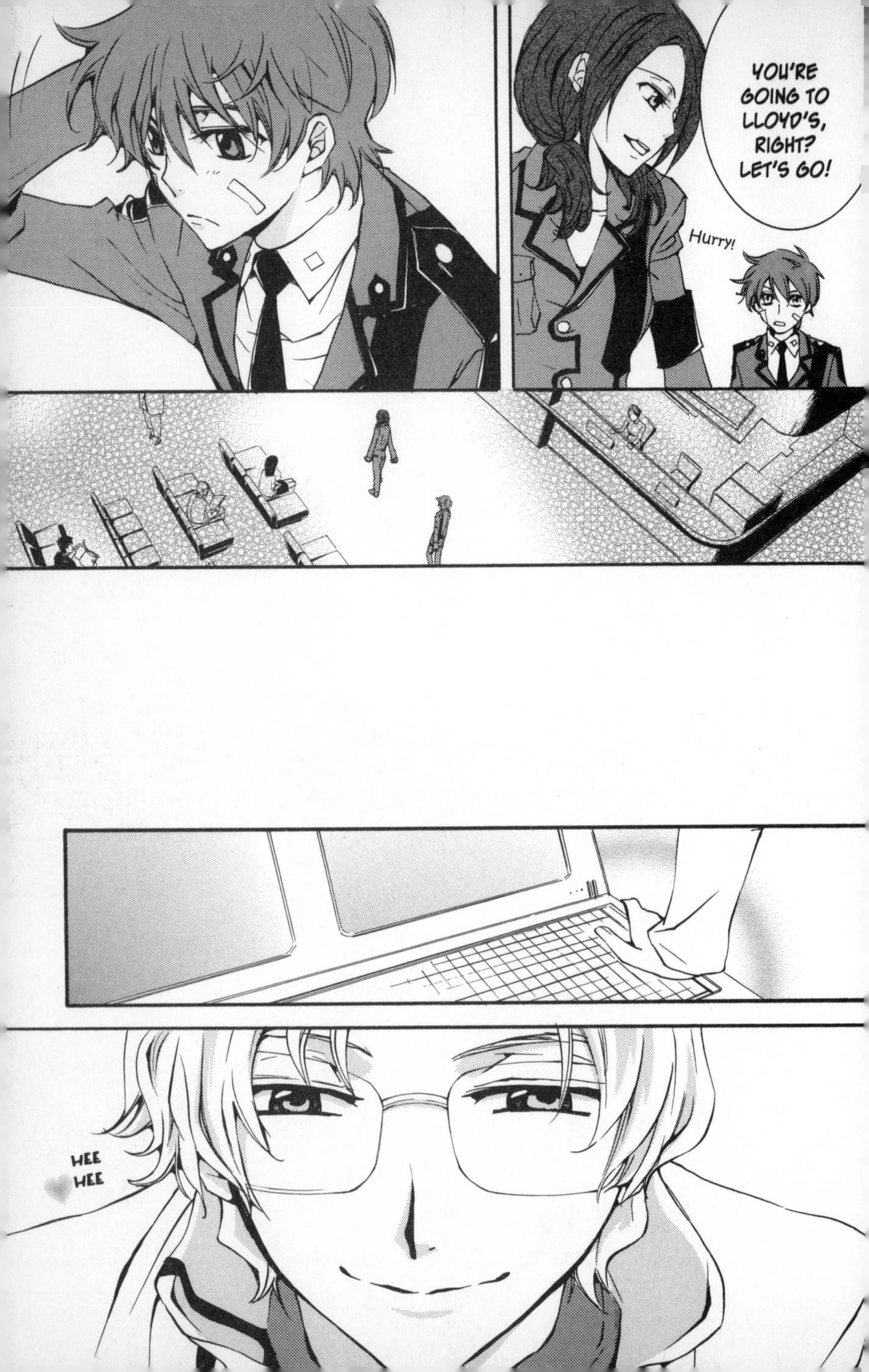
YOU'RE GOING TO LLOYD'S, RIGHT? LET'S GO!
Hurry!
HEE HEE

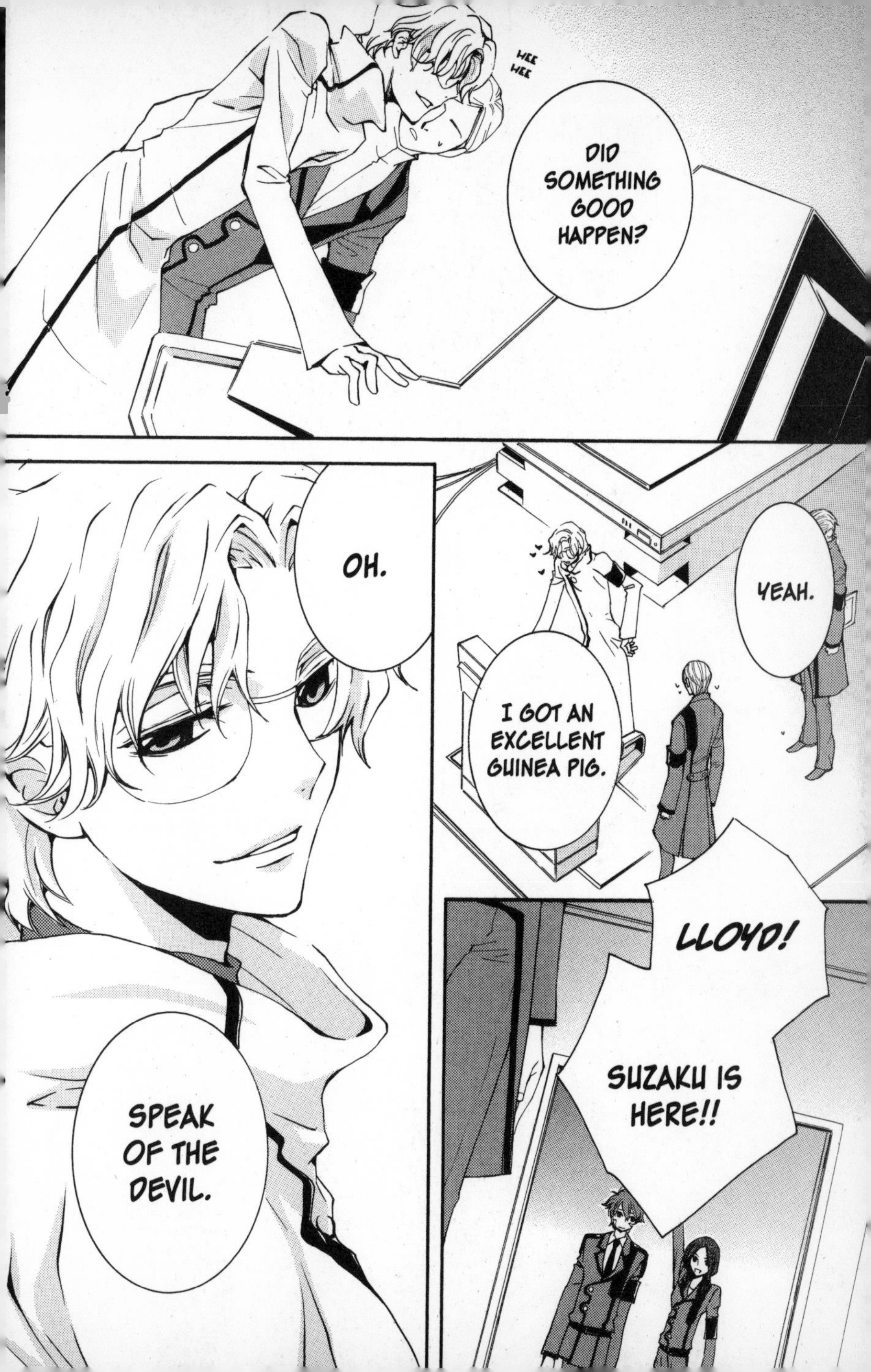
WEE WEE
DID SOMETHING GOOD HAPPEN?
YEAH.
I GOT AN EXCELLENT GUINEA PIG.
LLOYD!
SUZAKU IS HERE!!
OH.
SPEAK OF THE DEVIL.

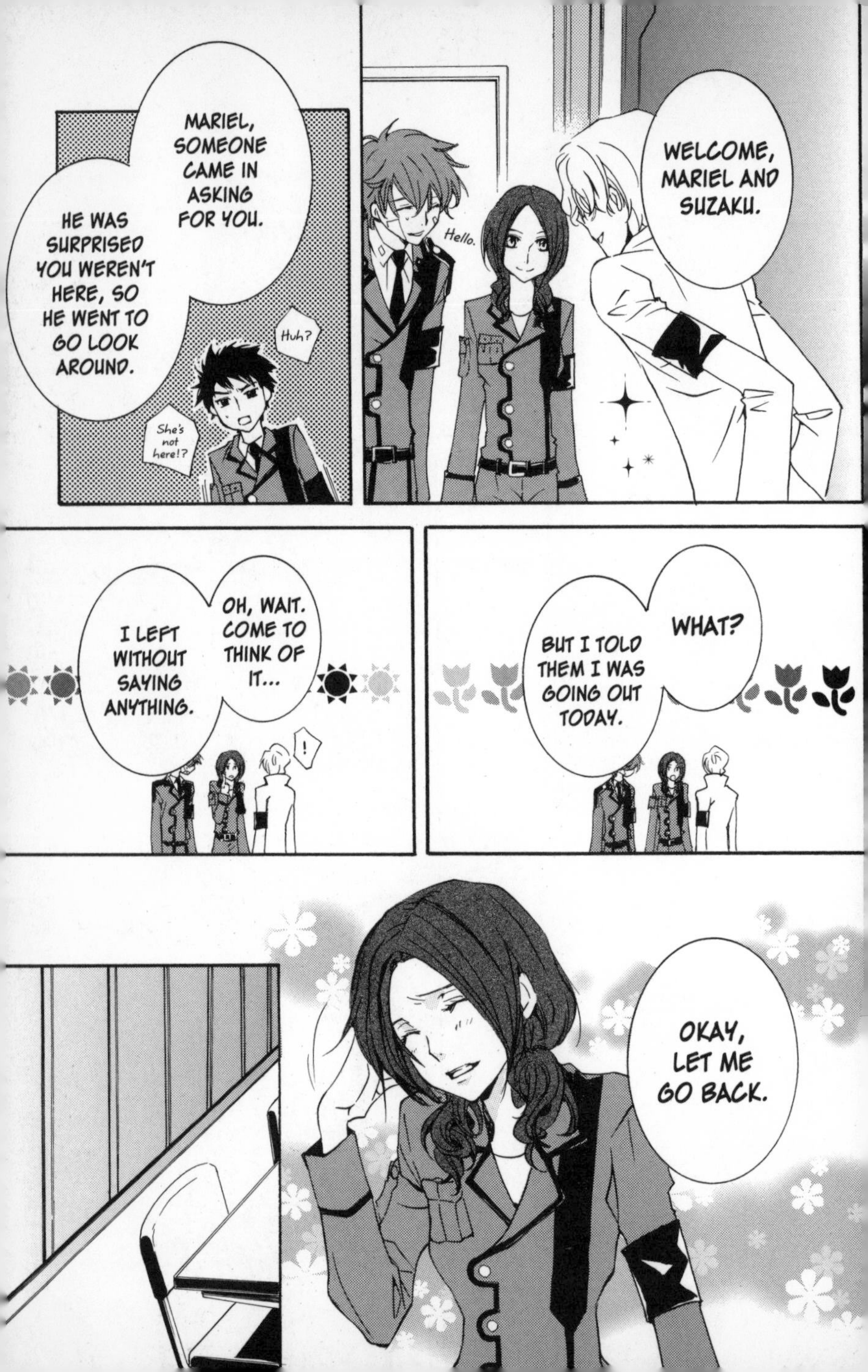
WELCOME, MARIEL AND SUZAKU.
Hello.
MARIEL, SOMEONE CAME IN ASKING FOR YOU.
HE WAS SURPRISED YOU WEREN'T HERE, SO HE WENT TO GO LOOK AROUND.
Huh?
She's not here!?
WHAT?
BUT I TOLD THEM I WAS GOING OUT TODAY.
OH, WAIT. COME TO THINK OF IT...
I LEFT WITHOUT SAYING ANYTHING.
!
OKAY, LET ME GO BACK.

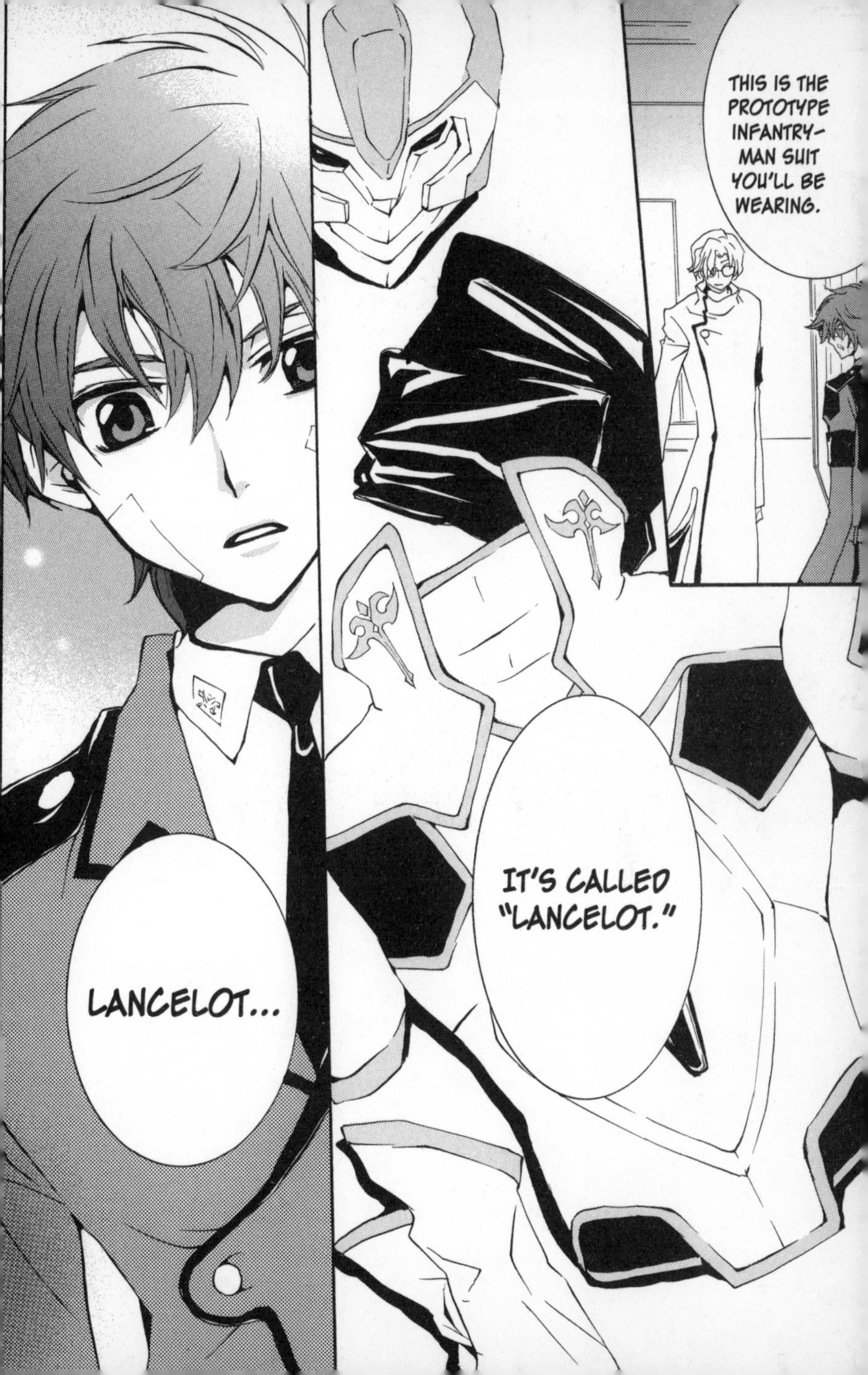
THIS IS THE PROTOTYPE INFANTRYMAN SUIT YOU'LL BE WEARING.
IT'S CALLED "LANCELOT."
LANCELOT...

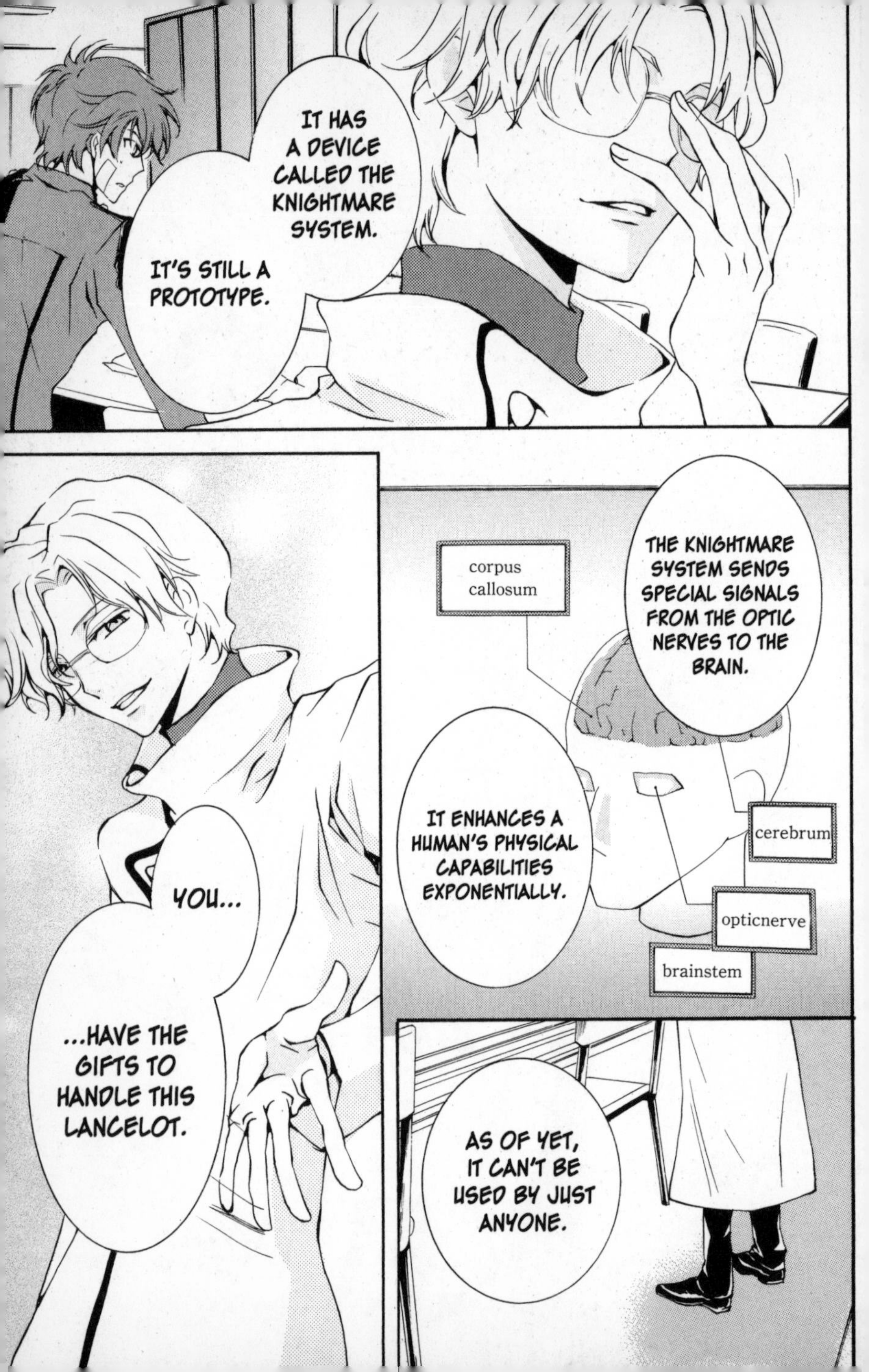
IT HAS A DEVICE CALLED THE KNIGHTMARE SYSTEM.
IT'S STILL A PROTOTYPE.
THE KNIGHTMARE SYSTEM SENDS SPECIAL SIGNALS FROM THE OPTIC NERVES TO THE BRAIN.
corpus callosum
IT ENHANCES A HUMAN'S PHYSICAL CAPABILITIES EXPONENTIALLY.
cerebrum
opticnerve
brainstem
AS OF YET, IT CAN'T BE USED BY JUST ANYONE.
YOU...
...HAVE THE GIFTS TO HANDLE THIS LANCELOT.

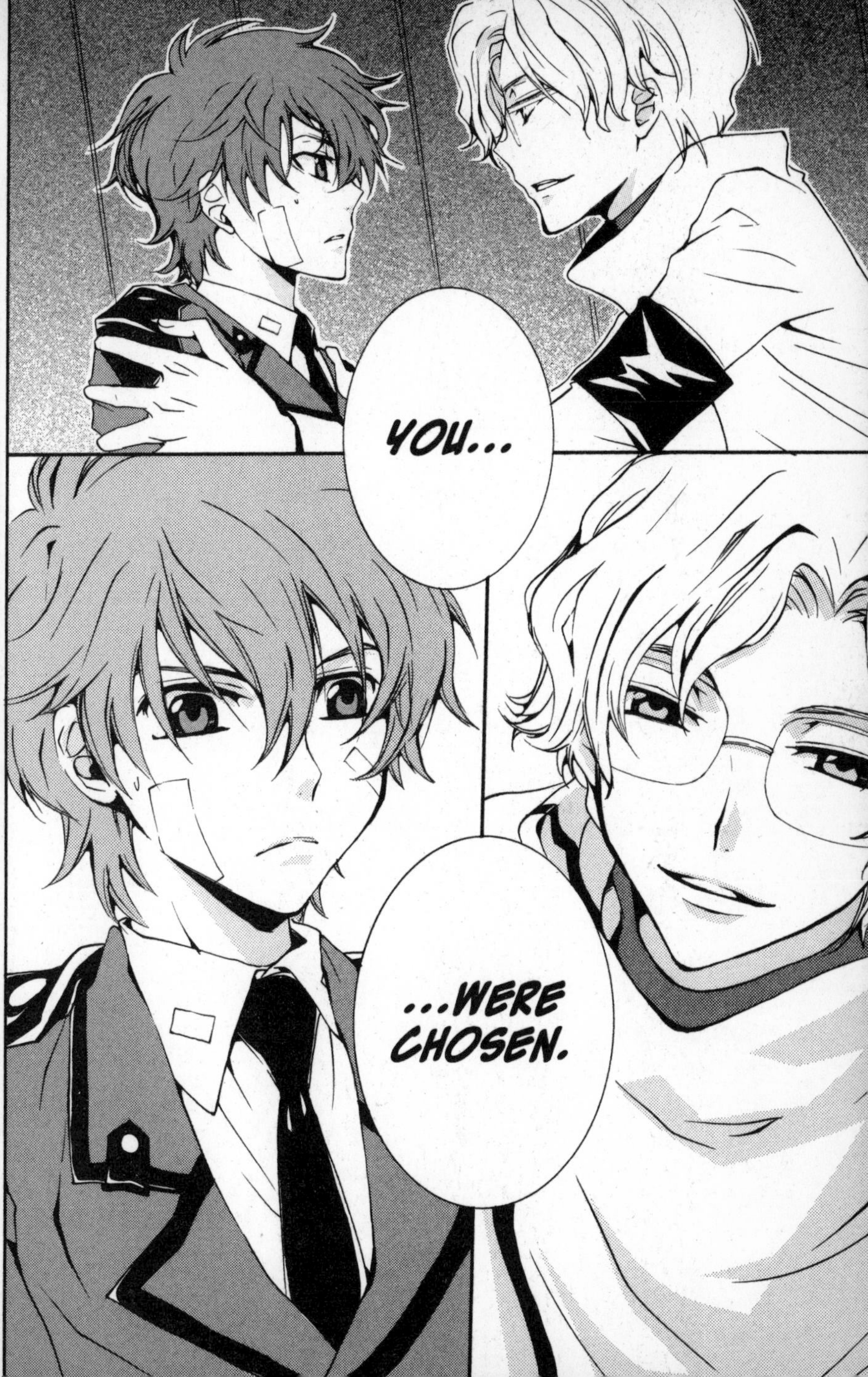
YOU...
...WERE CHOSEN.

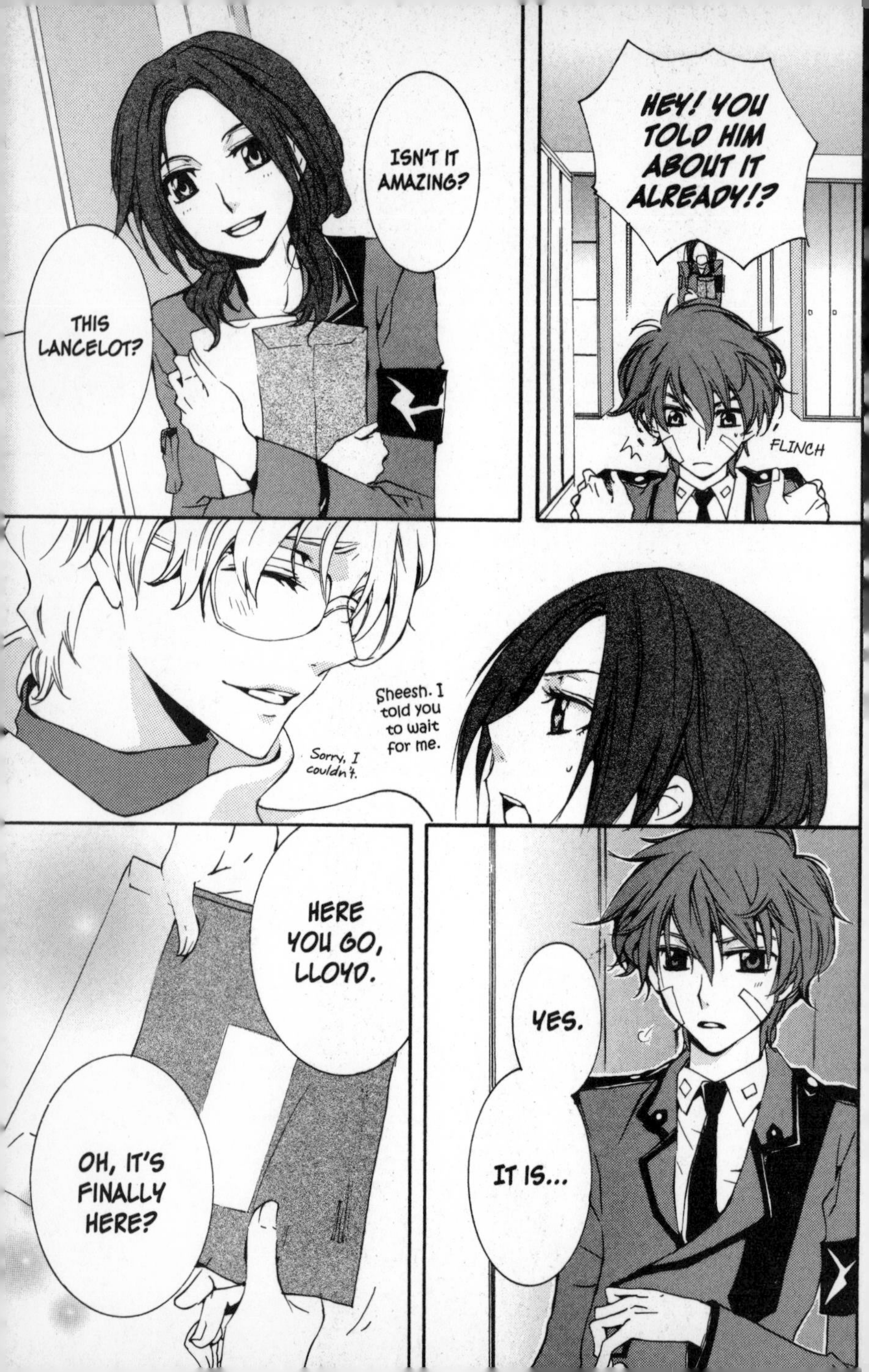
HEY! YOU TOLD HIM ABOUT IT ALREADY!?
FLINCH
ISN'T IT AMAZING?
THIS LANCELOT?
Sheesh. I told you to wait for me.
Sorry, I couldn't.
YES.
IT IS...
HERE YOU GO, LLOYD.
OH, IT'S FINALLY HERE?

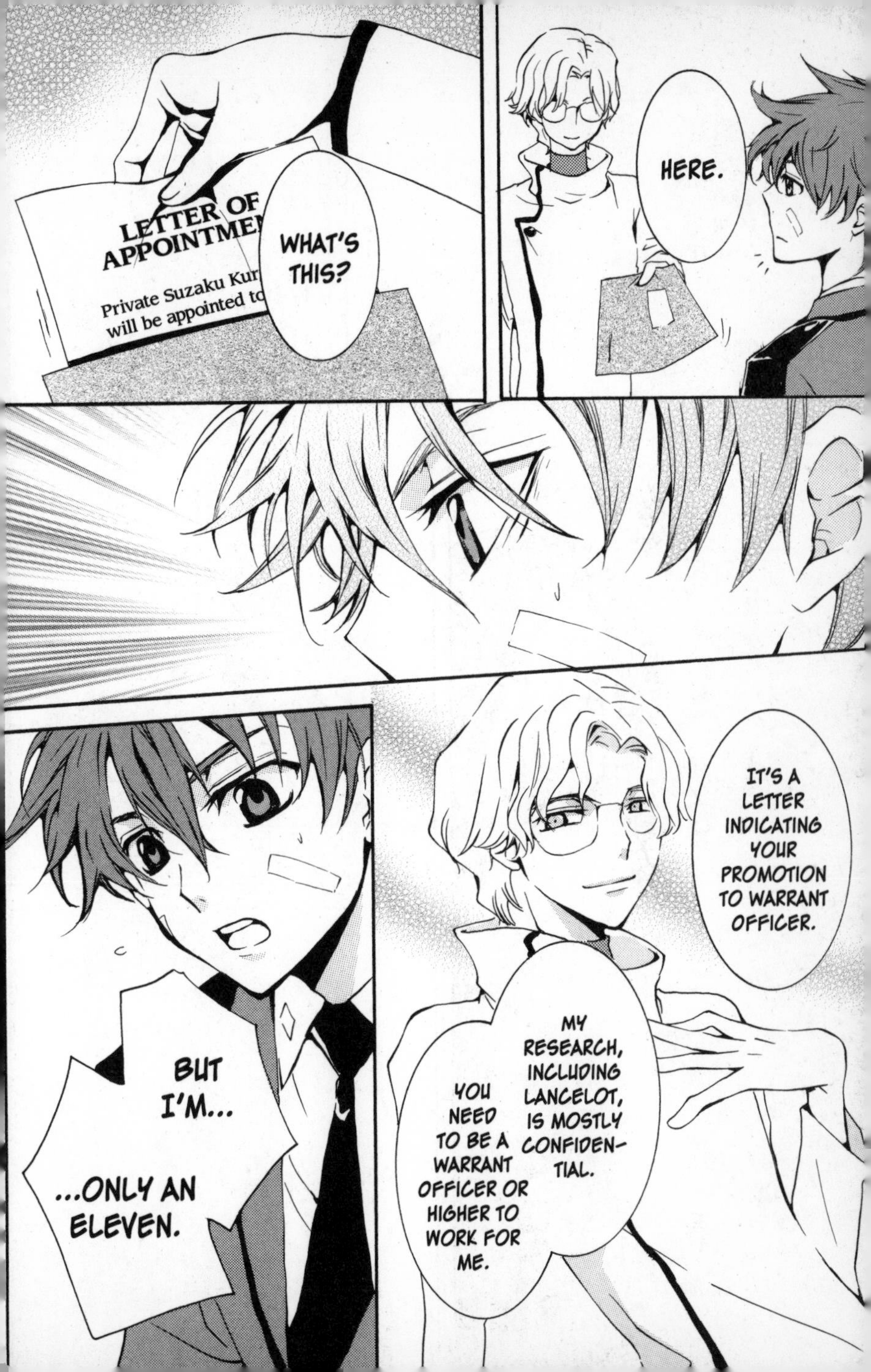
HERE.
LETTER OF APPOINTMEN
Private Suzaku Kur
will be appointed to
WHAT'S THIS?
IT'S A LETTER INDICATING YOUR PROMOTION TO WARRANT OFFICER.
MY RESEARCH, INCLUDING LANCELOT, IS MOSTLY CONFIDEN-TIAL.
YOU NEED TO BE A WARRANT OFFICER OR HIGHER TO WORK FOR ME.
BUT I'M...
...ONLY AN ELEVEN.

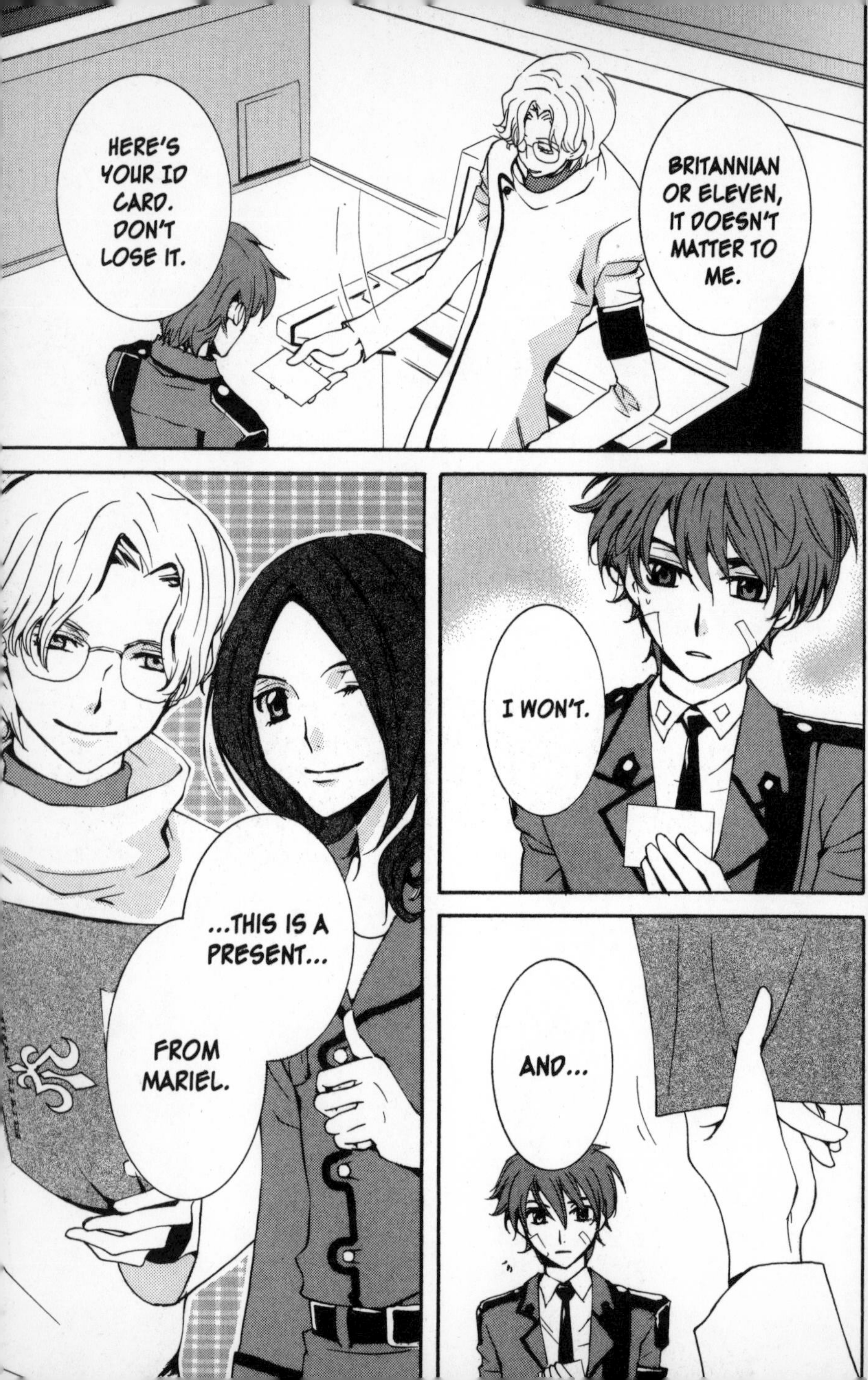
BRITANNIAN OR ELEVEN, IT DOESN'T MATTER TO ME.
HERE'S YOUR ID CARD. DON'T LOSE IT.
I WON'T.
AND...
...THIS IS A PRESENT...
FROM MARIEL.

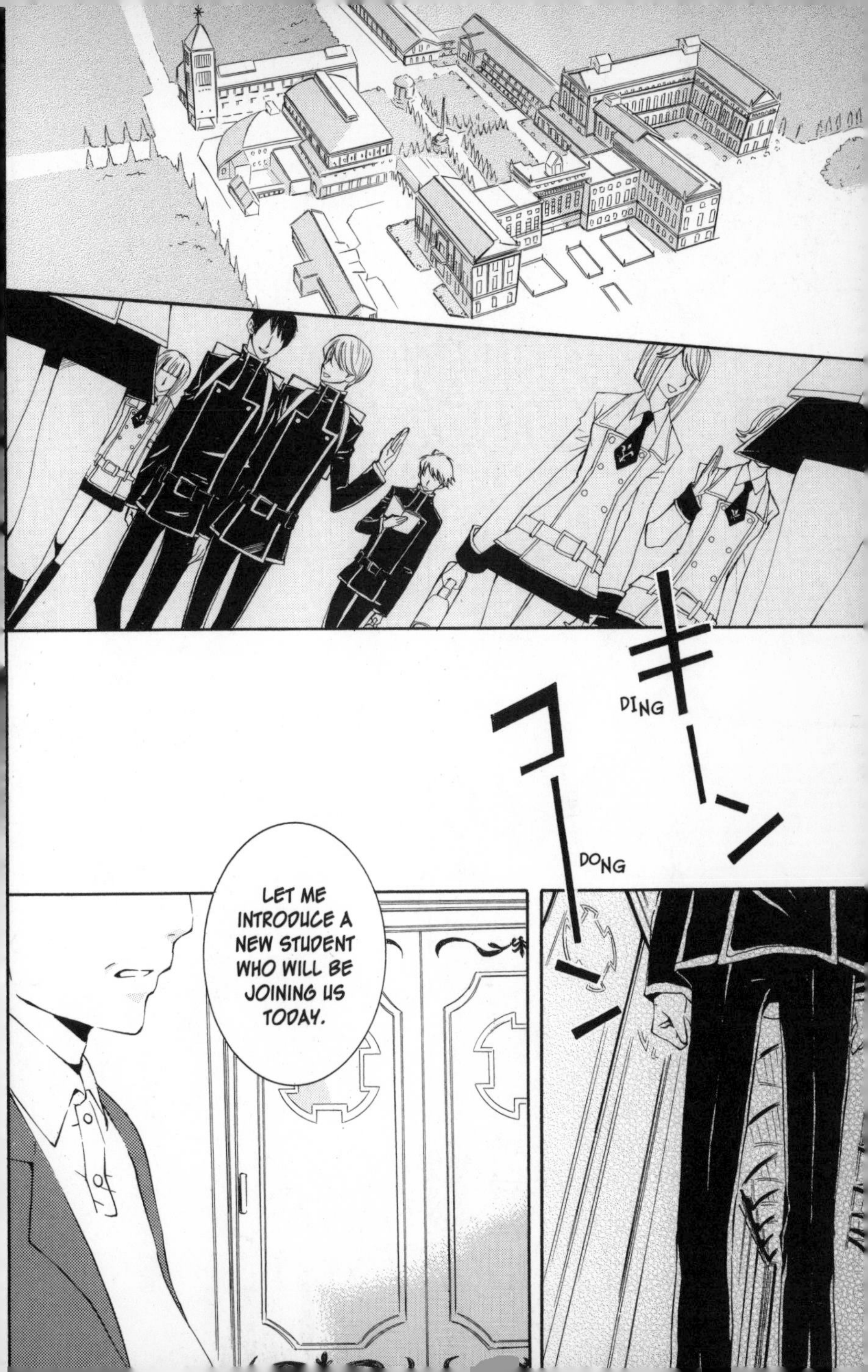
DING
DONG
LET ME INTRODUCE A NEW STUDENT WHO WILL BE JOINING US TODAY.

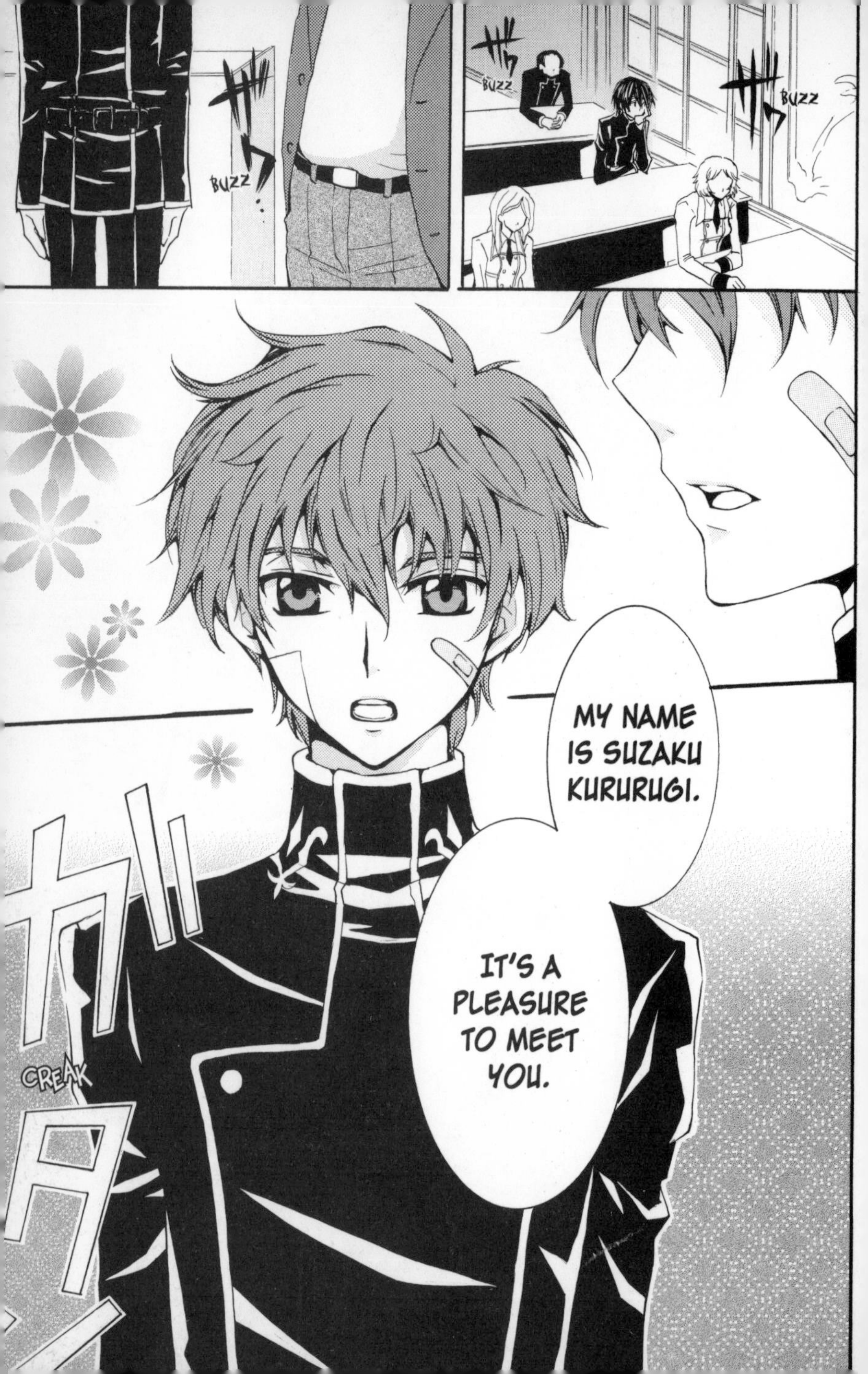
BUZZ
BUZZ
BUZZ
MY NAME IS SUZAKU KURURUGI.
IT'S A PLEASURE TO MEET YOU.
CREAK

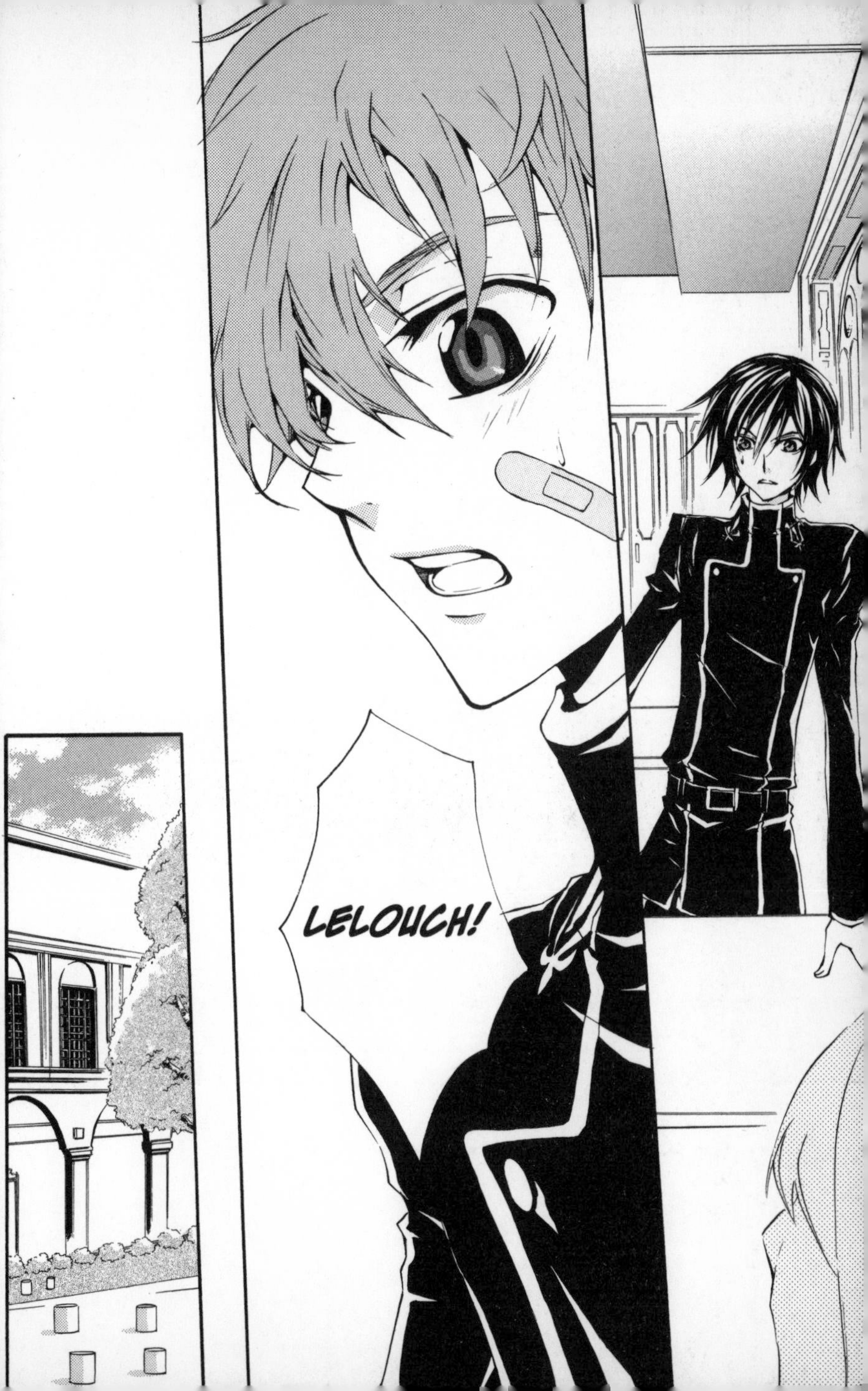
LELOUCH!

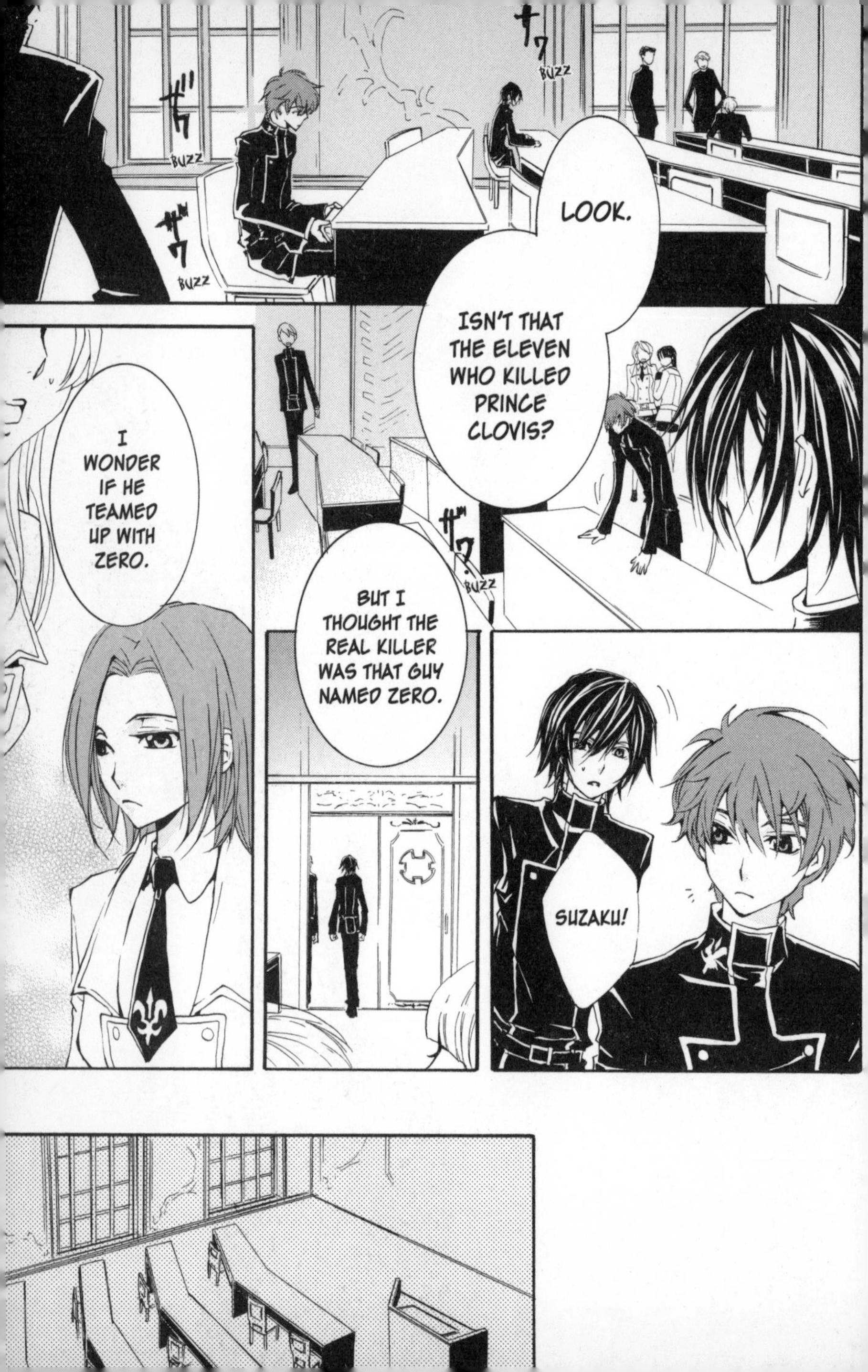
BUZZ
BUZZ
BUZZ
LOOK.
ISN'T THAT THE ELEVEN WHO KILLED PRINCE CLOVIS?
BUZZ
BUT I THOUGHT THE REAL KILLER WAS THAT GUY NAMED ZERO.
I WONDER IF HE TEAMED UP WITH ZERO.
SUZAKU!

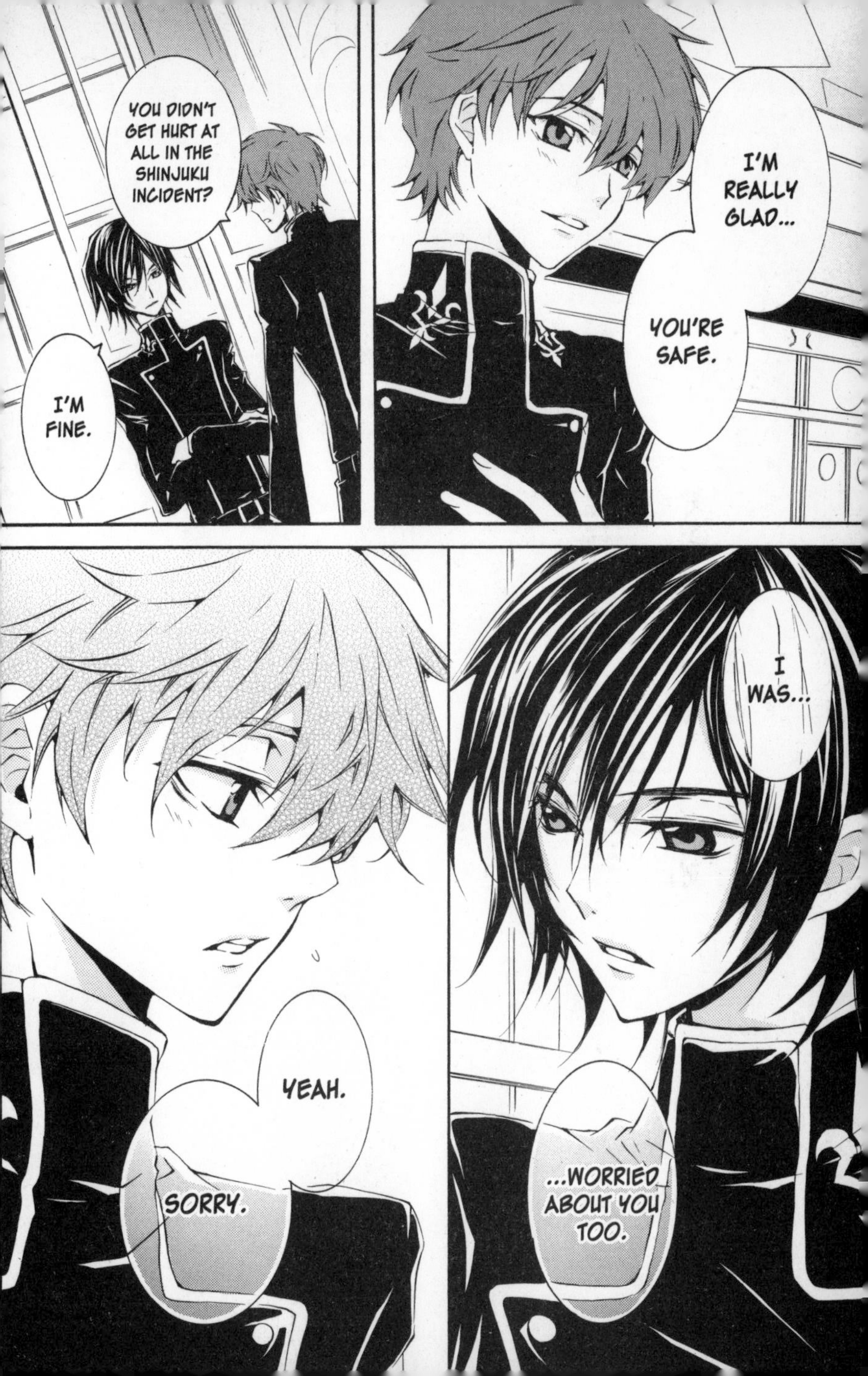
I'M REALLY GLAD...
YOU'RE SAFE.
YOU DIDN'T GET HURT AT ALL IN THE SHINJUKU INCIDENT?
I'M FINE.
I WAS...
...WORRIED ABOUT YOU TOO.
YEAH.
SORRY.

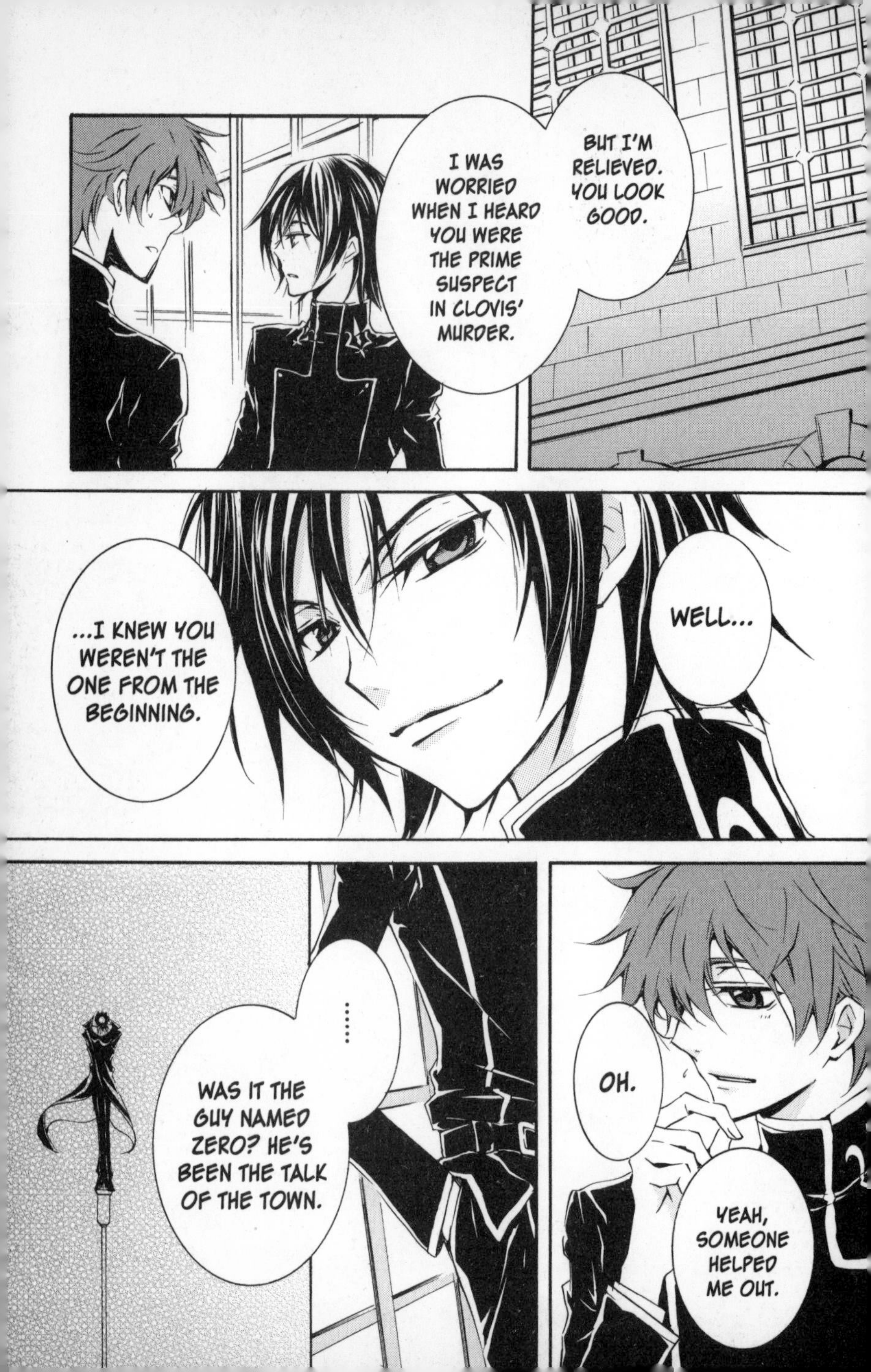
I WAS WORRIED WHEN I HEARD YOU WERE THE PRIME SUSPECT IN CLOVIS' MURDER.
BUT I'M RELIEVED. YOU LOOK GOOD.
WELL...
...I KNEW YOU WEREN'T THE ONE FROM THE BEGINNING.
OH.
YEAH, SOMEONE HELPED ME OUT.
......
WAS IT THE GUY NAMED ZERO? HE'S BEEN THE TALK OF THE TOWN.

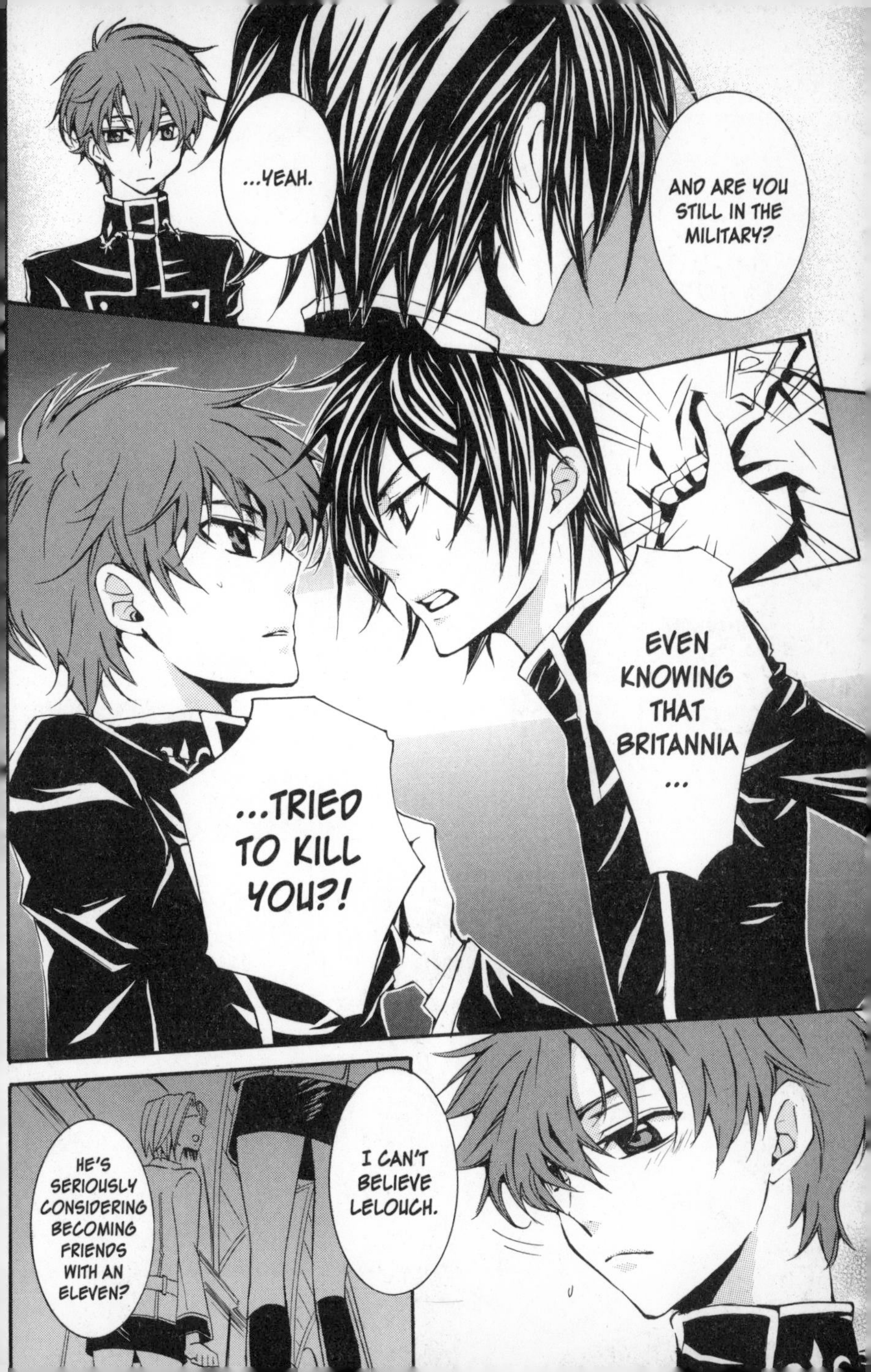
AND ARE YOU STILL IN THE MILITARY?
...YEAH.
EVEN KNOWING THAT BRITANNIA ...
...TRIED TO KILL YOU?!
I CAN'T BELIEVE LELOUCH.
HE'S SERIOUSLY CONSIDERING BECOMING FRIENDS WITH AN ELEVEN?

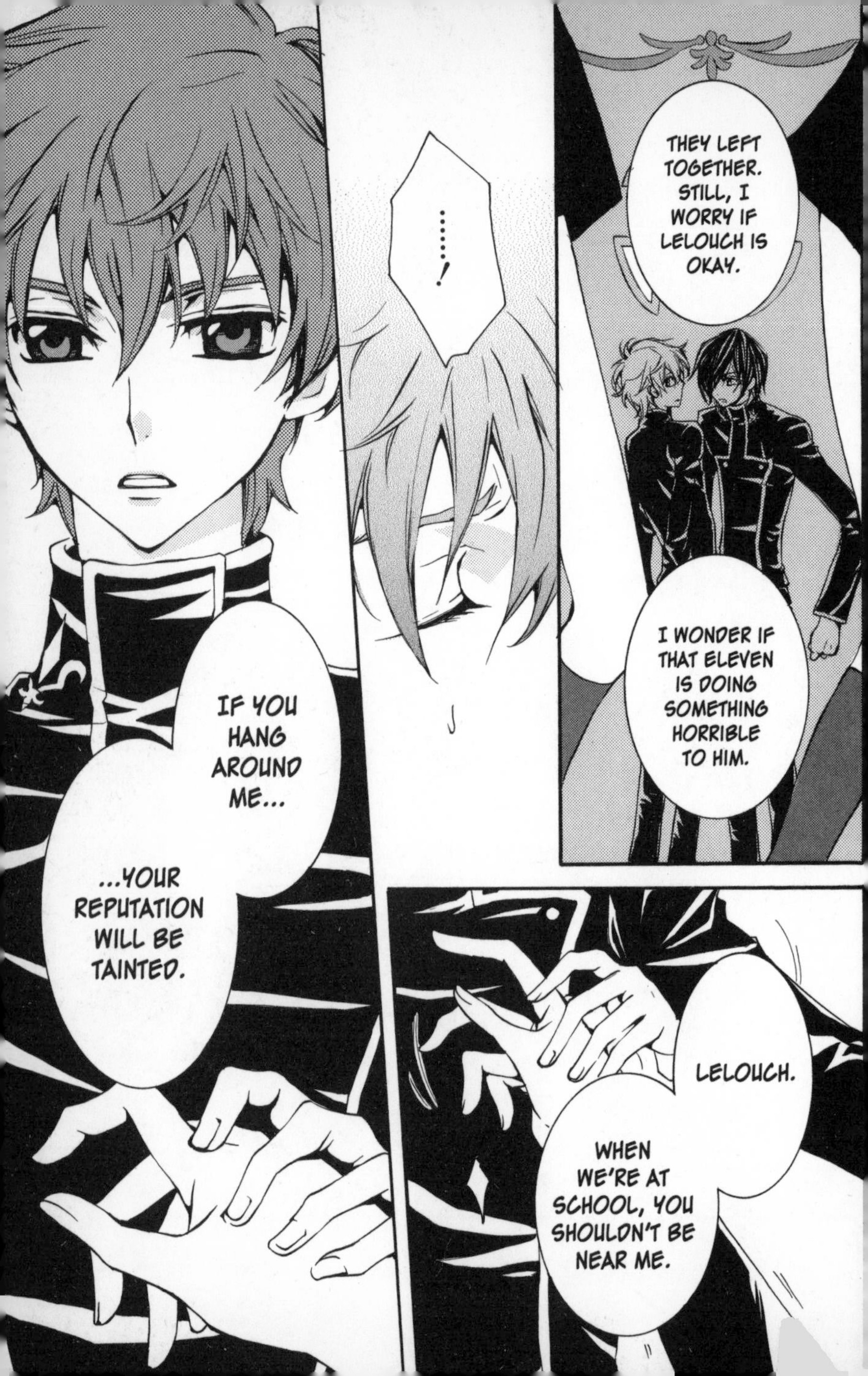
THEY LEFT TOGETHER. STILL, I WORRY IF LELOUCH IS OKAY.
I WONDER IF THAT ELEVEN IS DOING SOMETHING HORRIBLE TO HIM.
......!
LELOUCH.
WHEN WE'RE AT SCHOOL, YOU SHOULDN'T BE NEAR ME.
IF YOU HANG AROUND ME...
...YOUR REPUTATION WILL BE TAINTED.

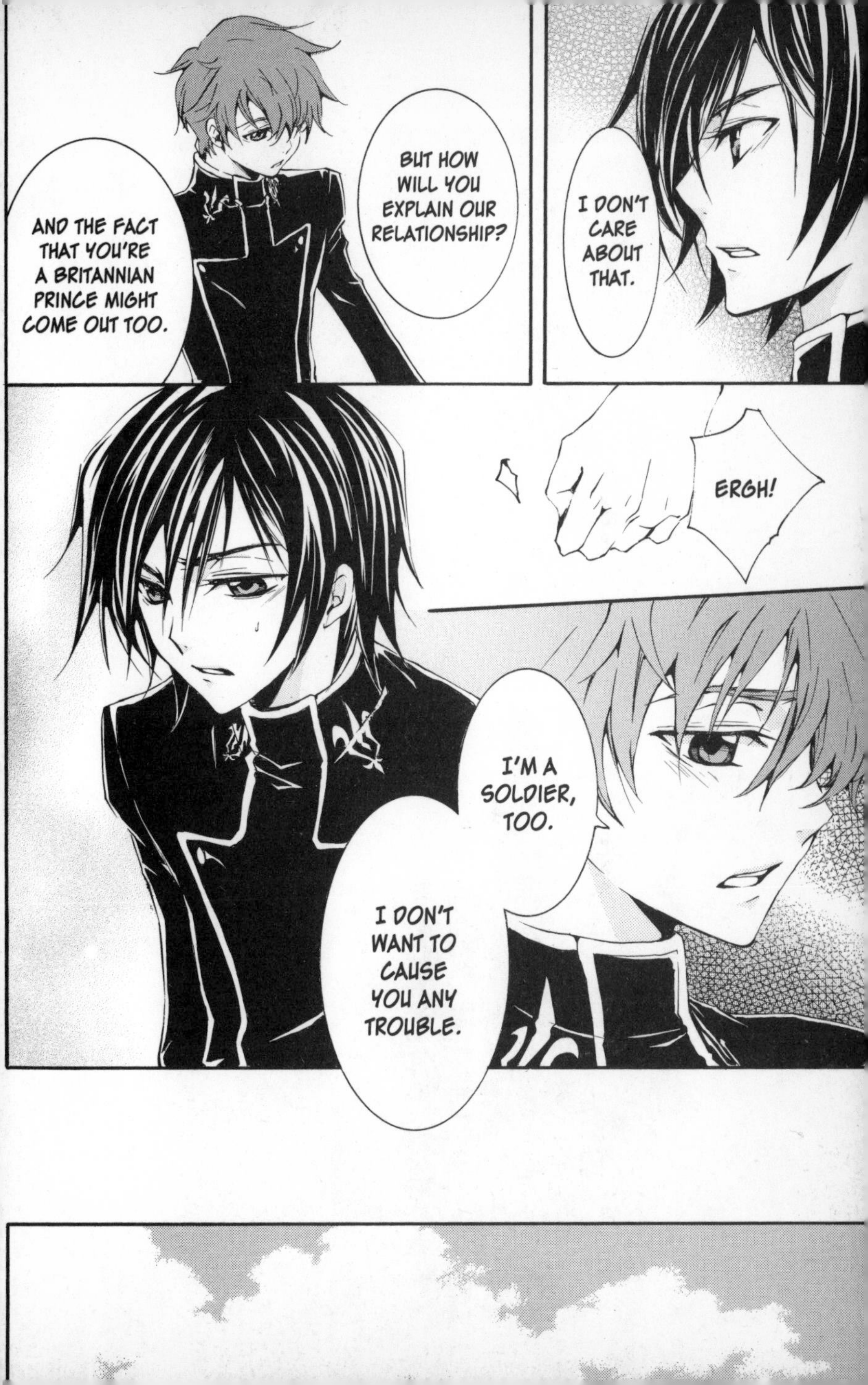
I DON'T CARE ABOUT THAT.
BUT HOW WILL YOU EXPLAIN OUR RELATIONSHIP?
AND THE FACT THAT YOU'RE A BRITANNIAN PRINCE MIGHT COME OUT TOO.
ERGH!
I'M A SOLDIER, TOO.
I DON'T WANT TO CAUSE YOU ANY TROUBLE.

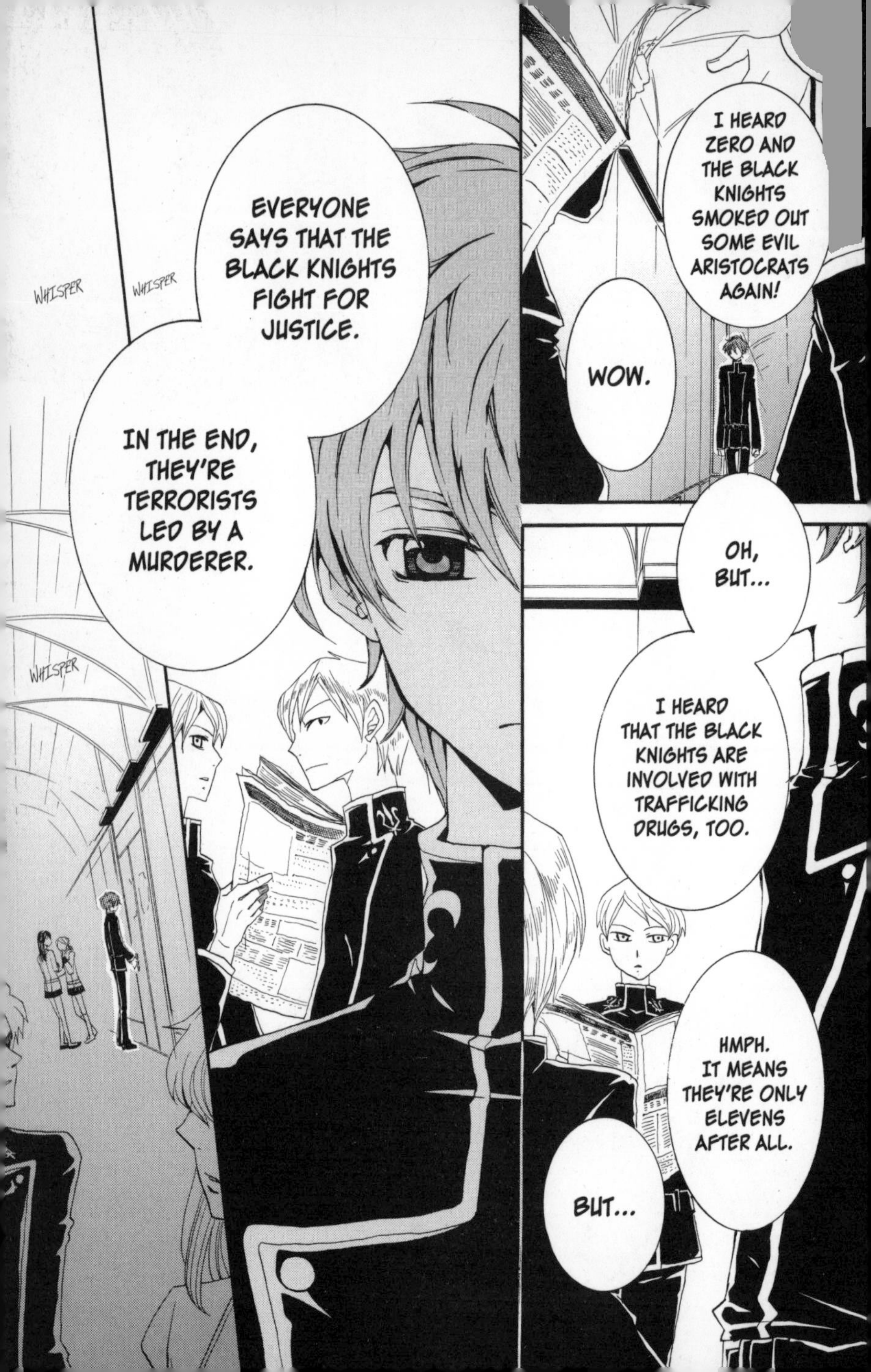

I HEARD ZERO AND THE BLACK KNIGHTS SMOKED OUT SOME EVIL ARISTOCRATS AGAIN!
WOW.
OH, BUT...
I HEARD THAT THE BLACK KNIGHTS ARE INVOLVED WITH TRAFFICKING DRUGS, TOO.
HMPH. IT MEANS THEY'RE ONLY ELEVENS AFTER ALL.
BUT...
EVERYONE SAYS THAT THE BLACK KNIGHTS FIGHT FOR JUSTICE.
WHISPER
WHISPER
IN THE END, THEY'RE TERRORISTS LED BY A MURDERER.
WHISPER

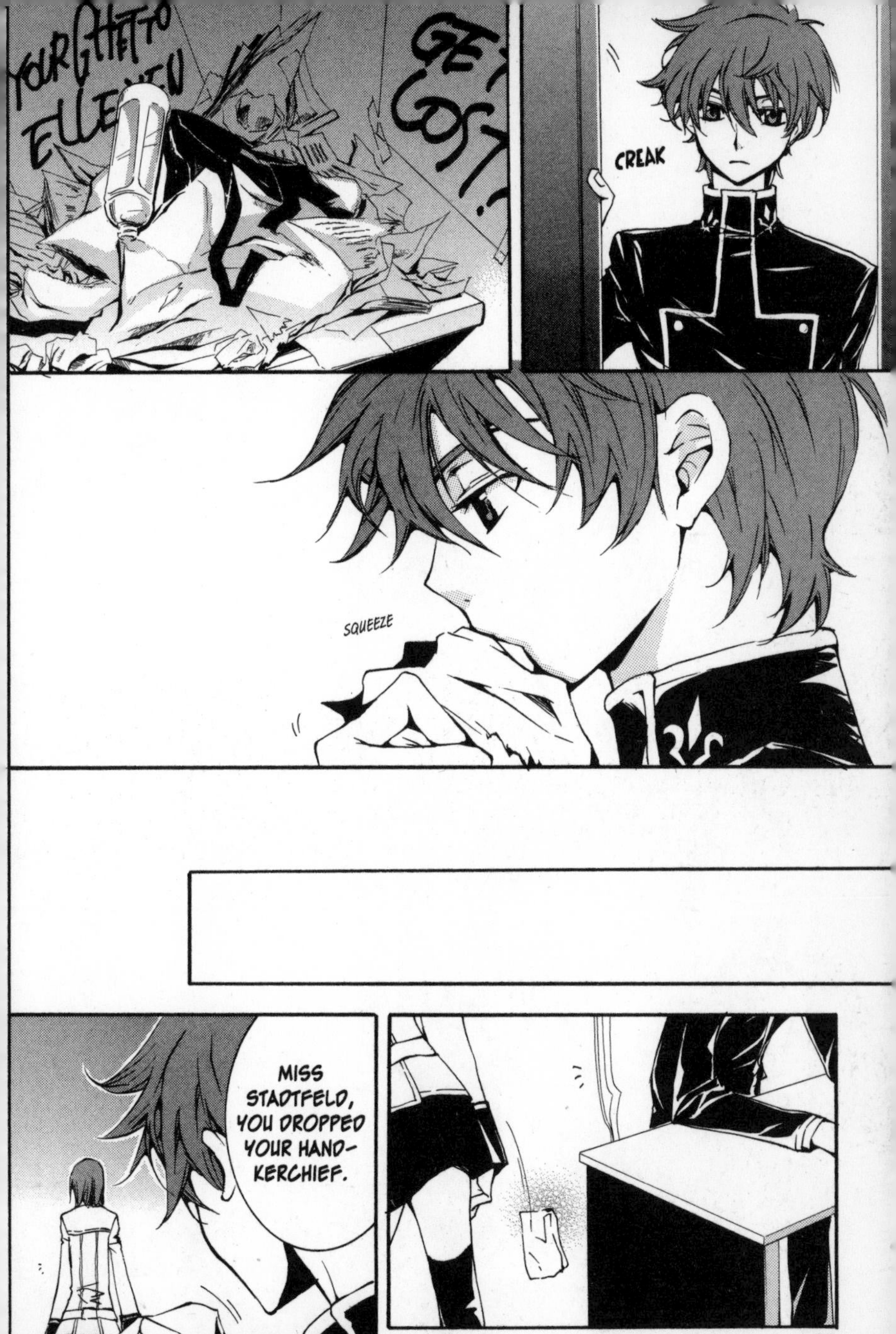
CREAK
YOUR GHETTO
SQUEEZE
MISS STADTFELD, YOU DROPPED YOUR HAND-KERCHIEF.

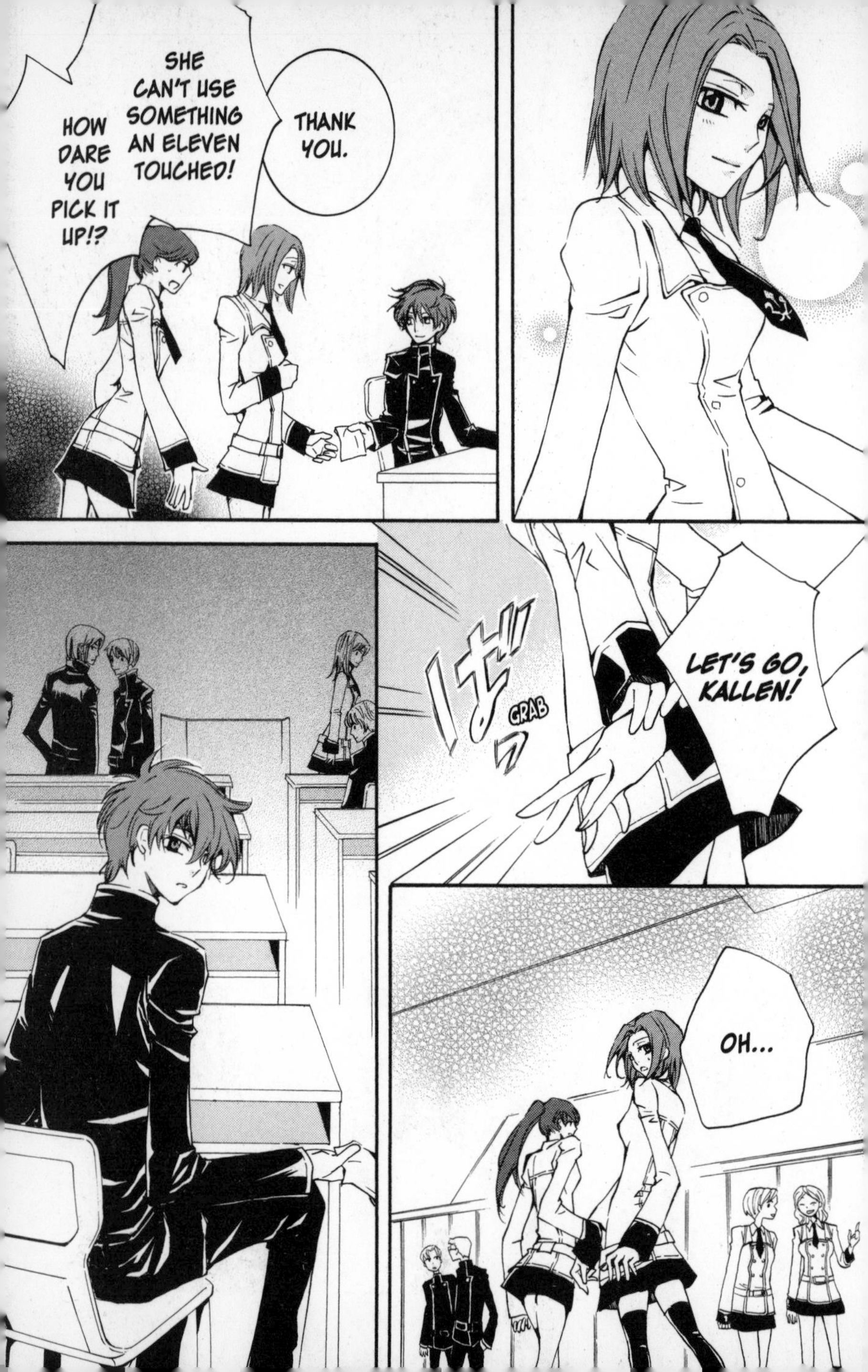
THANK YOU.
SHE CAN'T USE SOMETHING AN ELEVEN TOUCHED!
HOW DARE YOU PICK IT UP!?
LET'S GO, KALLEN!
GRAB
OH...

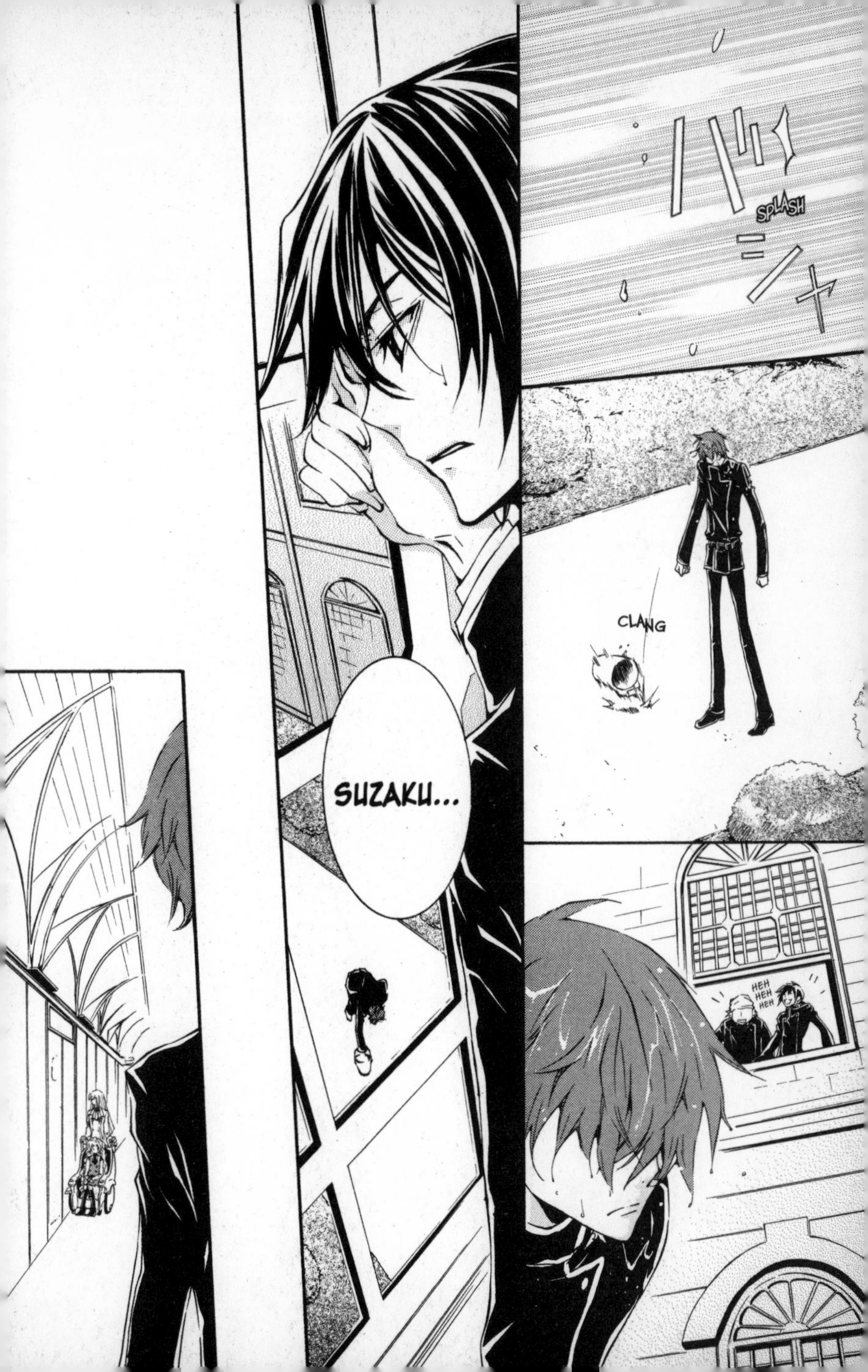
SPLASH
CLANG
HEH HEH HEH
SUZAKU...

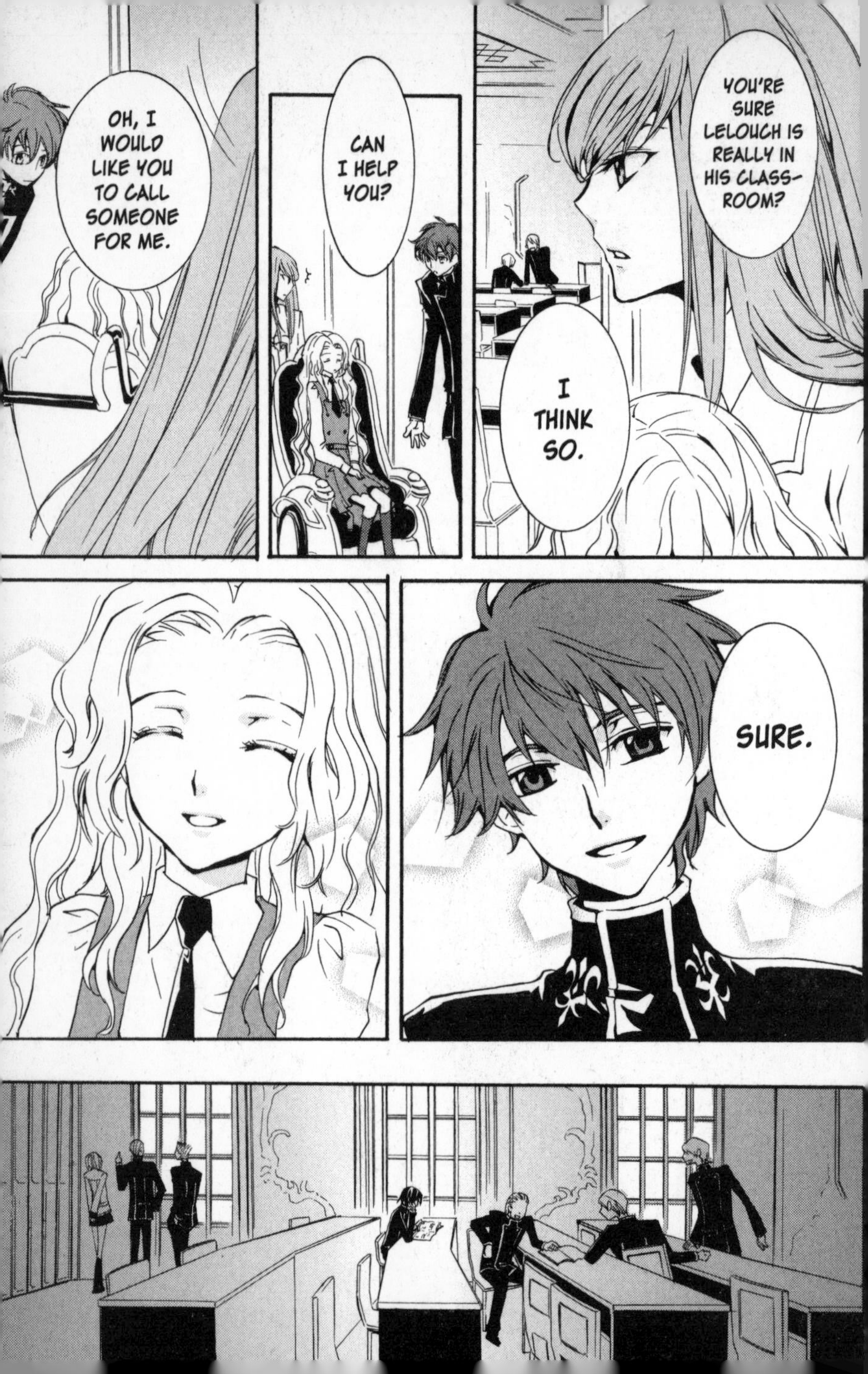
YOU'RE SURE LELOUCH IS REALLY IN HIS CLASS-ROOM?
I THINK SO.
CAN I HELP YOU?
OH, I WOULD LIKE YOU TO CALL SOMEONE FOR ME.
SURE.

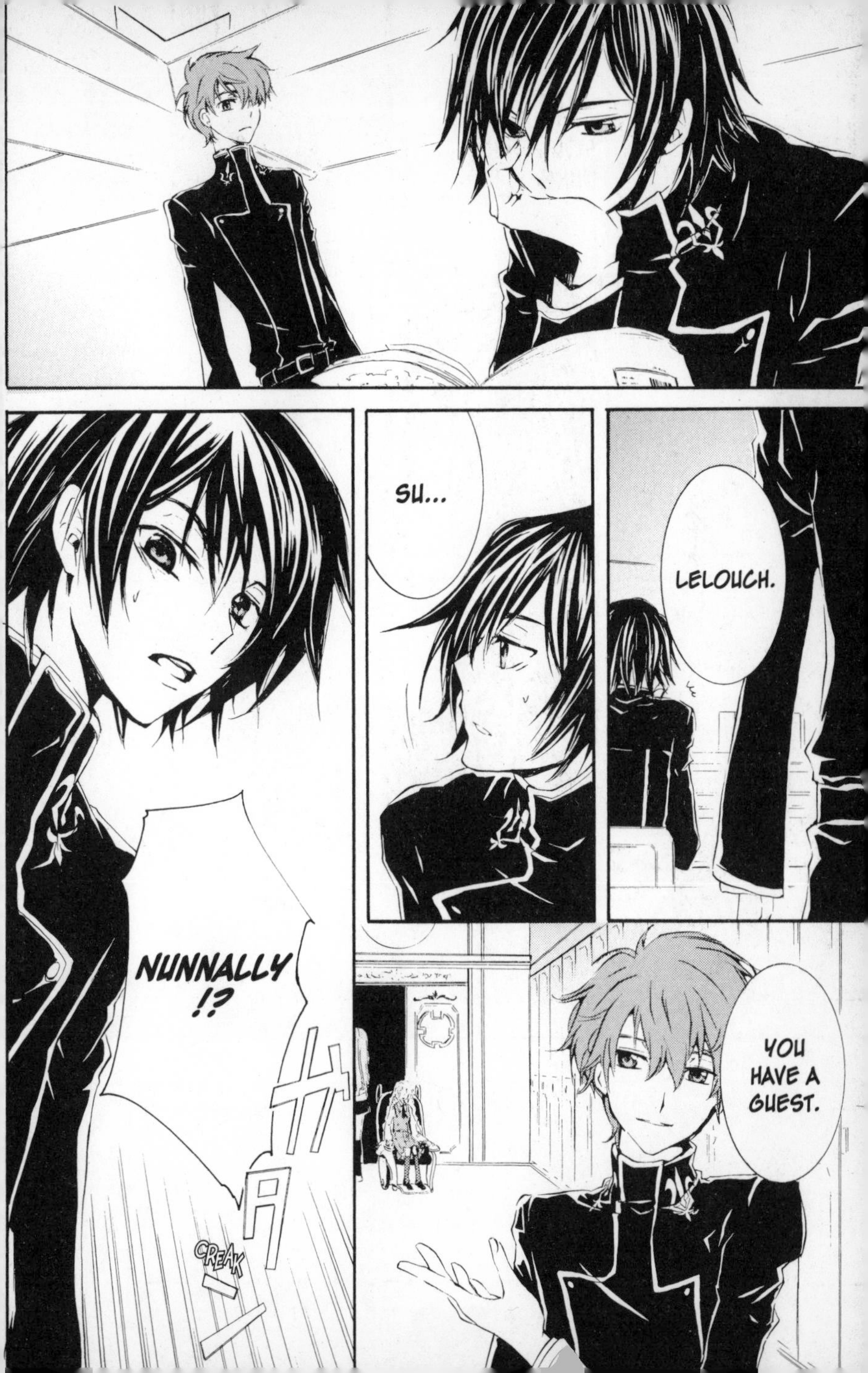
LELOUCH.
SU...
YOU HAVE A GUEST.
NUNNALLY !?
CREAK

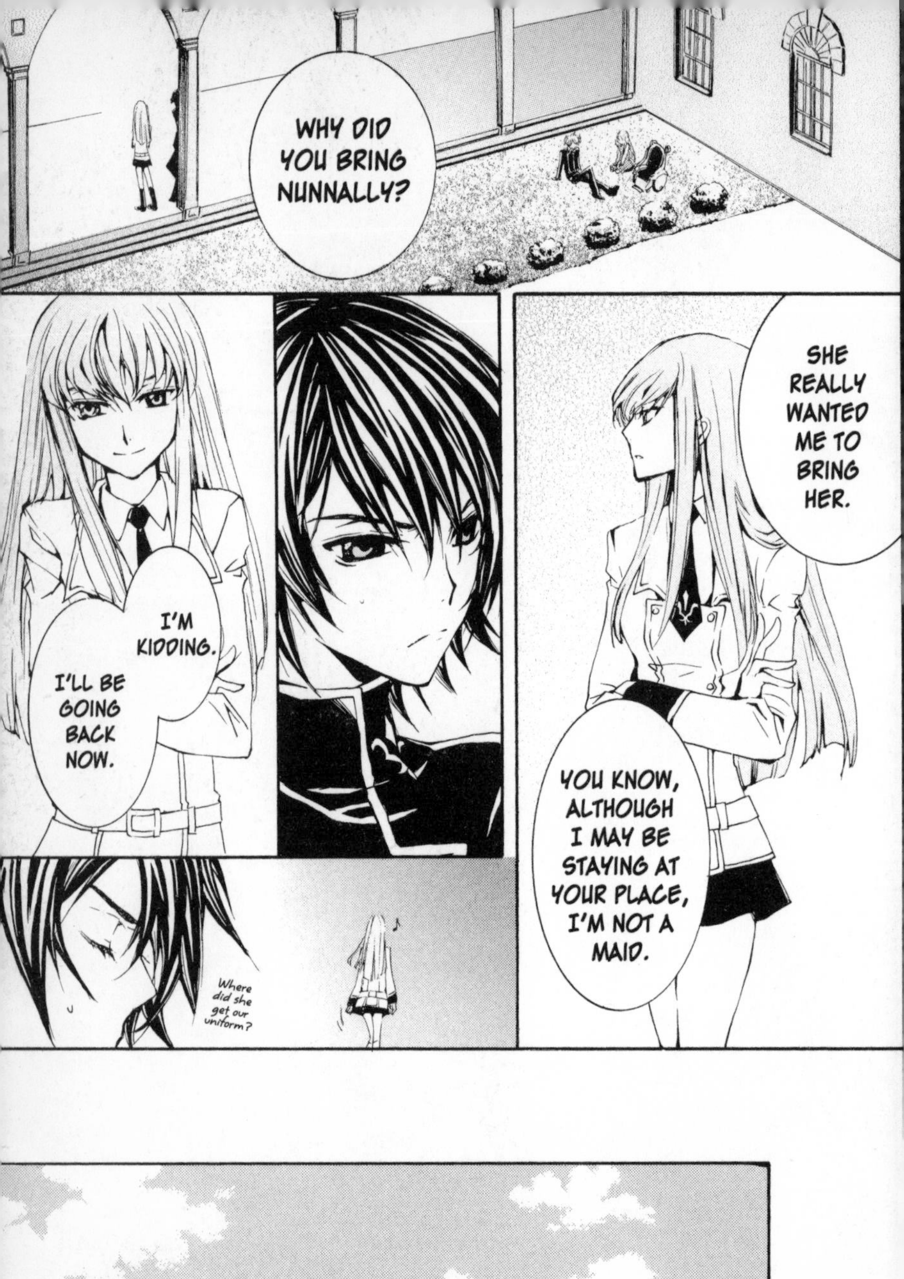
WHY DID YOU BRING NUNNALLY?
SHE REALLY WANTED ME TO BRING HER.
YOU KNOW, ALTHOUGH I MAY BE STAYING AT YOUR PLACE, I'M NOT A MAID.
I'M KIDDING.
I'LL BE GOING BACK NOW.
Where did she get our uniform?

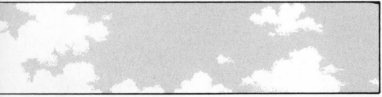

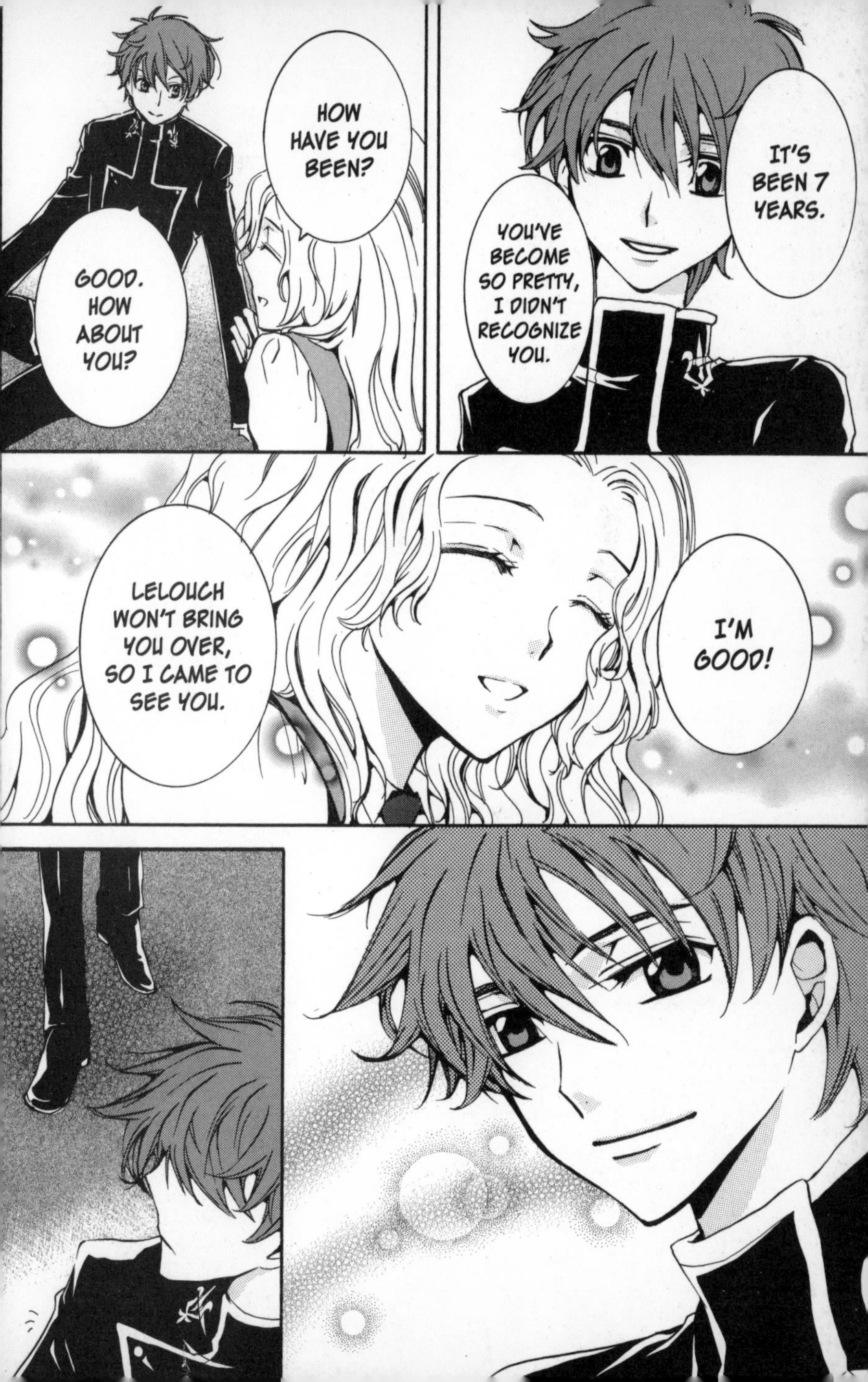
IT'S BEEN 7 YEARS.
YOU'VE BECOME SO PRETTY, I DIDN'T RECOGNIZE YOU.
HOW HAVE YOU BEEN?
GOOD. HOW ABOUT YOU?
I'M GOOD!
LELOUCH WON'T BRING YOU OVER, SO I CAME TO SEE YOU.

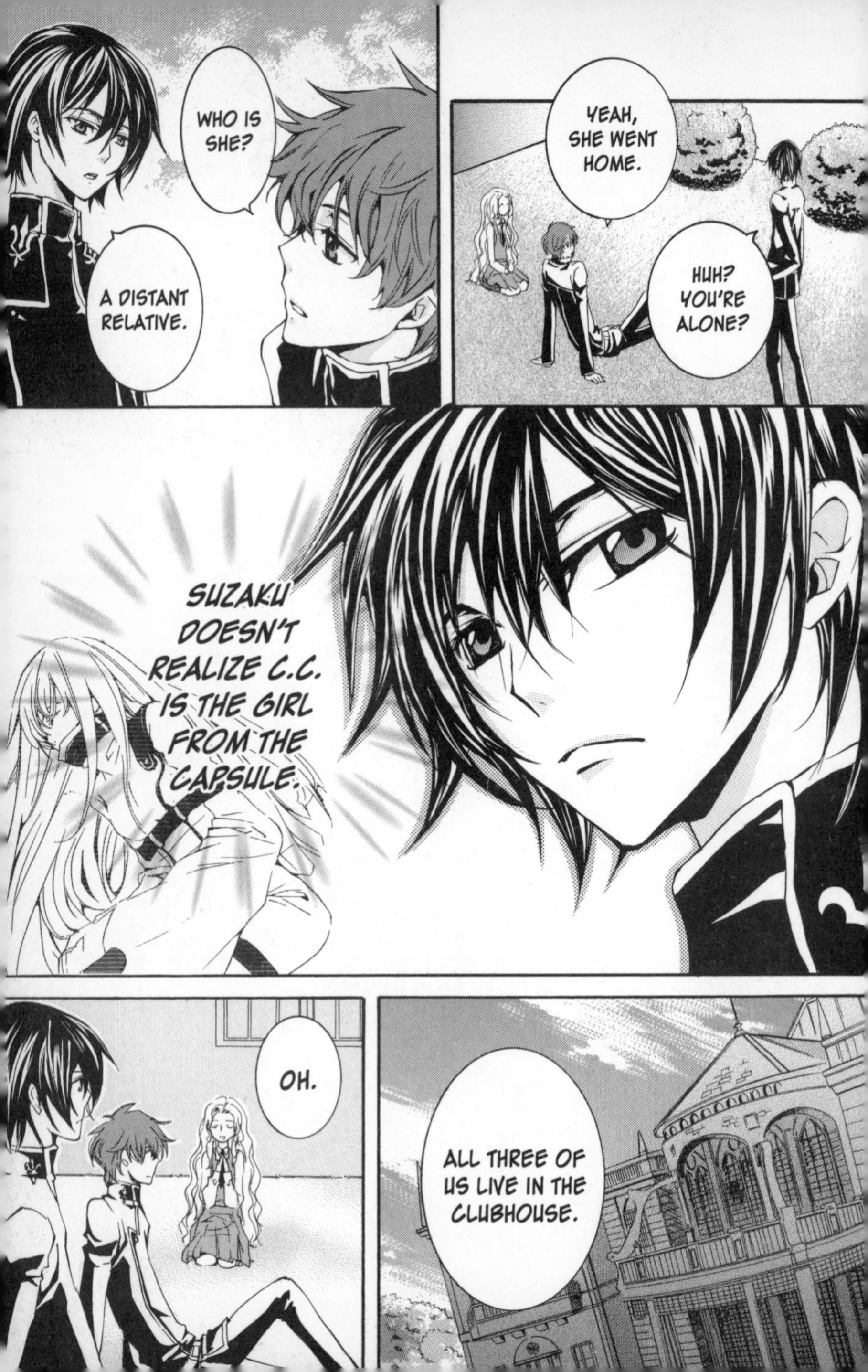
HUH? YOU'RE ALONE?
YEAH, SHE WENT HOME.
WHO IS SHE?
A DISTANT RELATIVE.
SUZAKU DOESN'T REALIZE C.C. IS THE GIRL FROM THE CAPSULE.
ALL THREE OF US LIVE IN THE CLUBHOUSE.
OH.

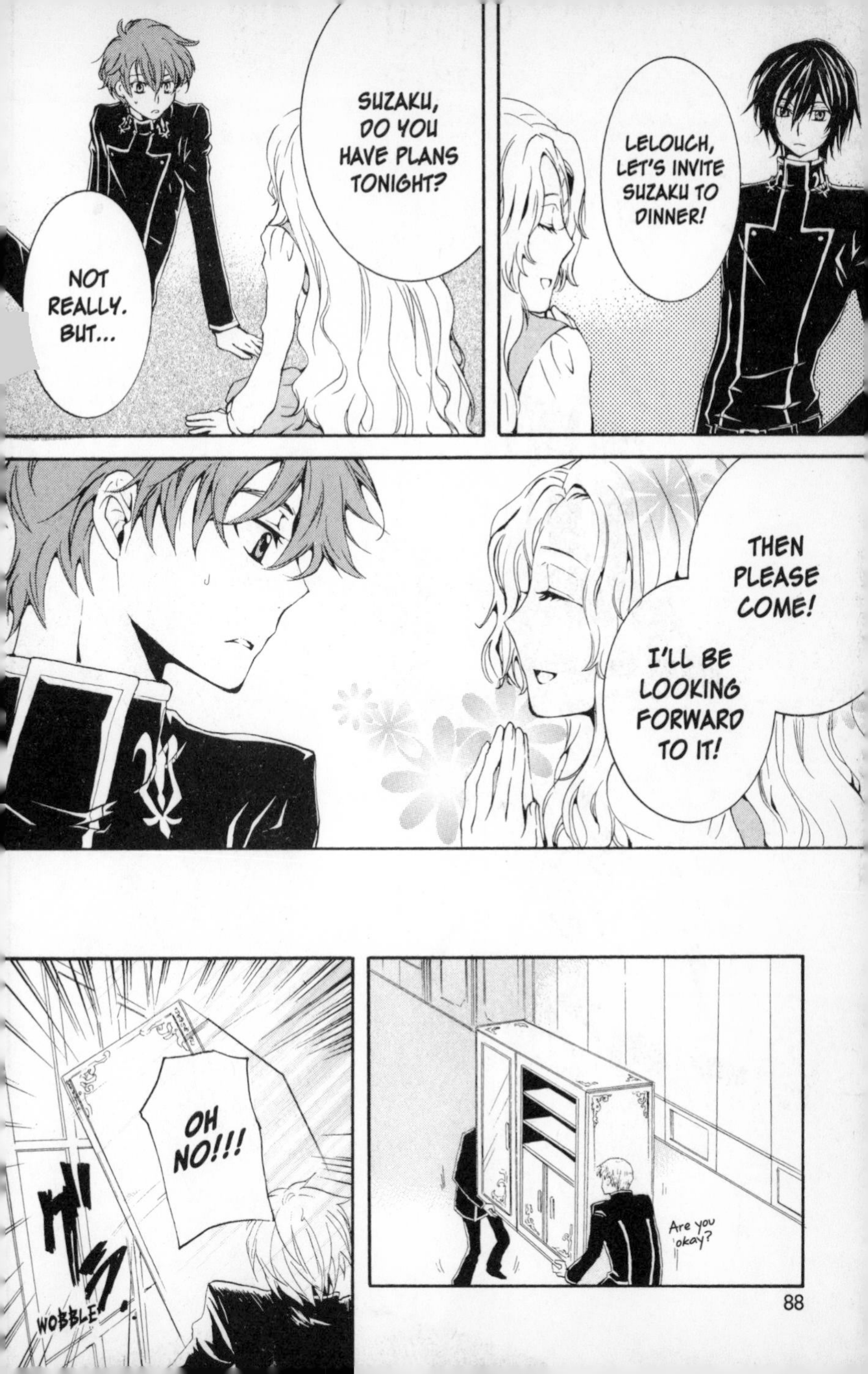
LELOUCH, LET'S INVITE SUZAKU TO DINNER!
SUZAKU, DO YOU HAVE PLANS TONIGHT?
NOT REALLY. BUT...
THEN PLEASE COME!
I'LL BE LOOKING FORWARD TO IT!
Are you okay?
OH NO!!!
WOBBLE

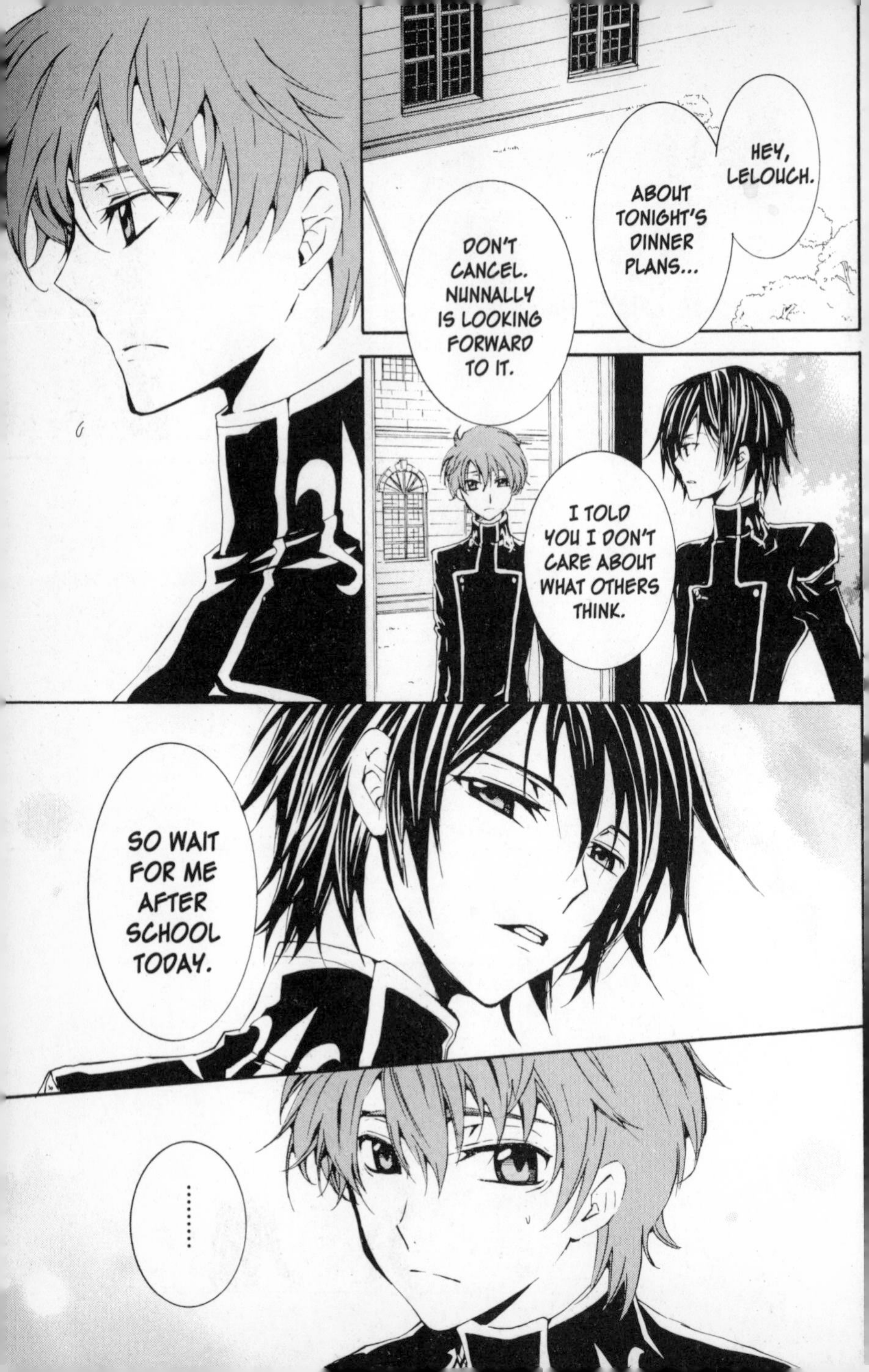
HEY, LELOUCH.
ABOUT TONIGHT'S DINNER PLANS...
DON'T CANCEL. NUNNALLY IS LOOKING FORWARD TO IT.
I TOLD YOU I DON'T CARE ABOUT WHAT OTHERS THINK.
SO WAIT FOR ME AFTER SCHOOL TODAY.
......

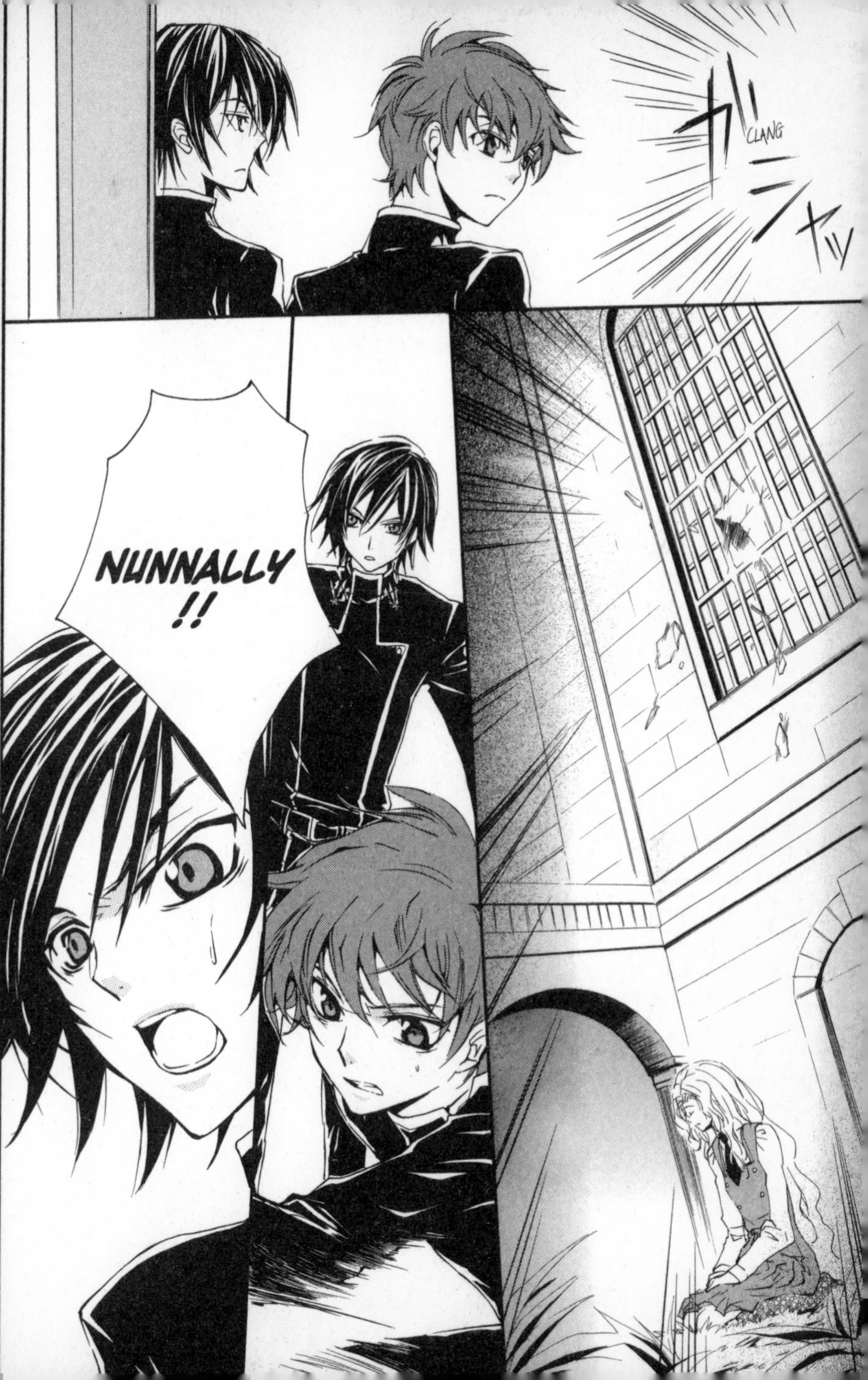
ガシャッ
CLANG
NUNNALLY !!

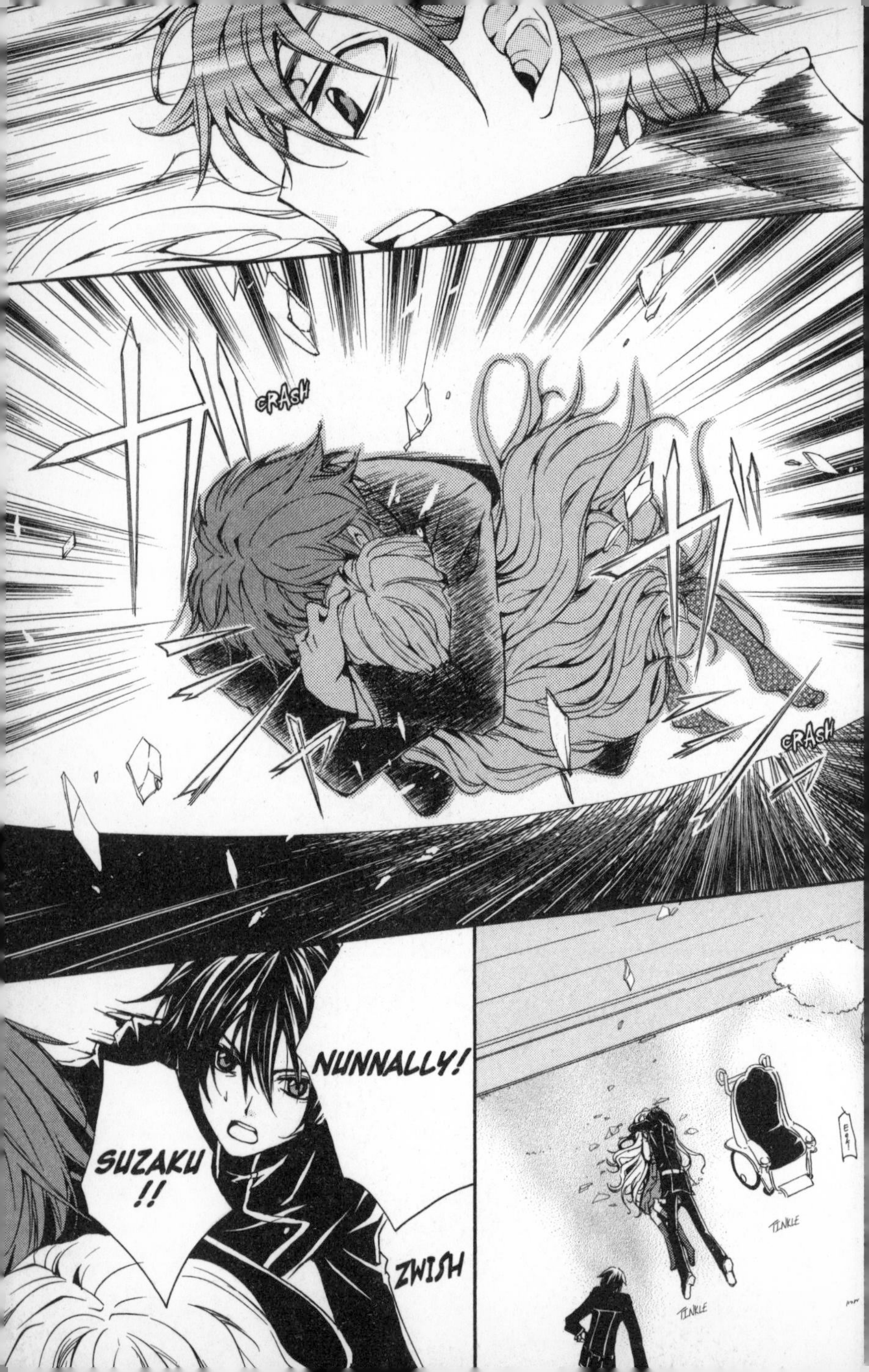
CRASH
CRASH
TINKLE
TINKLE
NUNNALLY!
SUZAKU !!
ZWISH

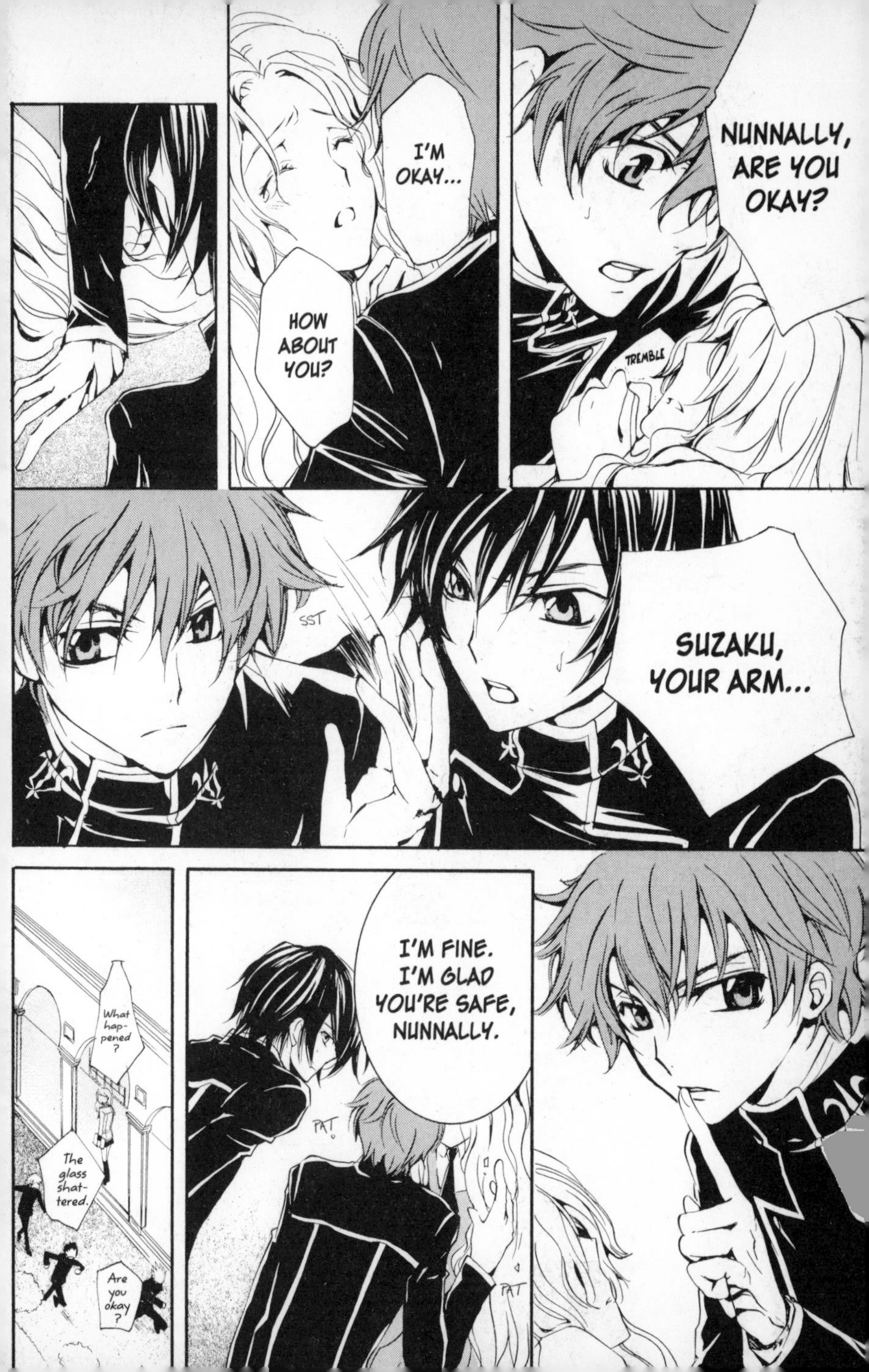
NUNNALLY, ARE YOU OKAY?
TREMBLE
I'M OKAY...
HOW ABOUT YOU?
SUZAKU, YOUR ARM...
SST
I'M FINE. I'M GLAD YOU'RE SAFE, NUNNALLY.
PAT
PAT
What hap-pened?
The glass shat-tered.
Are you okay?

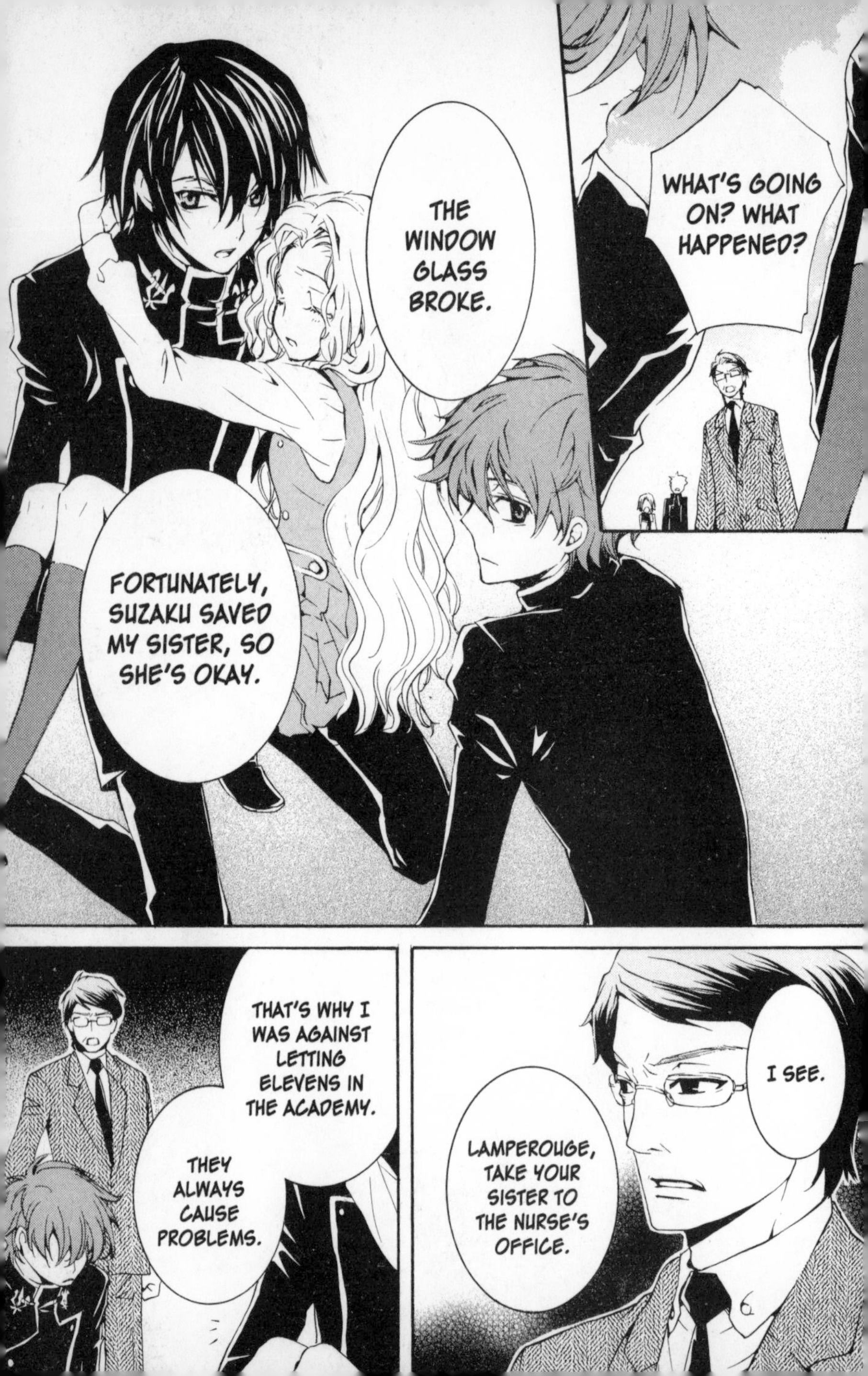
WHAT'S GOING ON? WHAT HAPPENED?
THE WINDOW GLASS BROKE.
FORTUNATELY, SUZAKU SAVED MY SISTER, SO SHE'S OKAY.
I SEE.
LAMPEROUGE, TAKE YOUR SISTER TO THE NURSE'S OFFICE.
THAT'S WHY I WAS AGAINST LETTING ELEVENS IN THE ACADEMY.
THEY ALWAYS CAUSE PROBLEMS.

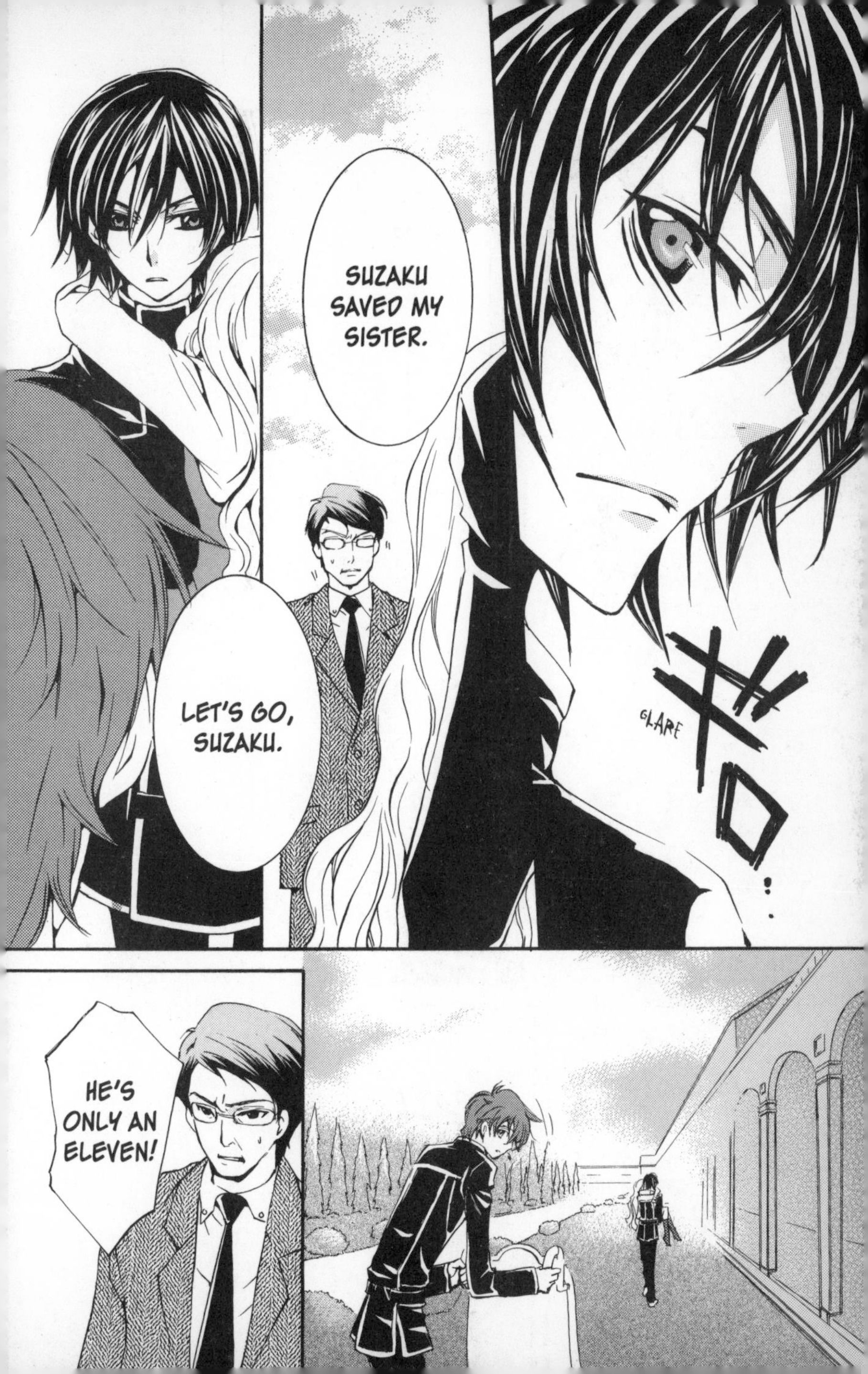
GLARE
SUZAKU SAVED MY SISTER.
LET'S GO, SUZAKU.
HE'S ONLY AN ELEVEN!

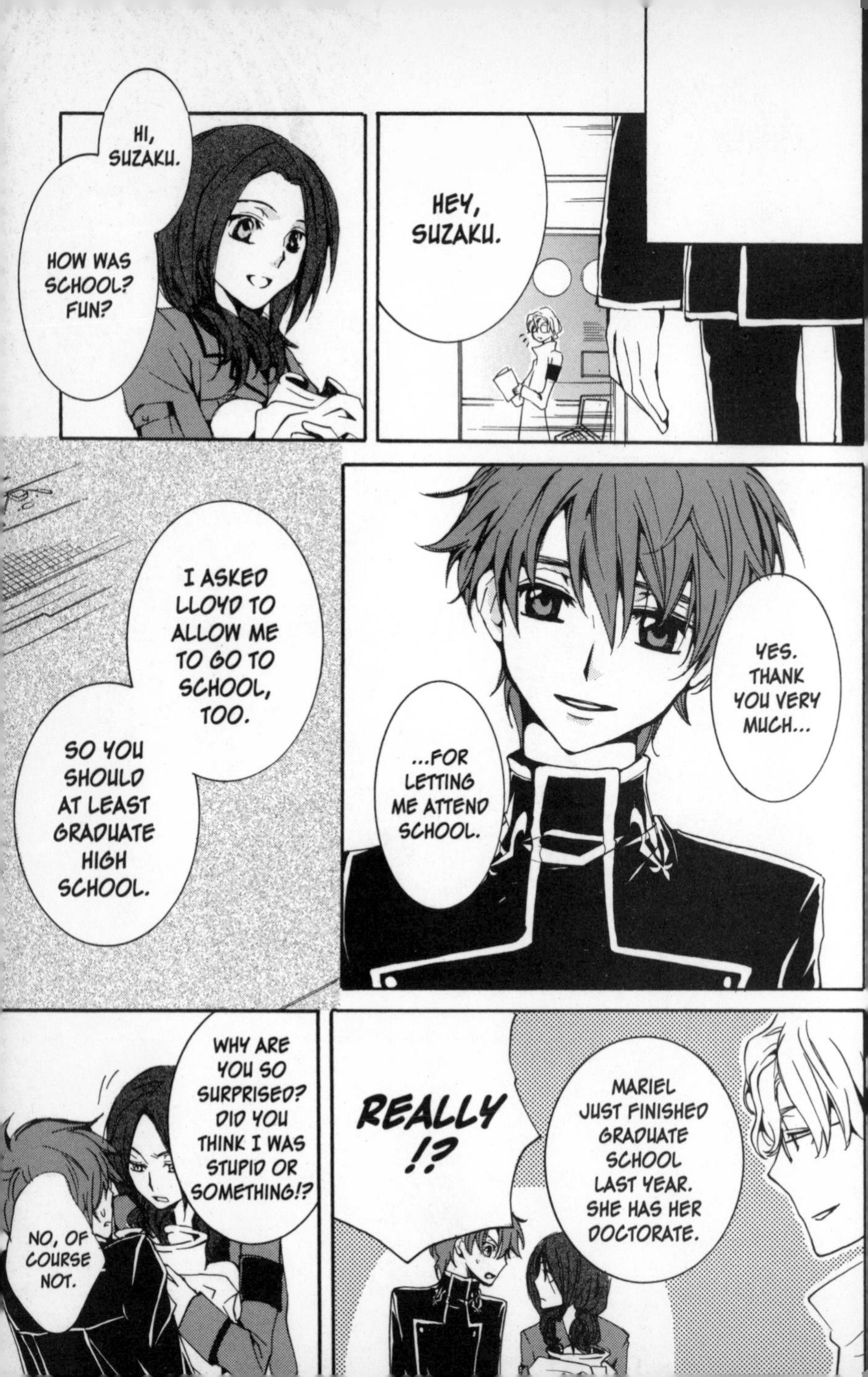
HEY, SUZAKU.
HI, SUZAKU.
HOW WAS SCHOOL? FUN?
YES. THANK YOU VERY MUCH...
...FOR LETTING ME ATTEND SCHOOL.
I ASKED LLOYD TO ALLOW ME TO GO TO SCHOOL, TOO.
SO YOU SHOULD AT LEAST GRADUATE HIGH SCHOOL.
MARIEL JUST FINISHED GRADUATE SCHOOL LAST YEAR. SHE HAS HER DOCTORATE.
REALLY !?
WHY ARE YOU SO SURPRISED? DID YOU THINK I WAS STUPID OR SOMETHING!?
NO, OF COURSE NOT.

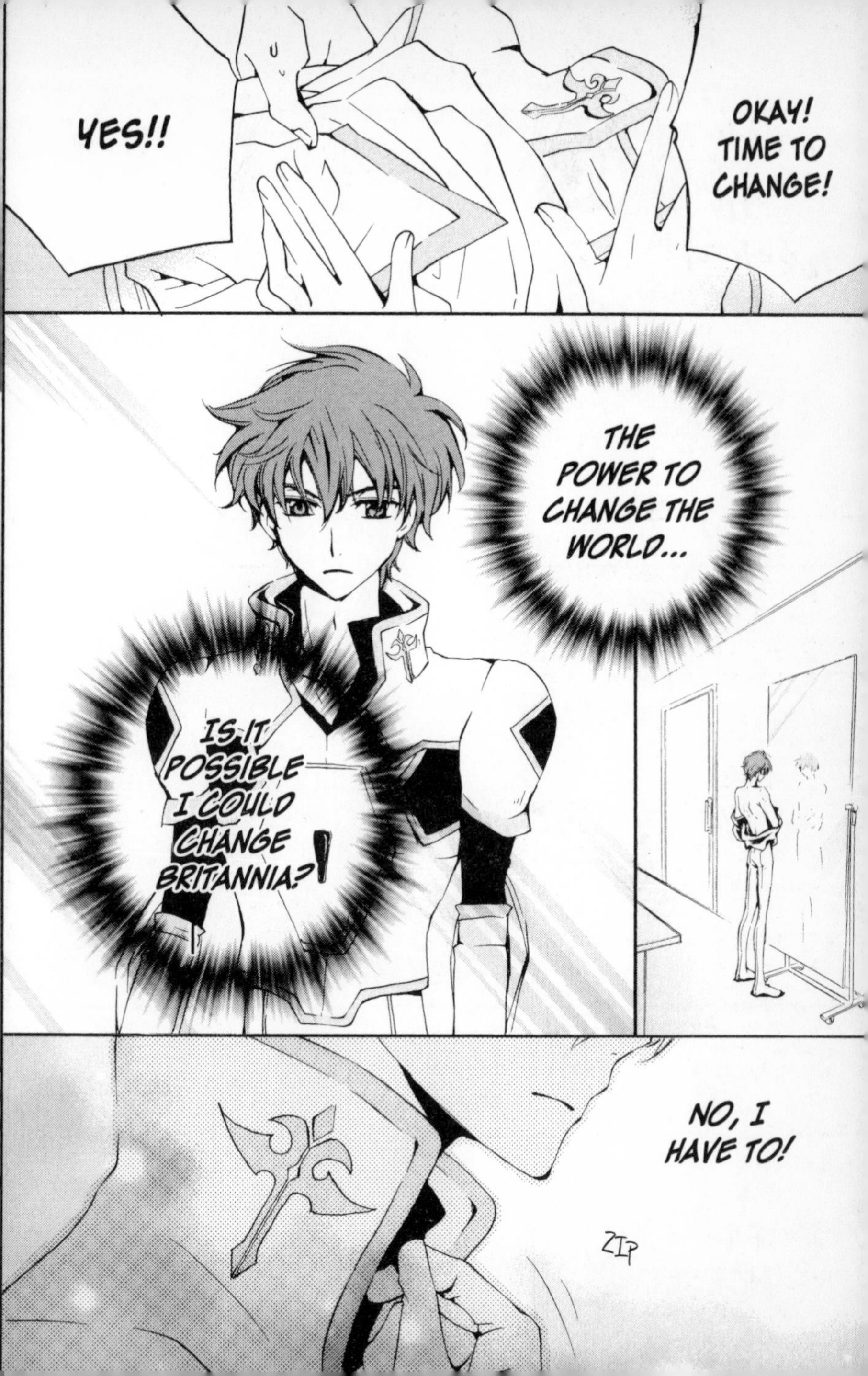
OKAY! TIME TO CHANGE!
YES!!
THE POWER TO CHANGE THE WORLD...
IS IT POSSIBLE I COULD CHANGE BRITANNIA?
NO, I HAVE TO!
ZIP

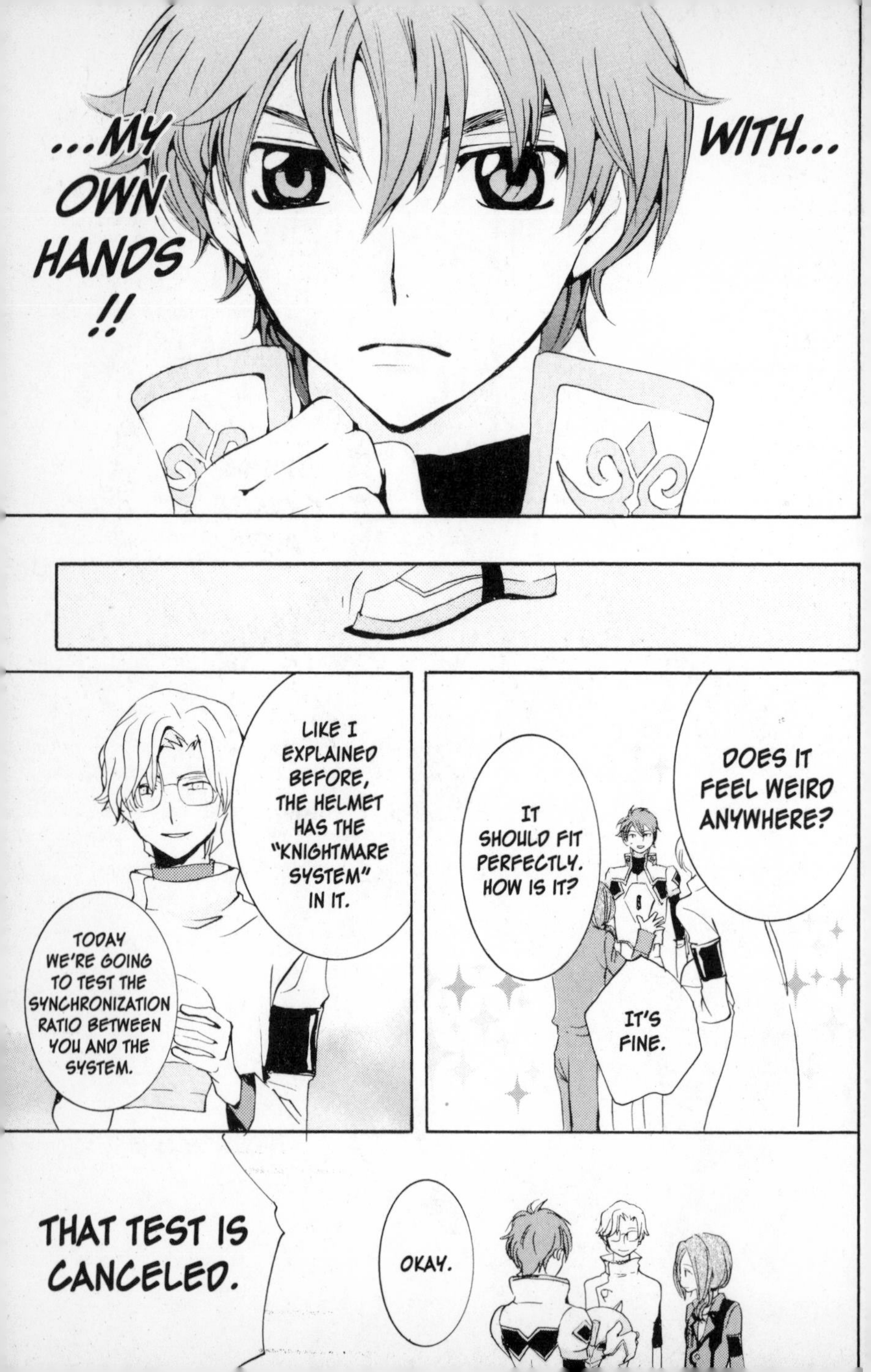
WITH...
...MY OWN HANDS!!
DOES IT FEEL WEIRD ANYWHERE?
IT SHOULD FIT PERFECTLY. HOW IS IT?
IT'S FINE.
LIKE I EXPLAINED BEFORE, THE HELMET HAS THE "KNIGHTMARE SYSTEM" IN IT.
TODAY WE'RE GOING TO TEST THE SYNCHRONIZATION RATIO BETWEEN YOU AND THE SYSTEM.
OKAY.
THAT TEST IS CANCELED.

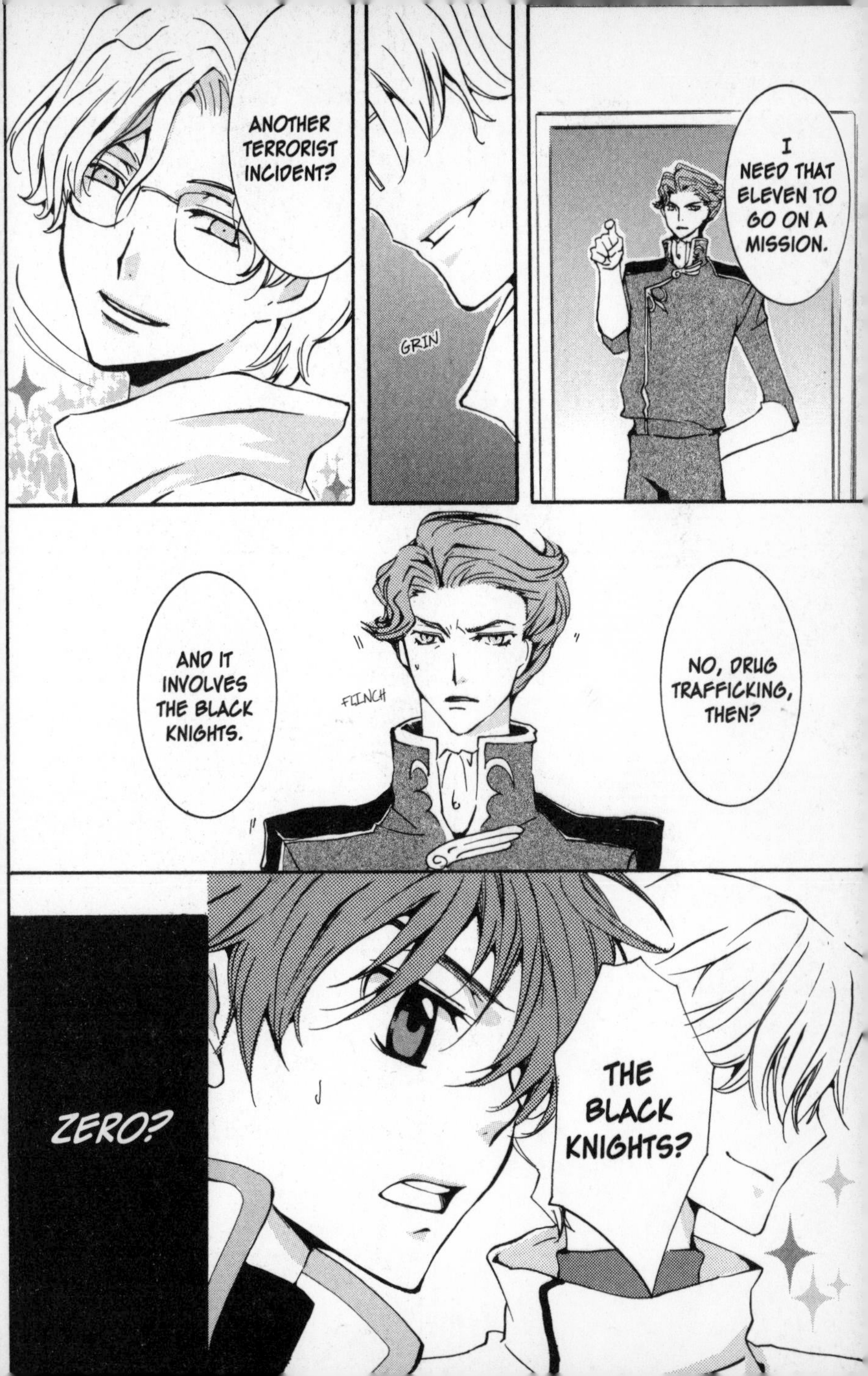
I NEED THAT ELEVEN TO GO ON A MISSION.
GRIN
ANOTHER TERRORIST INCIDENT?
NO, DRUG TRAFFICKING, THEN?
FLINCH
AND IT INVOLVES THE BLACK KNIGHTS.
THE BLACK KNIGHTS?
ZERO?

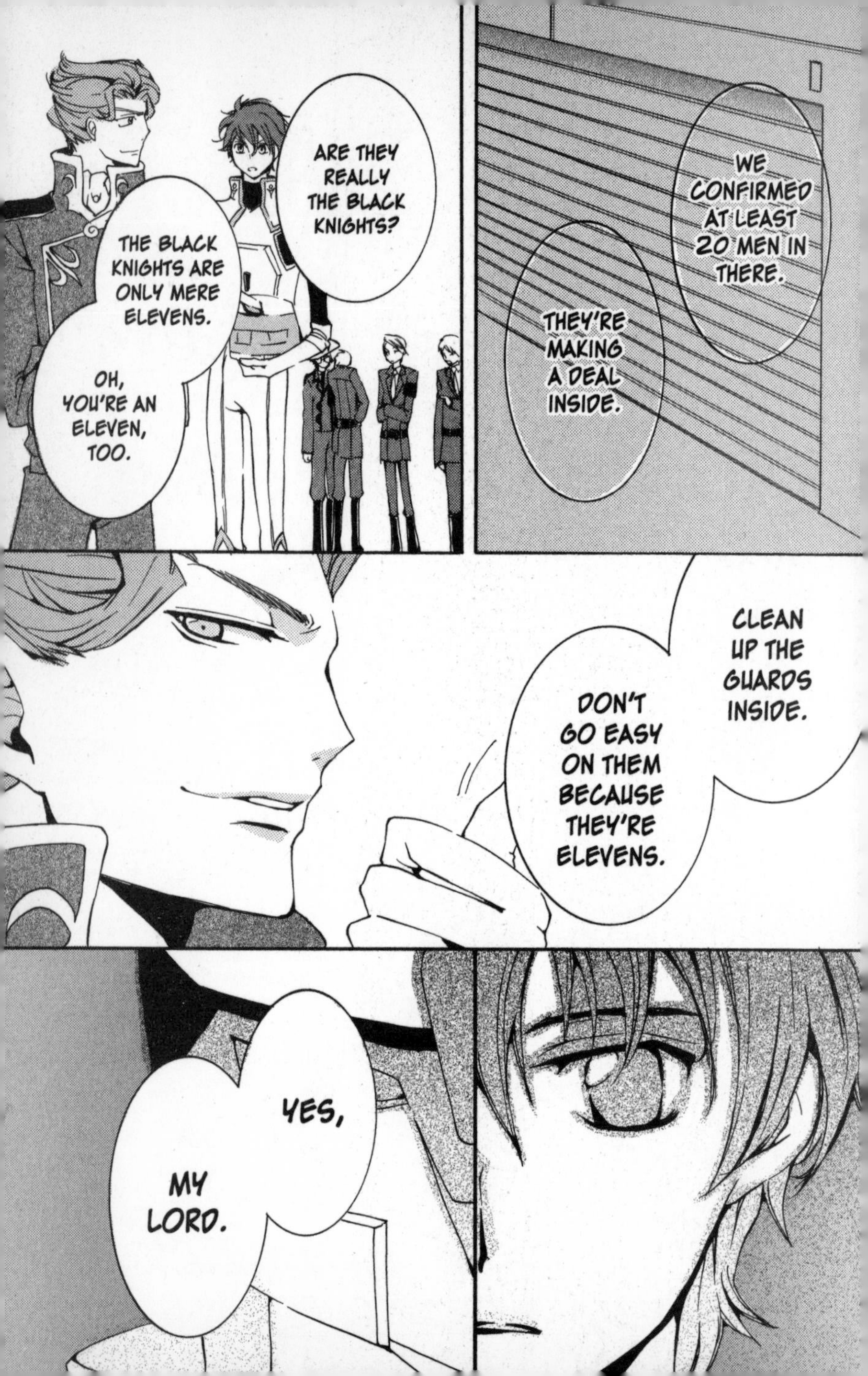
WE CONFIRMED AT LEAST 20 MEN IN THERE.
THEY'RE MAKING A DEAL INSIDE.
ARE THEY REALLY THE BLACK KNIGHTS?
THE BLACK KNIGHTS ARE ONLY MERE ELEVENS.
OH, YOU'RE AN ELEVEN, TOO.
CLEAN UP THE GUARDS INSIDE.
DON'T GO EASY ON THEM BECAUSE THEY'RE ELEVENS.
YES,
MY LORD.

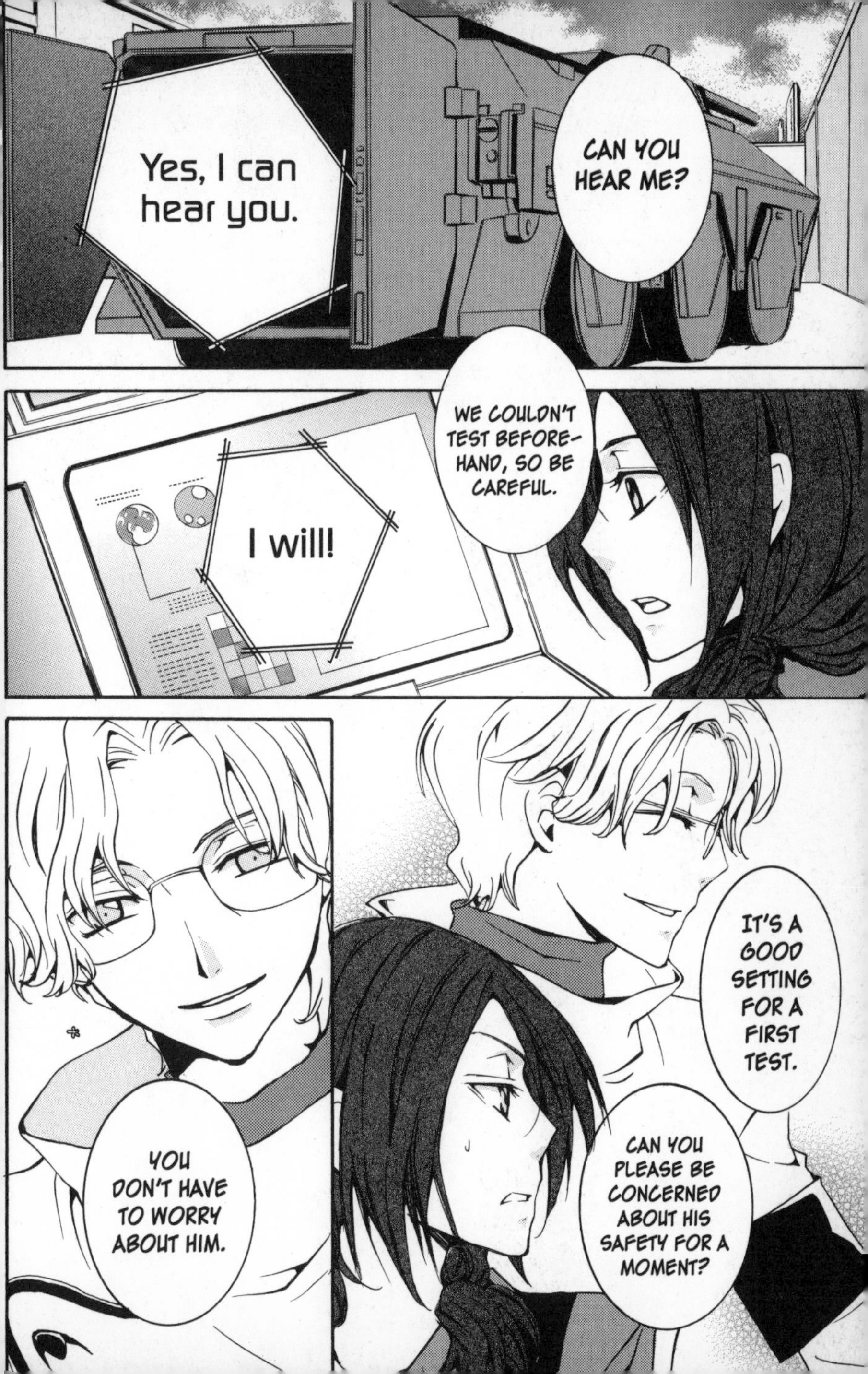
CAN YOU HEAR ME?
Yes, I can hear you.
WE COULDN'T TEST BEFORE-HAND, SO BE CAREFUL.
I will!
IT'S A GOOD SETTING FOR A FIRST TEST.
CAN YOU PLEASE BE CONCERNED ABOUT HIS SAFETY FOR A MOMENT?
YOU DON'T HAVE TO WORRY ABOUT HIM.

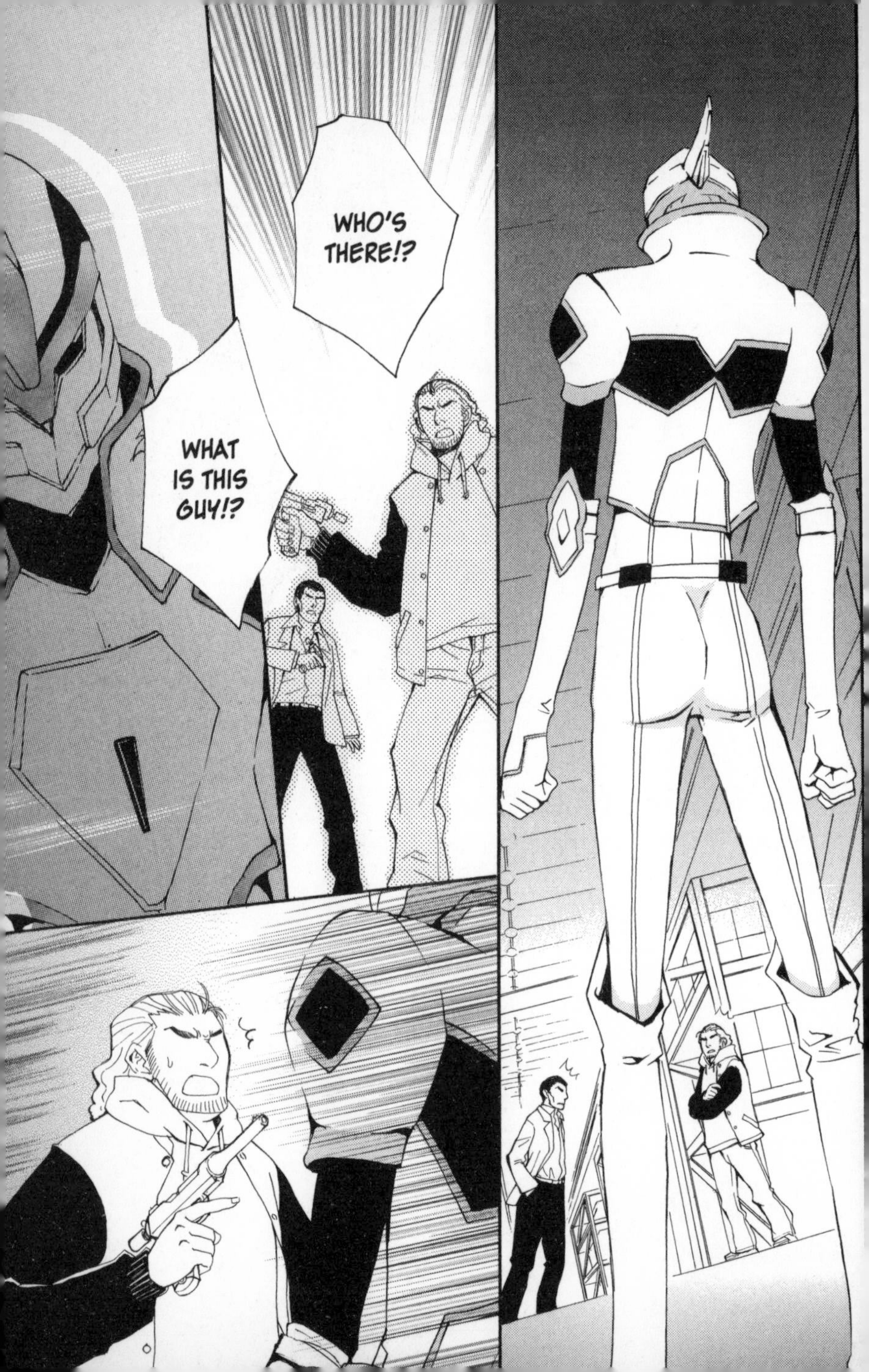
WHO'S THERE!?
WHAT IS THIS GUY!?

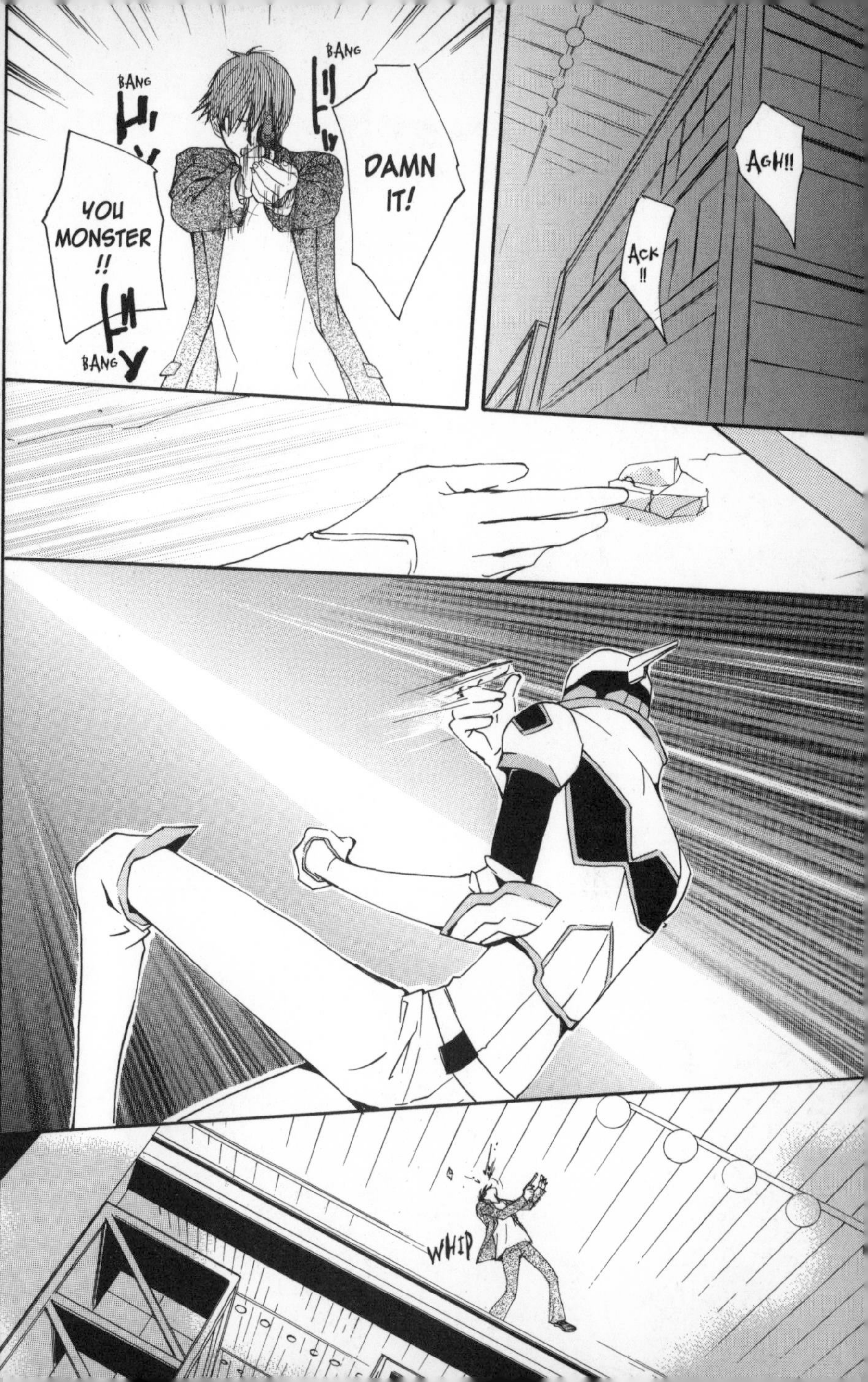
AGH!!
ACK!!
BANG
DAMN IT!
BANG
YOU MONSTER!!
BANG
WHIP

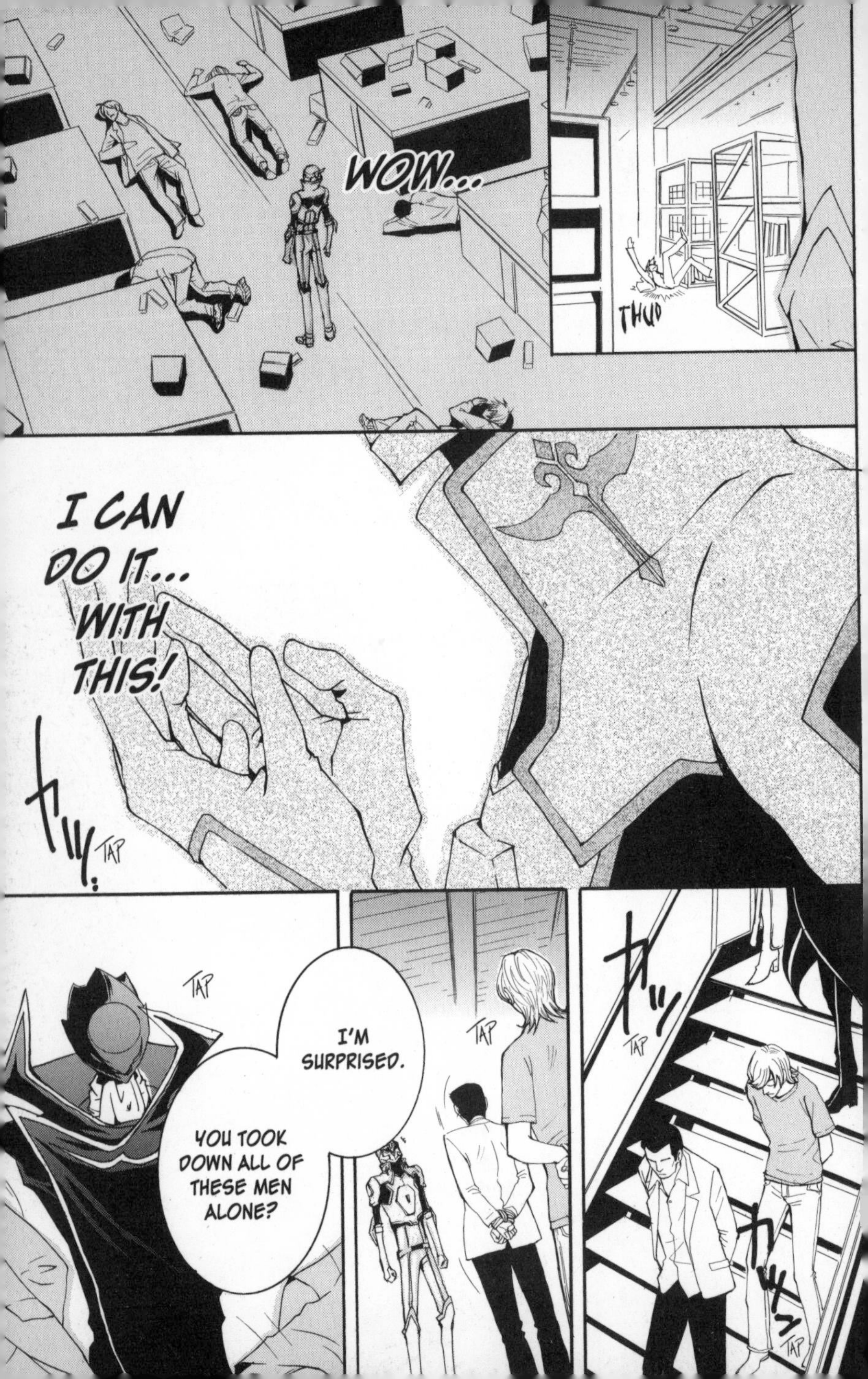
THUD
WOW...
I CAN DO IT... WITH THIS!
TAP
TAP
TAP
TAP
I'M SURPRISED.
YOU TOOK DOWN ALL OF THESE MEN ALONE?
TAP

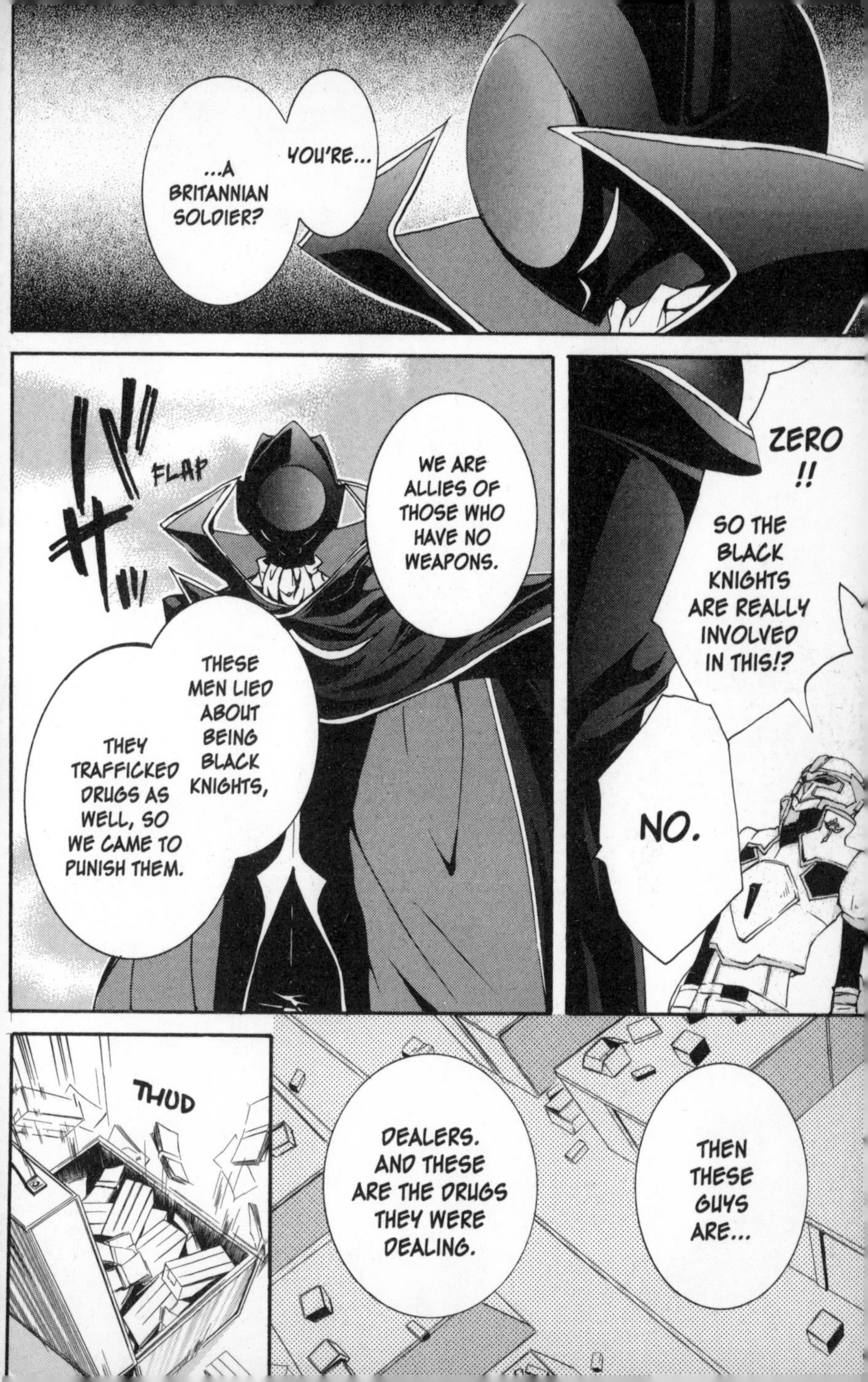
YOU'RE...
...A BRITANNIAN SOLDIER?
ZERO !!
SO THE BLACK KNIGHTS ARE REALLY INVOLVED IN THIS!?
NO.
FLAP
WE ARE ALLIES OF THOSE WHO HAVE NO WEAPONS.
THESE MEN LIED ABOUT BEING BLACK KNIGHTS,
THEY TRAFFICKED DRUGS AS WELL, SO WE CAME TO PUNISH THEM.
THEN THESE GUYS ARE...
DEALERS. AND THESE ARE THE DRUGS THEY WERE DEALING.
THUD

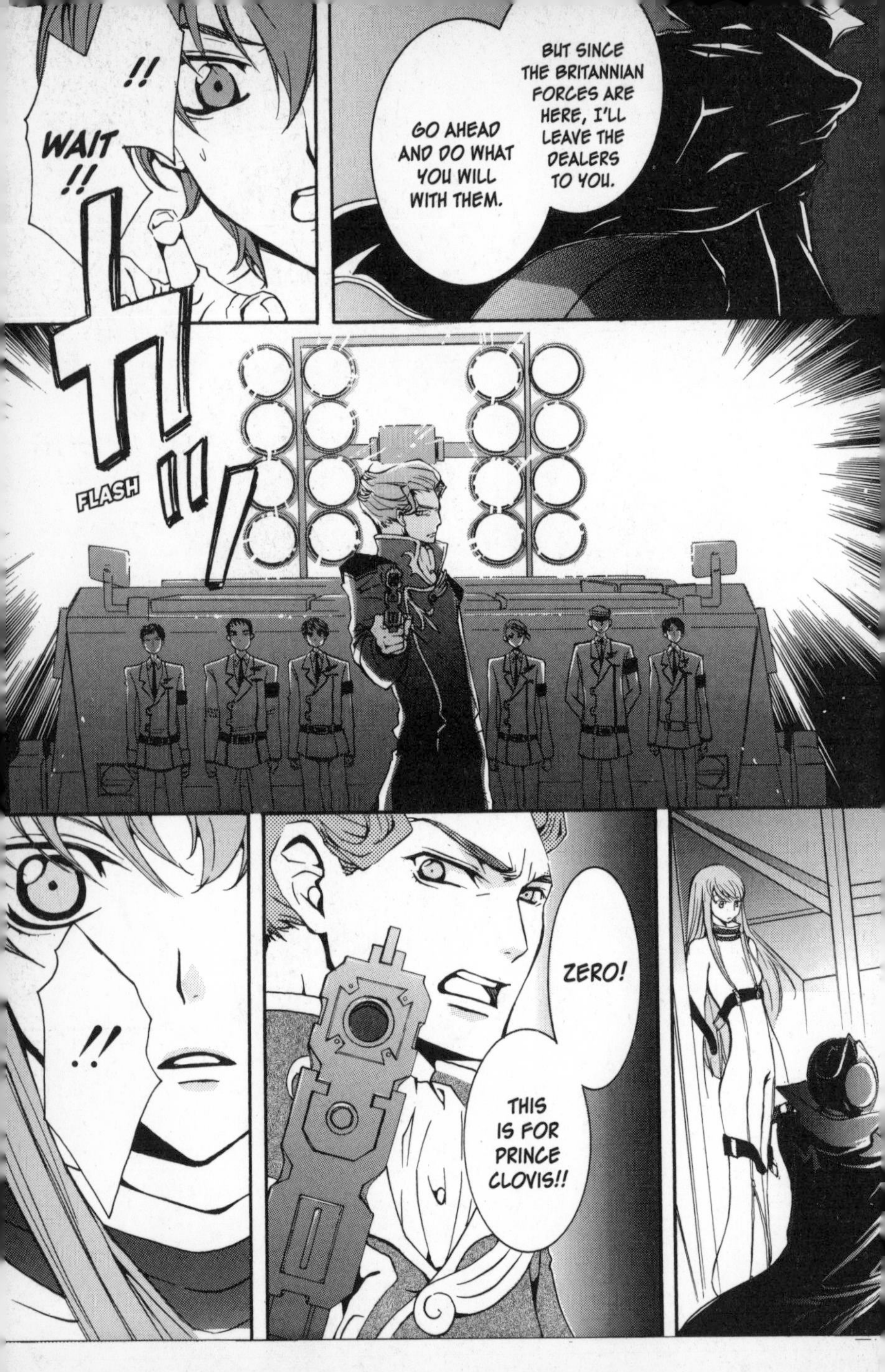
BUT SINCE THE BRITANNIAN FORCES ARE HERE, I'LL LEAVE THE DEALERS TO YOU.
GO AHEAD AND DO WHAT YOU WILL WITH THEM.
!!
WAIT!!
FLASH
ZERO!
THIS IS FOR PRINCE CLOVIS!!
!!

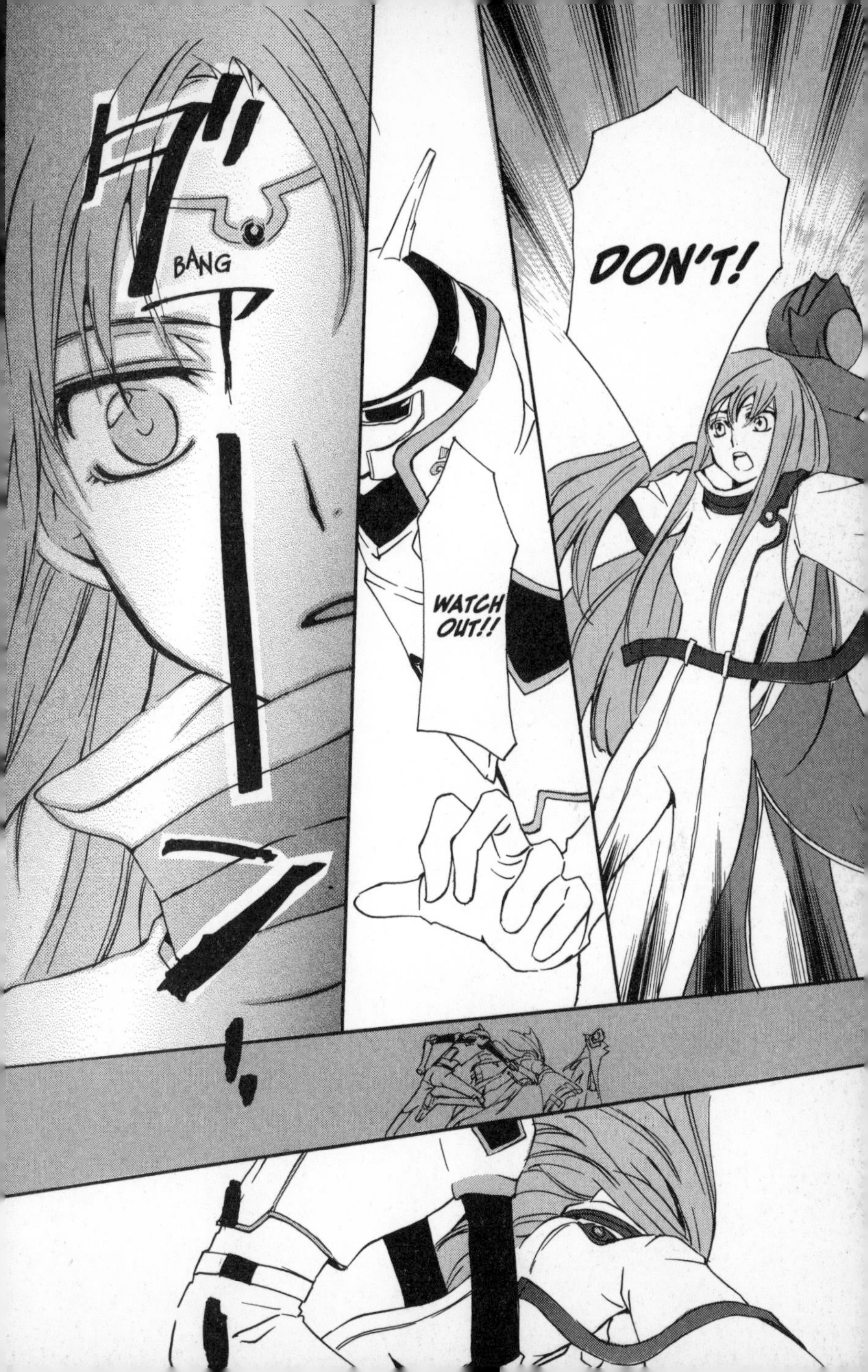
DON'T!
WATCH OUT!!
BANG

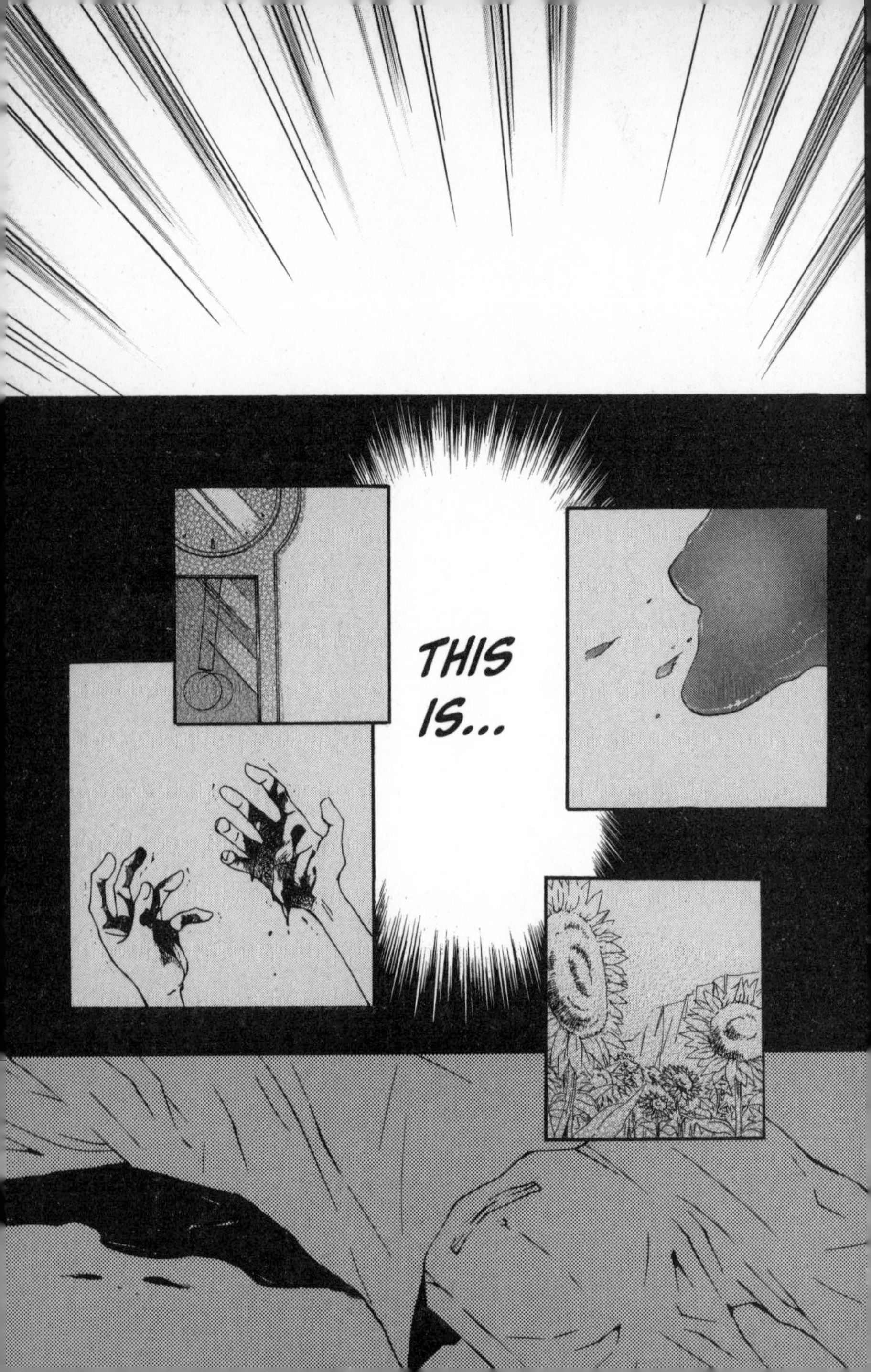
THIS IS...

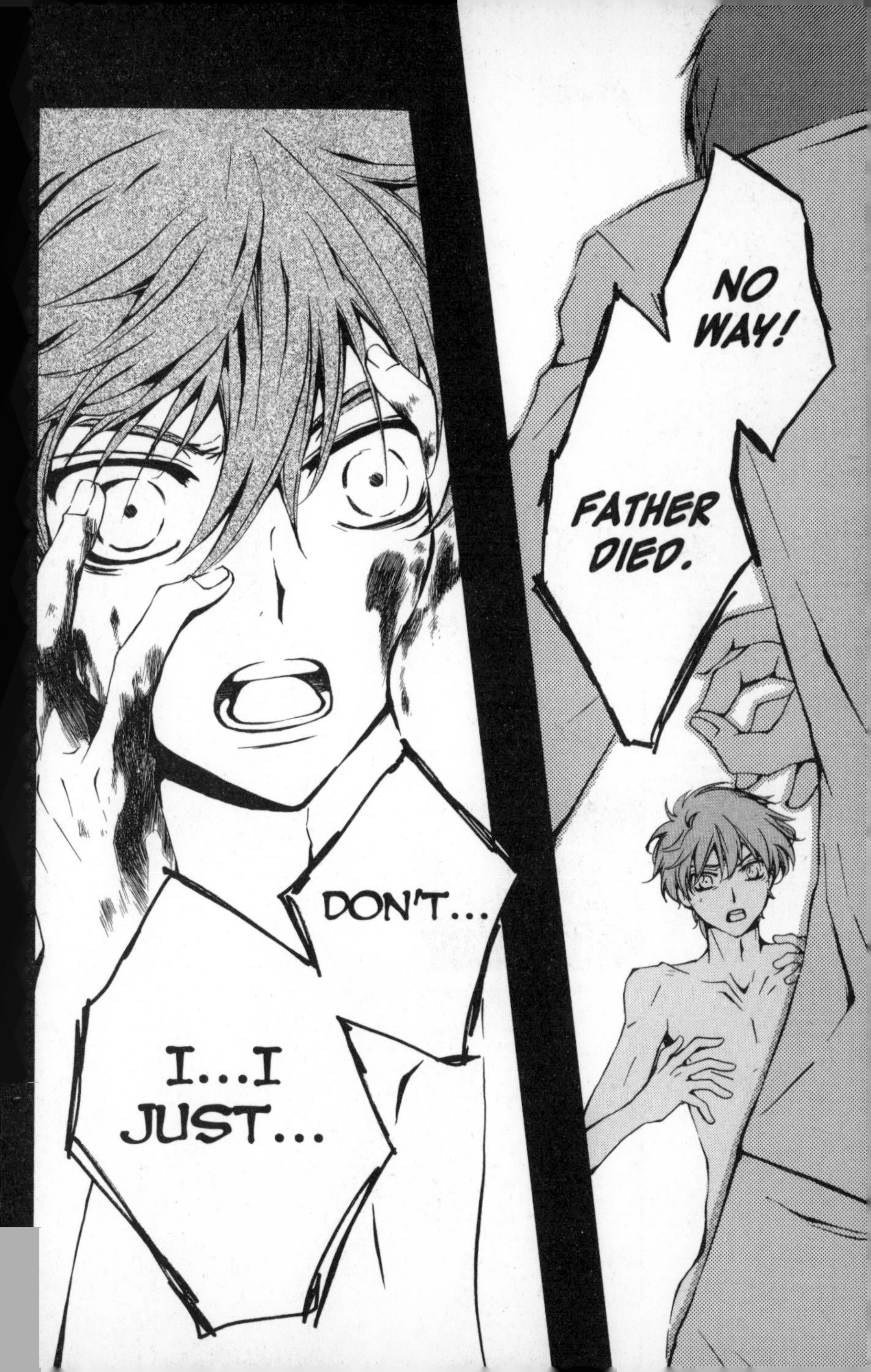
NO WAY!
FATHER DIED.
DON'T...
I...I JUST...

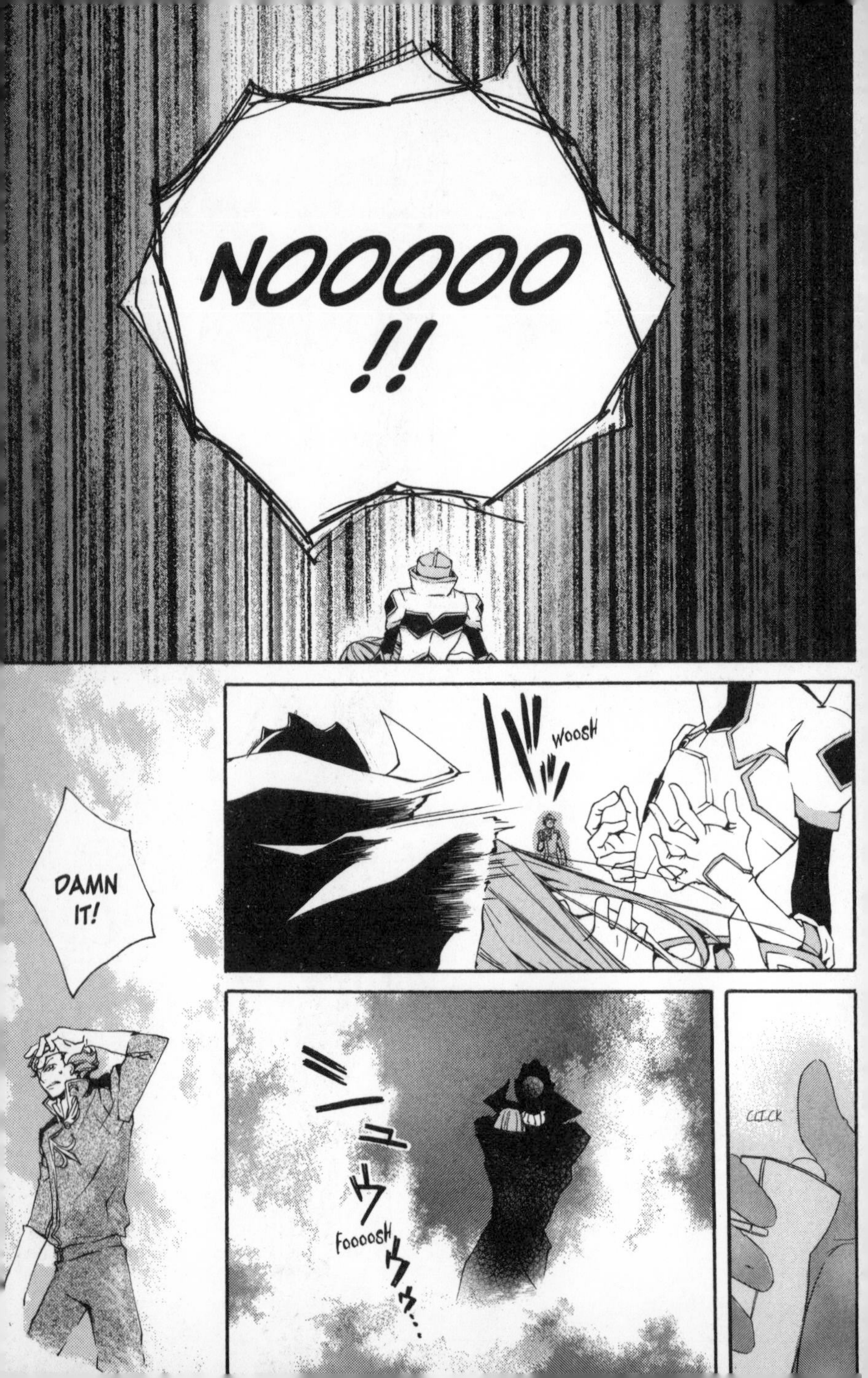
NOOOOO !!
WOOSH
CLICK
FOOOOSH
DAMN IT!

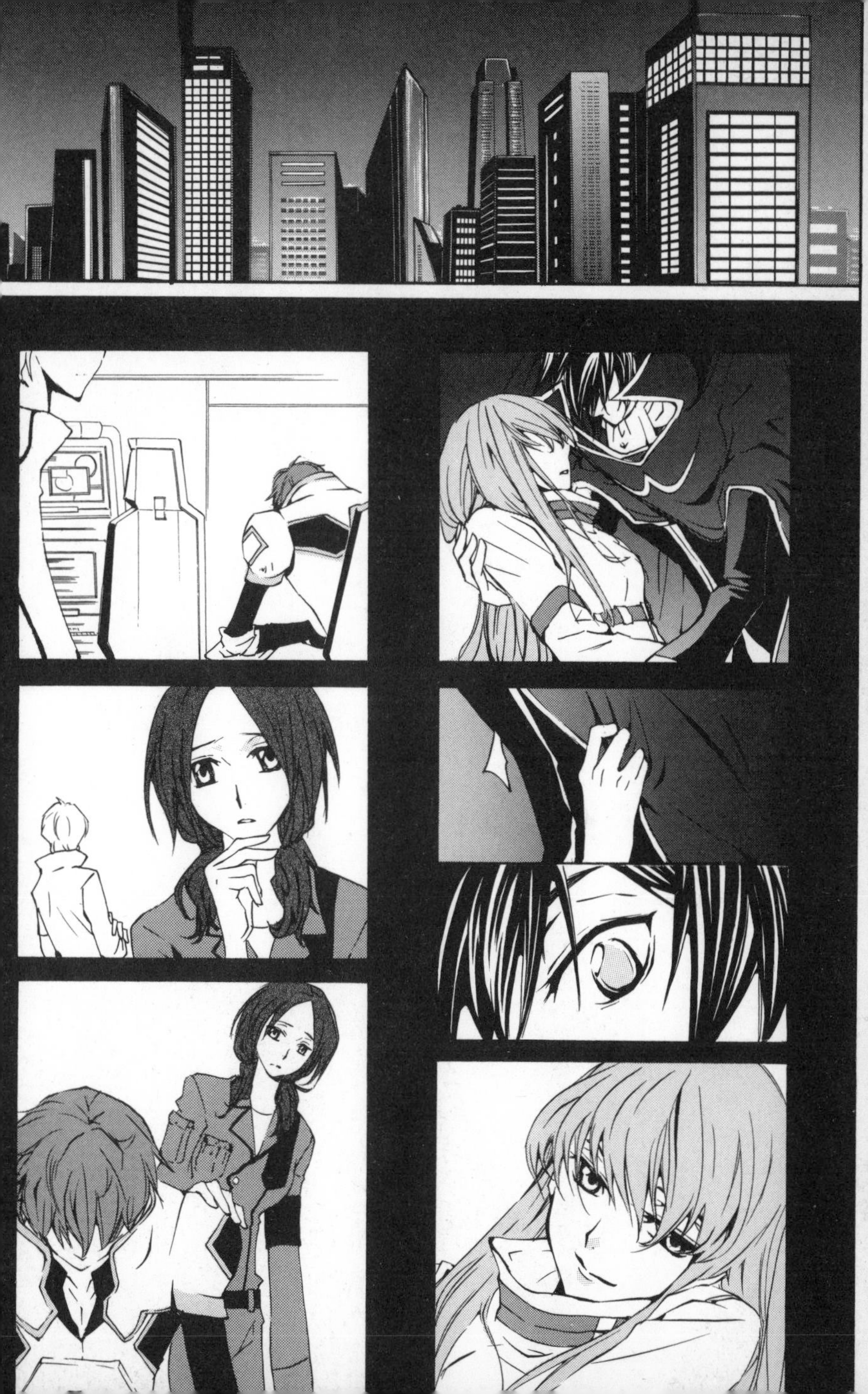

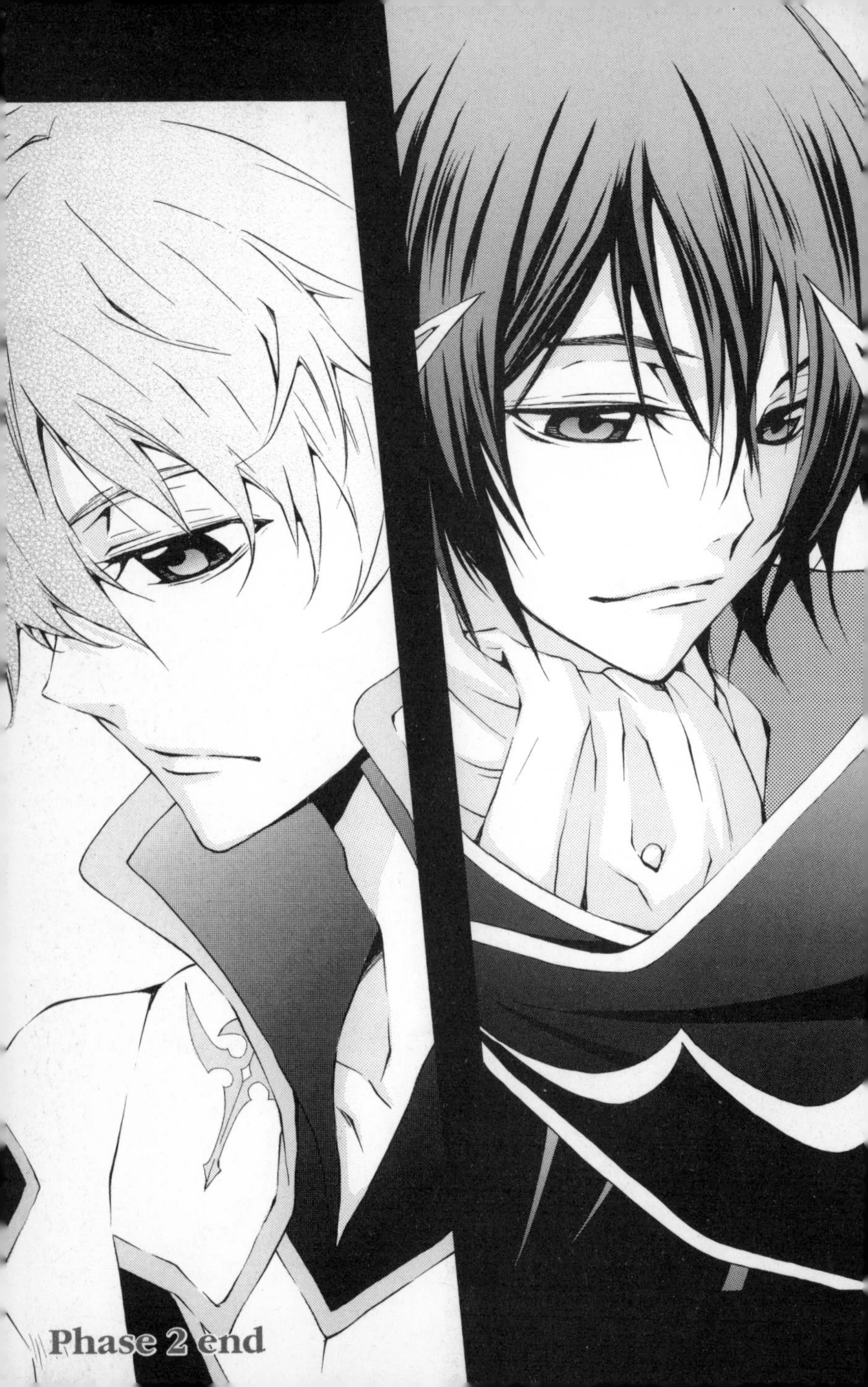
Phase 2 end

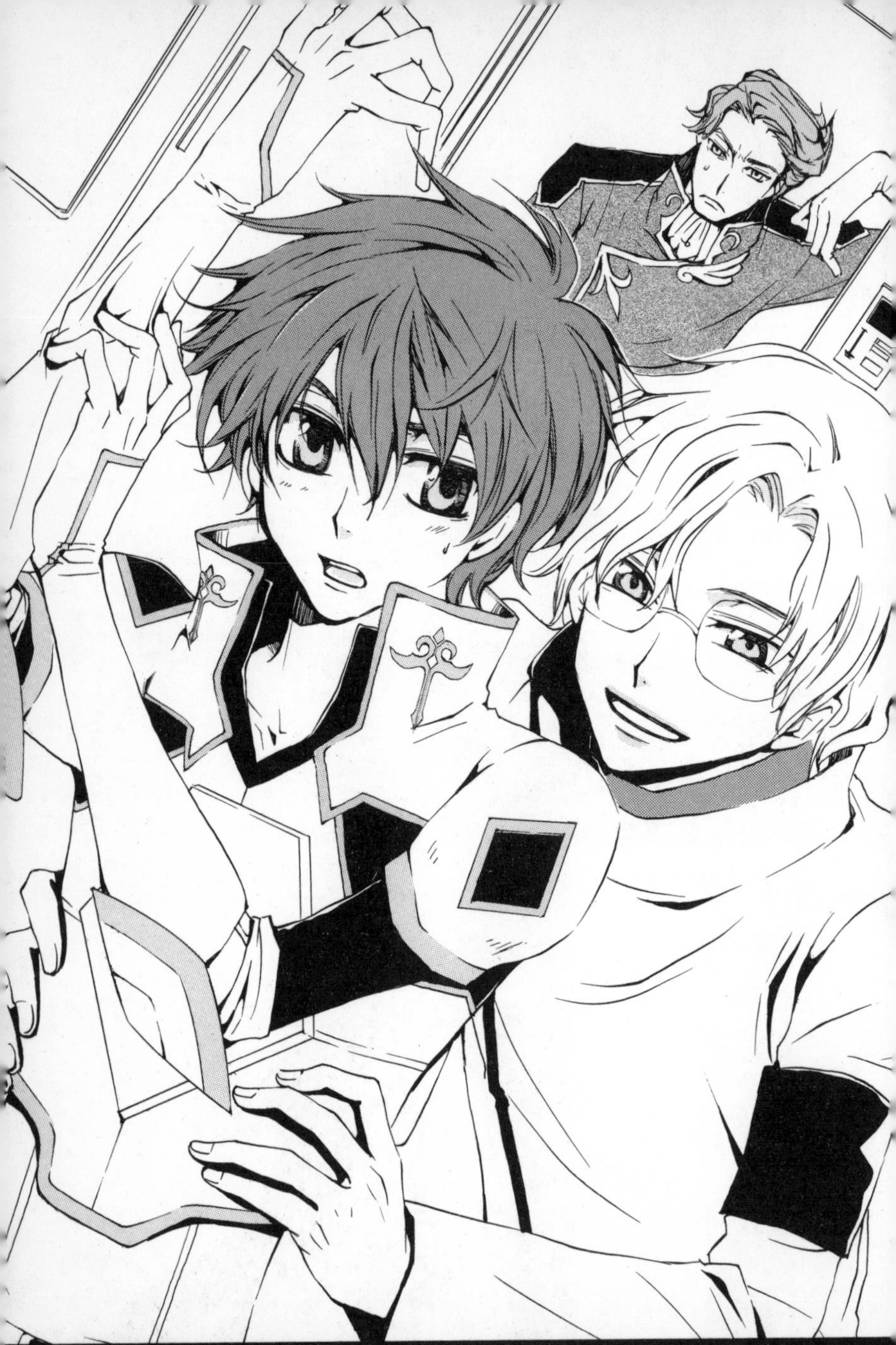

Phase 3

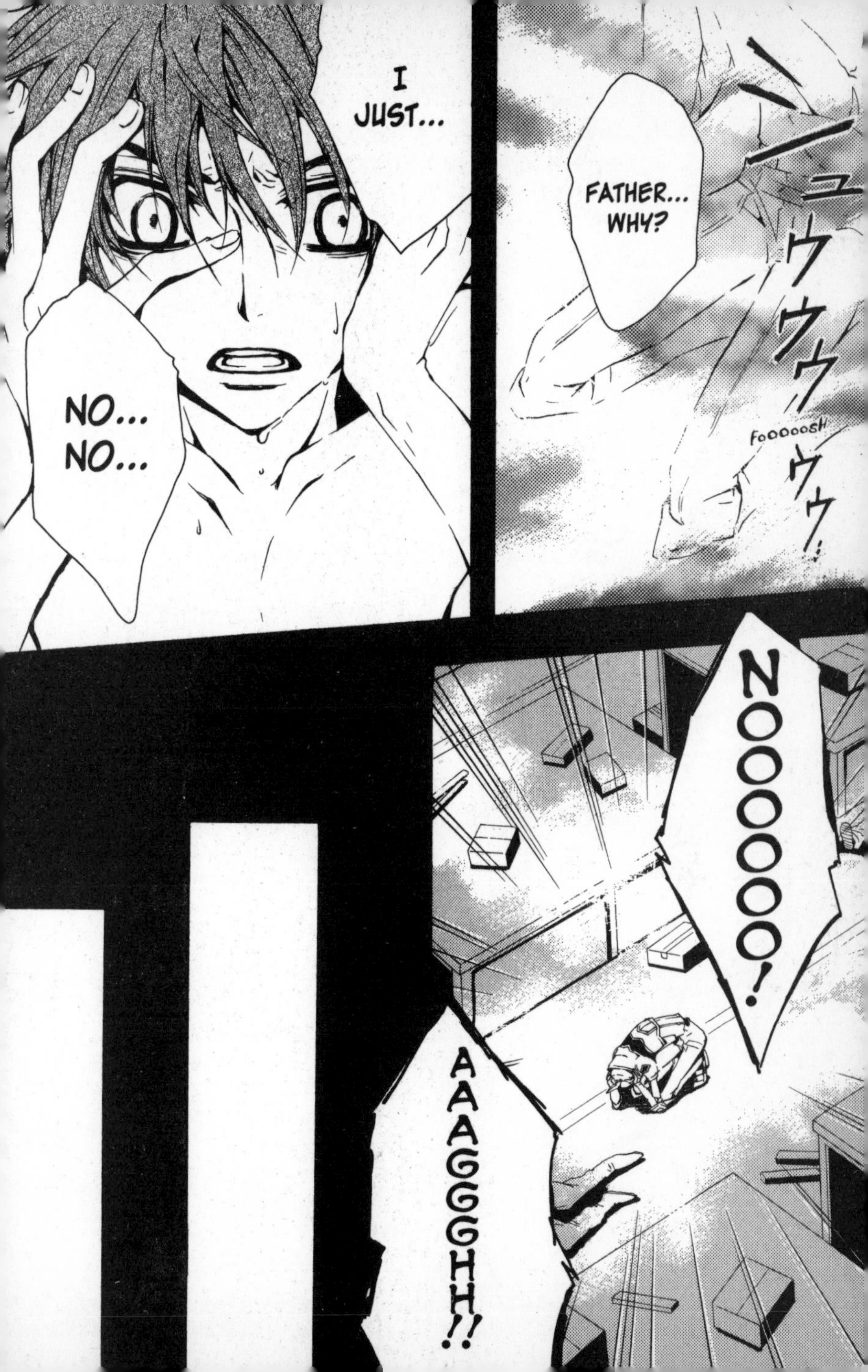
FATHER... WHY?
ユウウウウウ!
FOOOOOOSH
I JUST...
NO... NO...
NOOOOOOO!
AAAGGGHH!!

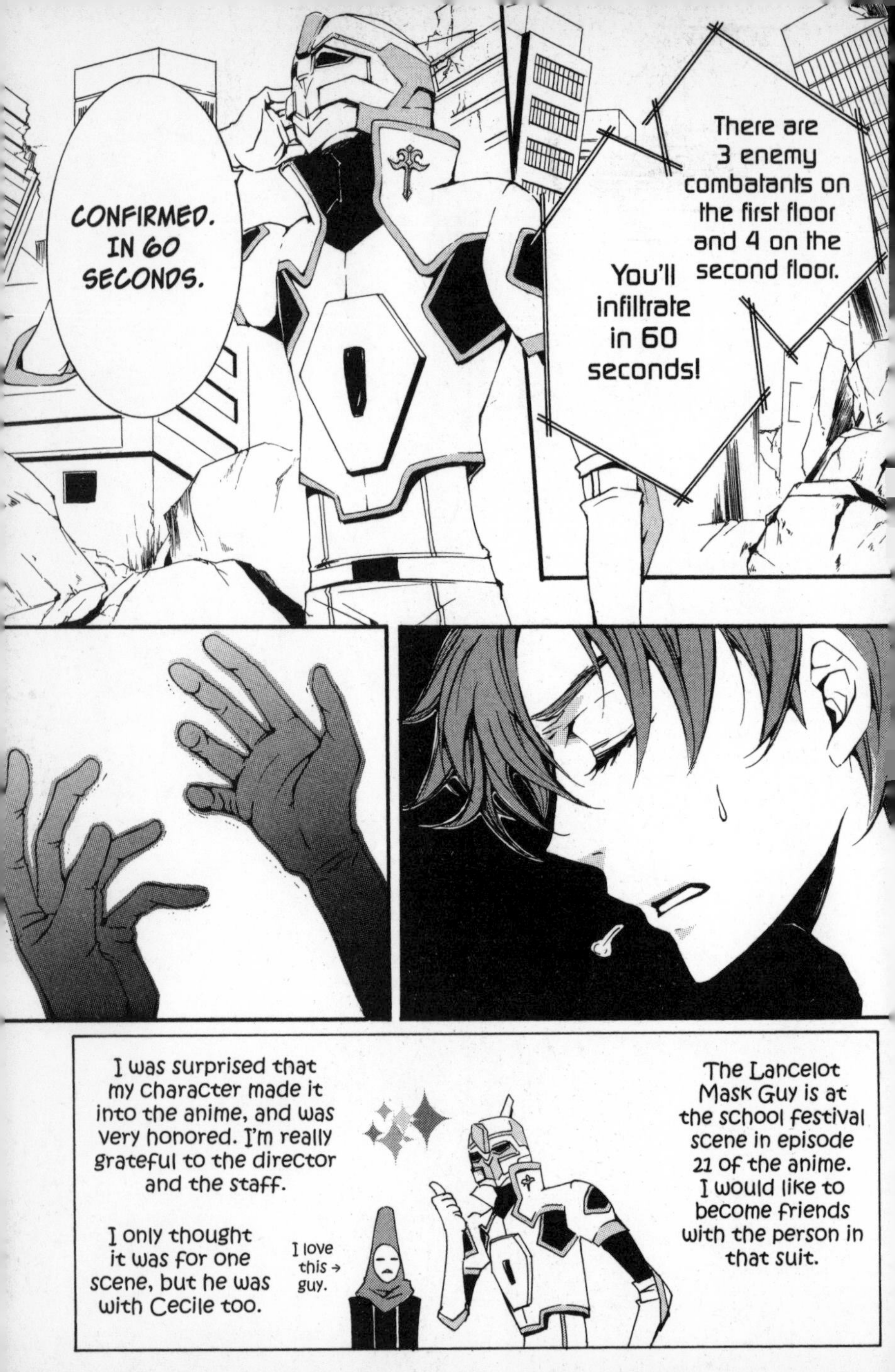
There are 3 enemy combatants on the first floor and 4 on the second floor.
You'll infiltrate in 60 seconds!
CONFIRMED. IN 60 SECONDS.
The Lancelot Mask Guy is at the school festival scene in episode 21 of the anime. I would like to become friends with the person in that suit.
I was surprised that my character made it into the anime, and was very honored. I'm really grateful to the director and the staff.
I love this → guy.
I only thought it was for one scene, but he was with Cecile too.

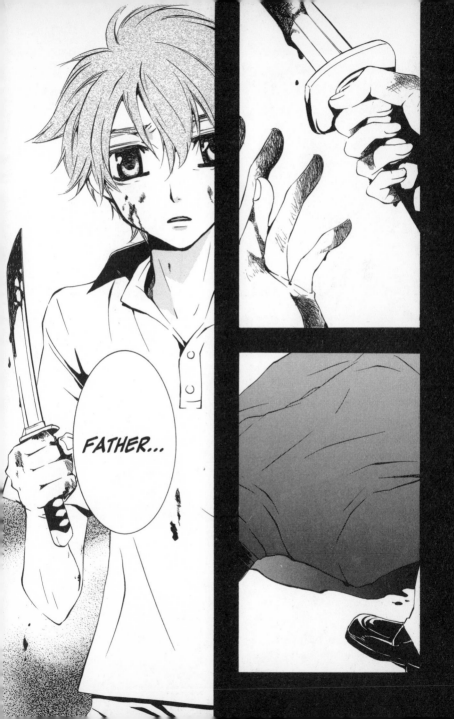

FATHER...

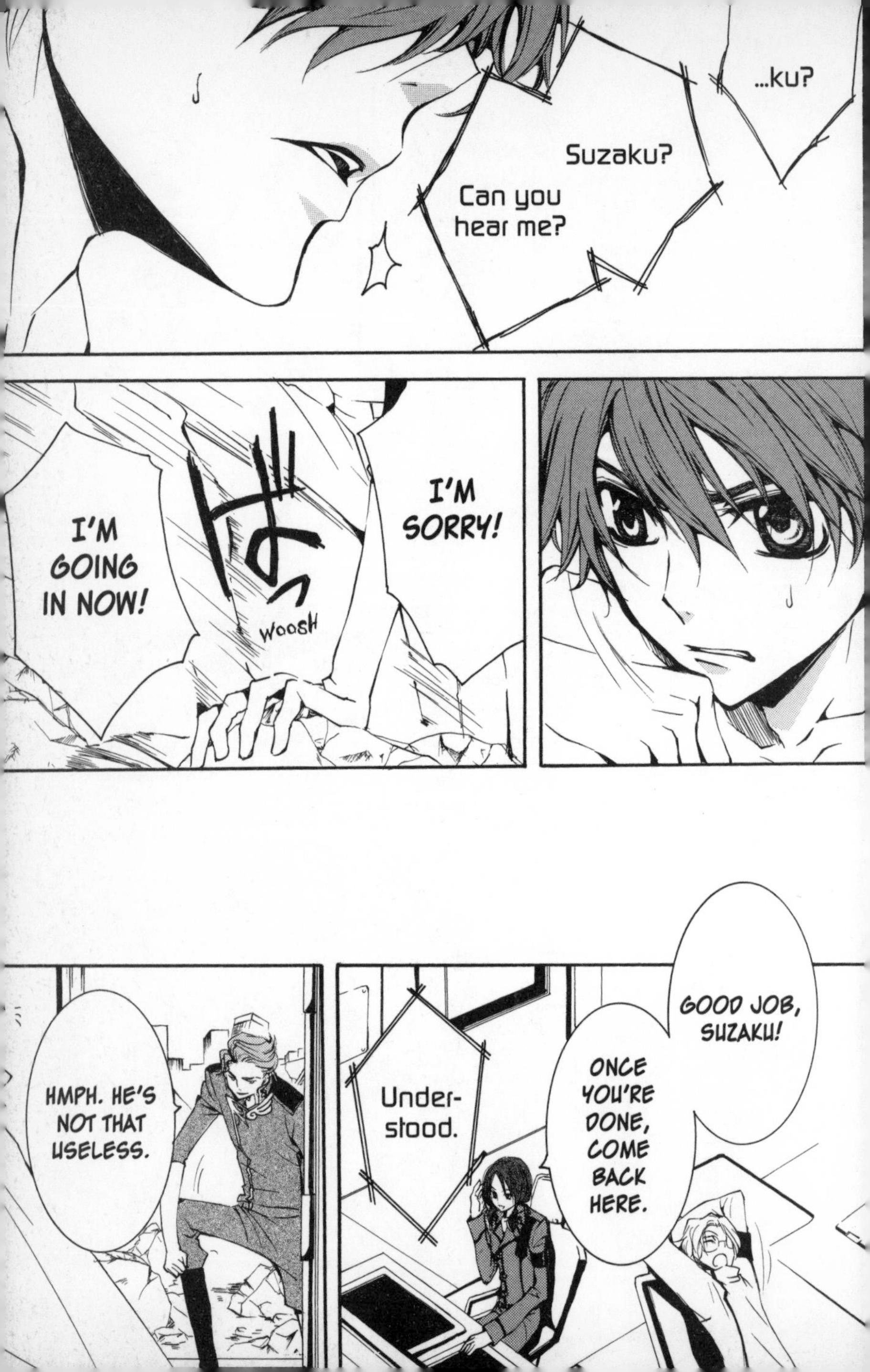
...ku?
Suzaku?
Can you hear me?
I'M SORRY!
ばっ
WOOSH
I'M GOING IN NOW!
GOOD JOB, SUZAKU!
ONCE YOU'RE DONE, COME BACK HERE.
Under-stood.
HMPH. HE'S NOT THAT USELESS.

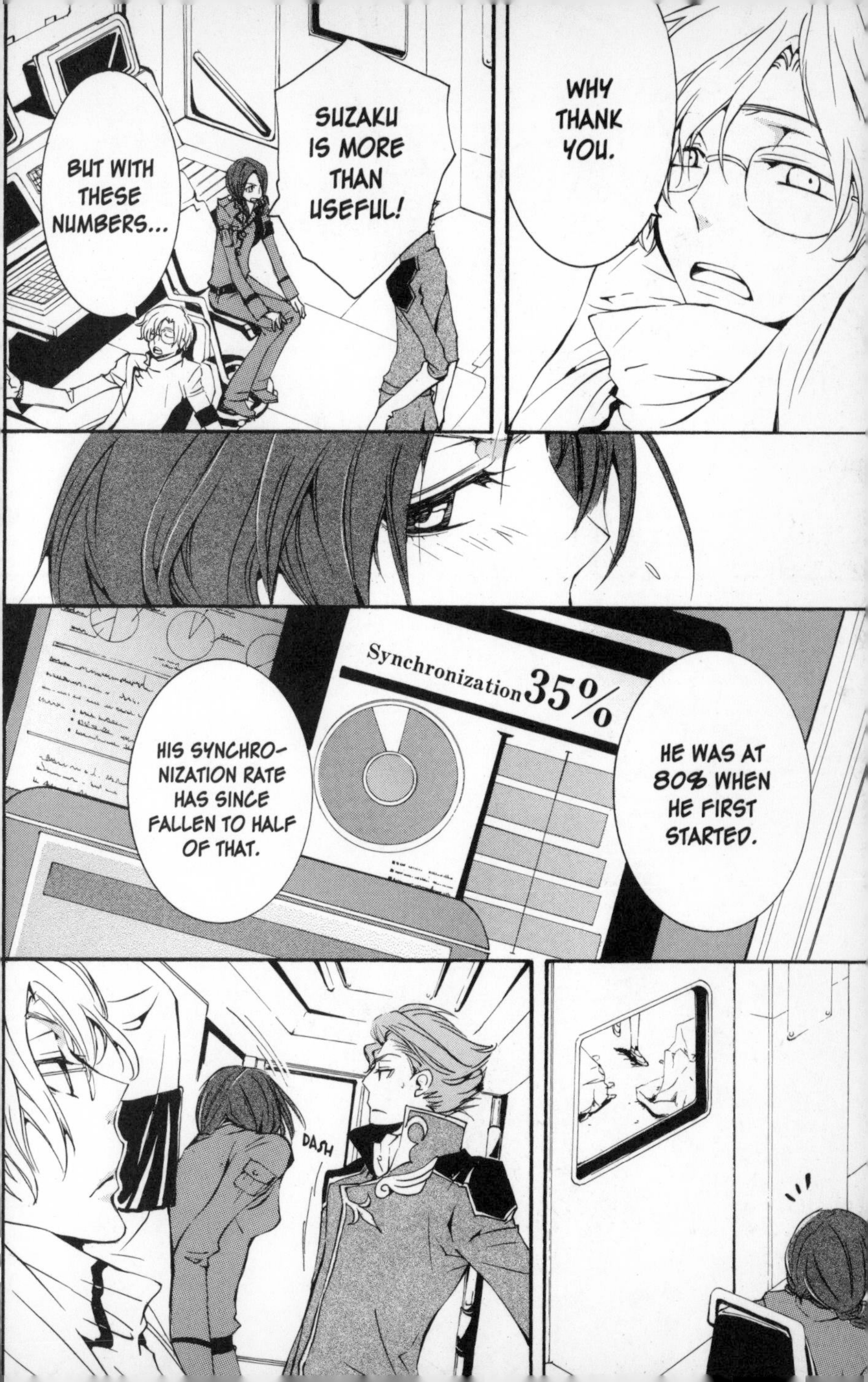
WHY THANK YOU.
SUZAKU IS MORE THAN USEFUL!
BUT WITH THESE NUMBERS...
Synchronization 35%
HE WAS AT 80% WHEN HE FIRST STARTED.
HIS SYNCHRONIZATION RATE HAS SINCE FALLEN TO HALF OF THAT.
DASH

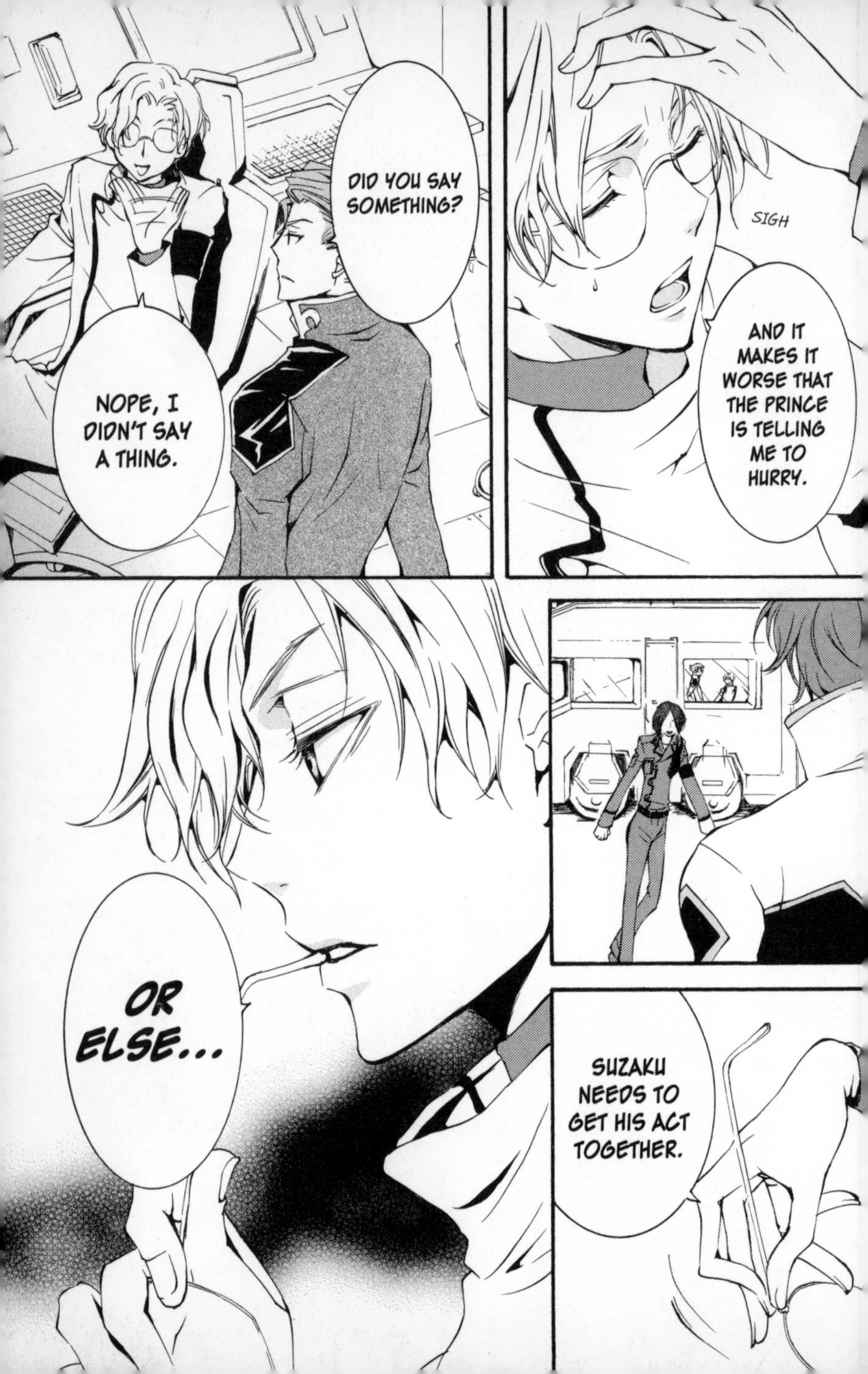
SIGH
AND IT MAKES IT WORSE THAT THE PRINCE IS TELLING ME TO HURRY.
DID YOU SAY SOMETHING?
NOPE, I DIDN'T SAY A THING.
SUZAKU NEEDS TO GET HIS ACT TOGETHER.
OR ELSE...

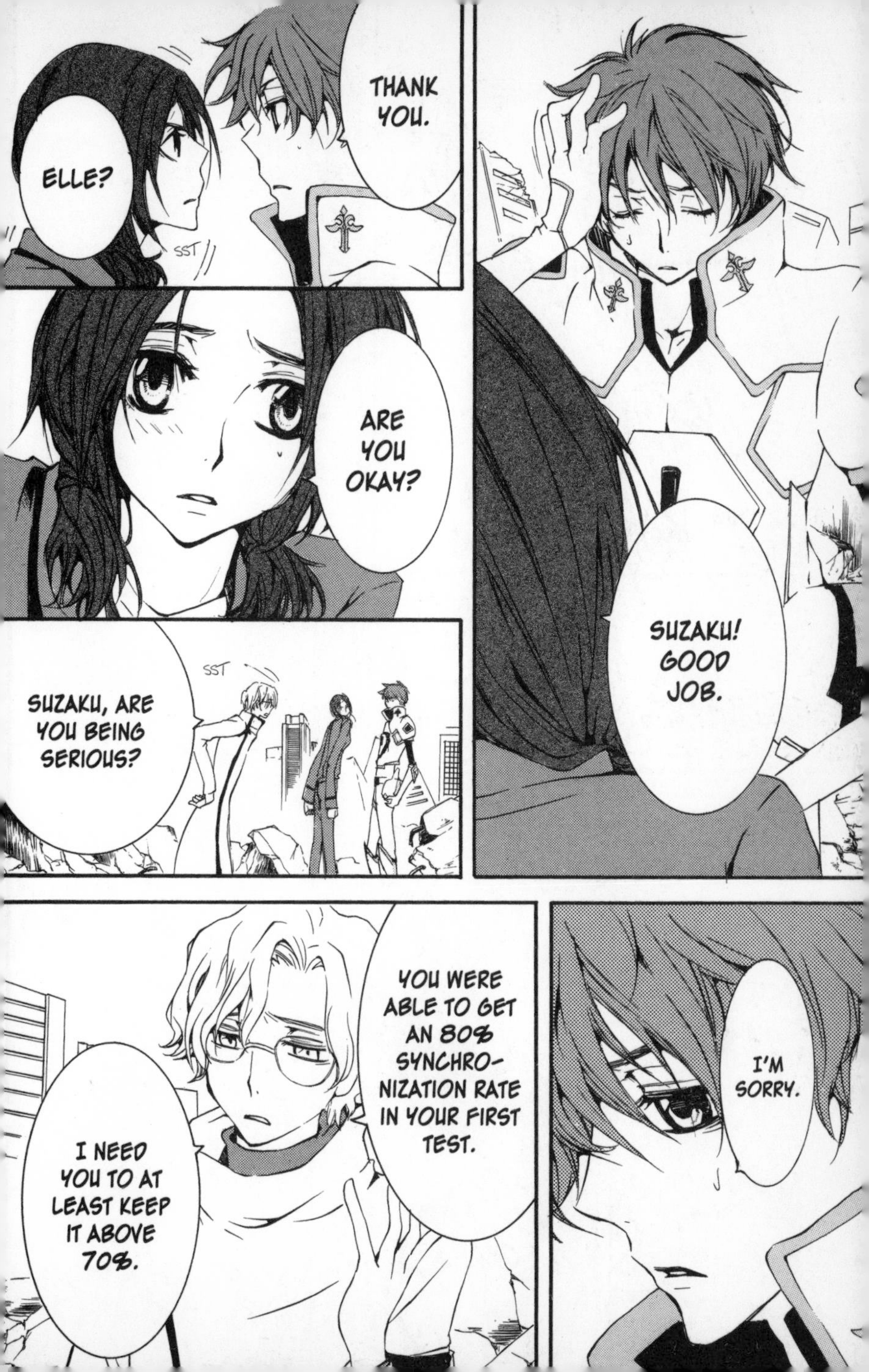
SUZAKU! GOOD JOB.
THANK YOU.
ELLE?
SST
ARE YOU OKAY?
SST
SUZAKU, ARE YOU BEING SERIOUS?
I'M SORRY.
YOU WERE ABLE TO GET AN 80% SYNCHRO-NIZATION RATE IN YOUR FIRST TEST.
I NEED YOU TO AT LEAST KEEP IT ABOVE 70%.

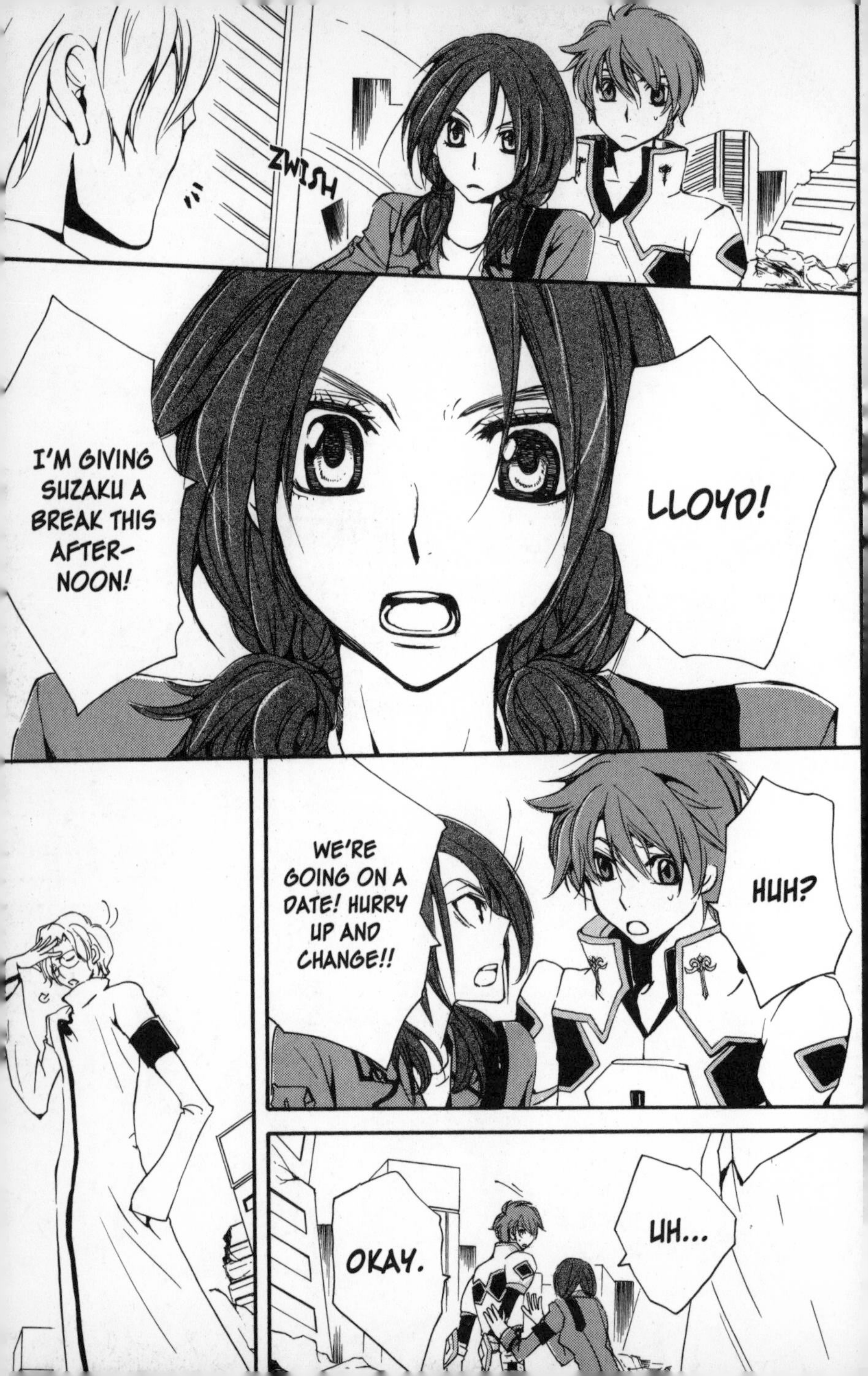
ZWISH
LLOYD!
I'M GIVING SUZAKU A BREAK THIS AFTER-NOON!
WE'RE GOING ON A DATE! HURRY UP AND CHANGE!!
HUH?
UH...
OKAY.

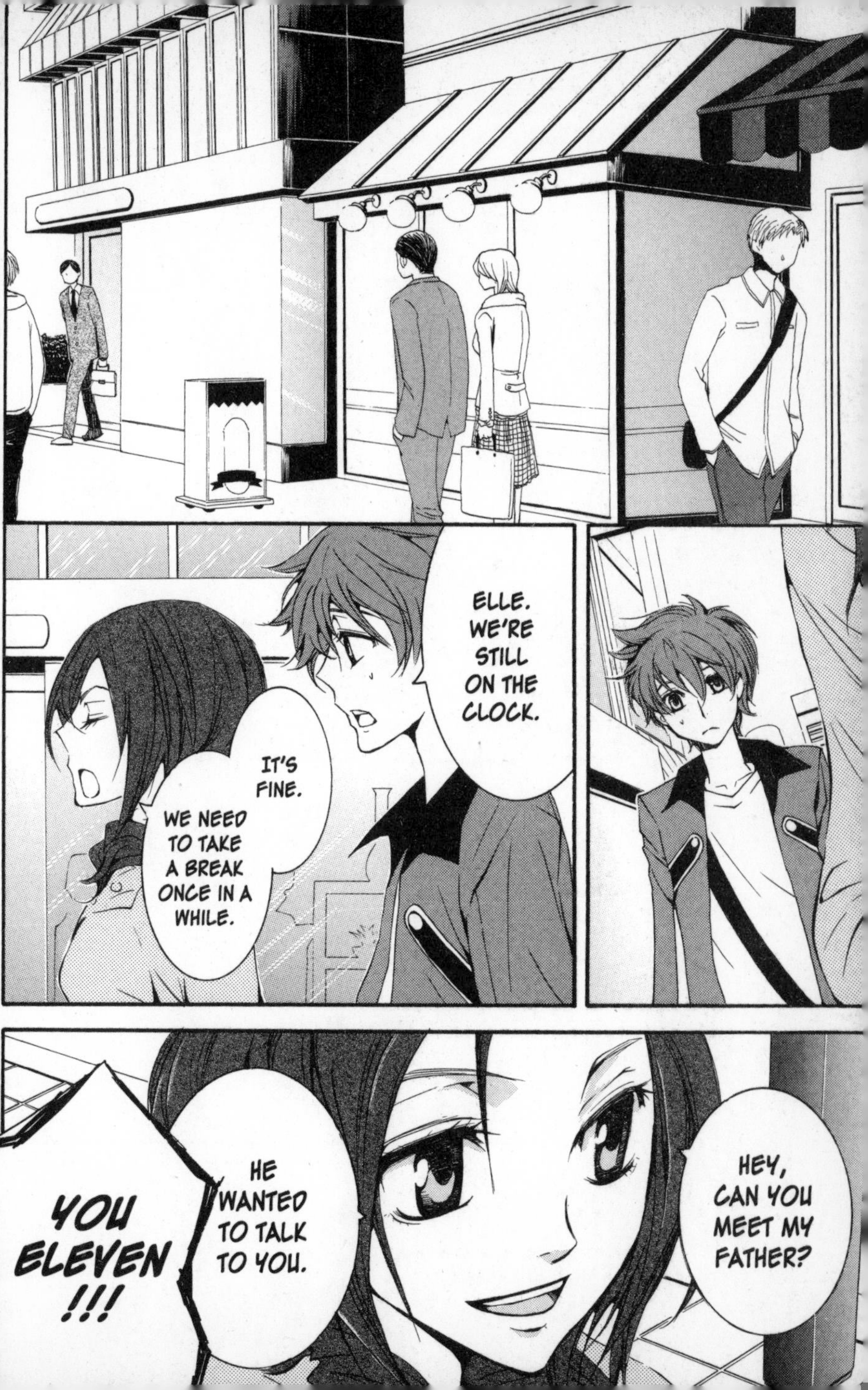
ELLE. WE'RE STILL ON THE CLOCK.
IT'S FINE.
WE NEED TO TAKE A BREAK ONCE IN A WHILE.
HEY, CAN YOU MEET MY FATHER?
HE WANTED TO TALK TO YOU.
YOU ELEVEN!!!

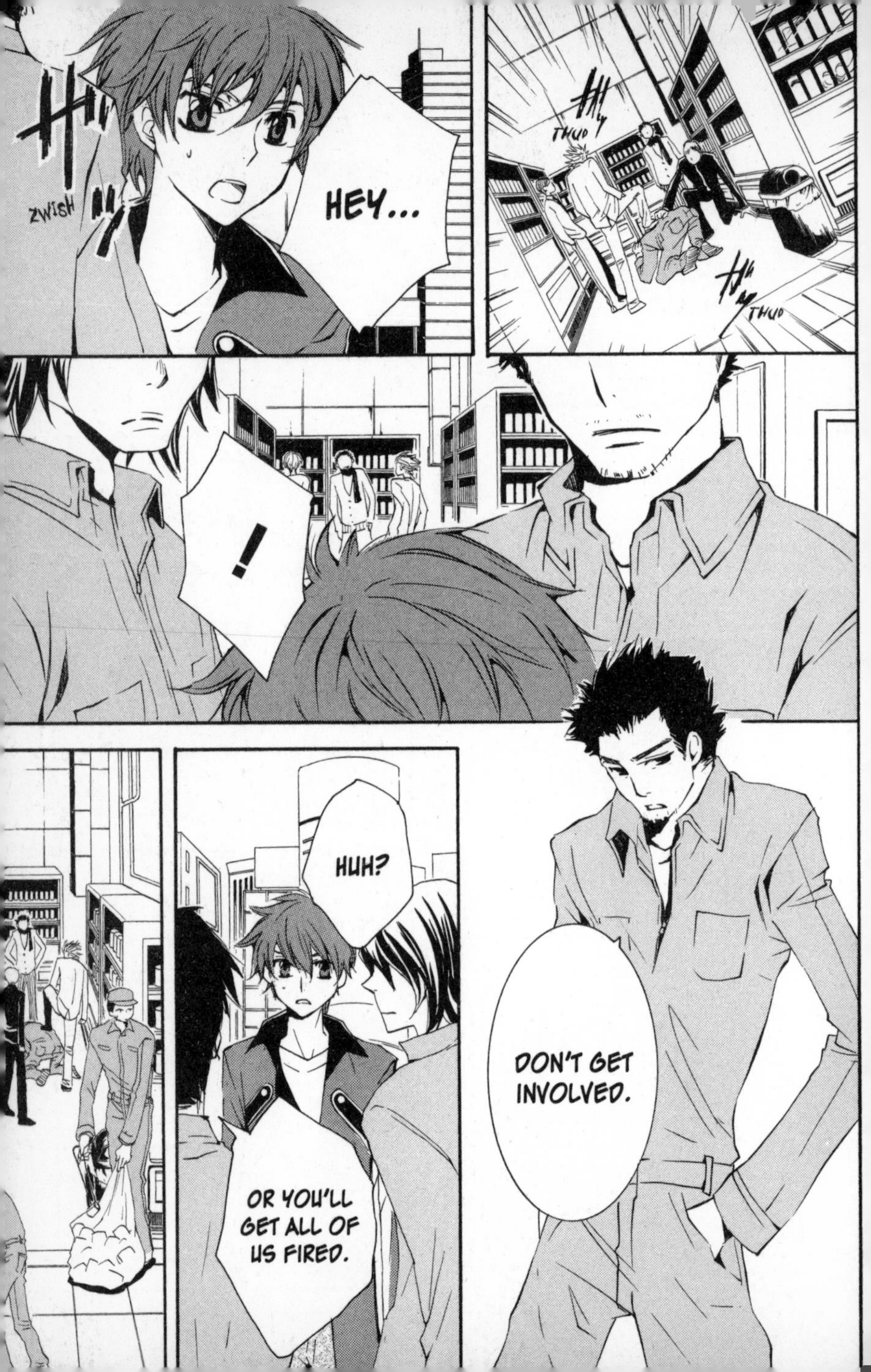
THUD
THUD
HEY...
ZWISH
!
DON'T GET INVOLVED.
HUH?
OR YOU'LL GET ALL OF US FIRED.

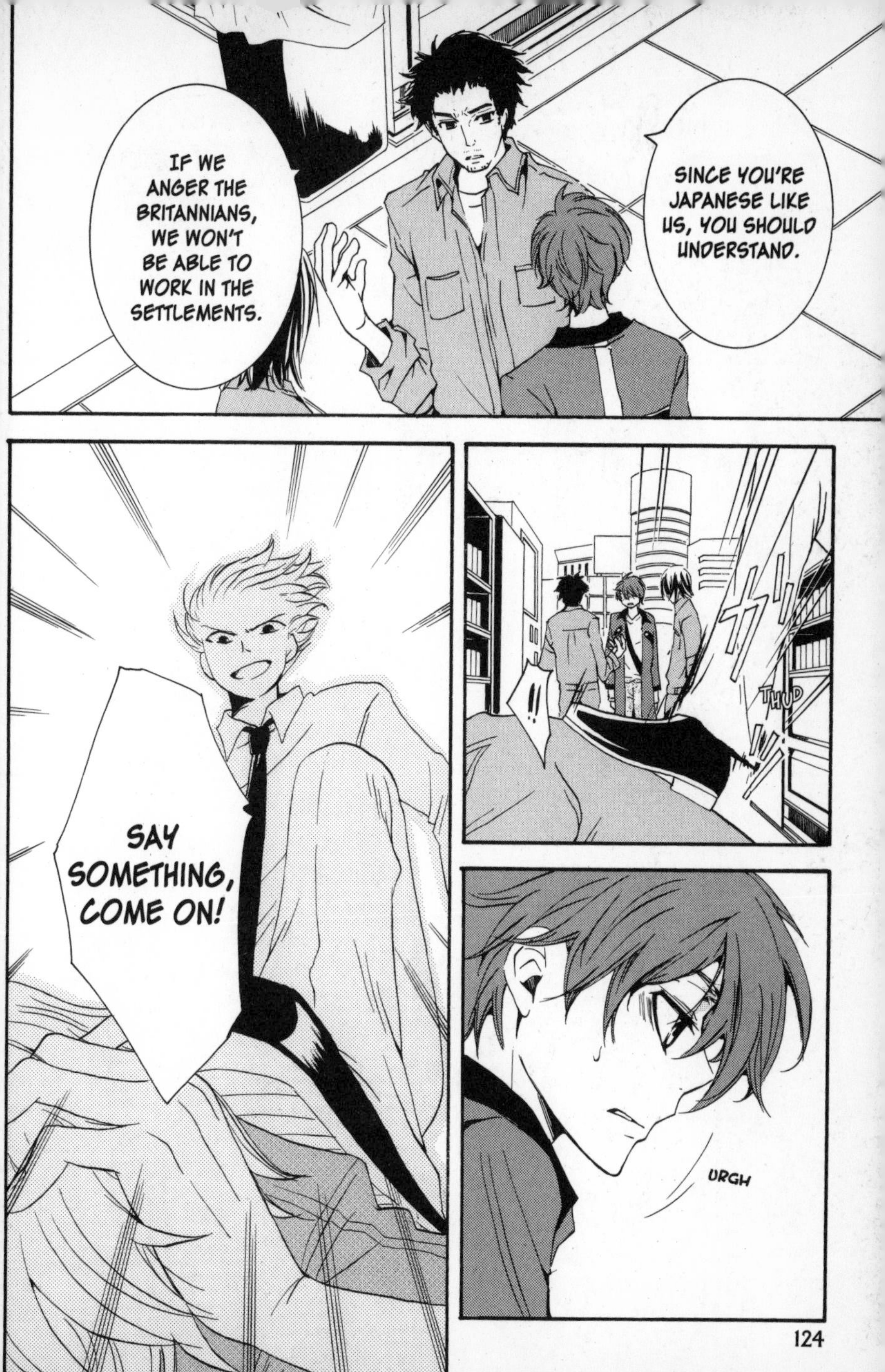
SINCE YOU'RE JAPANESE LIKE US, YOU SHOULD UNDERSTAND.
IF WE ANGER THE BRITANNIANS, WE WON'T BE ABLE TO WORK IN THE SETTLEMENTS.
!!
THUD
URGH
SAY SOMETHING, COME ON!

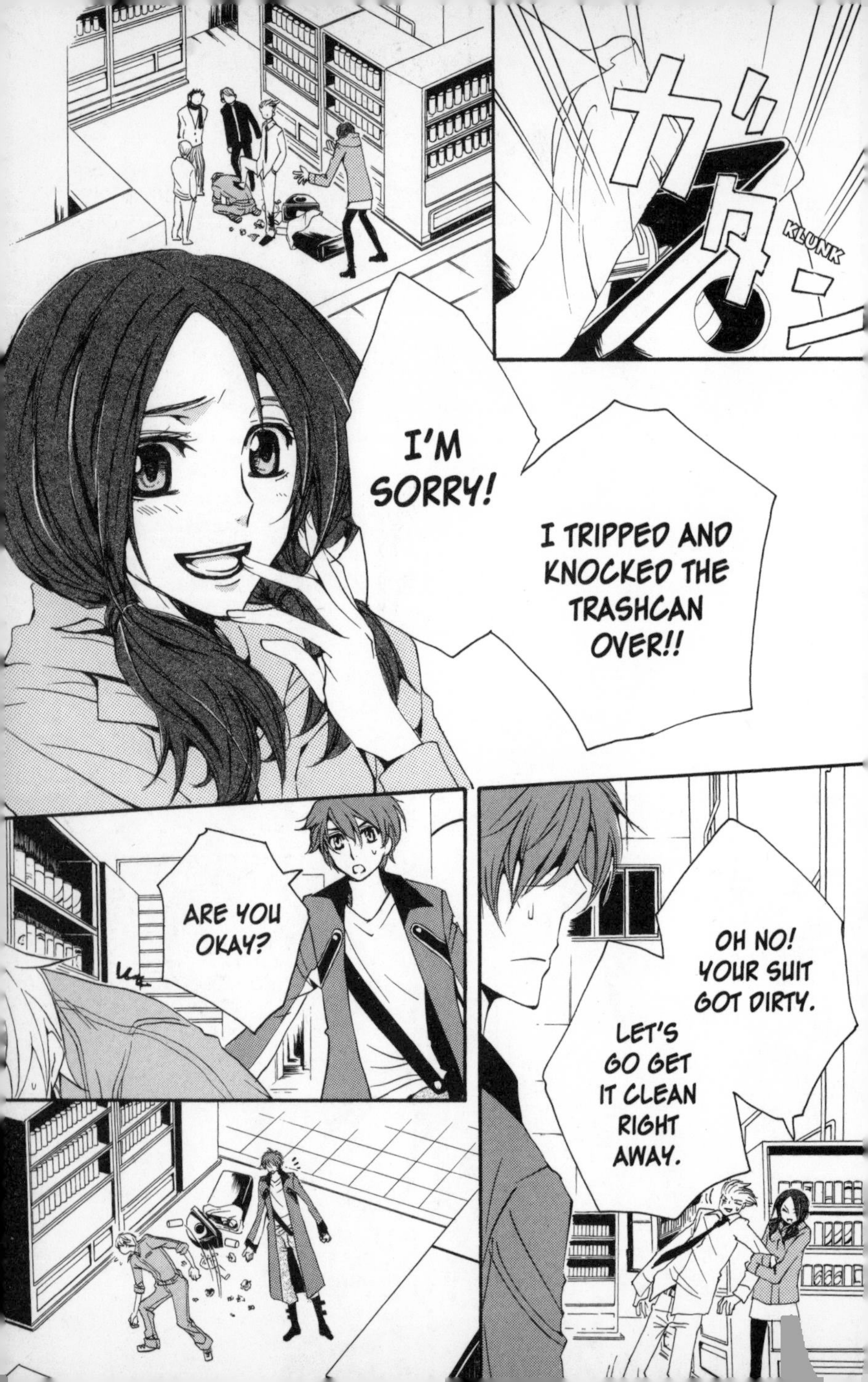
KLUNK
I'M SORRY!
I TRIPPED AND KNOCKED THE TRASHCAN OVER!!
OH NO! YOUR SUIT GOT DIRTY.
LET'S GO GET IT CLEAN RIGHT AWAY.
ARE YOU OKAY?

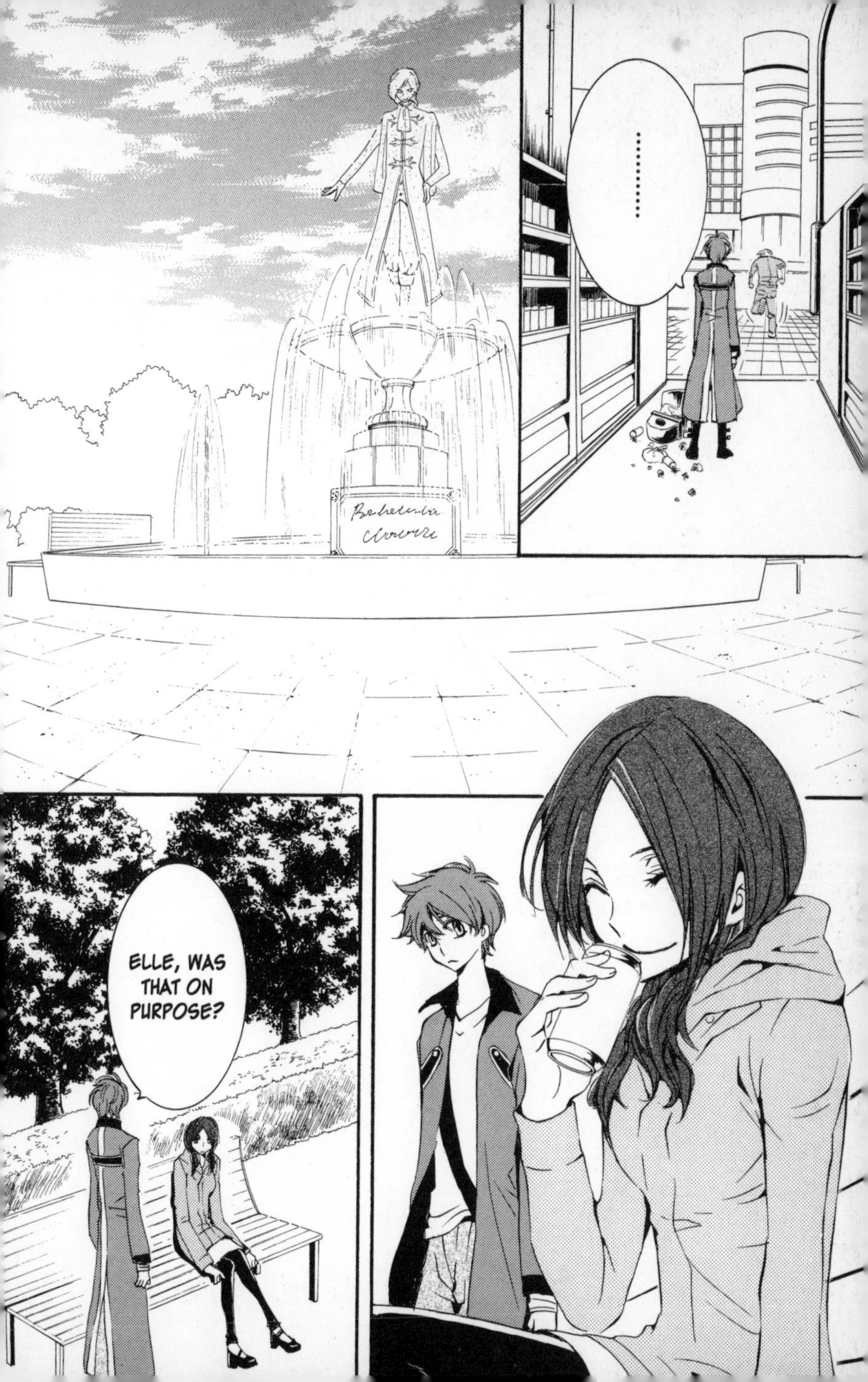
……
ELLE, WAS THAT ON PURPOSE?

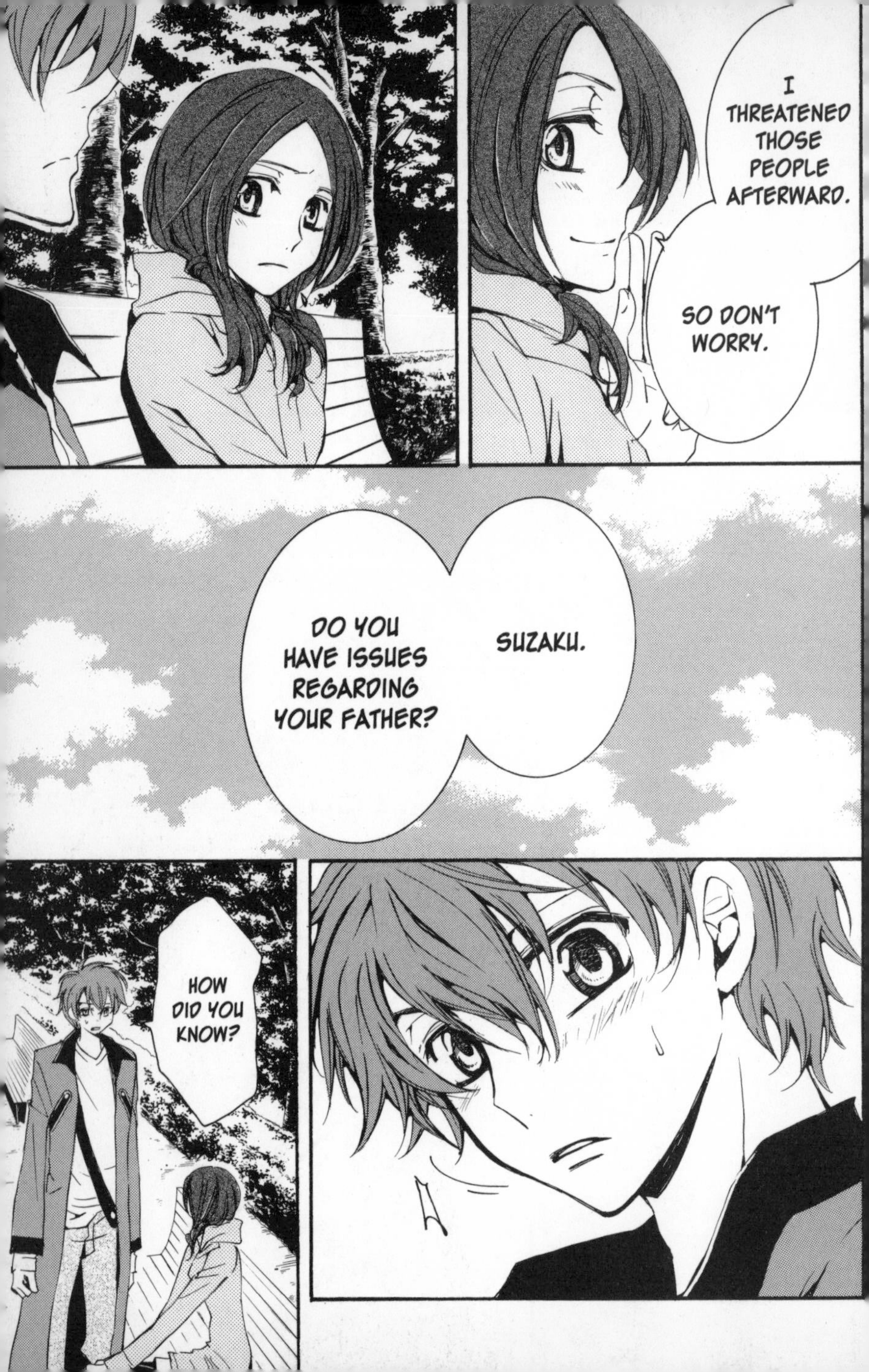
I THREATENED THOSE PEOPLE AFTERWARD.
SO DON'T WORRY.
SUZAKU.
DO YOU HAVE ISSUES REGARDING YOUR FATHER?
HOW DID YOU KNOW?

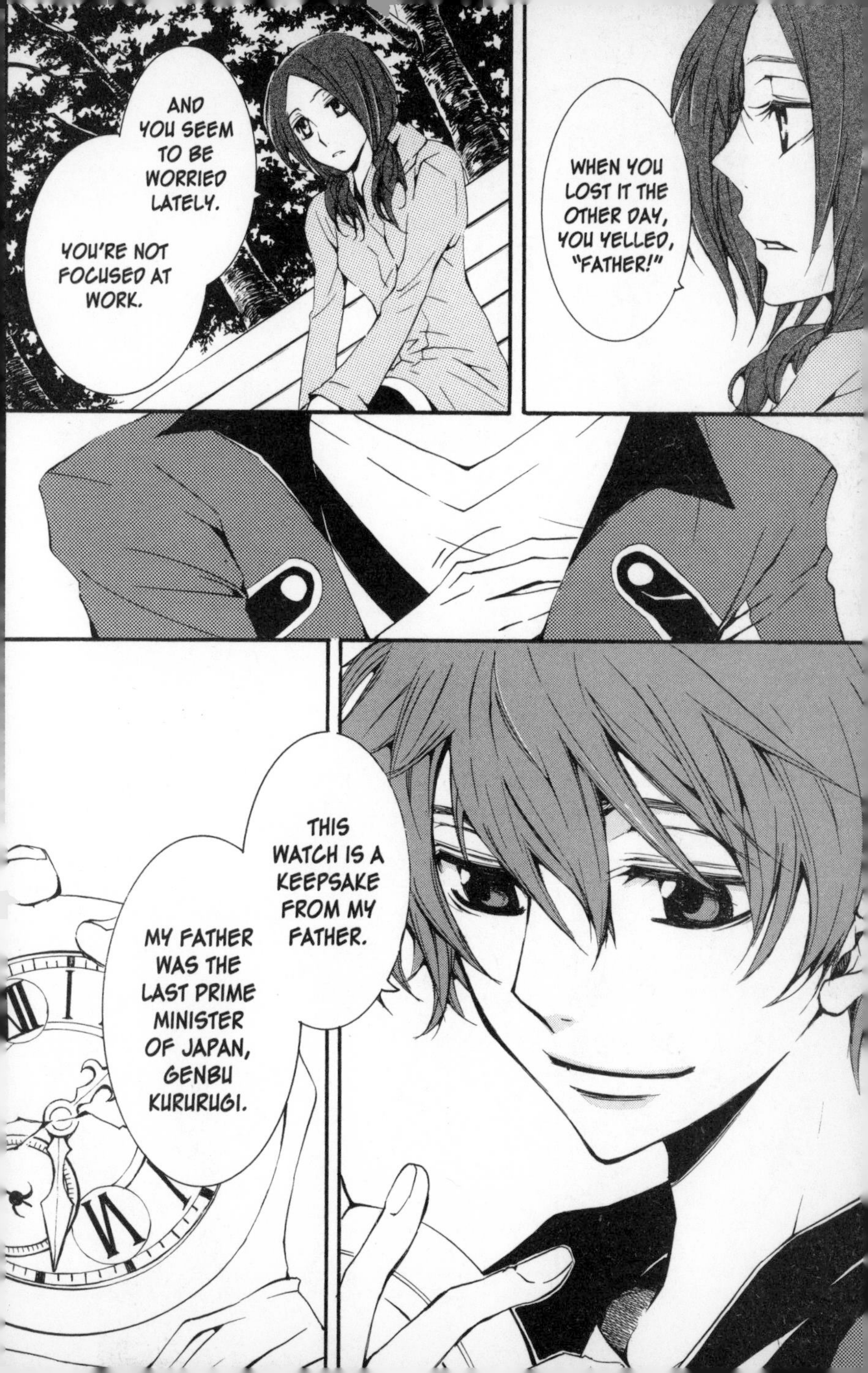
WHEN YOU LOST IT THE OTHER DAY, YOU YELLED, "FATHER!"
AND YOU SEEM TO BE WORRIED LATELY.
YOU'RE NOT FOCUSED AT WORK.
THIS WATCH IS A KEEPSAKE FROM MY FATHER.
MY FATHER WAS THE LAST PRIME MINISTER OF JAPAN, GENBU KURURUGI.

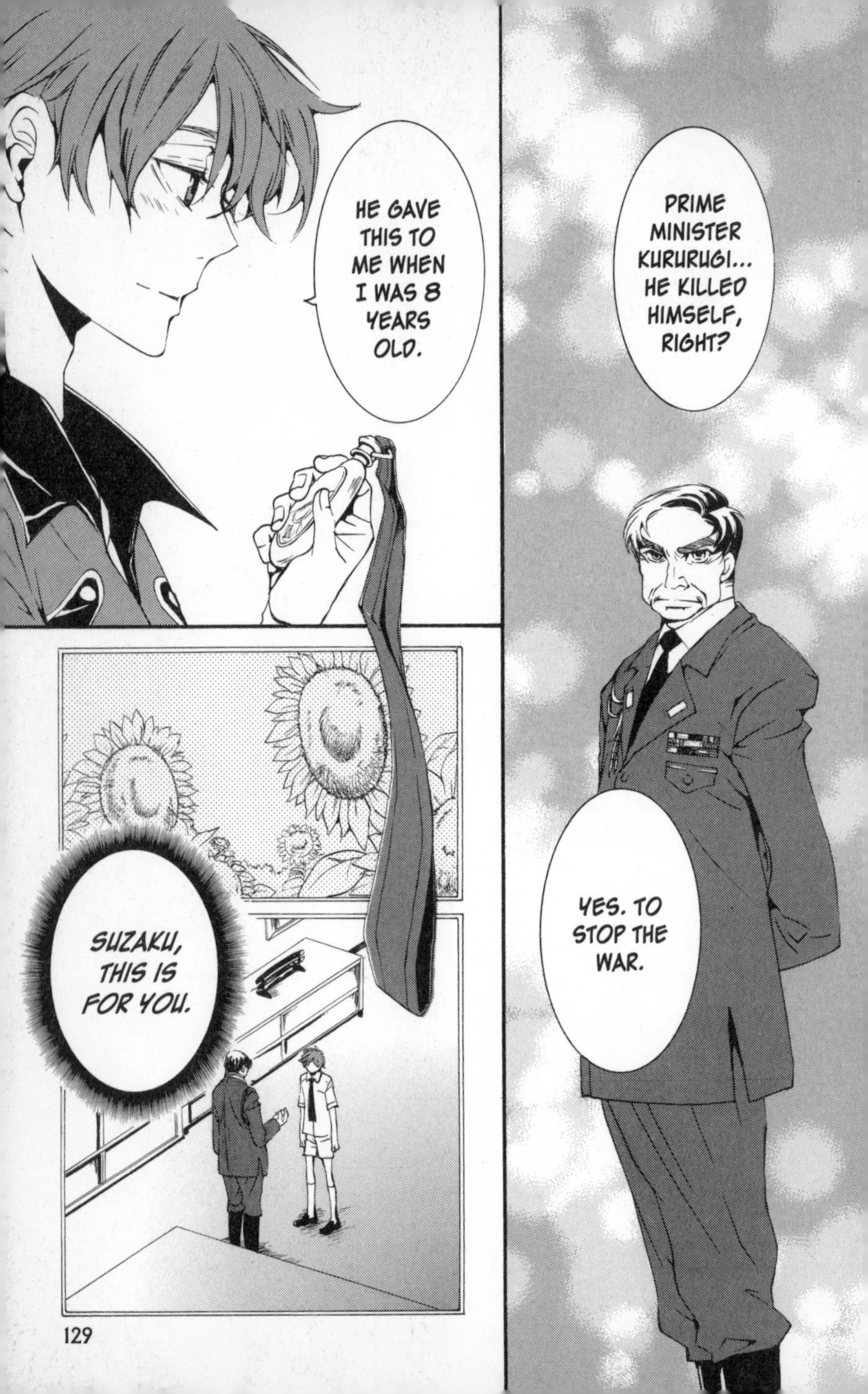
PRIME MINISTER KURURUGI... HE KILLED HIMSELF, RIGHT?
YES. TO STOP THE WAR.
HE GAVE THIS TO ME WHEN I WAS 8 YEARS OLD.
SUZAKU, THIS IS FOR YOU.

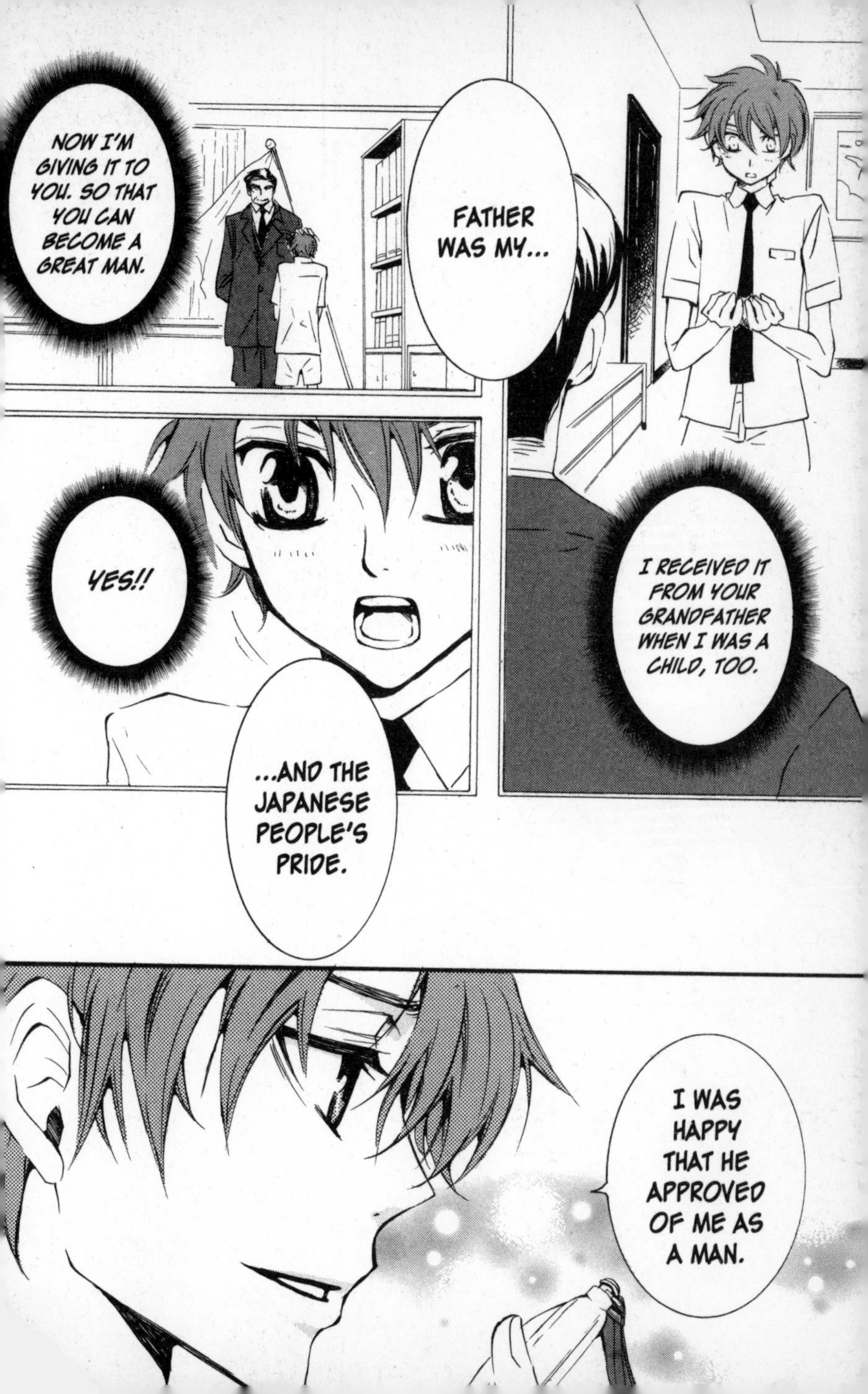
FATHER WAS MY...
I RECEIVED IT FROM YOUR GRANDFATHER WHEN I WAS A CHILD, TOO.
NOW I'M GIVING IT TO YOU. SO THAT YOU CAN BECOME A GREAT MAN.
YES!!
...AND THE JAPANESE PEOPLE'S PRIDE.
I WAS HAPPY THAT HE APPROVED OF ME AS A MAN.

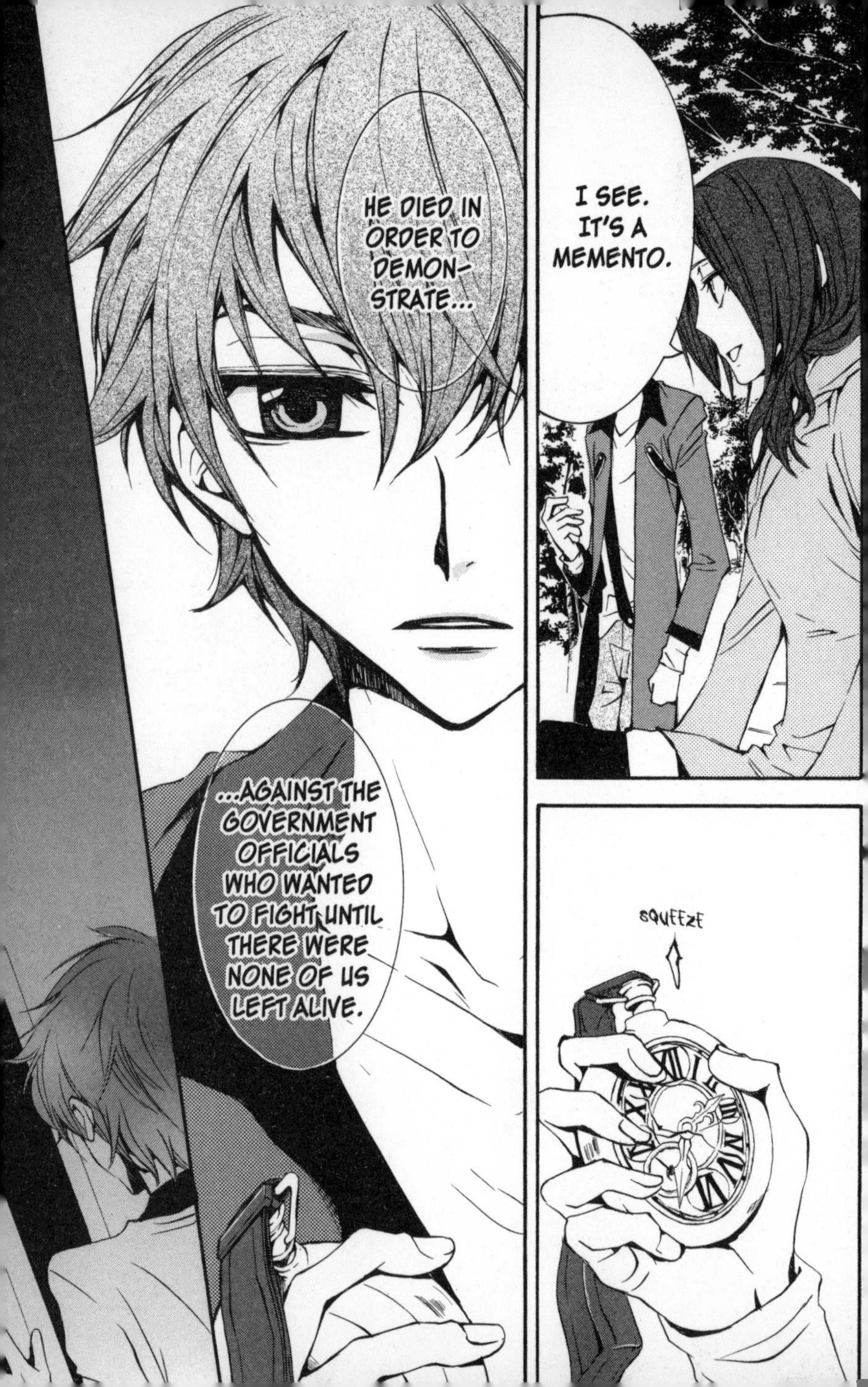
I SEE. IT'S A MEMENTO.
SQUEEZE
HE DIED IN ORDER TO DEMON-STRATE...
...AGAINST THE GOVERNMENT OFFICIALS WHO WANTED TO FIGHT UNTIL THERE WERE NONE OF US LEFT ALIVE.

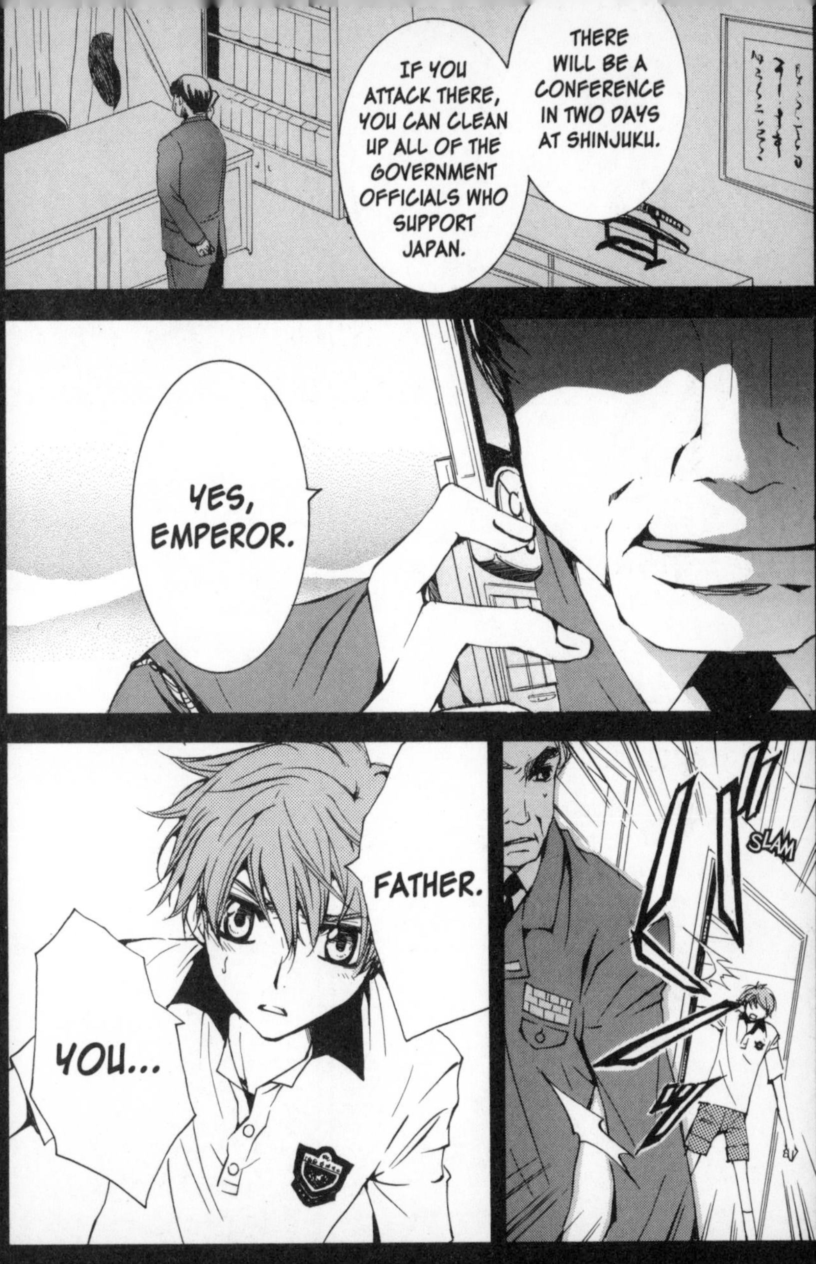
THERE WILL BE A CONFERENCE IN TWO DAYS AT SHINJUKU.
IF YOU ATTACK THERE, YOU CAN CLEAN UP ALL OF THE GOVERNMENT OFFICIALS WHO SUPPORT JAPAN.
YES, EMPEROR.
SLAM
FATHER.
YOU...

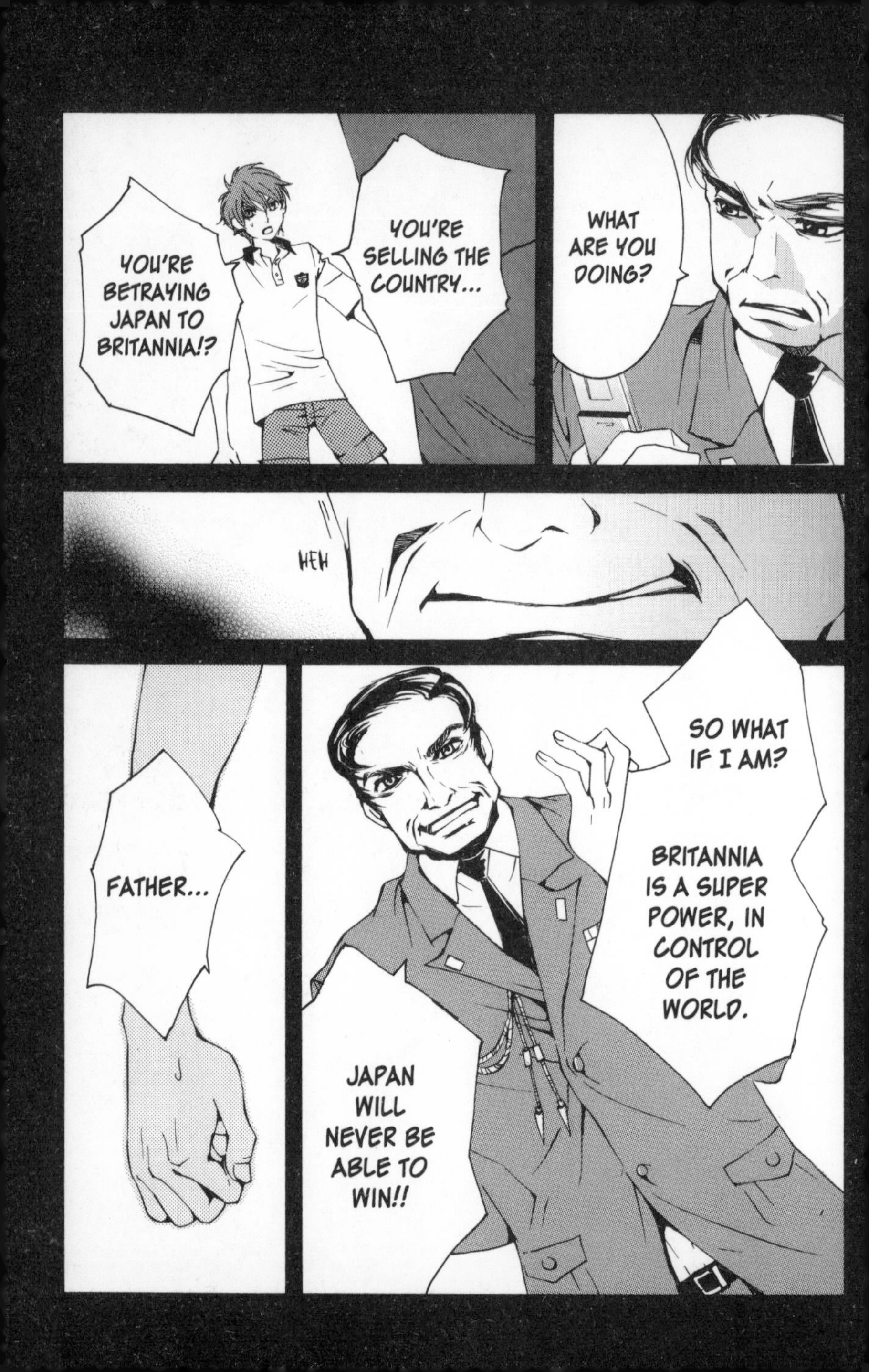
WHAT ARE YOU DOING?
YOU'RE SELLING THE COUNTRY...
YOU'RE BETRAYING JAPAN TO BRITANNIA!?
HEH
SO WHAT IF I AM?
BRITANNIA IS A SUPER POWER, IN CONTROL OF THE WORLD.
JAPAN WILL NEVER BE ABLE TO WIN!!
FATHER...

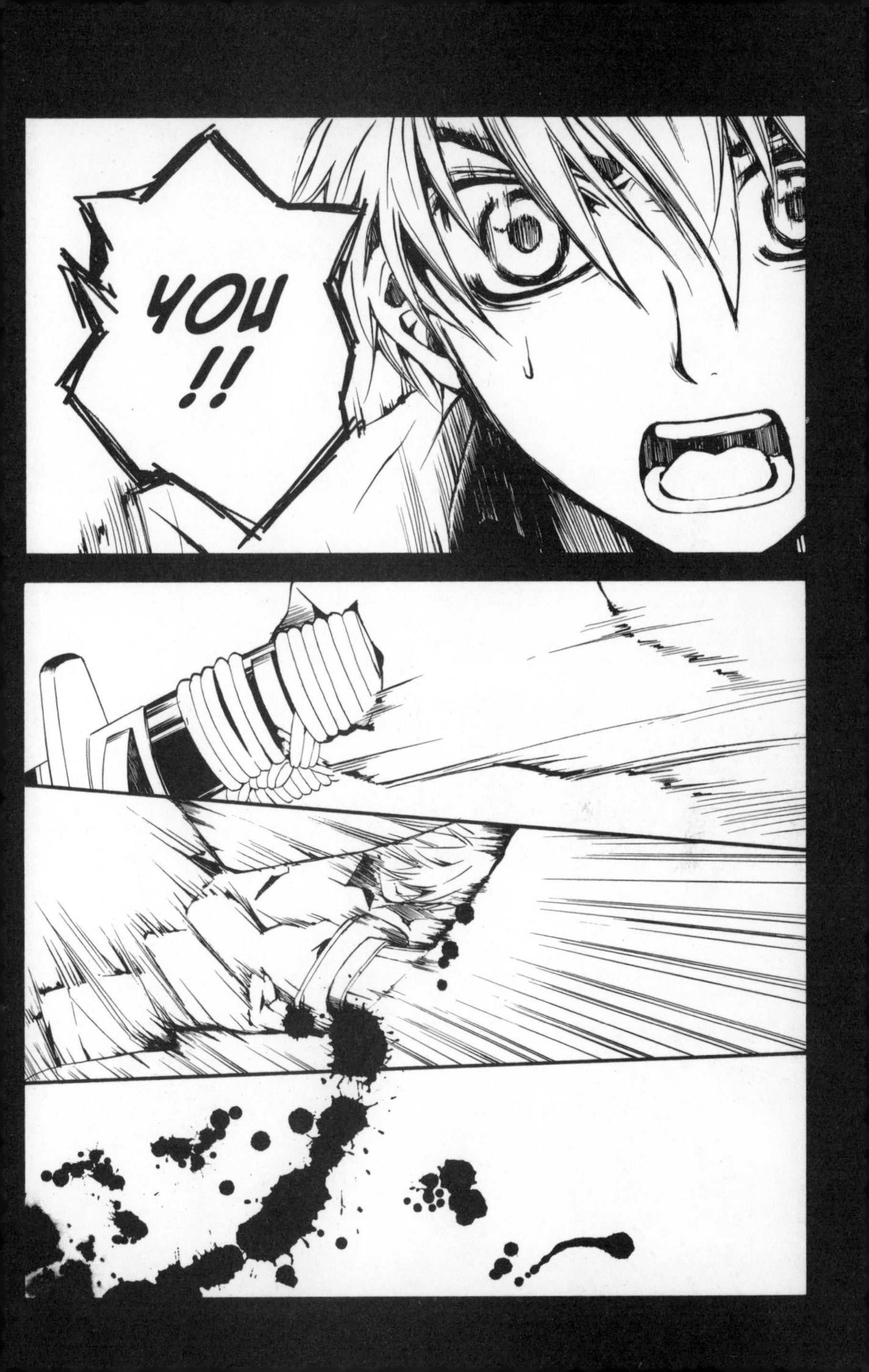
YOU !!

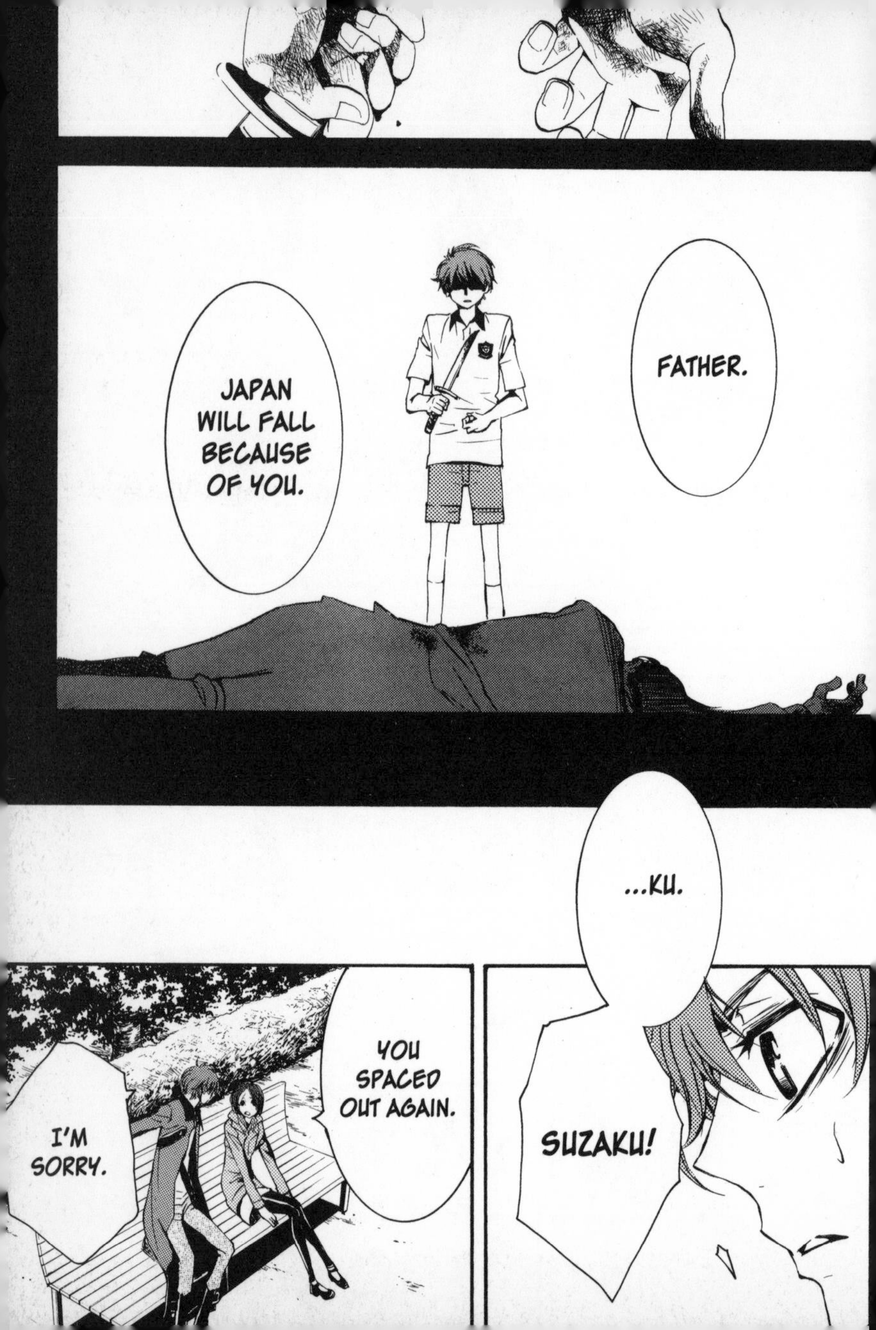
FATHER.
JAPAN WILL FALL BECAUSE OF YOU.
...KU.
SUZAKU!
YOU SPACED OUT AGAIN.
I'M SORRY.

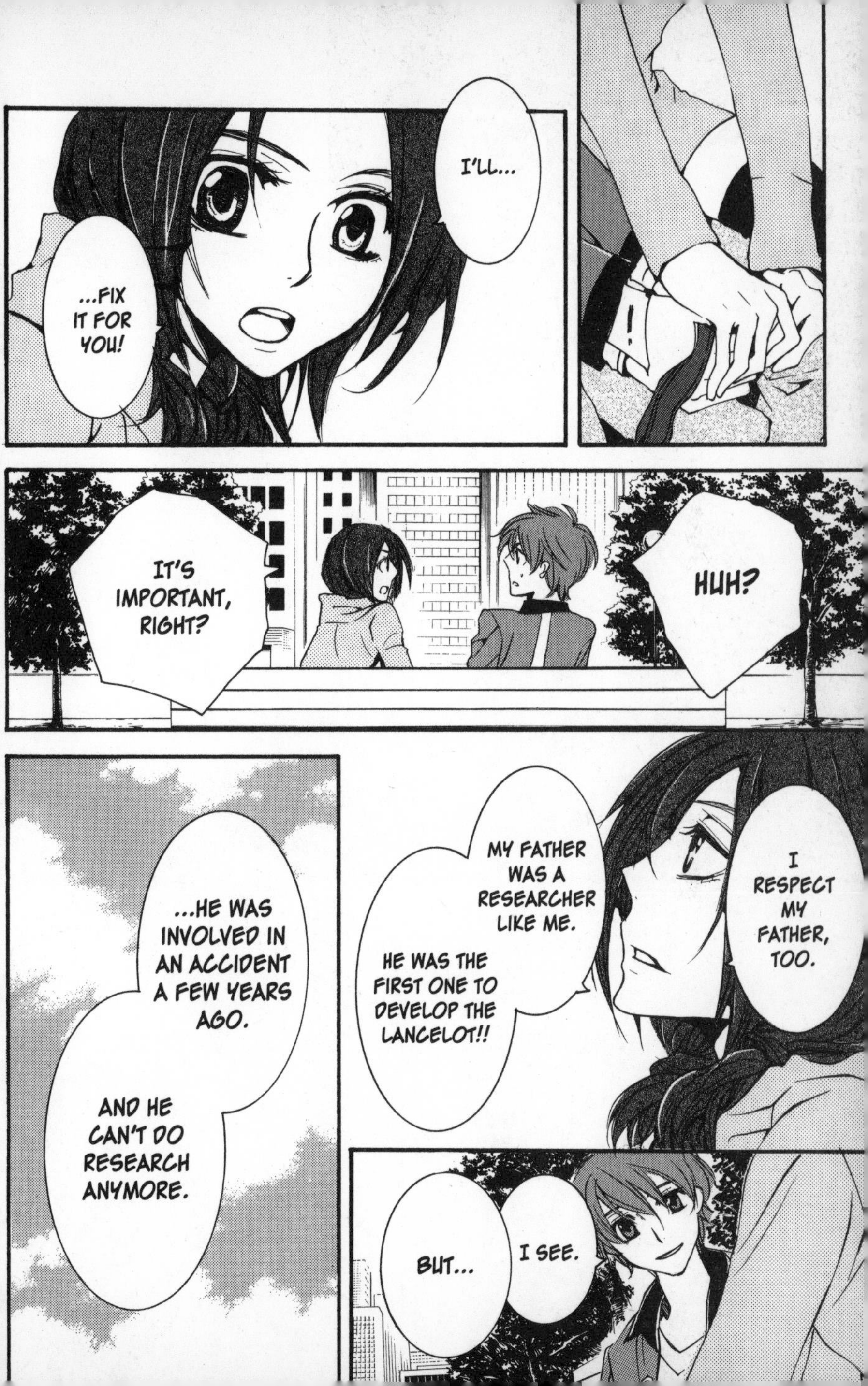
I'LL...
...FIX IT FOR YOU!
HUH?
IT'S IMPORTANT, RIGHT?
I RESPECT MY FATHER, TOO.
MY FATHER WAS A RESEARCHER LIKE ME.
HE WAS THE FIRST ONE TO DEVELOP THE LANCELOT!!
I SEE.
BUT...
...HE WAS INVOLVED IN AN ACCIDENT A FEW YEARS AGO.
AND HE CAN'T DO RESEARCH ANYMORE.

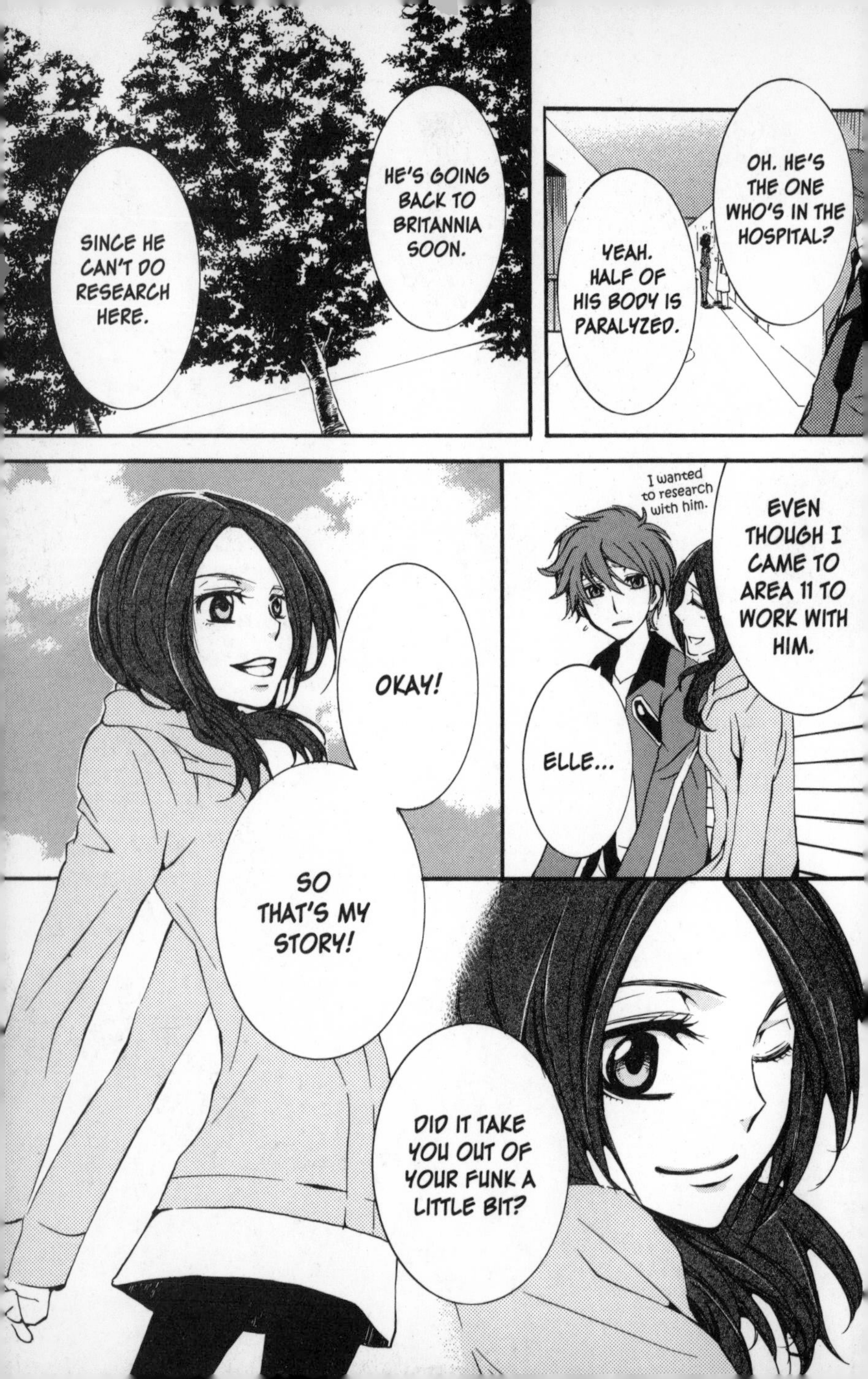
OH. HE'S THE ONE WHO'S IN THE HOSPITAL?
YEAH. HALF OF HIS BODY IS PARALYZED.
HE'S GOING BACK TO BRITANNIA SOON.
SINCE HE CAN'T DO RESEARCH HERE.
EVEN THOUGH I CAME TO AREA 11 TO WORK WITH HIM.
I wanted to research with him.
ELLE...
OKAY!
SO THAT'S MY STORY!
DID IT TAKE YOU OUT OF YOUR FUNK A LITTLE BIT?

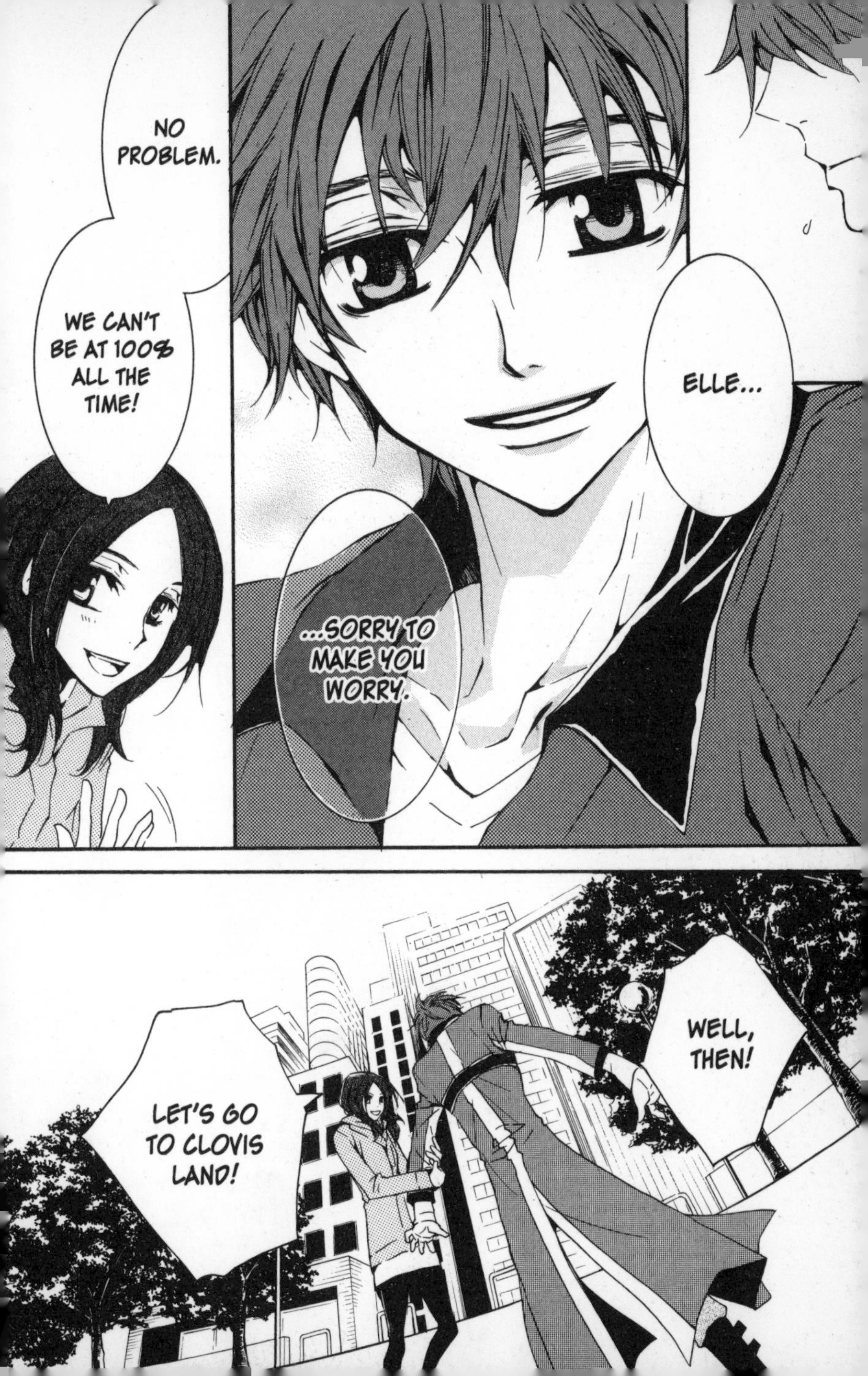
ELLE...
...SORRY TO MAKE YOU WORRY.
NO PROBLEM.
WE CAN'T BE AT 100% ALL THE TIME!
WELL, THEN!
LET'S GO TO CLOVIS LAND!

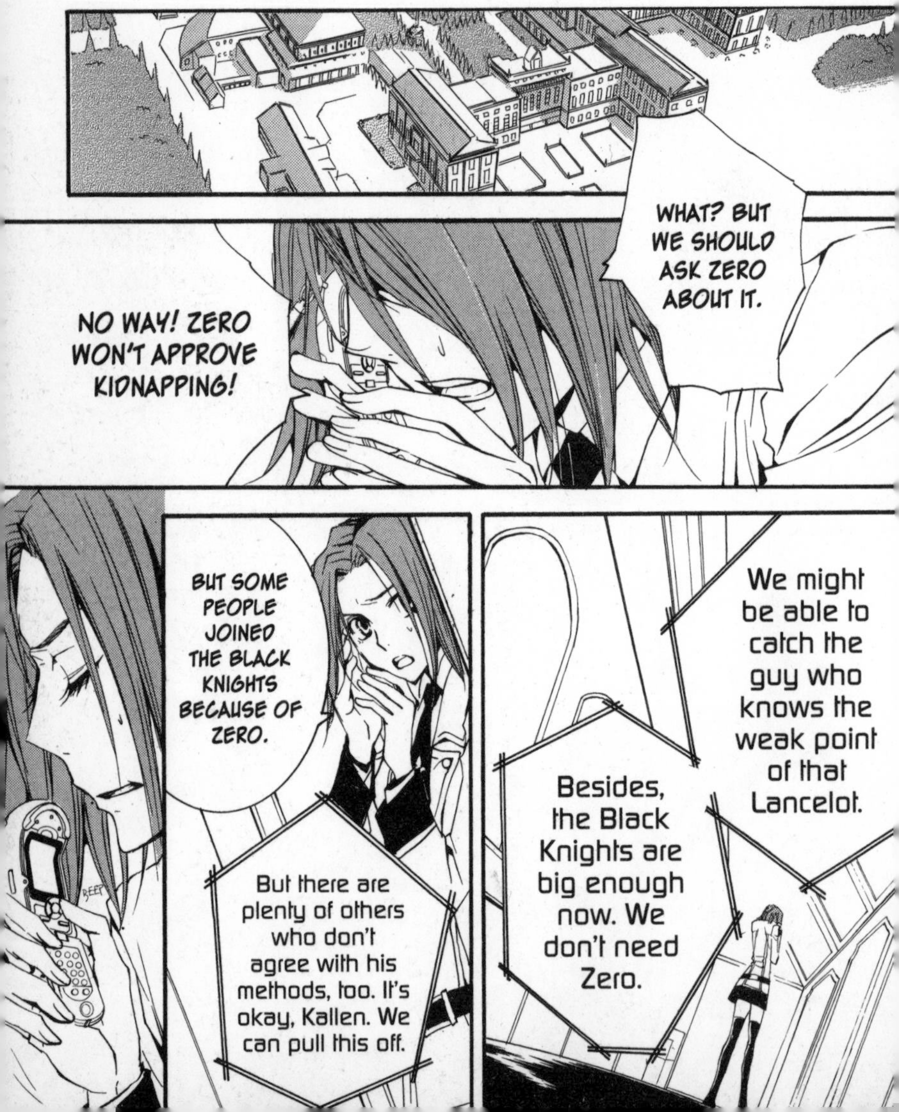
WHAT? BUT WE SHOULD ASK ZERO ABOUT IT.
NO WAY! ZERO WON'T APPROVE KIDNAPPING!
We might be able to catch the guy who knows the weak point of that Lancelot.
Besides, the Black Knights are big enough now. We don't need Zero.
BUT SOME PEOPLE JOINED THE BLACK KNIGHTS BECAUSE OF ZERO.
But there are plenty of others who don't agree with his methods, too. It's okay, Kallen. We can pull this off.

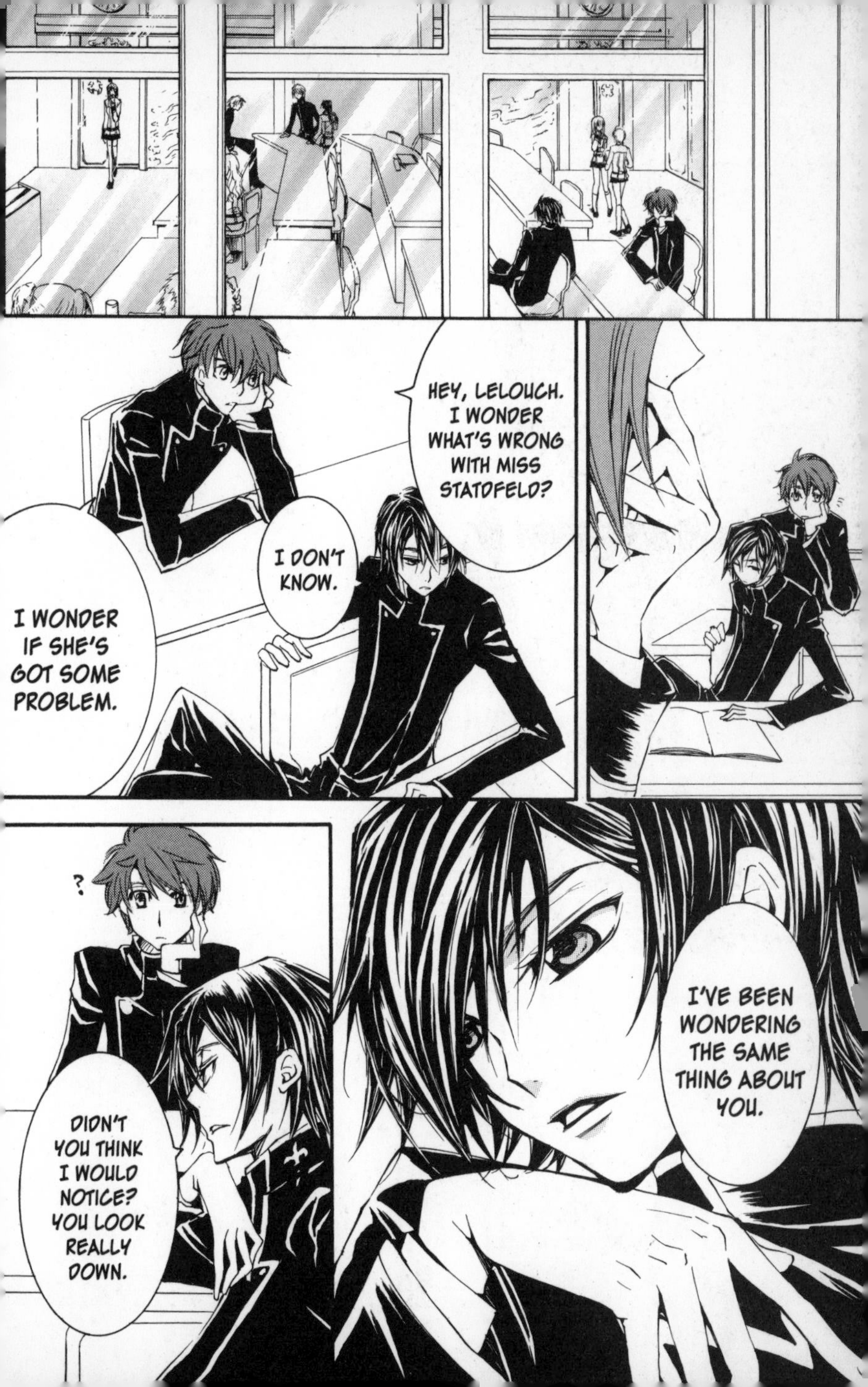
HEY, LELOUCH. I WONDER WHAT'S WRONG WITH MISS STATDFELD?
I DON'T KNOW.
I WONDER IF SHE'S GOT SOME PROBLEM.
I'VE BEEN WONDERING THE SAME THING ABOUT YOU.
?
DIDN'T YOU THINK I WOULD NOTICE? YOU LOOK REALLY DOWN.

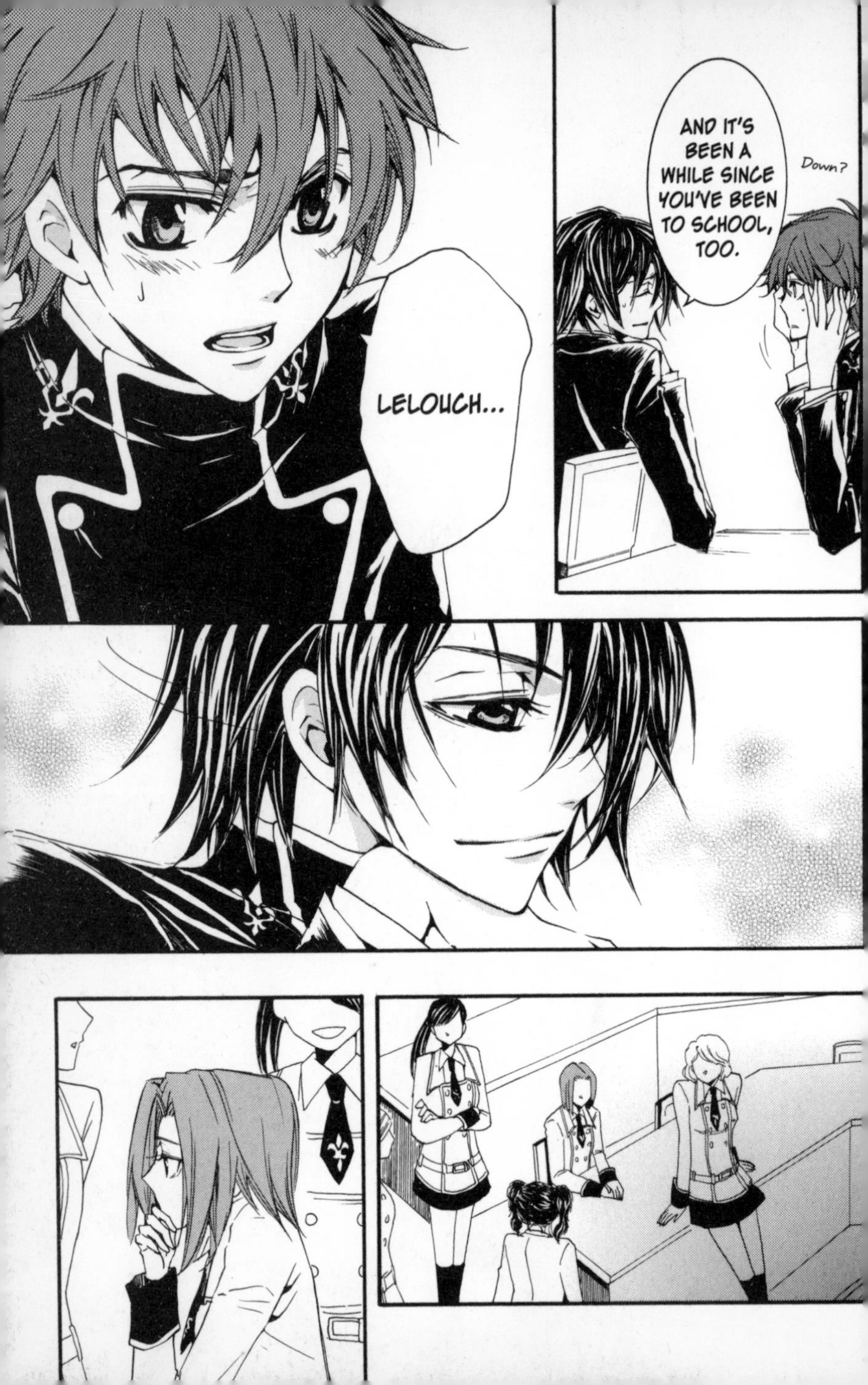
AND IT'S BEEN A WHILE SINCE YOU'VE BEEN TO SCHOOL, TOO.
Down?
LELOUCH...

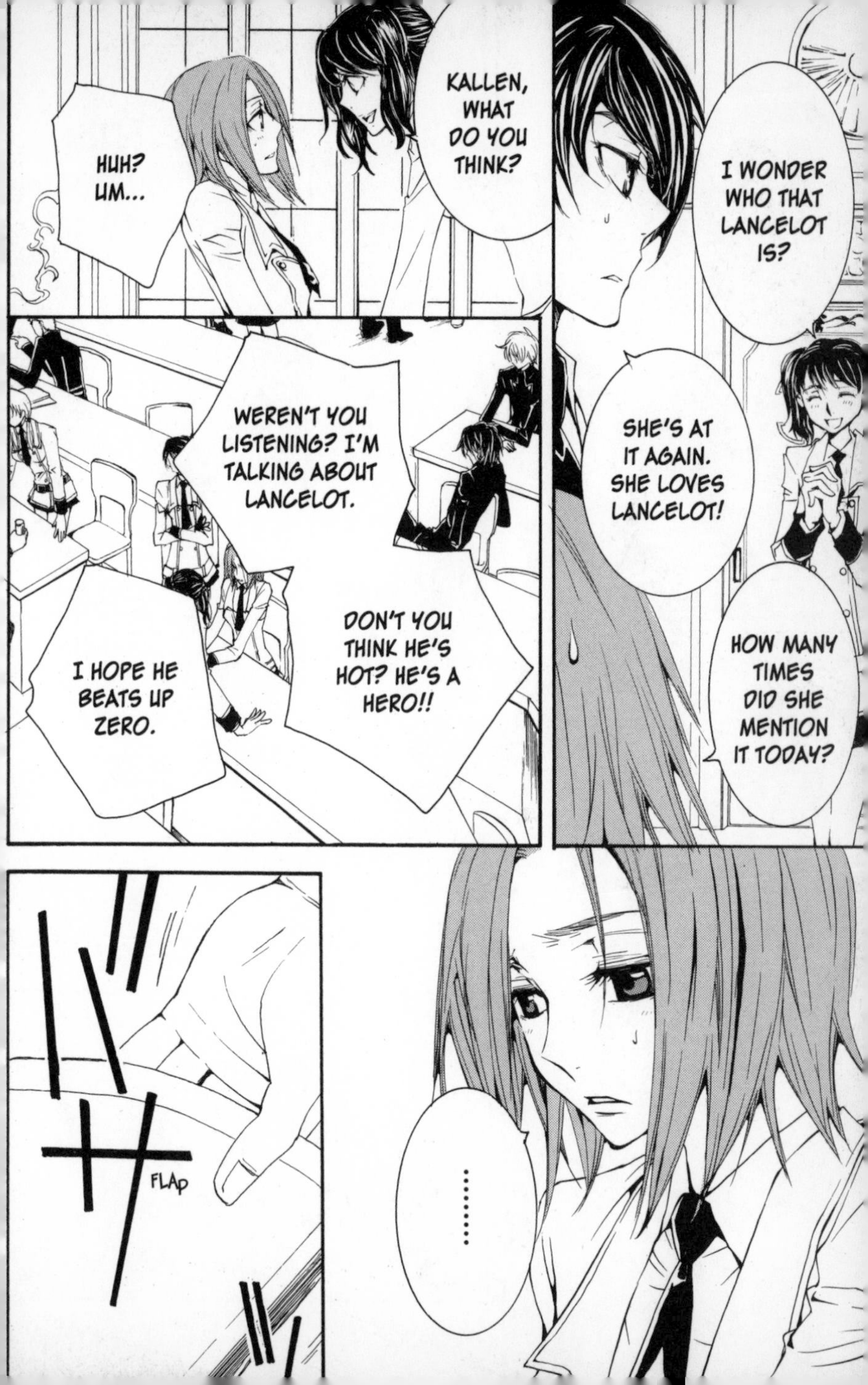
I WONDER WHO THAT LANCELOT IS?
SHE'S AT IT AGAIN. SHE LOVES LANCELOT!
HOW MANY TIMES DID SHE MENTION IT TODAY?
KALLEN, WHAT DO YOU THINK?
HUH? UM...
WEREN'T YOU LISTENING? I'M TALKING ABOUT LANCELOT.
DON'T YOU THINK HE'S HOT? HE'S A HERO!!
I HOPE HE BEATS UP ZERO.
....
FLAP

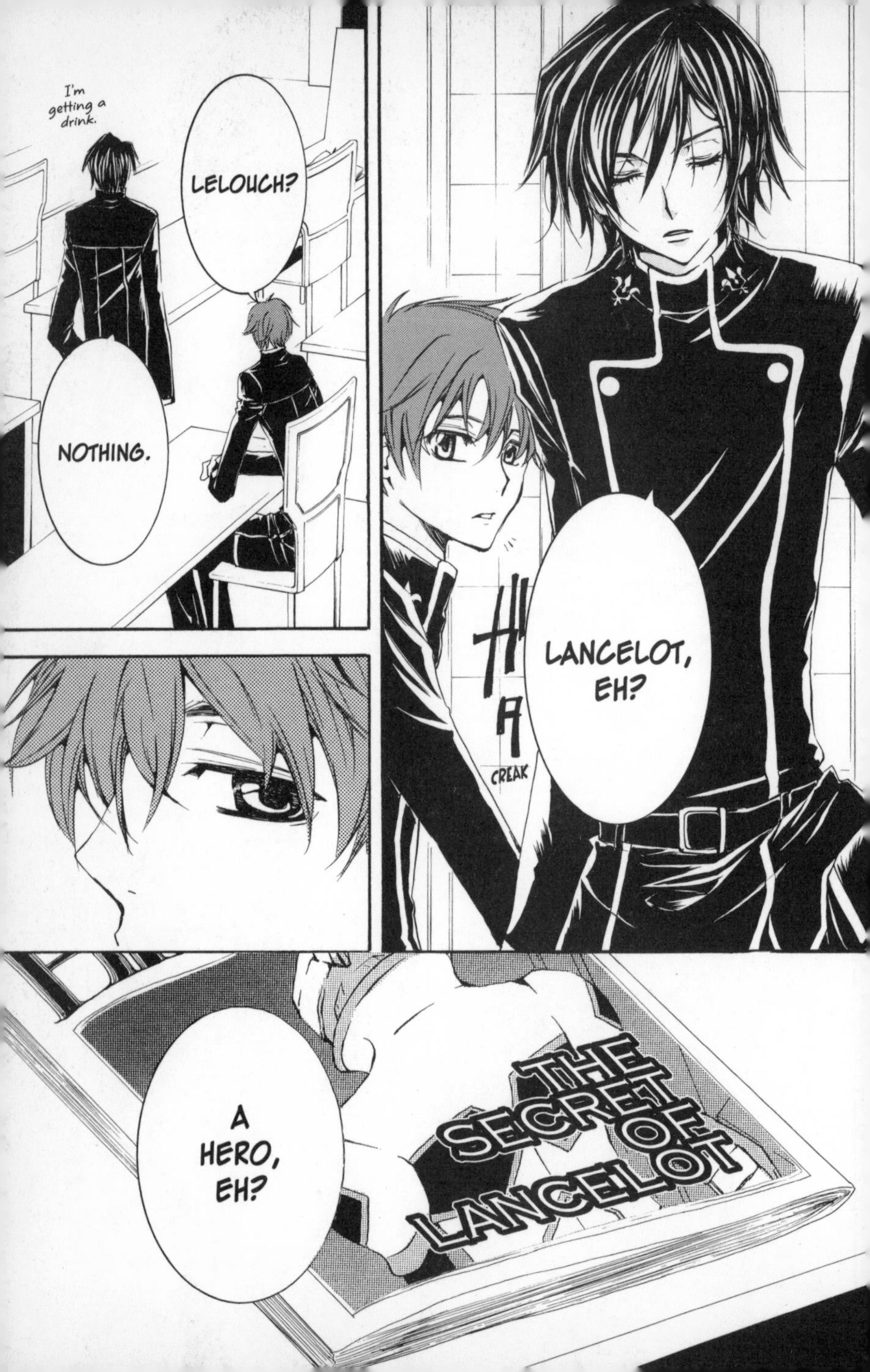
LANCELOT, EH?
CREAK
I'm getting a drink.
LELOUCH?
NOTHING.
A HERO, EH?
THE SECRET OF LANCELOT

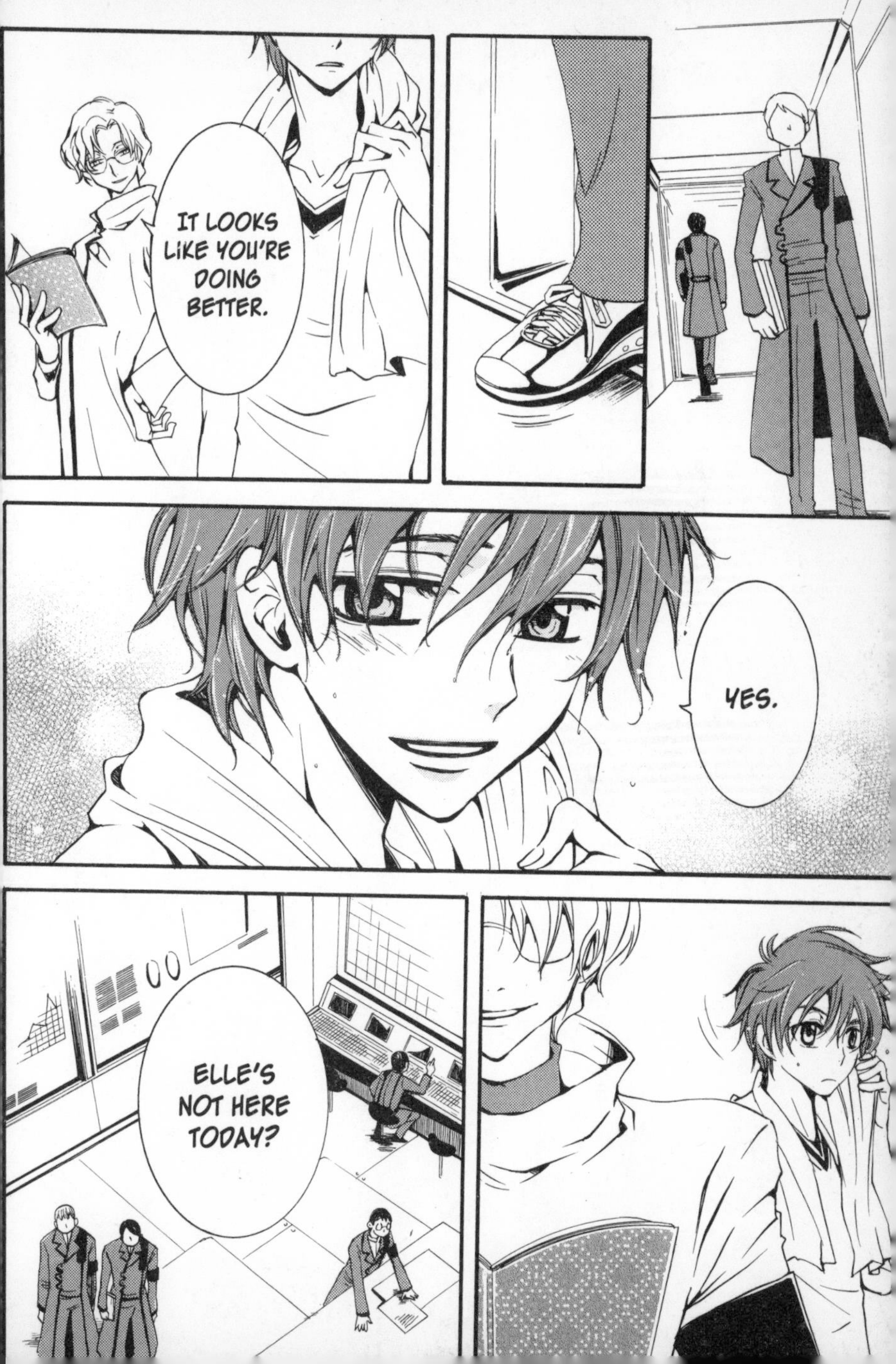
IT LOOKS LIKE YOU'RE DOING BETTER.
YES.
ELLE'S NOT HERE TODAY?

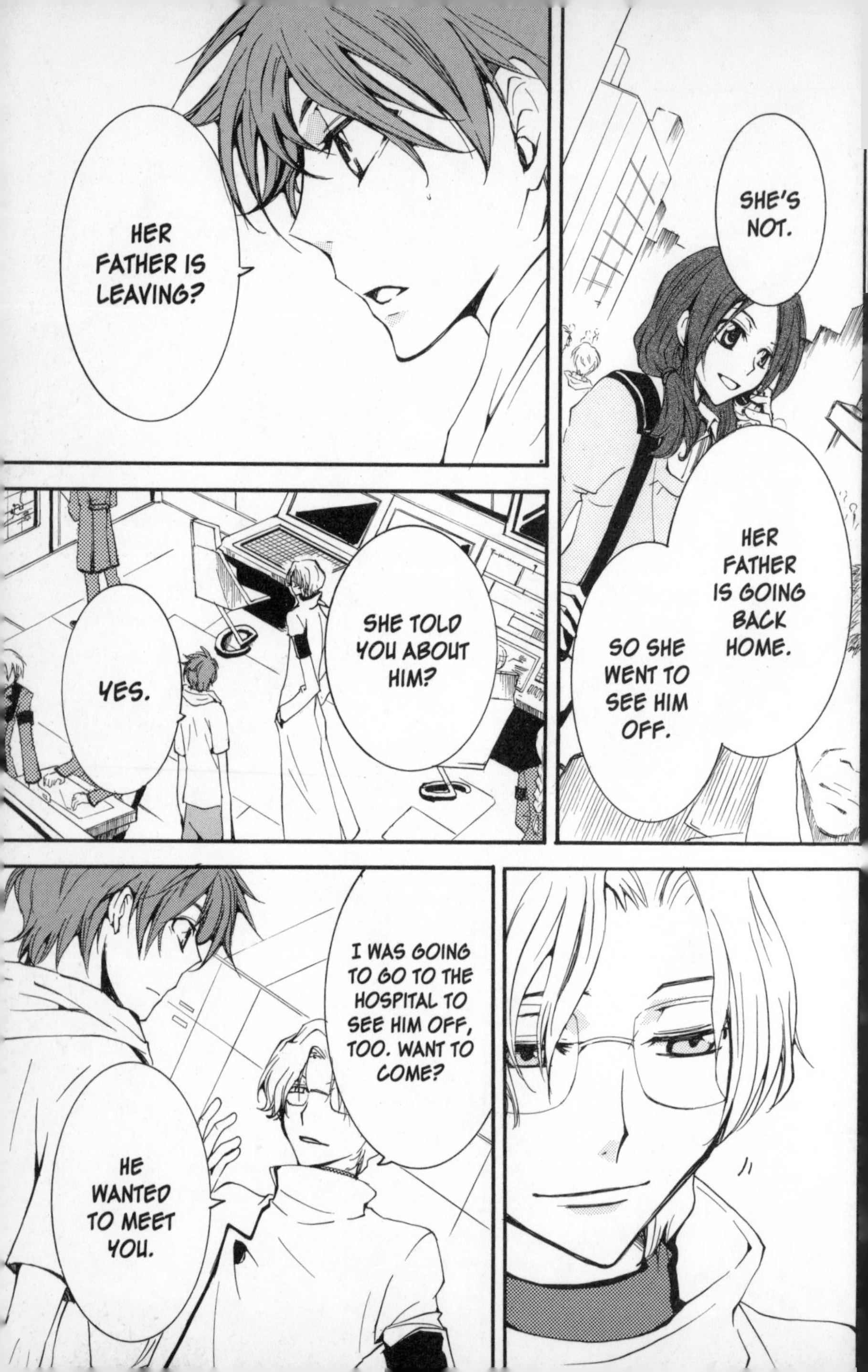
SHE'S NOT.
HER FATHER IS GOING BACK HOME.
SO SHE WENT TO SEE HIM OFF.
HER FATHER IS LEAVING?
SHE TOLD YOU ABOUT HIM?
YES.
I WAS GOING TO GO TO THE HOSPITAL TO SEE HIM OFF, TOO. WANT TO COME?
HE WANTED TO MEET YOU.

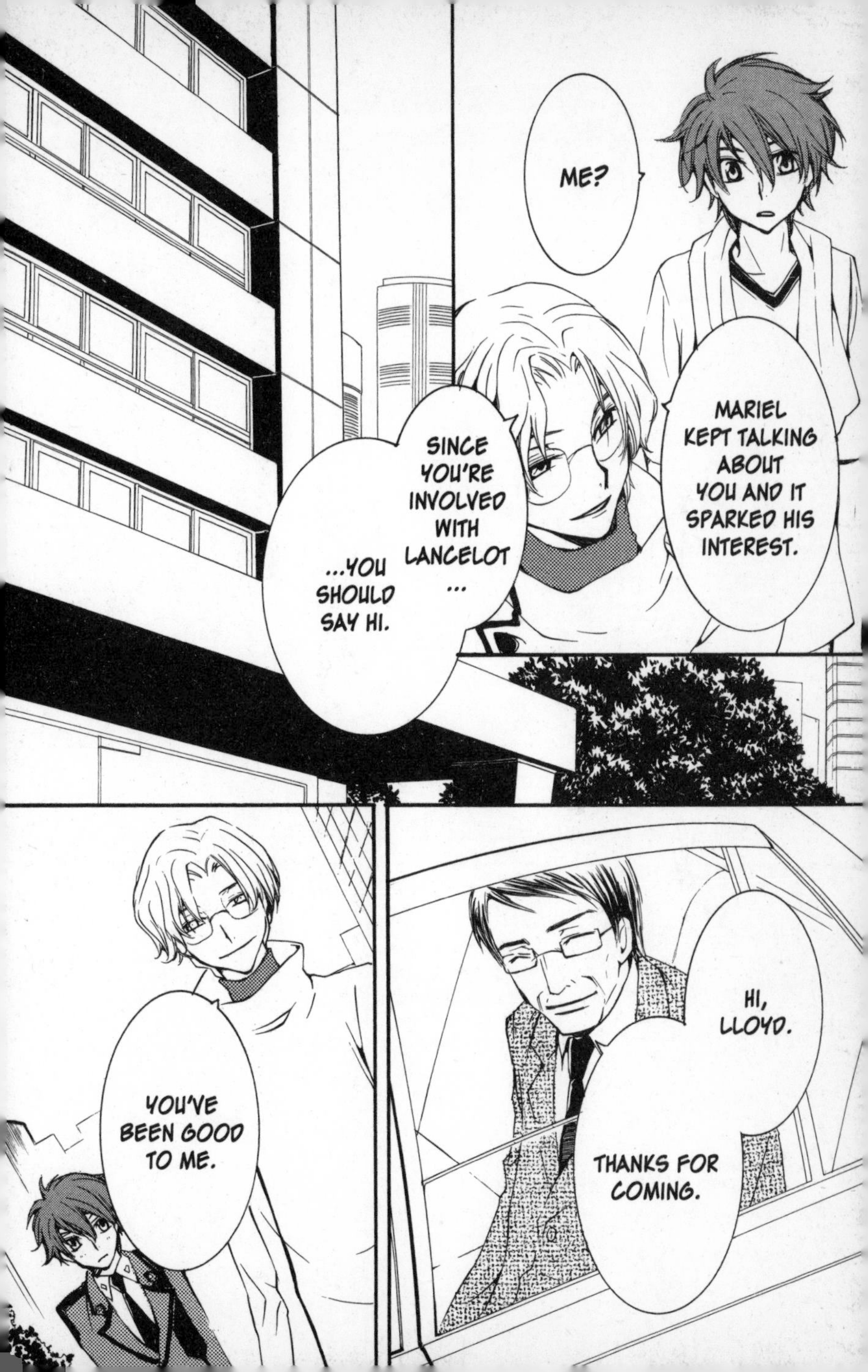
ME?
MARIEL KEPT TALKING ABOUT YOU AND IT SPARKED HIS INTEREST.
SINCE YOU'RE INVOLVED WITH LANCELOT ...
...YOU SHOULD SAY HI.
HI, LLOYD.
THANKS FOR COMING.
YOU'VE BEEN GOOD TO ME.

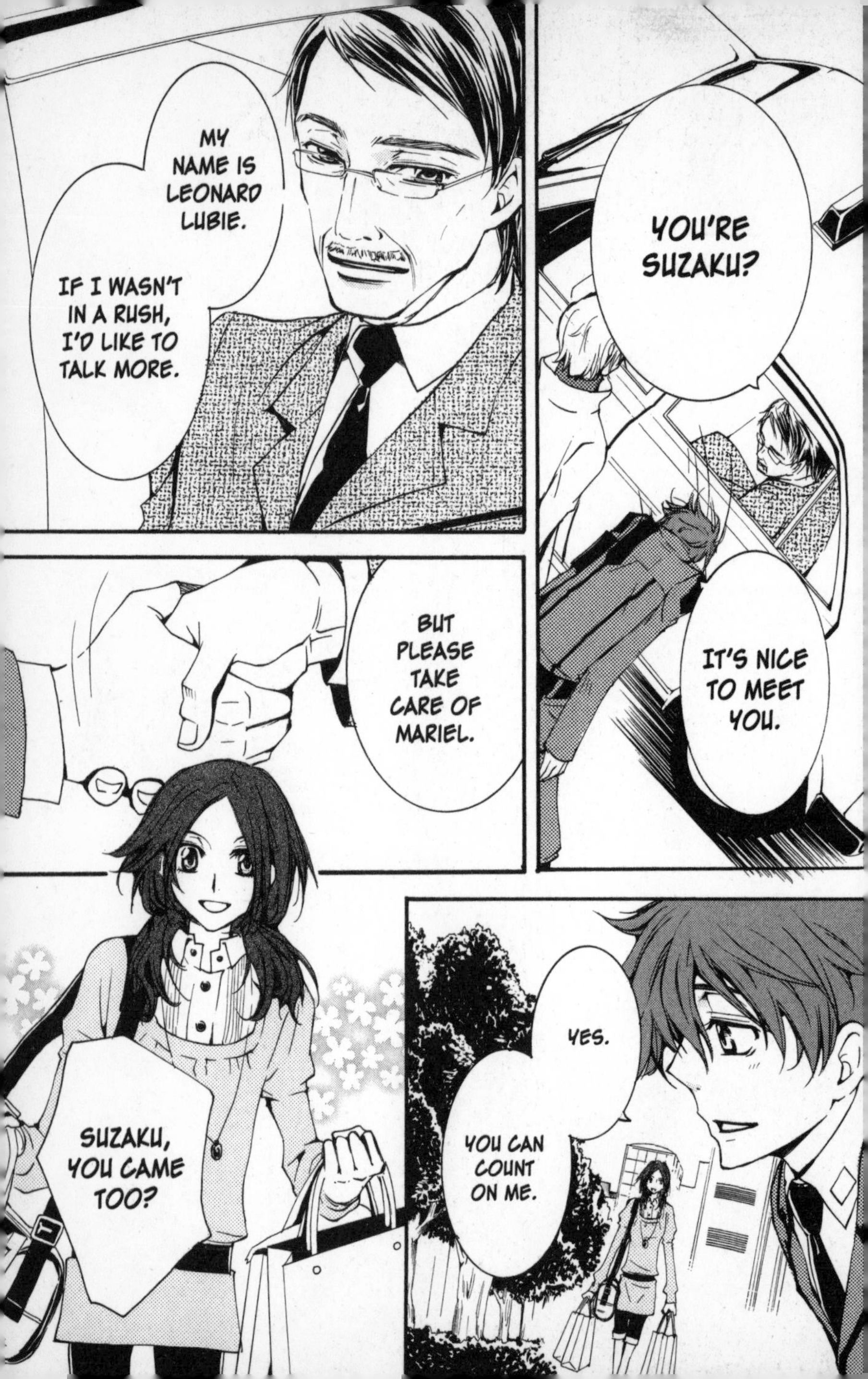
YOU'RE SUZAKU?
IT'S NICE TO MEET YOU.
MY NAME IS LEONARD LUBIE.
IF I WASN'T IN A RUSH, I'D LIKE TO TALK MORE.
BUT PLEASE TAKE CARE OF MARIEL.
YES.
YOU CAN COUNT ON ME.
SUZAKU, YOU CAME TOO?

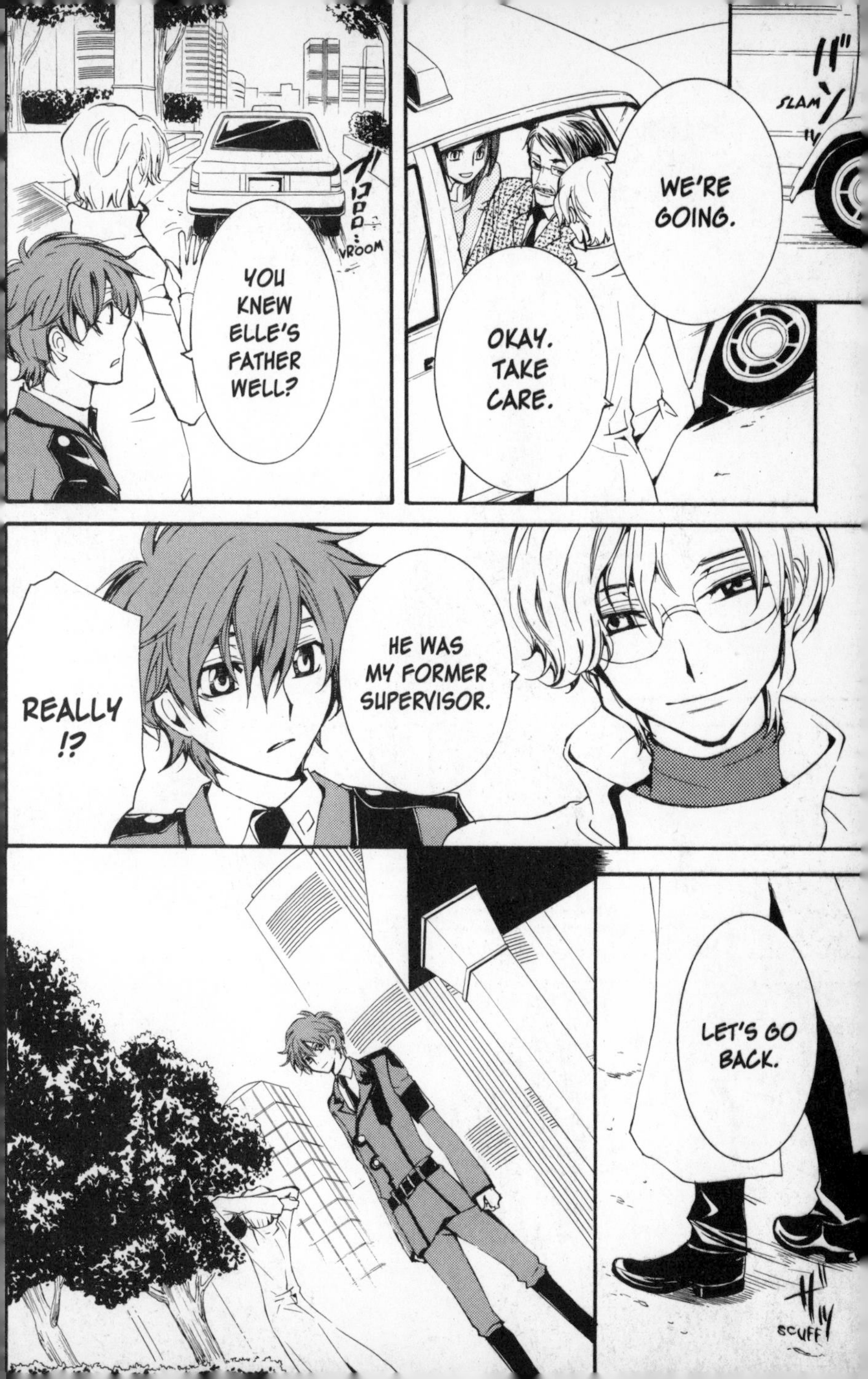
SLAM
WE'RE GOING.
OKAY. TAKE CARE.
VROOM
YOU KNEW ELLE'S FATHER WELL?
HE WAS MY FORMER SUPERVISOR.
REALLY !?
LET'S GO BACK.
SCUFF

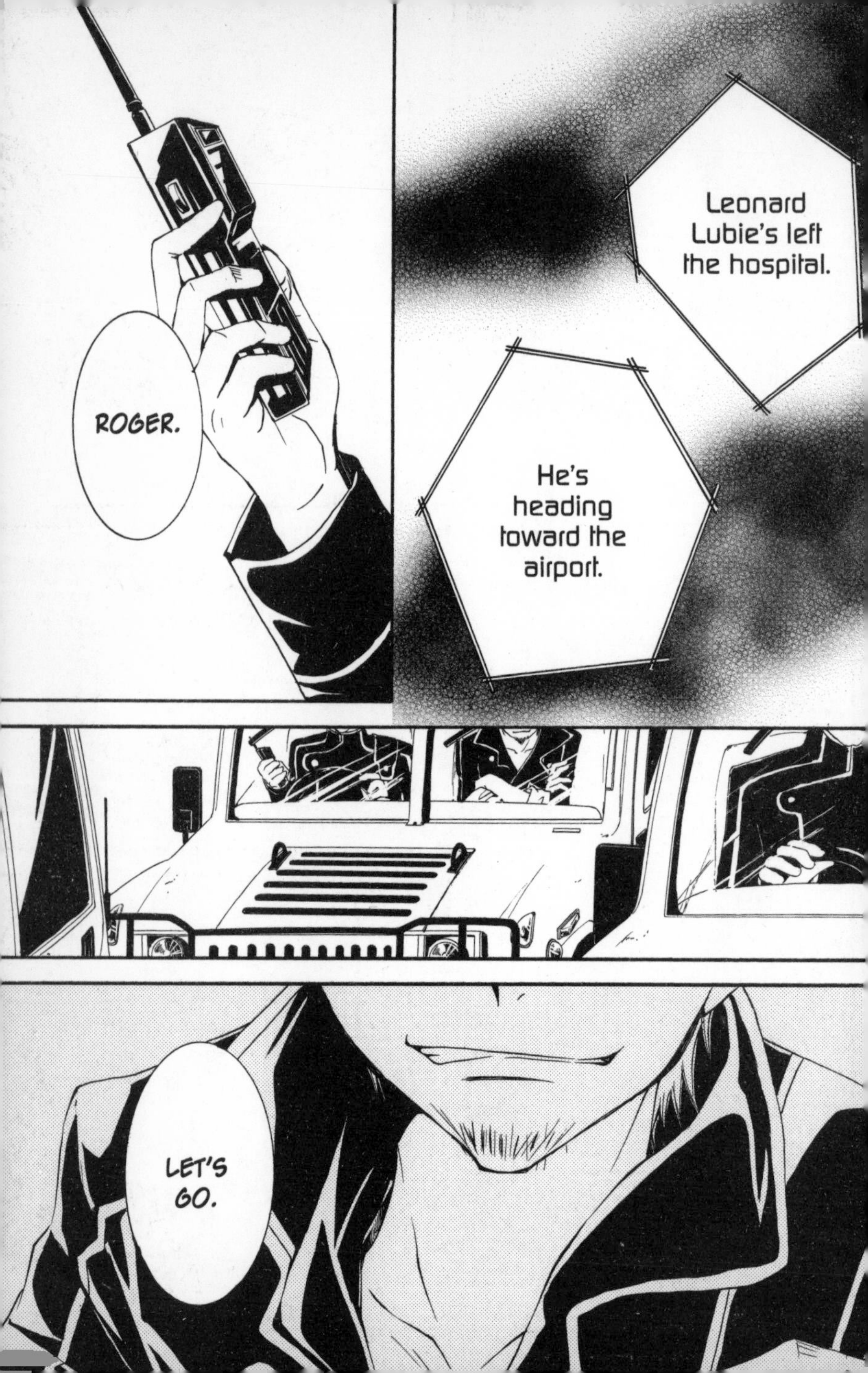
Leonard Lubie's left the hospital.
He's heading toward the airport.
ROGER.
LET'S GO.

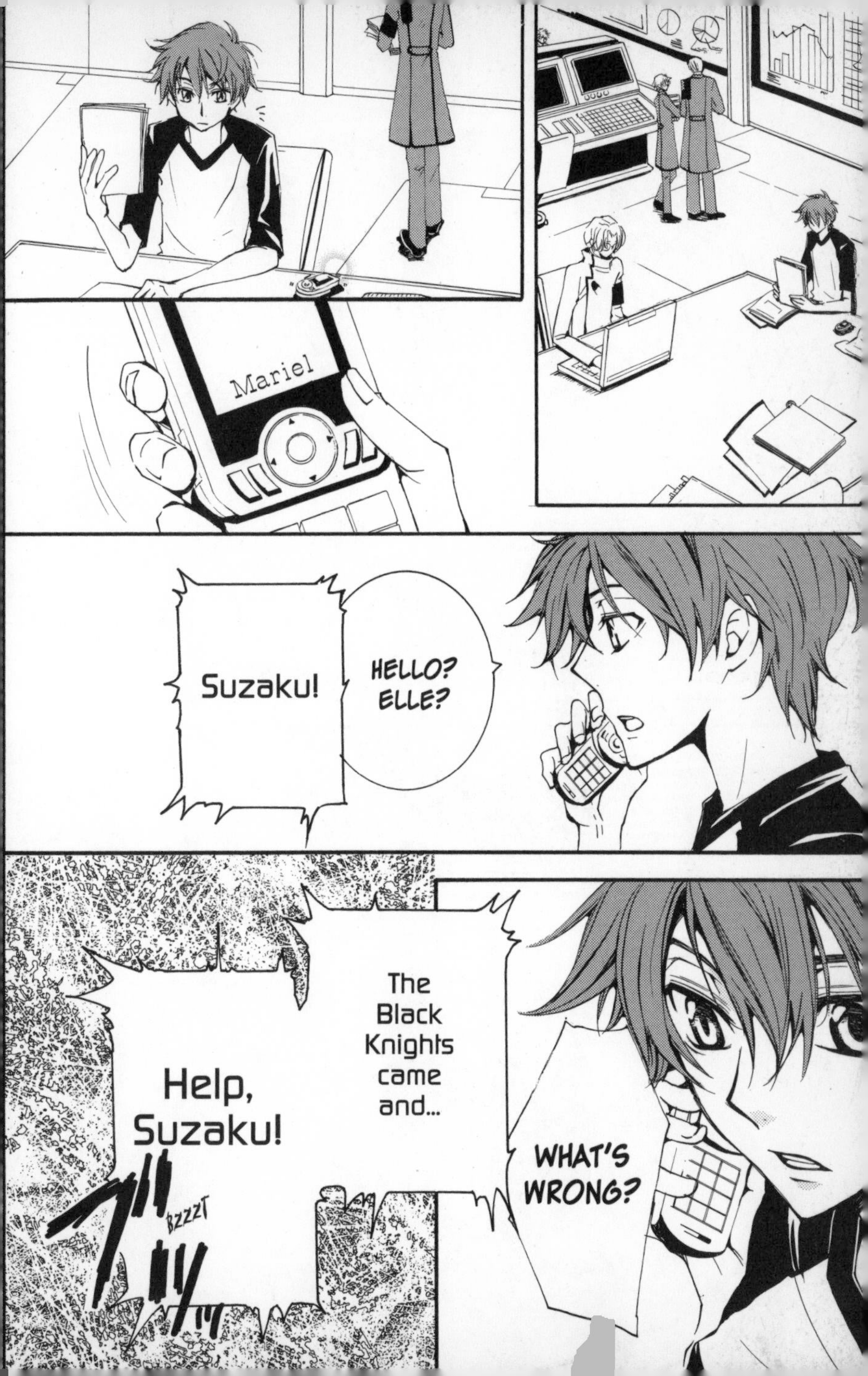
Mariel
HELLO? ELLE?
Suzaku!
WHAT'S WRONG?
The Black Knights came and...
Help, Suzaku!
BZZZT

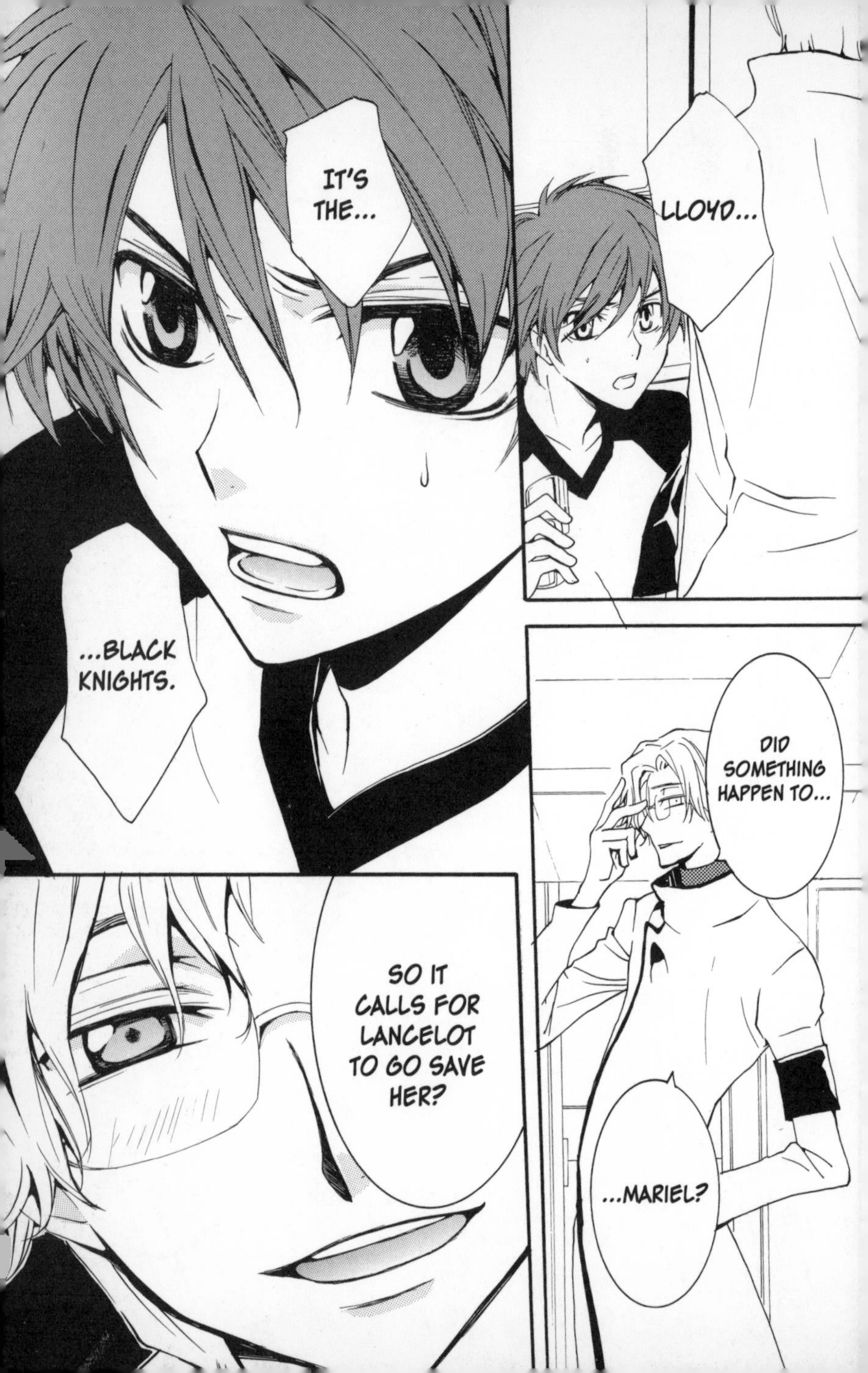
LLOYD...
DID SOMETHING HAPPEN TO...
...MARIEL?
IT'S THE...
...BLACK KNIGHTS.
SO IT CALLS FOR LANCELOT TO GO SAVE HER?

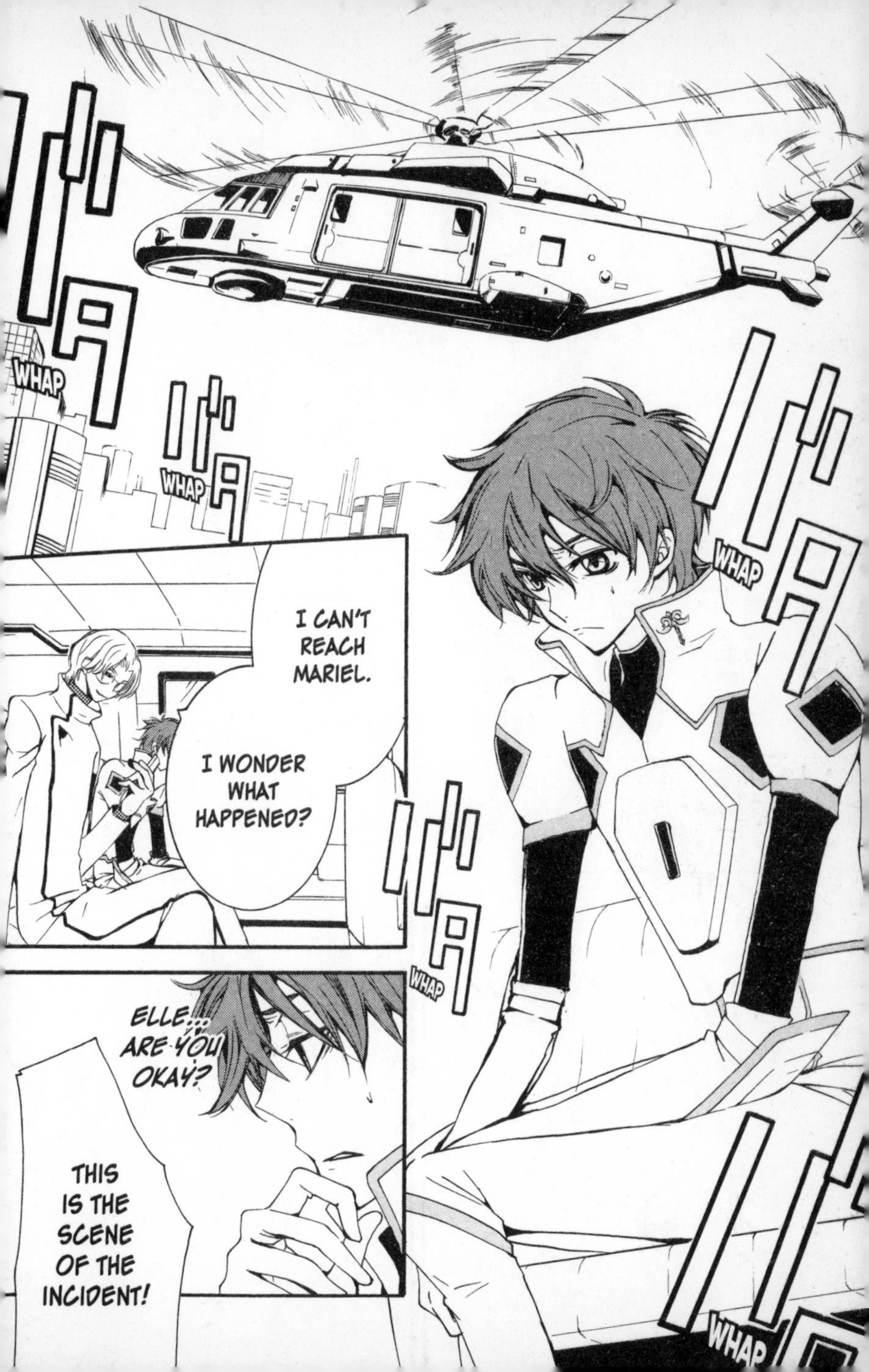
WHAP
WHAP
WHAP
WHAP
WHAP
I CAN'T REACH MARIEL.
I WONDER WHAT HAPPENED?
ELLE... ARE YOU OKAY?
THIS IS THE SCENE OF THE INCIDENT!

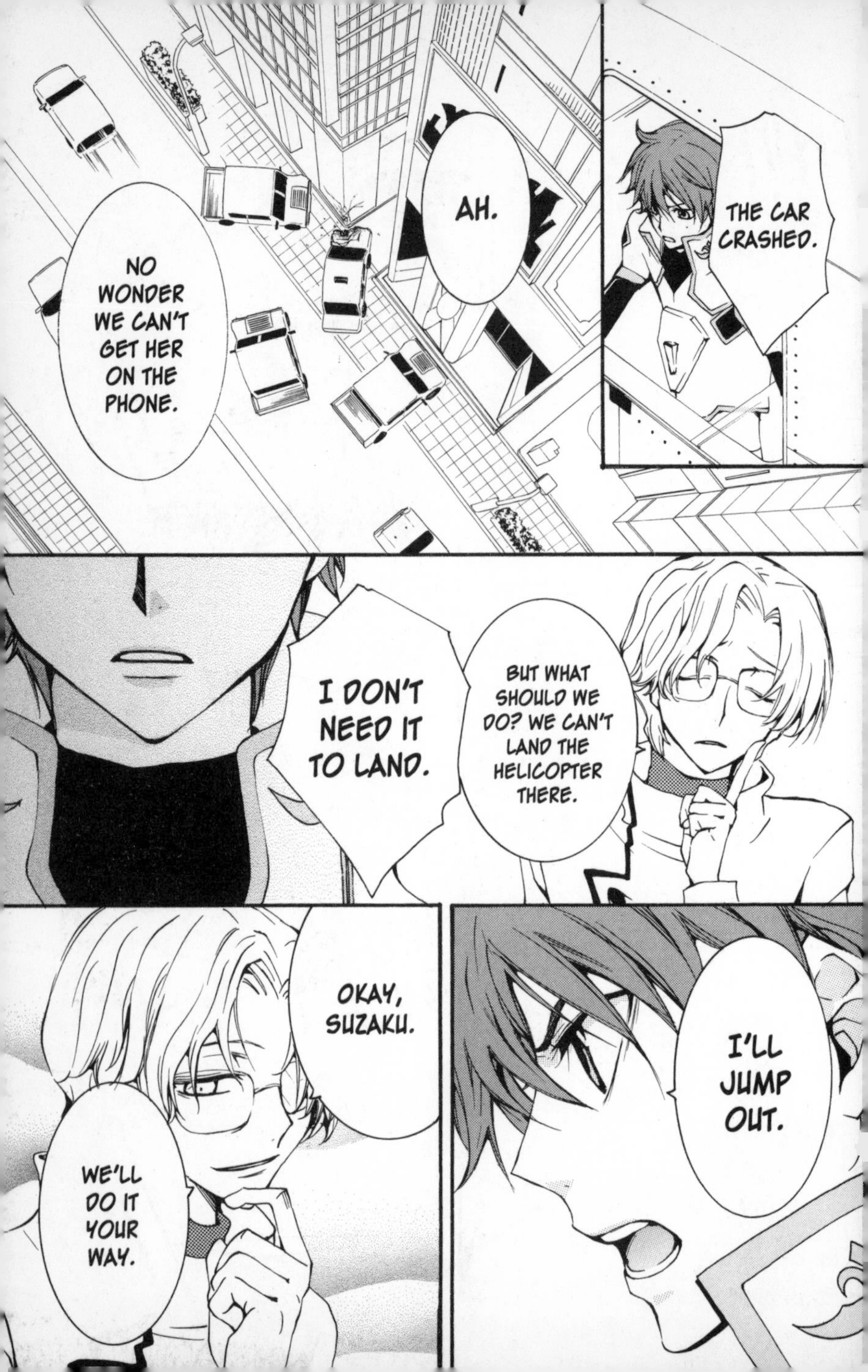
THE CAR CRASHED.
AH.
NO WONDER WE CAN'T GET HER ON THE PHONE.
BUT WHAT SHOULD WE DO? WE CAN'T LAND THE HELICOPTER THERE.
I DON'T NEED IT TO LAND.
I'LL JUMP OUT.
OKAY, SUZAKU.
WE'LL DO IT YOUR WAY.

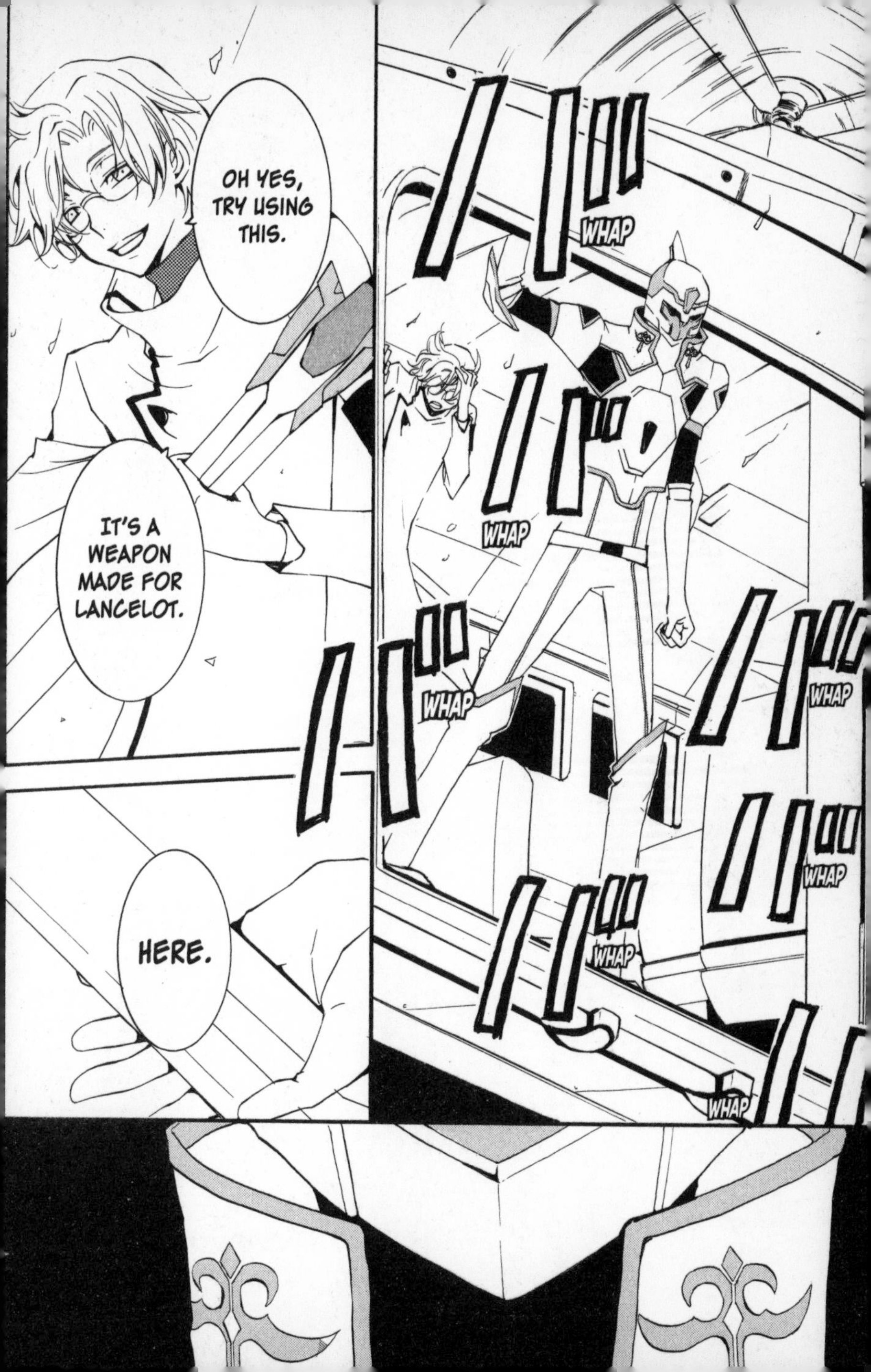
WHAP
WHAP
WHAP
WHAP
WHAP
WHAP
WHAP
OH YES, TRY USING THIS.
IT'S A WEAPON MADE FOR LANCELOT.
HERE.

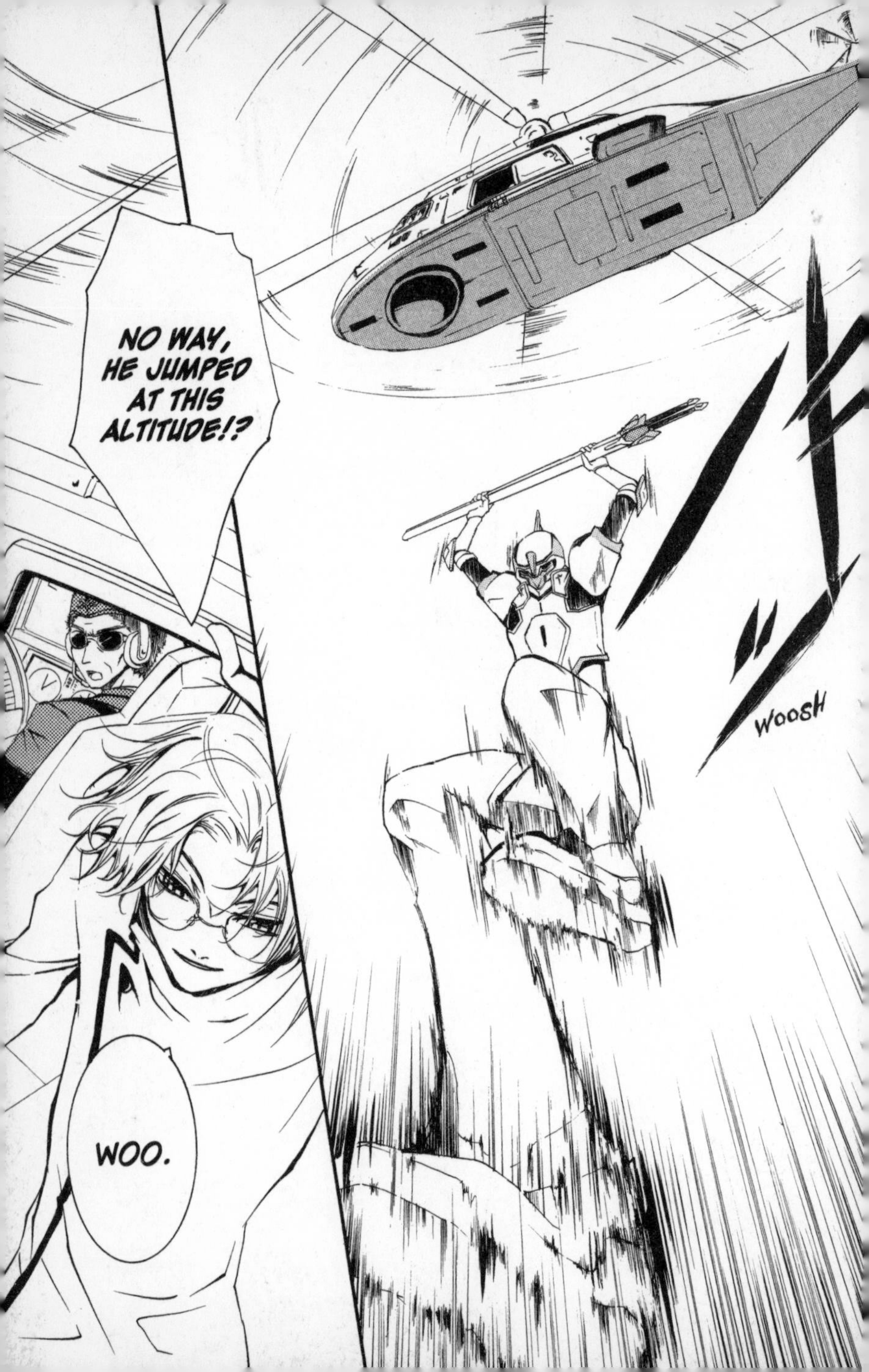
WOOSH
NO WAY, HE JUMPED AT THIS ALTITUDE!?
WOO.

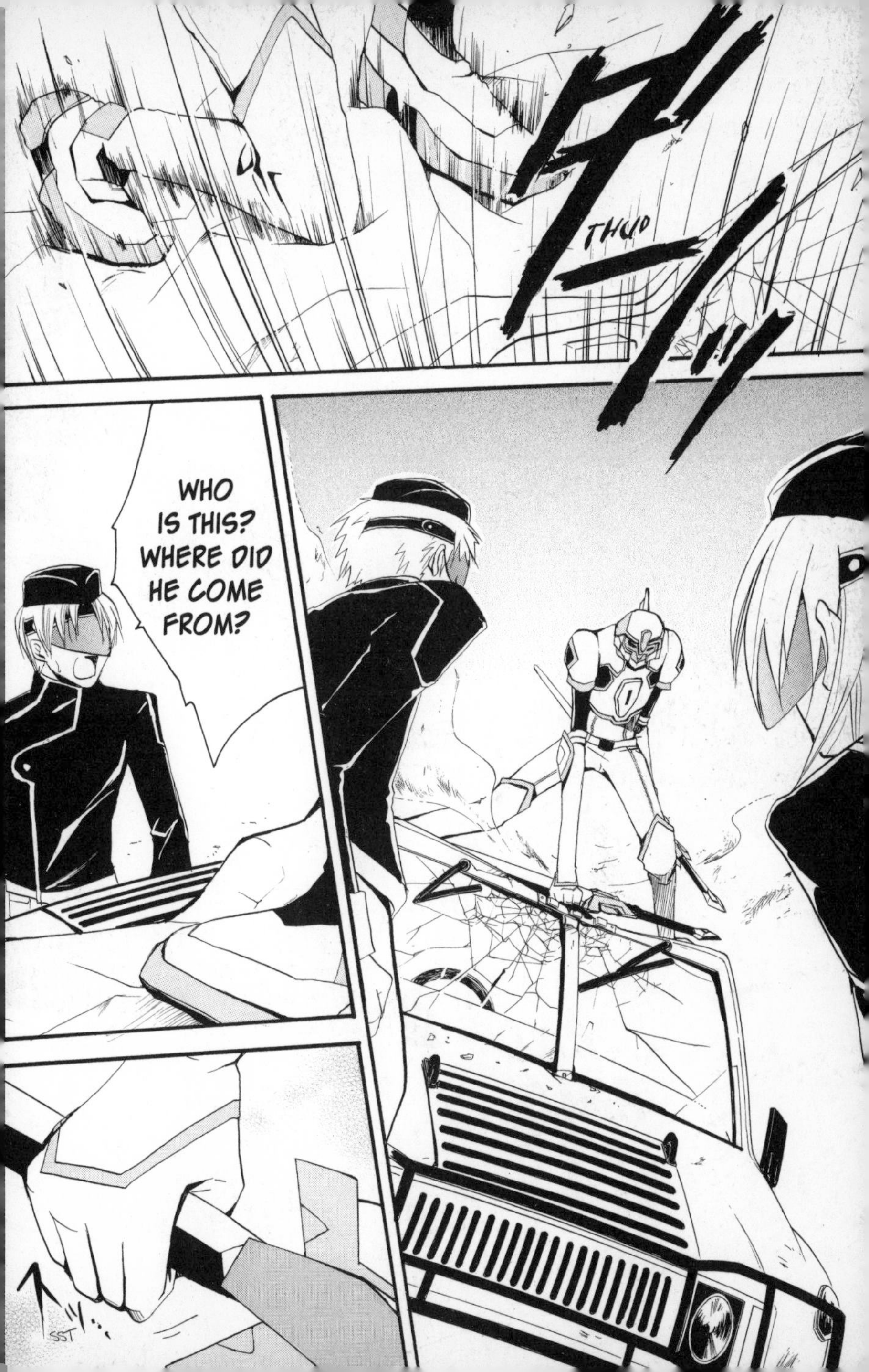
THUD
WHO IS THIS? WHERE DID HE COME FROM?
SST

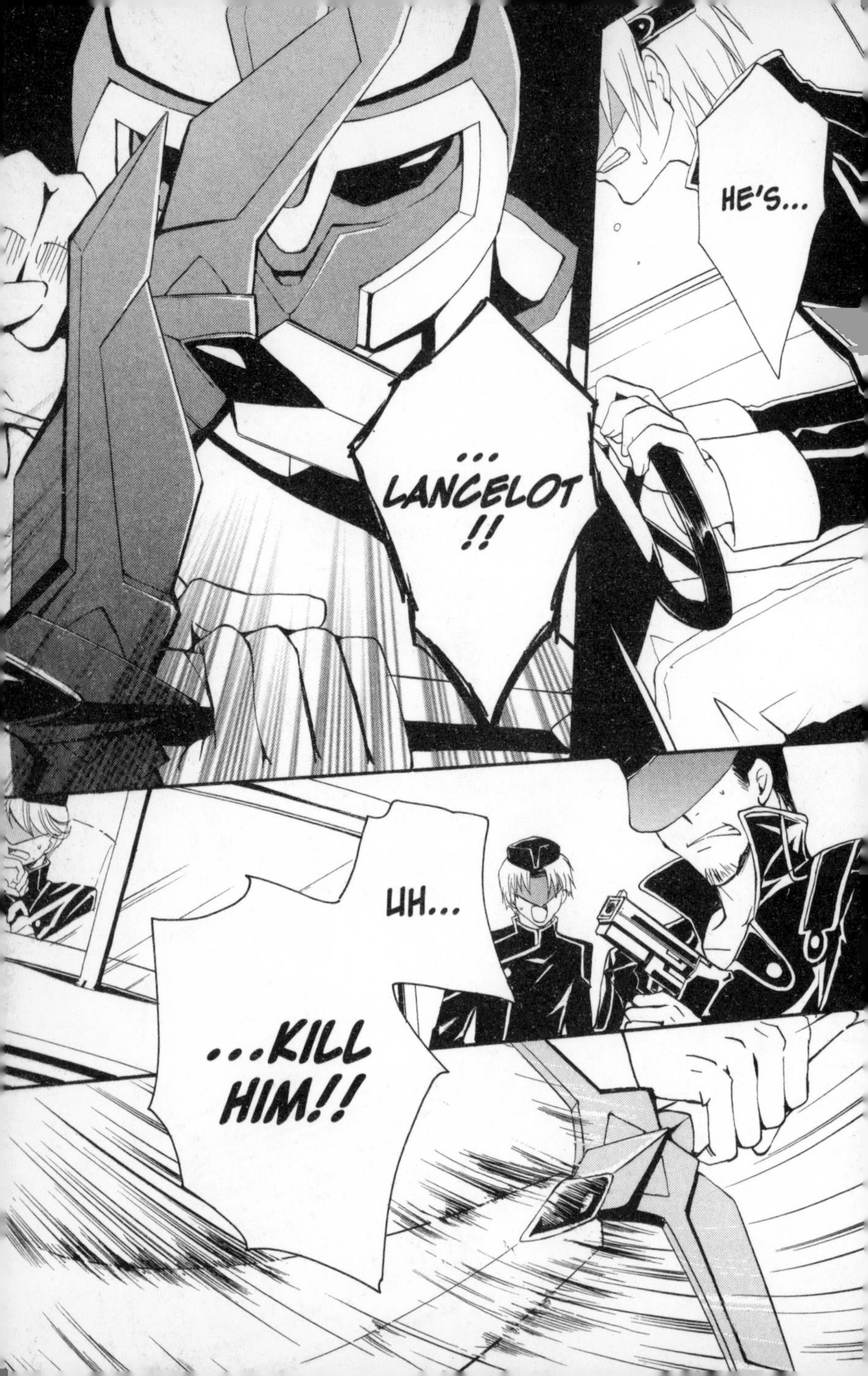
HE'S...
...LANCELOT!!
UH...
...KILL HIM!!

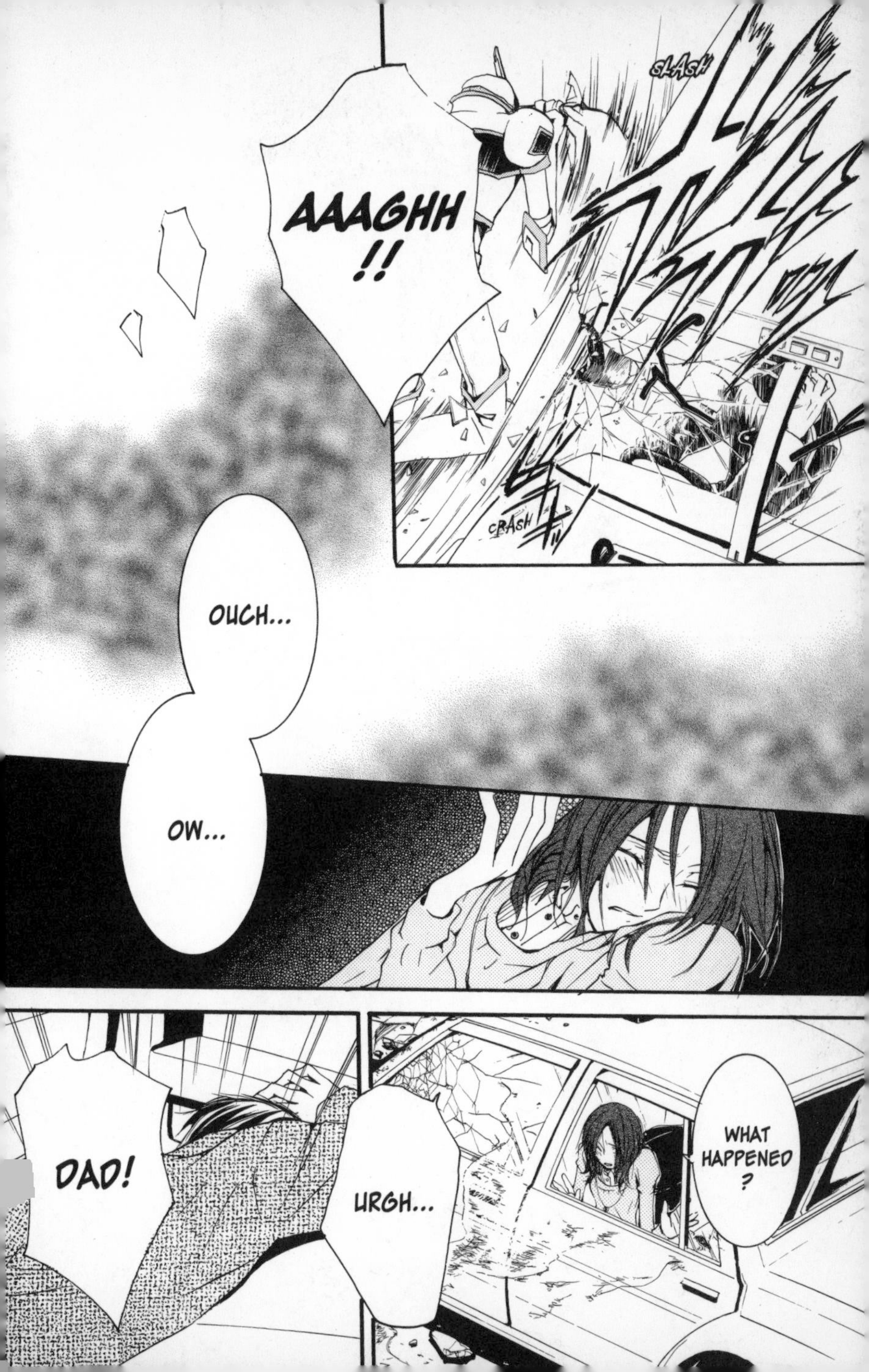
SLASH
AAAGHH!!
CRASH
OUCH...
OW...
WHAT HAPPENED?
URGH...
DAD!

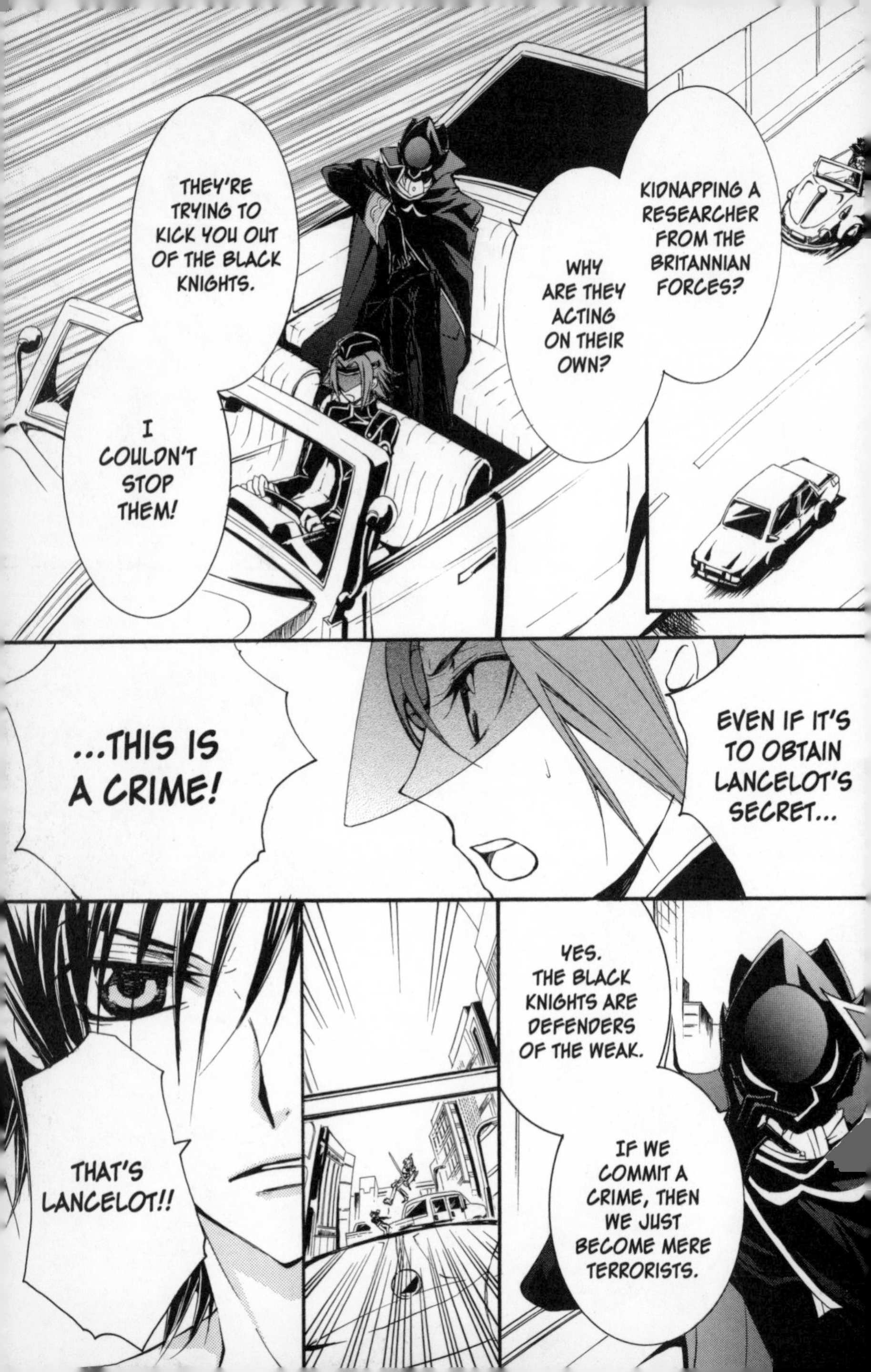
KIDNAPPING A RESEARCHER FROM THE BRITANNIAN FORCES?
WHY ARE THEY ACTING ON THEIR OWN?
THEY'RE TRYING TO KICK YOU OUT OF THE BLACK KNIGHTS.
I COULDN'T STOP THEM!
EVEN IF IT'S TO OBTAIN LANCELOT'S SECRET...
...THIS IS A CRIME!
YES. THE BLACK KNIGHTS ARE DEFENDERS OF THE WEAK.
IF WE COMMIT A CRIME, THEN WE JUST BECOME MERE TERRORISTS.
THAT'S LANCELOT!!

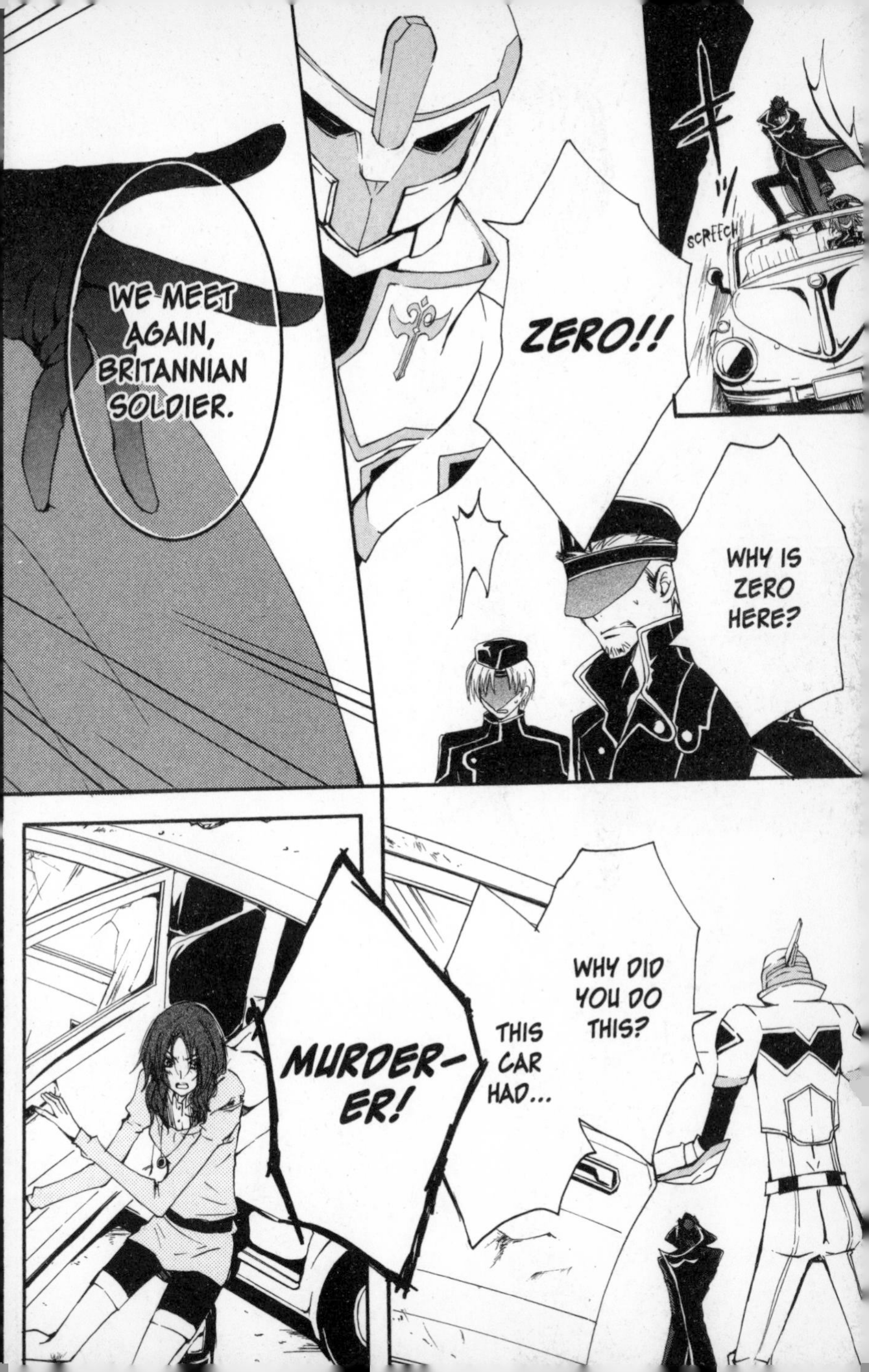
SCREECH
ZERO!!
WHY IS ZERO HERE?
WE MEET AGAIN, BRITANNIAN SOLDIER.
WHY DID YOU DO THIS?
THIS CAR HAD...
MURDER-ER!

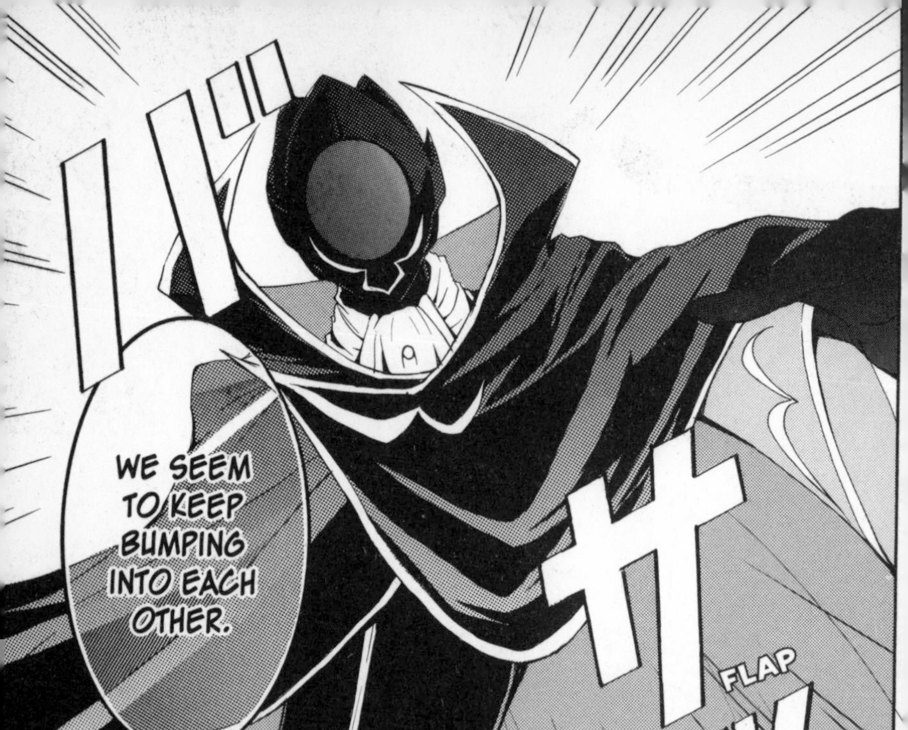
WE SEEM TO KEEP BUMPING INTO EACH OTHER.
FLAP

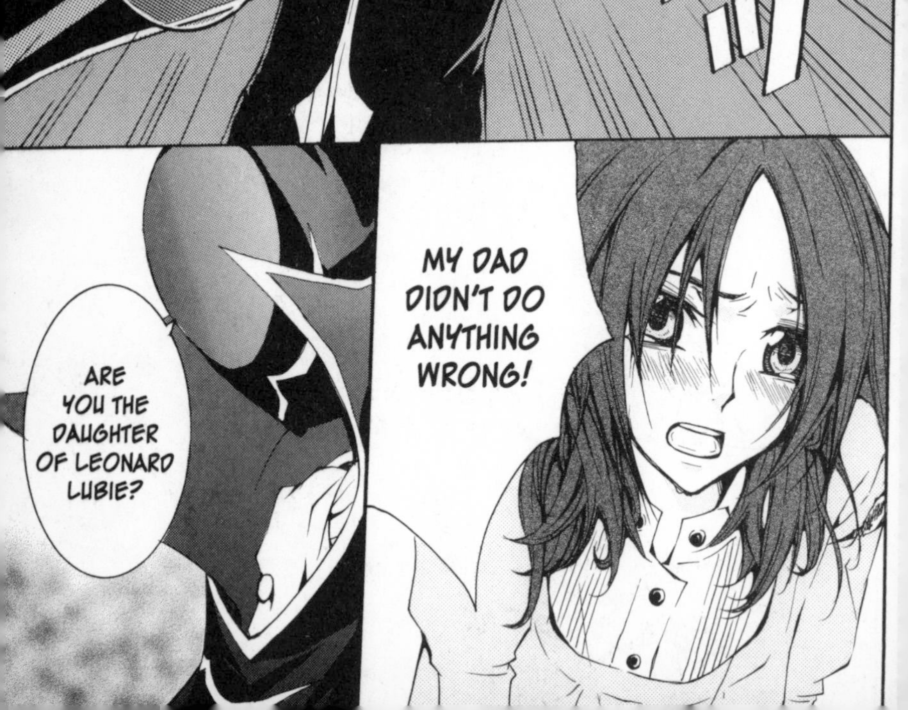
MY DAD DIDN'T DO ANYTHING WRONG!
ARE YOU THE DAUGHTER OF LEONARD LUBIE?

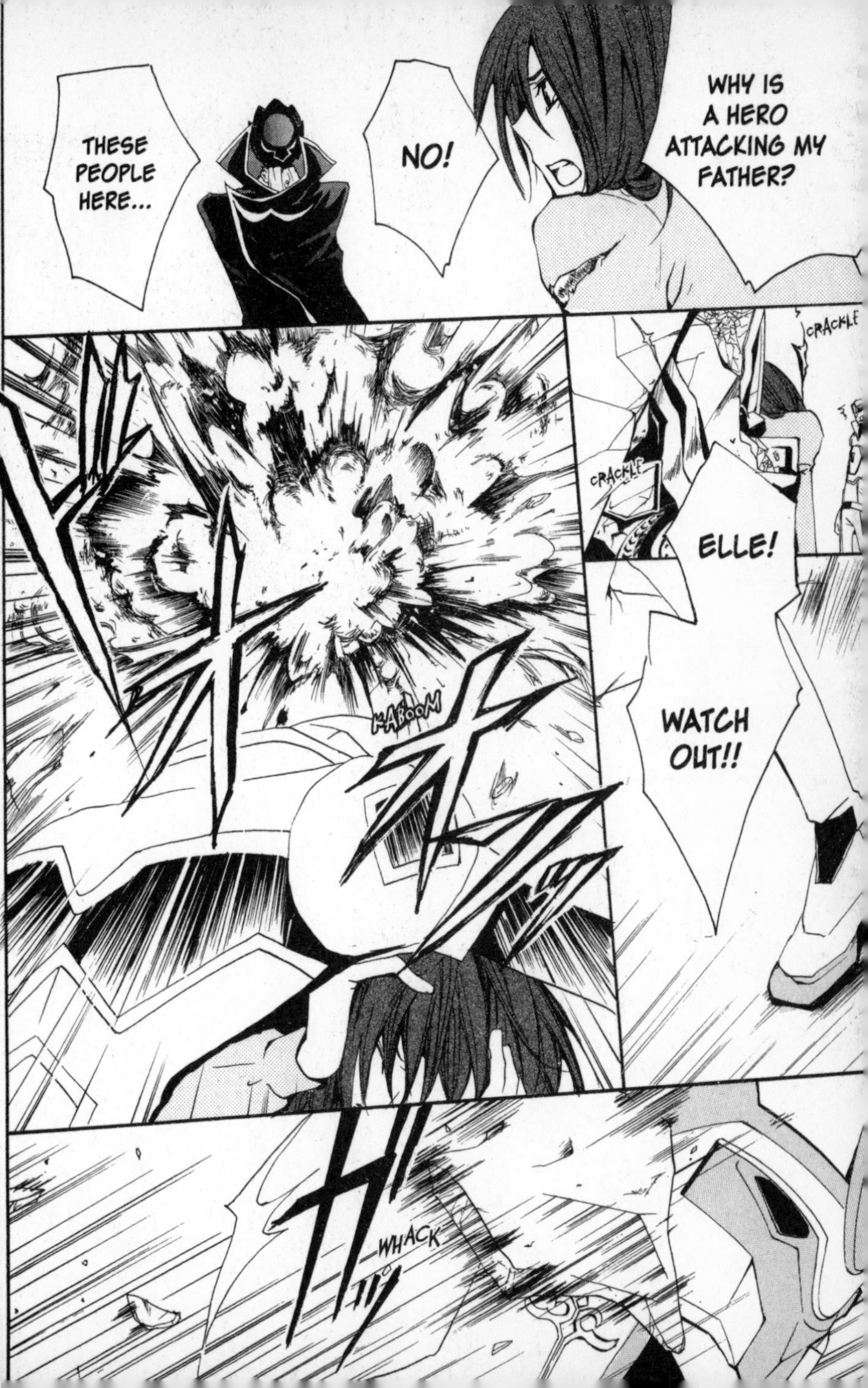
WHY IS A HERO ATTACKING MY FATHER?
NO!
THESE PEOPLE HERE...
CRACKLE
CRACKLE
ELLE!
WATCH OUT!!
KABOOM
WHACK

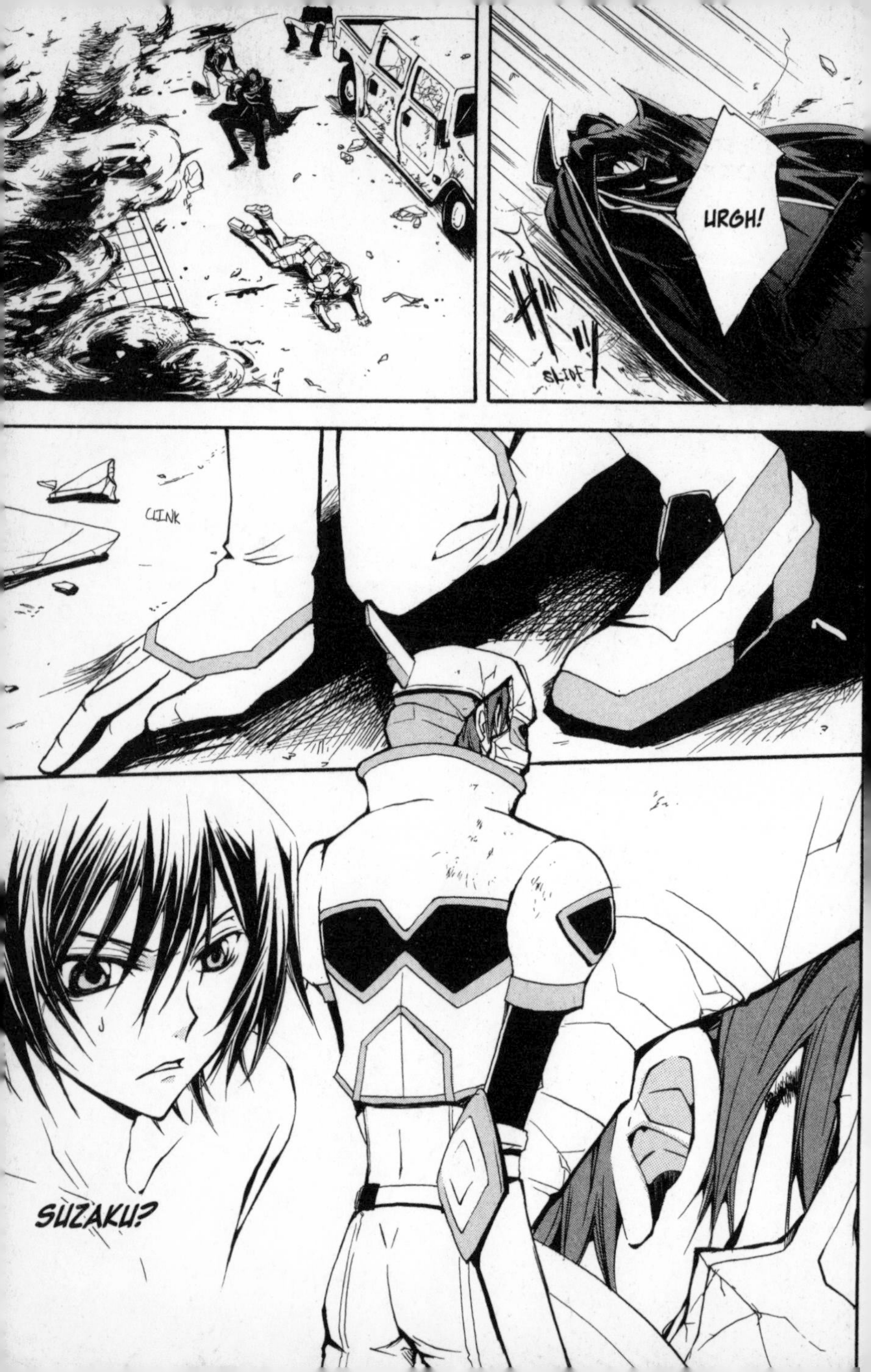
URGH!
SLIDE
CLINK
SUZAKU?

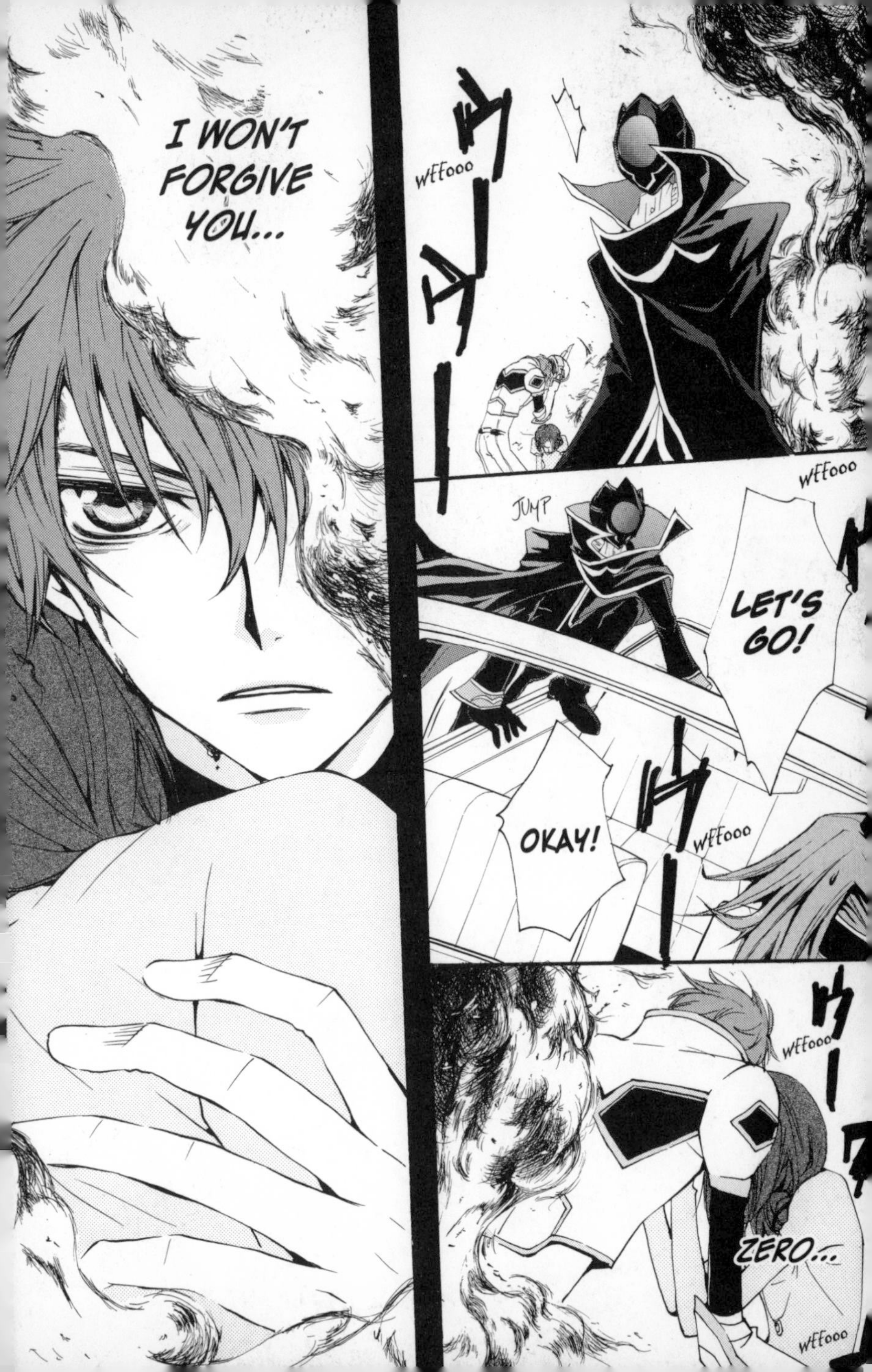
wEEooo
wEEooo
LET'S GO!
JUMP
OKAY!
wEEooo
wEEooo
ZERO...
wEEooo
I WON'T FORGIVE YOU...

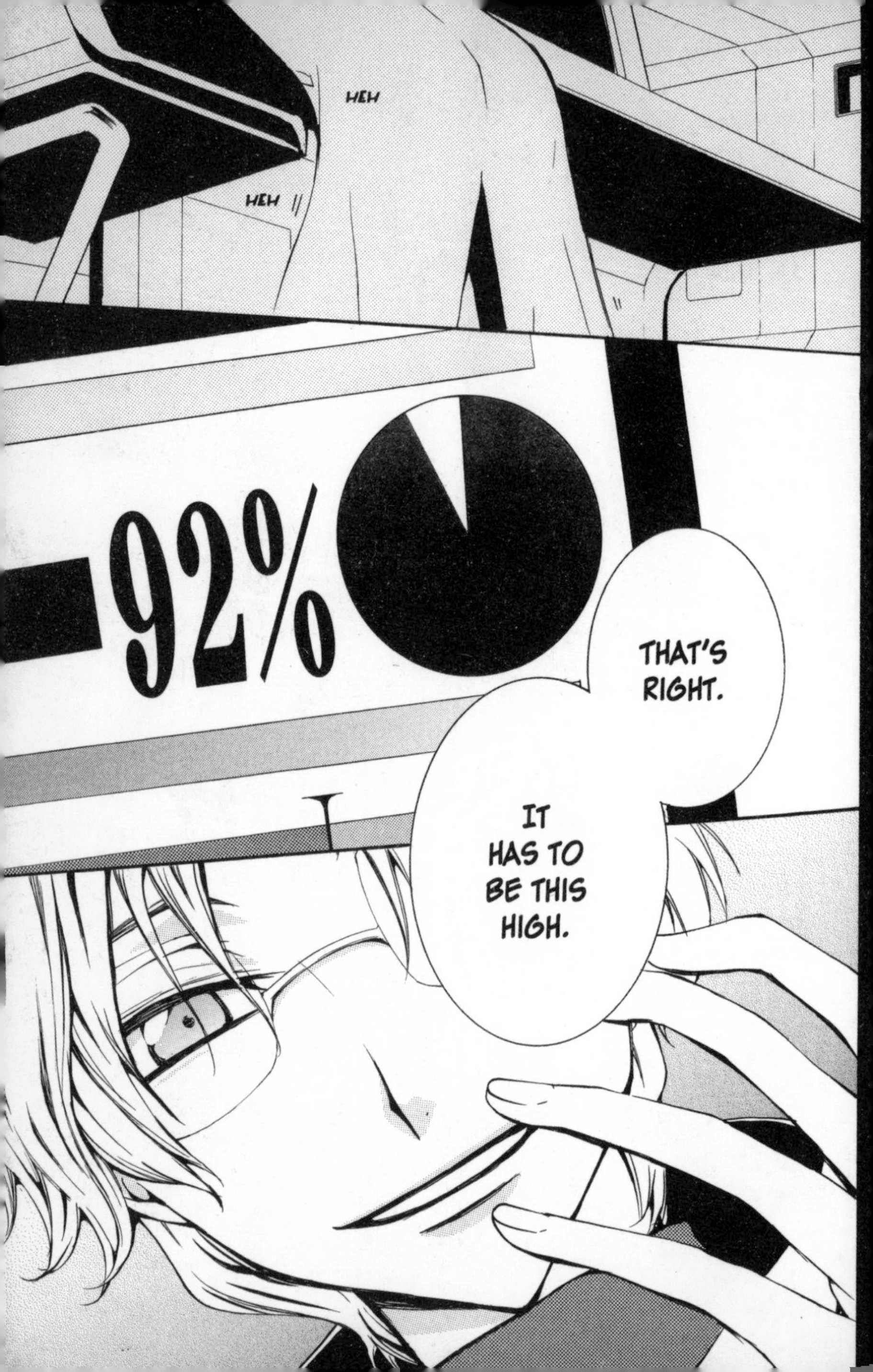
HEH
HEH
92%
THAT'S RIGHT.
IT HAS TO BE THIS HIGH.

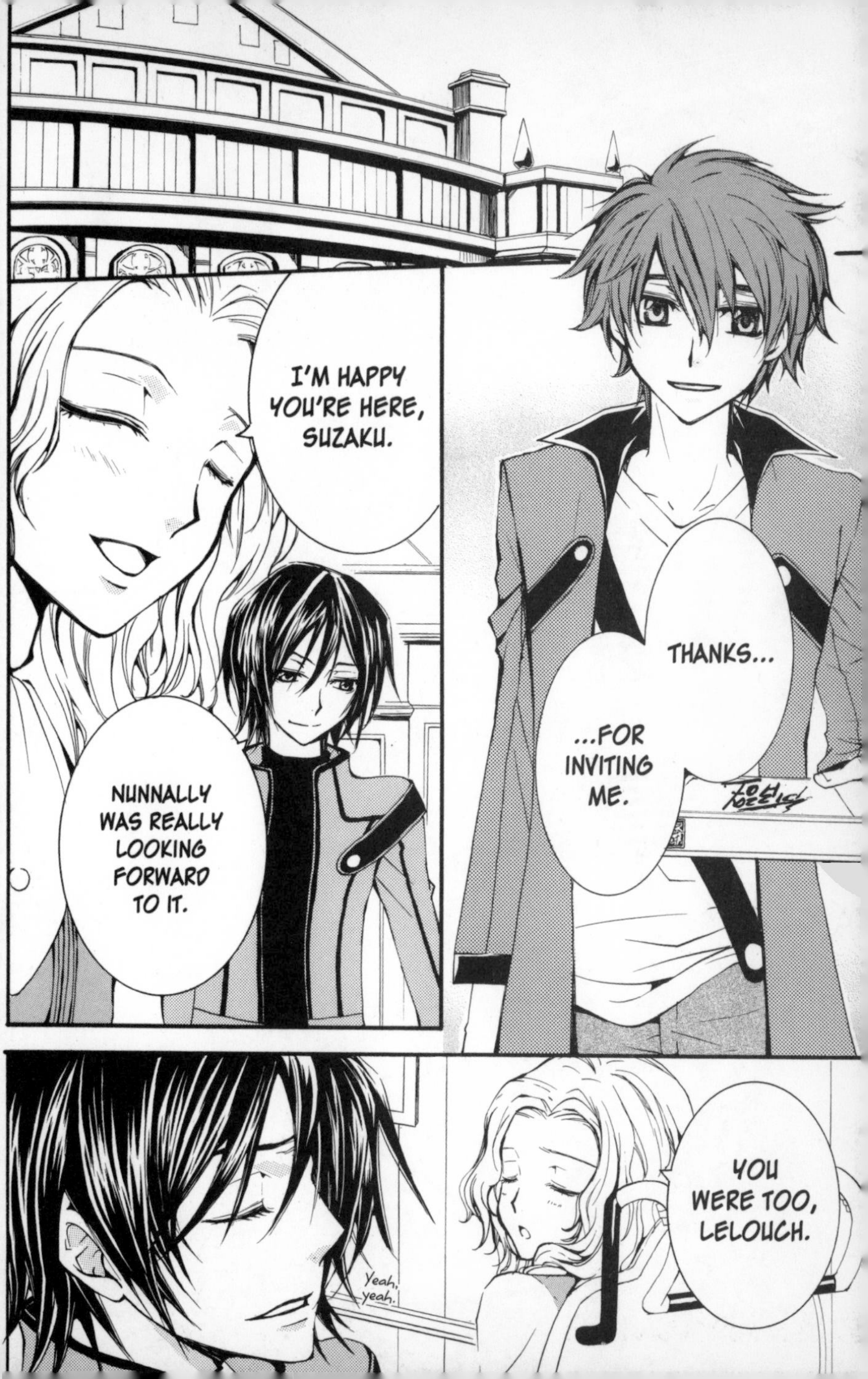
I'M HAPPY YOU'RE HERE, SUZAKU.
NUNNALLY WAS REALLY LOOKING FORWARD TO IT.
THANKS...
...FOR INVITING ME.
YOU WERE TOO, LELOUCH.
Yeah, yeah.

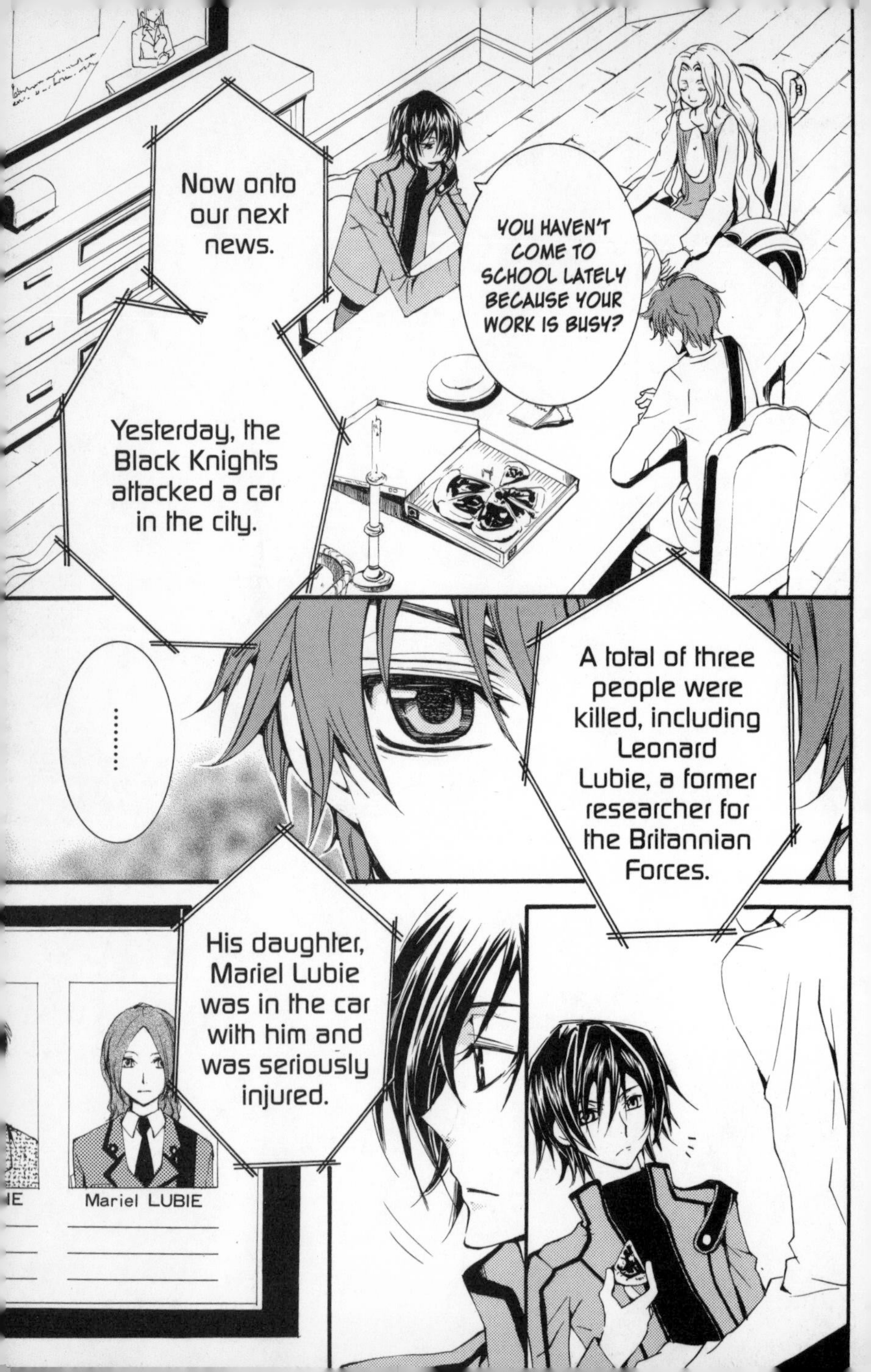
YOU HAVEN'T COME TO SCHOOL LATELY BECAUSE YOUR WORK IS BUSY?
Now onto our next news.
Yesterday, the Black Knights attacked a car in the city.
A total of three people were killed, including Leonard Lubie, a former researcher for the Britannian Forces.
......
His daughter, Mariel Lubie was in the car with him and was seriously injured.
Mariel LUBIE
IE

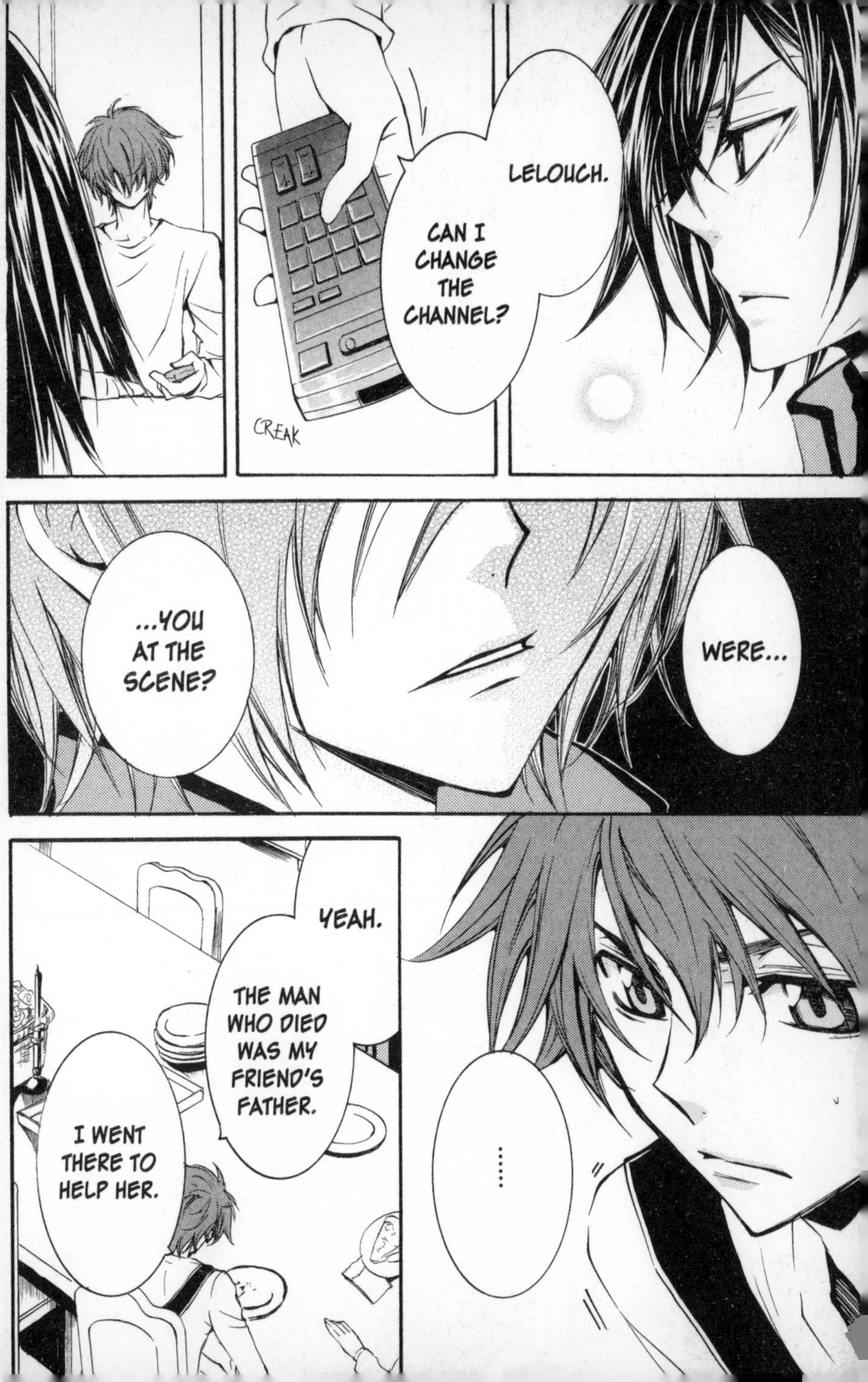
LELOUCH.
CAN I CHANGE THE CHANNEL?
CREAK
WERE...
...YOU AT THE SCENE?
......
YEAH.
THE MAN WHO DIED WAS MY FRIEND'S FATHER.
I WENT THERE TO HELP HER.

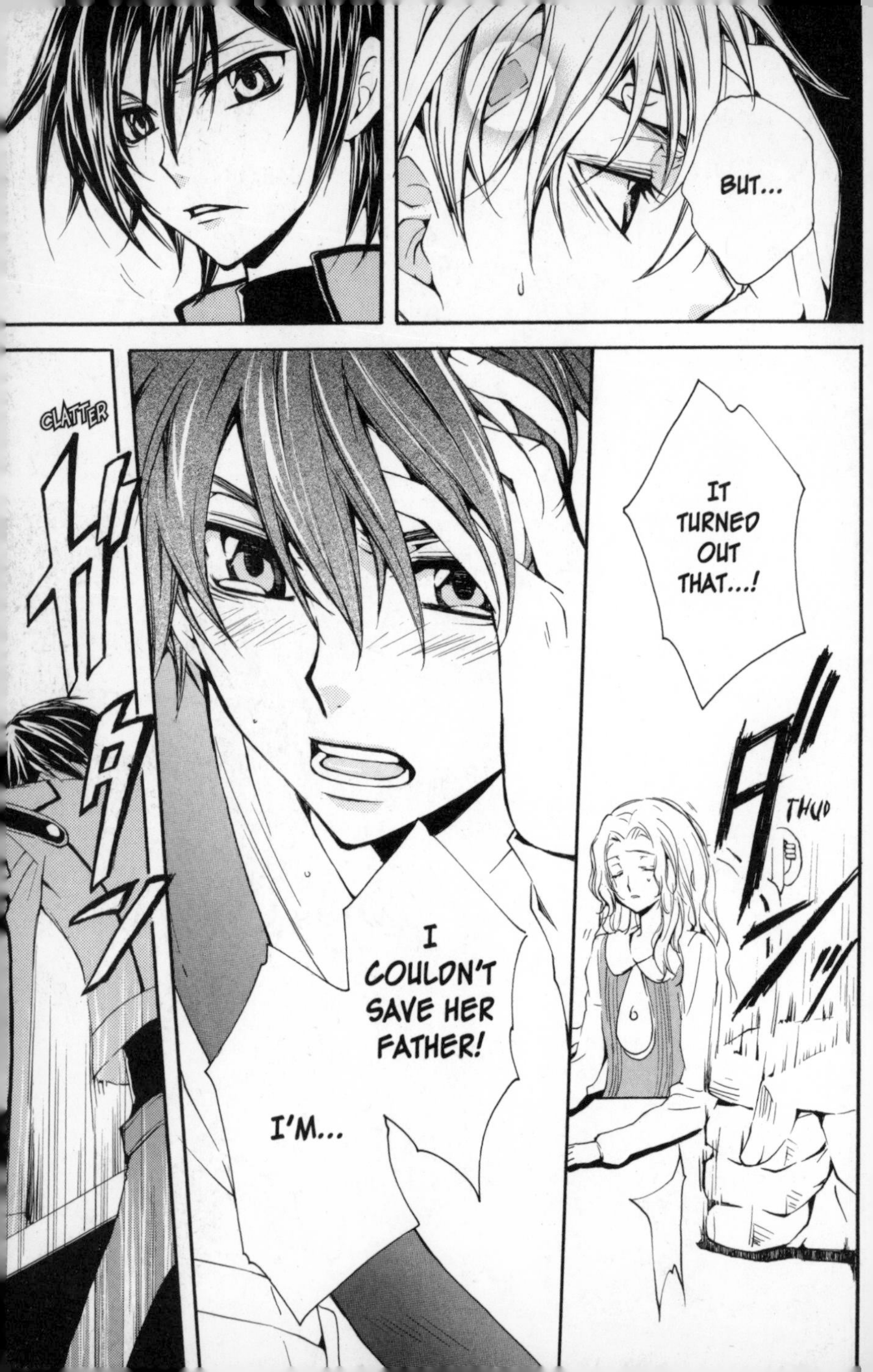
BUT...
IT TURNED OUT THAT...!
THUD
I COULDN'T SAVE HER FATHER!
I'M...
CLATTER

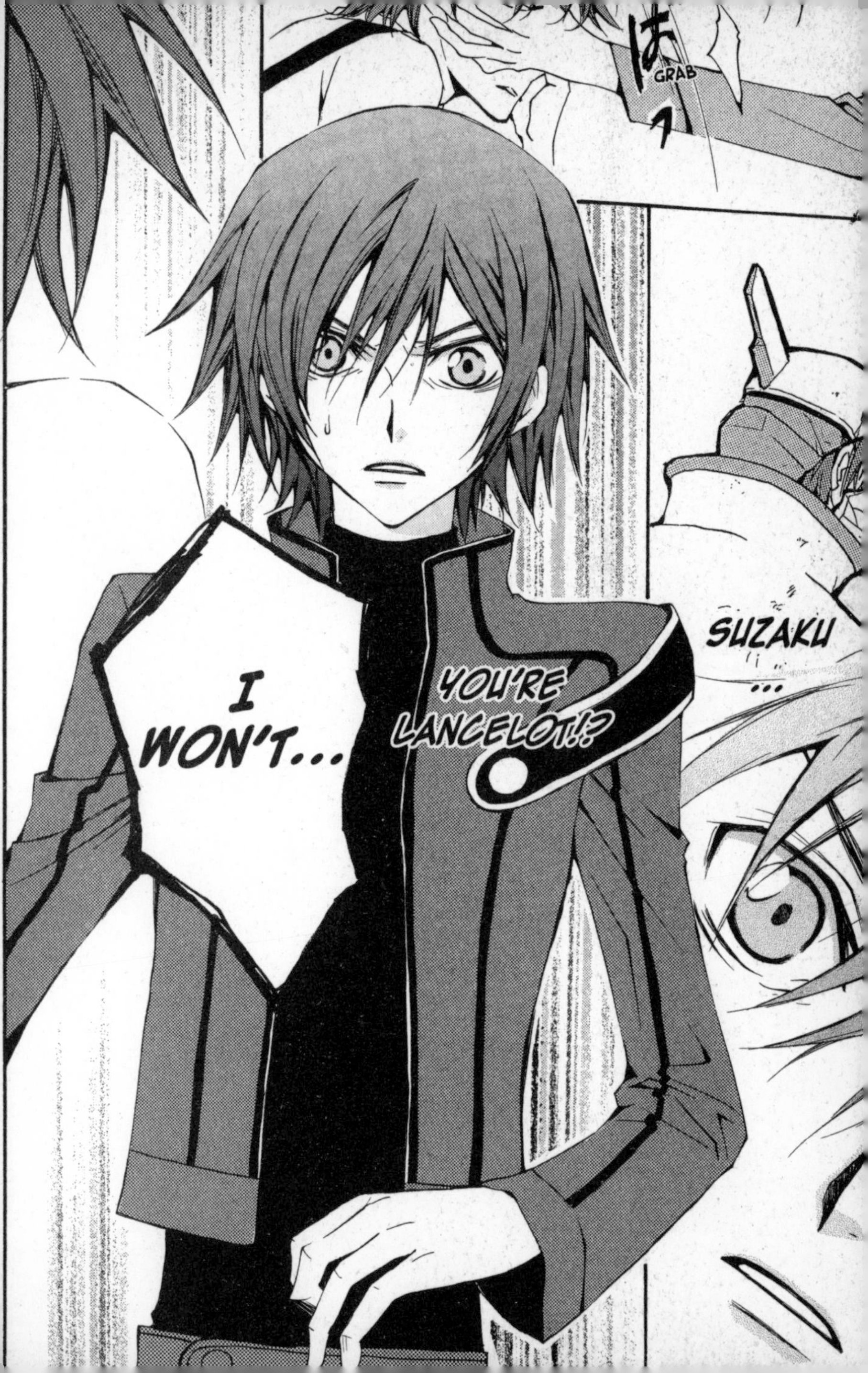
GRAB
SUZAKU...
YOU'RE LANCELOT!?
I WON'T...

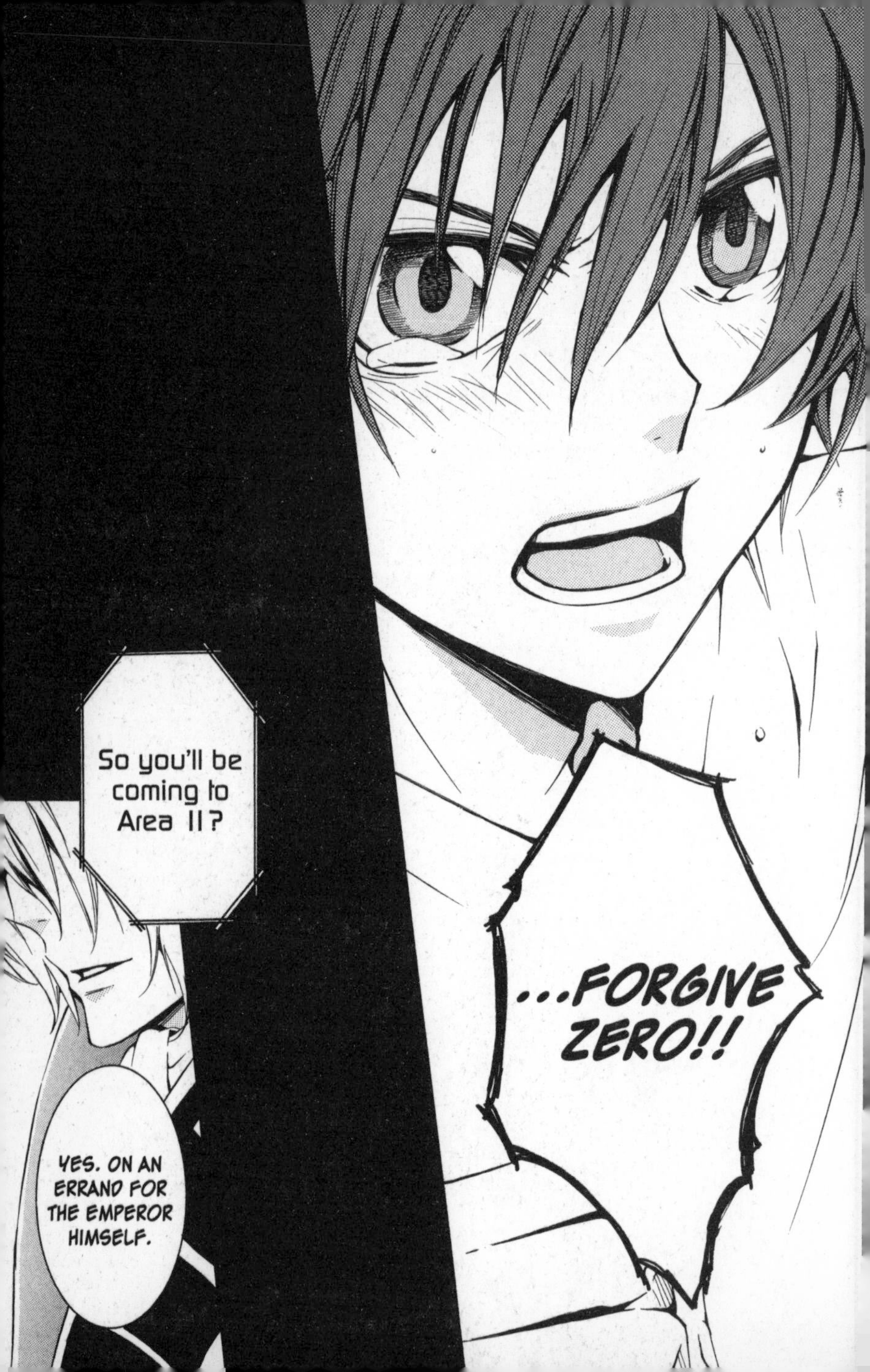
...FORGIVE ZERO!!
So you'll be coming to Area 11?
YES. ON AN ERRAND FOR THE EMPEROR HIMSELF.

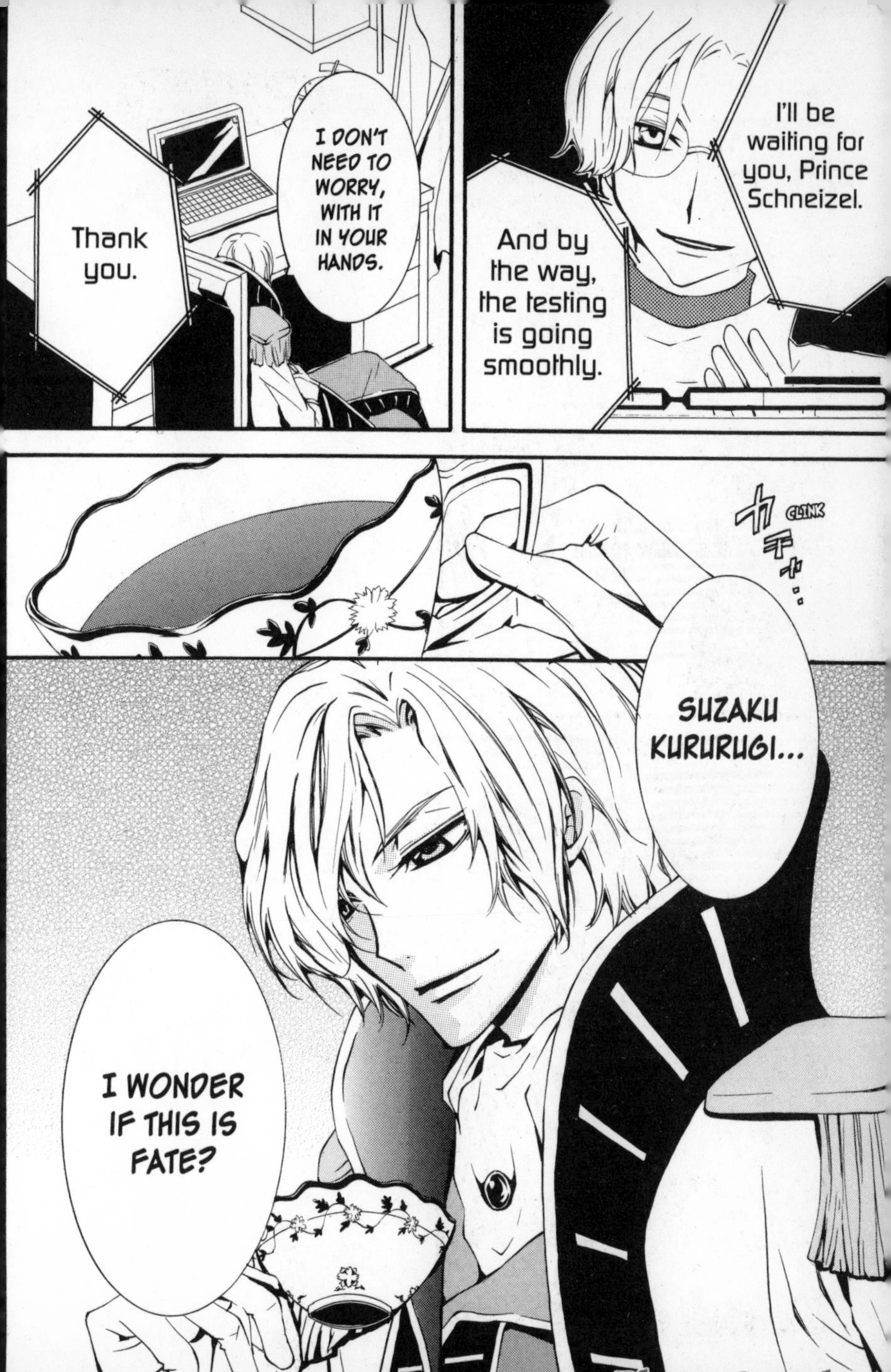
I'll be waiting for you, Prince Schneizel.
And by the way, the testing is going smoothly.
I DON'T NEED TO WORRY, WITH IT IN YOUR HANDS.
Thank you.
カチャ
CLINK
SUZAKU KURURUGI...
I WONDER IF THIS IS FATE?

Phase 3 end

Extra

BONUS COMICS

CHOP
CHOP
CHOP

YOU'RE PRETTY GOOD, SUZAKU.

DID THEY TEACH YOU IN THE MILITARY?

TO
ATO
ATO

ONION
ONION

USUALLY WE EAT AT THE CAFETERIA.

AND EVEN IF WE COOK, I ONLY PREPARE THE INGREDIENTS.

95 GEACHU !!!

What's that?

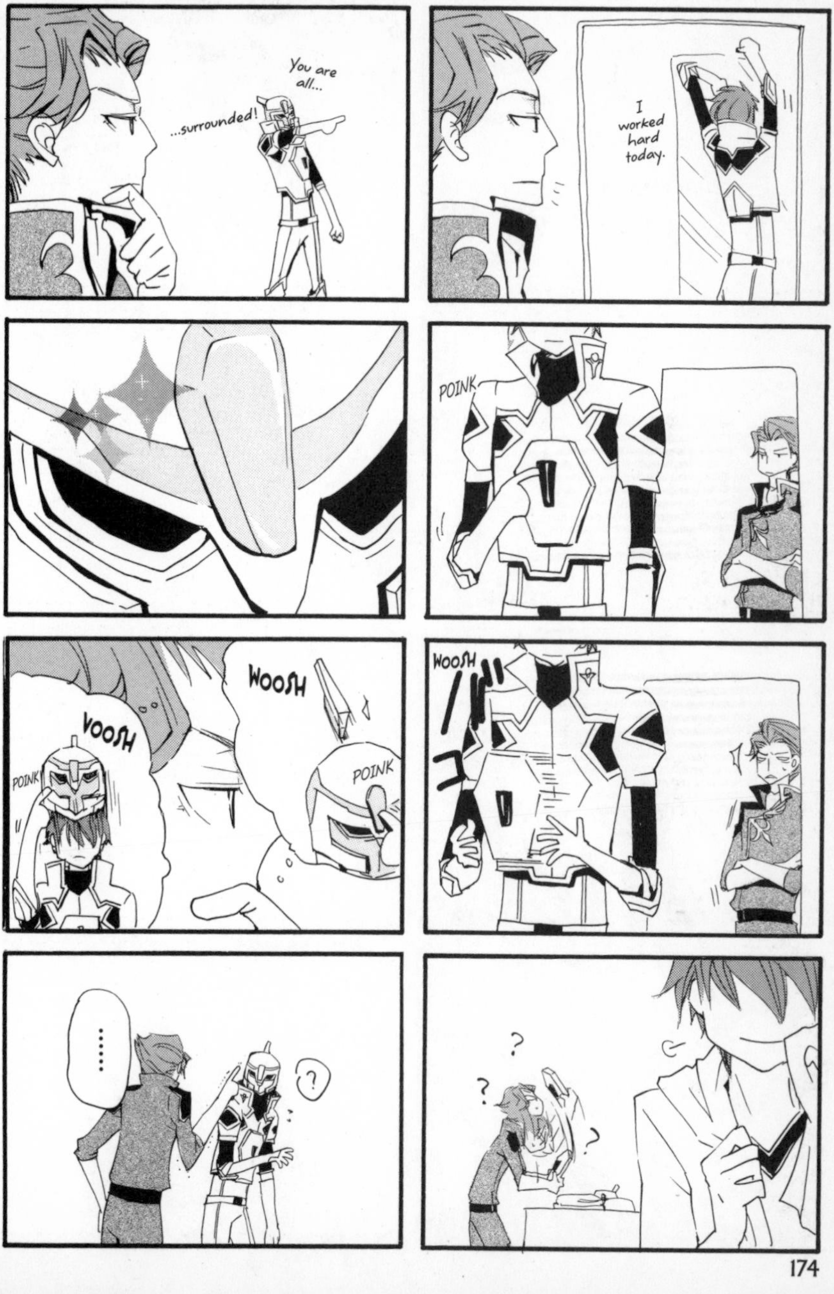
I worked hard today.
You are all...
...surrounded!
POINK
WOOSH
WOOSH
WOOSH
POINK
POINK
?
?
?
......
?

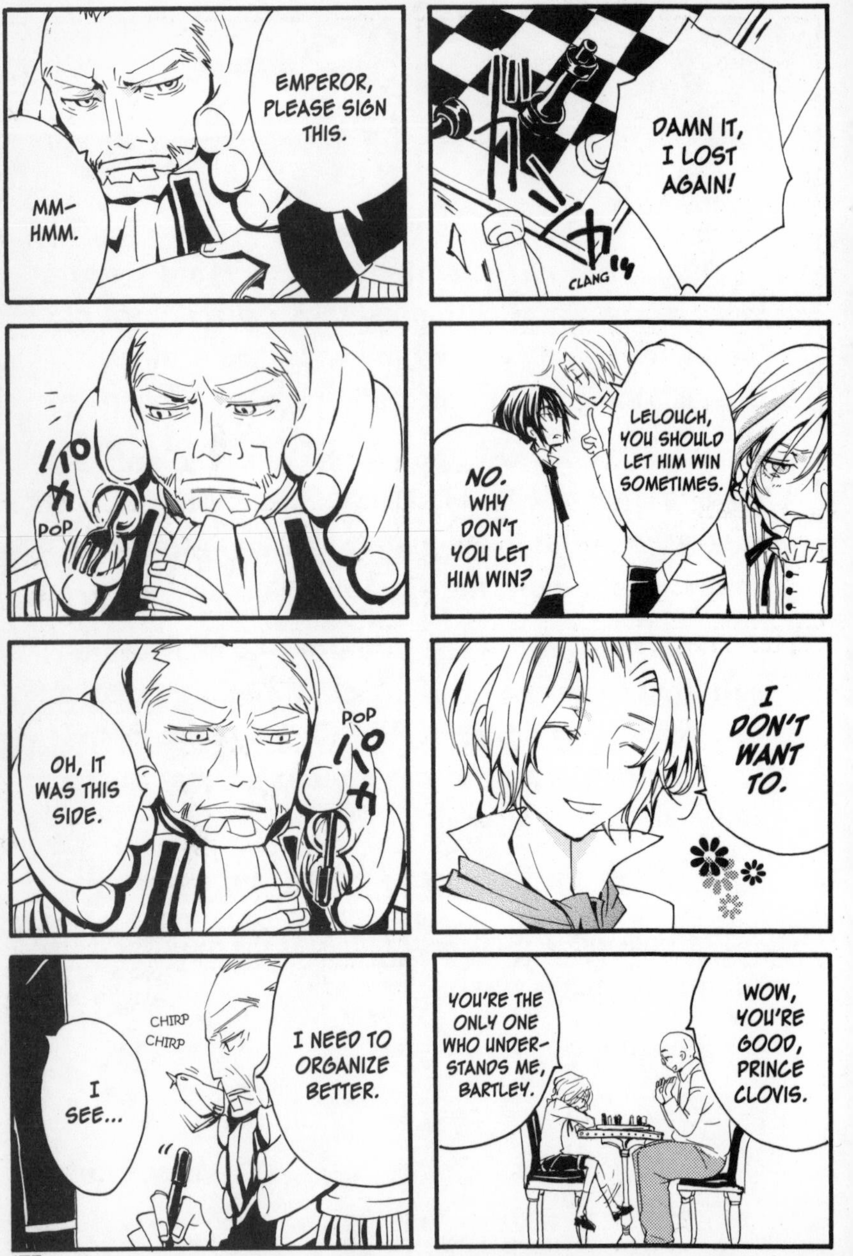
DAMN IT, I LOST AGAIN!
CLANG
EMPEROR, PLEASE SIGN THIS.
MM-HMM.
LELOUCH, YOU SHOULD LET HIM WIN SOMETIMES.
NO. WHY DON'T YOU LET HIM WIN?
POP
I DON'T WANT TO.
POP
OH, IT WAS THIS SIDE.
WOW, YOU'RE GOOD, PRINCE CLOVIS.
YOU'RE THE ONLY ONE WHO UNDER-STANDS ME, BARTLEY.
I NEED TO ORGANIZE BETTER.
CHIRP CHIRP
I SEE...

AFTERWORD

Hello, I am Atsuro Yomino.

I've always drawn manga freely at my own pace, so working with deadlines caused a lot of problems that impacted many people. I'm really sorry. Thank you for helping me out so much.

When I was working on Phase 1, the anime hadn't started yet, so I still hadn't captured Suzaku as I did in the later chapters. But I'm still studying. I'll work hard to improve.

This "Suzaku of the Counterattack" is quite different from the original story and may take a few readers by surprise, but I hope you can see it as a story in a different dimension that focuses on Suzaku.

And I'm sorry that I'm in love with Clovis.

In volume 2, Schneizel should be making a lot of appearances, too.

Please look forward to it.

Atsuro Yomino